MT SAN JACINTO COLLEGE
SAN JACINTO CAMPUS LIBRARY
1499 N STATE ST
SAN JACINTO, CA 92583

Poverty, Hunger, and Democracy in Africa

Also by David Bigman

COPING WITH HUNGER: *Toward a System of Food Security and Price Stabilization*

EXCHANGE RATE AND TRADE INSTABILITY: *Causes, Consequences and Remedies (co-editor with T. Taya)*

FLEXIBLE EXCHANGE RATES AND THE STATE OF WORLD TRADE AND PAYMENTS *(co-editor with T. Taya)*

FOOD POLICIES AND FOOD SECURITY UNDER INSTABILITY: *Modeling and Analysis*

FOOD SECURITY AND FOOD INVENTORIES IN DEVELOPING COUNTRIES: *Issues and Policies (co-editor with P. Berck)*

THE FUNCTIONING OF FLEXIBLE EXCHANGE RATES: *Theory, Evidence, and Policy Implications (co-editor with T. Taya)*

GEOGRAPHICAL TARGETING FOR POVERTY ALLEVIATION: *Methodology and Applications (co-editor with H. Fofack)*

GLOBALIZATION AND THE LEAST DEVELOPED COUNTRIES: *Potentials and Pitfalls*

THE IMPACT OF GLOBALIZATION ON STRATEGIES OF RURAL DEVELOPMENT AND POVERTY ALLEVIATION IN DEVELOPING COUNTRIES *(editor)*

Poverty, Hunger, and Democracy in Africa

Potential and Limitations of Democracy in Cementing Multiethnic Societies

David Bigman

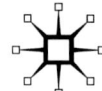

© David Bigman 2011
Foreword (1) © John E. Endicott 2011
Foreword (2) © Arie Kuyvenhoven 2011

All rights reserved. No reproduction, copy or transmission of this publication may be made without written permission.

No portion of this publication may be reproduced, copied or transmitted save with written permission or in accordance with the provisions of the Copyright, Designs and Patents Act 1988, or under the terms of any licence permitting limited copying issued by the Copyright Licensing Agency, Saffron House, 6–10 Kirby Street, London EC1N 8TS.

Any person who does any unauthorized act in relation to this publication may be liable to criminal prosecution and civil claims for damages.

The author has asserted his right to be identified as the author of this work in accordance with the Copyright, Designs and Patents Act 1988.

First published in 2011 by
PALGRAVE MACMILLAN

Palgrave Macmillan in the UK is an imprint of Macmillan Publishers Limited, registered in England, company number 785998, of Houndmills, Basingstoke, Hampshire RG21 6XS.

Palgrave Macmillan in the US is a division of St Martin's Press LLC, 175 Fifth Avenue, New York, NY 10010.

Palgrave Macmillan is the global academic imprint of the above companies and has companies and representatives throughout the world.

Palgrave® and Macmillan® are registered trademarks in the United States, the United Kingdom, Europe and other countries.

ISBN: 978–0–230–20528–4 hardback

This book is printed on paper suitable for recycling and made from fully managed and sustained forest sources. Logging, pulping and manufacturing processes are expected to conform to the environmental regulations of the country of origin.

A catalogue record for this book is available from the British Library.

A catalog record for this book is available from the Library of Congress.

10 9 8 7 6 5 4 3 2 1
20 19 18 17 16 15 14 13 12 11

Printed and bound in the United State of America

Contents

List of Tables	ix
List of Figures	x
List of Maps	xi
List of Boxes	xii
List of Abbreviations	xiii
Acknowledgments	xv
Preface	xvii
Foreword John Endicott	xxi
Foreword Arie Kuyvenhoven	xxiii

Part I Introduction and Background

Introduction — 3

1.1 The Black Man's Burden — 31

From hopeful independence to stagnation	32
From prolonged stagnation to a decade of miraculous growth	34
New investment opportunities and capital flows to Africa	37
Will the commodity crisis and the global recession end Africa's recovery?	40
Despite the continent's growth and the more prudent economic policies, poverty continues to rise	42
The threat of global warming	46
The growing gap between countries, and growing inequalities between people	47
Africa's agenda in the coming decade	51
Notes	54

Part II Coping with Escalating Food Insecurity

2.1 The Threat of Climatic Changes — 57

The haunting Malthusian predicament: the water crisis	59

How relevant are Malthus's "principles of production and population"?	61
The Neo-Malthusian vision of the limits to growth	63

2.2 Can Africa Feed Its People? 65

The Millennium Development Goals: can they end hunger?	65
Is Africa reaching limits to growth?	69
Can African farmers produce enough food?	75
How can African farmers increase their yields?	83
Coping with hunger: a global imperative	91

2.3 Is Africa Doomed to Permanent Food Crises? 100

Some lessons from the food crisis of 2007–08	100
How can the African countries cope with local food shortages?	109
Can the food crisis happen again?	113
Notes	116

Part III Africa's Poverty Traps and Obstacles to Growth

3.1 The Geographical and Man-Made Obstacles 121

The myth of a poverty trap in landlocked countries	127
The potential strategy for landlocked countries— regional trade agreements	132
Africa's most crippling obstacle: decaying infrastructure	138
The "resource curse"	142
Nigeria's resource curse	148

3.2 The Demographic and Social Changes and the Urbanization of Poverty 154

Rural–urban migration and growing urban population	154
The urbanization of poverty	158
The dilemma: promoting urban industrialization or alleviating rural poverty	159
Notes	169

Part IV Civil Conflicts, Wars and Democracy: Will Democracy Inflame or Help to Settle Civil Conflicts?

4.1 The Roots and Long-Term Effects of Africa's Wars and Civil Conflicts 175

The tribal roots of civil conflicts	177

	Conflicts caused by deprivation and exclusion	180
	The tribal wars in the Great Lakes region	188
	The legacy of colonial borders	197
	Has poverty been the cause of conflicts and wars in Africa?	202
4.2	**The Impact of Wars and Civil Conflicts on Africa's Growth and Poverty**	**206**
	Africa's missing billions	208
	The threat of rising inequalities	210
	Africa's "fragile" and "failed" states	214
	Conditions for aid to fragile states	218
	Criteria of governance	223
	The role of state institutions	226
	Building the state institutions	230
	The deterioration of the African state institutions	232
	Does the public trust the public institutions?	236
	The impediments of the endemic corruption	238
4.3	**Will Democracy Settle or Intensify Civil Conflicts?**	**244**
	The debate over Western-style democracy	245
	Countries' experiences with the transition to democracy	248
	Africans' mistrust in democracy	252
	Do elections intensify tribal conflicts?	255
	Reducing civil conflicts: external "nation building" interventions vs. internal public pressure	260
	Sierra Leone: mission accomplished—with external intervention	269
	Conclusion	273
	Notes	274

Part V The Fourth Wave of Democratization: Will Democracy Cement the African Multiethnic Nation State?

5.1	**The Transition of the African Countries to Democracy**	**277**
	The structure of the tribal society	280
	From the tribal society to the state	284
	Africa's greatest curse: its autocratic leaders	289
	Ending the addiction to aid	293

5.2	Can Democracy Help the African States to Cement Their Multiethnic Societies?	294
	Alternative scenarios of future political developments	295
	The shape of the democratic reforms in Africa	299
	The dubious significance of democratic elections	301
	Notes	308

References	310
Index	315

Tables

1.1	Sub-Saharan Africa: selected macroeconomic indicators (as percent of GDP)	42
1.2	The share and growth of the poor population in South Asia and in SSA (poverty line 2005 PPP and $1.25/day)	44
1.3	Poverty rates in selected African countries (International poverty lines at 2005 prices and exchange rates)	46
2.1	World trade in staple foods—average 2007–09	84
2.2	Measures of chronic and mild poverty and indicators of income inequality in selected African countries (estimates for 2005; income per capita in 2000 prices and exchange rates)	93
2.3	Correlation coefficients between key per-person indicators	96
2.4	The annual rise in commodity prices	104
2.5	Commodity futures price increases (March 2003–March 2008)	105
3.1	Natural resources and access to the coast in the African countries	123
3.2	Costs of trade across borders	133
3.3	Distribution of cropland and rural population by market access zones (in percent)	140
3.4	Infrastructure of personal services in developing countries	141
3.5	Demographic trends in the world and in SSA: 1950–2050	157
3.6	Urban and rural poverty in SSA (Poverty line is US$1 a day in 1993 international purchasing power parity)	158
3.7	The costs of starting a business	163
4.1	List of African fragile states	216
4.2	OECD criteria of fragile states	217
4.3	African countries' indicators of governance global competitiveness (2007–08); ease of doing business (2008); corruption (2008); political stability (2008)	224

Figures

1.1	Percentage change of real GDP in SSA and in the world	35
1.2	Foreign investments in SSA countries	37
1.3	Inflows of FDI to the African 33 LDCs (in billions US$)	38
1.4	Stock Market Index in "New Frontiers" Economies	39
1.5	The share of main regions in the world's poor population (not including Eastern Europe)	43
1.6	Incidence of chronic and moderate poverty in SSA 1990–2005	45
1.7a	Coefficient of variation of mean per capita incomes in main country groups	48
1.7b	GDP and consumption per capita in the SSA countries, 2005	48
1.7c	The ratio between income per capita of the top and the bottom income deciles in 35 SSA countries, 2005	49
1.8	Trends of real GDP per capita of the oil exporting countries (US$ at 2000 prices and exchange rates)	50
2.1a	Proportion of people living on less than $1.25 a day: 1990 and 2005 (%)	67
2.1b	The proportion of undernourished people in the developing regions (%)	68
2.2	The number of hungry people in the world (00 thousands)	69
2.3	The change in the distribution of chronic proverty: 1990–2005 Number in (Millions) and proverty Incidence (%) (poverty line $1 per day in 2005 prices and exchange rate)	79
2.4	The commodity boom and bust: 2005–08	101
2.5	The share of investors in the commodity Future Markets, 2008	106
3.1	The increase in urbanization: 1950–2050	155
3.2.	The rate of urbanization in SSA (percent of the urban population)	156
4.1	Changes in the income gap between the countries of SSA (Measured in current US$ per capita)	213
4.2	Indicators of public sector ethics	226
4.3	Percent of respondents who had little or no trust in the president	237
4.4	Prevalence of bribery in selected countries	241
4.5	Average GDP per capita in Sierra Leone in US$ (in 2000 prices and exchange rates)	270

Maps

1.1	Africa	2
3.1	Nigeria	148
4.1	African Countries in Conflict: 1990–2005 (Dark Areas)	177
4.2	Kenya	179
4.3	Côte d'Ivoire	183
4.4	Sudan	184
4.5	Congo Democratic Republic	190
4.6	Rwanda	191
4.7	The Horn of Africa	222
4.8	Sierra Leone	270

Boxes

1.1	African emergence from prolonged stagnation	36
1.2	The "Frontier Economies"	38
2.1	Chronicles of food emergencies: an ominous look into the future	57
2.2	The limits to growth	60
2.3	Millennium development goals	66
2.4	The human face of the food crisis in the horn of Africa	71
2.5	Lingering African perceptions of structural adjustment programs	74
2.6	Guidelines for the agricultural development program in SSA	86
2.7	FAO–OECD: concerns about food security will remain high	88
2.8	Comprehensive Africa Agricultural Development Program (CAADP): general guidelines	89
2.9	Alliance for a Green Revolution in Africa (AGRA)	90
2.10	Countries' price stabilization policy measures	107
3.1	Nigeria	148
3.2	Oil wealth in Nigeria leaves the majority behind	152
4.1	Kenya	179
4.2	Sudan	184
4.3	Rwanda and Congo Dem. Rep.	190
4.4	Africa's view on western-style democracy	246
4.5	Sierra Leone	270

Abbreviations

AEC	African Economic Community
AGOA	US African Growth and Opportunity Act
APC	All Peoples Congress (Sierra Leone)
ATC	Agreement on Textiles and Clothing
AU	African Union
BBL	Billion Barrels of Light Oil
CCSP	US Climate Change Science Program
CGIAR	Consultative Group on International Agricultural Research
CIA	US Central Intelligence Agency
CIF/FOB	Cost+insurance+freight/cost-free on board
COMESA	Common Market for Eastern and Southern Africa
CONGO D.R.	Congo Democratic Republic—Congo Kinshasa
CONGO R.	Congo Republic—Congo Brazzaville
CPA	The Comprehensive Peace Agreement (in Sudan)
CPIA	Country Policy and Institutional Assessment (World Bank)
DFID	UK Department for International Development
DRC	Democratic Republic of the Congo
EAC	East African Community
EPRDF	Ethiopian Peoples' Revolutionary Democratic Front
EPZs	Export Processing Zones
EU	European Union
FAO	Food and Agriculture Organization of the United Nations
FDI	Foreign Direct Investments
FPI	Front Populaire Ivoirien
FTA	Free Trade Area
G-8	Group of eight rich countries: Canada, France, Germany, Italy, Japan, Russia, the United Kingdom, and the United States
GATT	General Agreement on Tariffs and Trade
GDP	Gross Domestic Product
GM	Genetically Modified
GNI	Gross National Income
HDI	Human Development Index
HIPC	Heavily Indebted Poor Countries Initiative
HIV/AIDS	Human Immunodeficiency Virus/Acquired Immunodeficiency Syndrome
IDA	International Development Association (World Bank)
IFAD	International Fund for Agricultural Development
IFPRI	International Food Policy Research Institute

IMF	International Monetary Fund
IPCC	Intergovernmental Panel on Climate Change
ISNAR	International Service for National Agricultural Research
LAC	Latin America and the Caribbean
LDCs	Least Developed Countries
MDGs	UN Millennium Development Goals
MDRI	Multilateral Debt Relief Initiative
MERCOSUR	*Mercado Común del Sur* (Southern Common Market): A regional trade agreement among key Latin American countries (Brazil, Argentina, Paraguay, and Uruguay and several associate members)
MFA	Multi-Fiber Arrangement
MFN	Most Favored Nation
MNJ	Nigerien Movement for Justice (in Niger)
MPLA	Popular Movement for the Liberation of Angola
NEPAD	New Partnership for Africa's Development
NEW	National Elections Watch (Sierra Leone)
NGO	Non-governmental Organization
OAU	Organization of African Unity
ODA	Official Development Assistance
OECD	Organization for Economic Cooperation and Development
OIC	Organization of the Islamic Conference
OPEC	Organization of Petroleum Exporting Countries
PPP	Purchasing Power Parity
PTA	Preferential Trade Agreement
RUF	Revolutionary United Front (Sierra Leone)
SADC	Southern African Development Community
SLA	Sudan Liberation Army
SSA	Sub-Saharan Africa
TPLF	Tigray People's Liberation Front
UN	United Nations
UNCTAD	United Nations Conference on Trade and Development
UNDC	United Nations Development Corporation
UNESCO	United Nations Educational, Scientific and Cultural Organization
WDR	World Development Report (World Bank)
WEO	World Economic Outlook (IMF)
WFP	World Food Program
WMO	World Meteorological Organization
WTO	World Trade Organization

Acknowledgments

My objective in this book was to draw a vision of the African continent in the coming decade that takes into account not only the very positive trends in the economies of many African countries after decades of stagnation, but also the far-reaching changes in social conditions that are making Africa an urban continent, and the promising but still very tentative changes in the regimes of many African countries as they make a transition to democracy. When I submitted the proposal for the book to Palgrave in 2007, the rise in oil prices was no longer viewed as a "correction" after many years in which these prices were unusually high, but nobody could imagine what was still in store. The food prices just started to climb, and initially this was considered to be beneficial to small farmers since it would increase their incomes. These and other developments in the commodity markets seemed at the time to be temporary bumps on the road of African countries to a much more promising future by accelerating their growth, improving their standard of living, and reducing their poverty.

The full and unprecedented dimensions of the commodity boom and subsequent bust became evident only in 2008. That crisis was followed by a spiral of crises in world markets that were not related to, or affected by, the African countries themselves, but nonetheless had a deep impact on their economies and people. The ground on which I built my thesis when I wrote the first draft of the book was shaking, and many of the premises that were the foundations of the vision I perceived for Africa's development in the coming decade no longer existed on planet earth, where the African continent is floating after the earth-shaking metamorphosis it went through as an effect of these series of global crises. I, therefore, had to write and rewrite and then rewrite again several parts of the book in order to keep it as relevant as I could. I am well aware changes will continue to take place, and some parts will unavoidably be read as "what would or could have happened if...."

Although Africa had no effect on the turmoil in the global economy, the results of this mayhem were most devastating for the African countries and the African people. On top of all this, the continent is going through major changes of its own in terms of economic, social, and political conditions. More than half a century after African countries gained their independence from colonial rule, many of them are still going through internal wars of independence to achieve personal freedom, get rid of autocratic leaders, and form the stable structure of a state.

In writing this book I owe my deepest thanks to my wife, Petra, who helped me throughout this process despite our frequent disagreements, starting from our disagreement on the first title I chose for the book, when I submitted the proposal, to our most recent disagreement on the title I chose when I submitted its final version, and every iota in between. But if you find the book worthwhile reading, it is at least as much thanks to her.

I am also thankful to the colleagues and experts who assisted me with comments on the content of the various chapters and in my personal struggle with Vista (for which I should blame no one except perhaps for Microsoft). I am also grateful to several editors who helped me through their meticulous work to give the book its final shape and form.

I would also like to express my gratitude to Dr. John Endicott, president of Woosong University, who made my last and most grueling months when I struggled with the final version of the book as a Visiting Professor at SolBridge International School of Business much easier and friendlier.

Finally, I would like to thank the two editors at Palgrave Macmillan, Gemma Papageorgiou and Taiba Batool, who ignored (through no fault of their own) my repeated delays in submitting the manuscript and helped me throughout this process.

Preface

My acquaintance with the economies and the economic problems of the African continent started in the late 1970s, when I worked in the World Bank with my friend and mentor at the time, Shlomo Reutlinger, on the food problems of the African people as an effect of recurring droughts and food shortages. With the stunning success of the Green Revolution in Asia, there was no shortage of food in the world, and yet hundreds of thousands of people in Africa have been exposed to periodic and recurring famine and hunger, and tens of thousands have perished. At around that time, many African countries were forced by the debt crisis that paralyzed their economies (and the function of their governments) to seek aid from the World Bank and IMF, and this aid was given under stiff *conditionalities* to restructure their economies according to specific guidelines that became cumulatively known as the "Washington Consensus."

The basic approach of research groups at the World Bank and at the other international research organizations that worked on Africa was to design a development strategy based on the most advanced economic models of the time in order to enable the African governments to benefit from the cumulative knowledge in economics and economic modeling that had been developed at the elite universities in the West by that time. This, it was hoped, would allow the African countries and other developing countries to accelerate their growth and reduce their poverty most rapidly, and over time join the community of the developed countries.

The continued stagnation and deepening poverty during the 1980s made it clear that the African countries were not able to implement disciplined fiscal policies and effective monetary policy, and the main reasons given at that time were the lack of adequate institutions to monitor and audit their governments' income and expenditures, the very limited experience of their central banks, which had, as a consequence, no power to influence monetary policy. As a result, the emphasis of the reforms shifted from the design of effective governmental policies to the design of effective government institutions, the central bank, and other public institutions. These institutions, their rules and regulations and modes of operation, were designed more or less along the lines of the same institutions in Western countries.

One key ingredient in the basic approach to the design of these reforms was missing in both the first and the second rounds: a deeper familiarity and interaction with the local population in order to understand their social order, their legal systems, and, more generally, their systems of governance. Obviously, these systems in tribal societies are fundamentally different from those in the Western world, and even the concept of the nation-state, the foundation of our system of governance, was foreign to them. Nevertheless, these people have strong allegiances to their tribes; their tribes have well-disciplined social orders and legal systems governed by tribal elders and by their long heritage.

In the design of the reforms, these people did not exist as individuals and as a community. They were like tabula rasa that had to be structured, and their organizations had to be formed from raw material. Wittingly or unwittingly, the basic approach was: "We" the West bring them the best knowledge that has been accumulated, the best models of economic policies that have been developed, and the most effective institutions for the implementation of policies that have evolved in our countries for many years. If they implement policies according to these models, design and restructure their institutions along the lines of Western institutions for the creation of effective government institutions, and conduct democratic elections along the Western style, they would be able to build their economies, their systems of governance and, thus, their nations and join the civilized world.

I must admit that I had much the same approach in most of my previous writings on Africa. In my work on this book, particularly in the parts concerned with the prospects and risks of democratization, I realized that one important dimension, perhaps the most important dimension, is missing in this analysis: What about the African people? Questions about *their* systems of governance, *their* social orders, *their* legal systems, are usually perceived as the domain of anthropologists; but in the design of a new system of governance or a new style of elections, their social order has been completely erased, and their difficulties adjusting to new and largely foreign systems by fundamentally changing the social order so strongly embedded in their heritage has been completely ignored.

It is true that the African tribes as embryonic states failed with a single gunshot of the Arab slave-traders. Most failed not because they were too small; even the larger tribes that formed a kingdom and were larger than, and had more people than, say, Holland, failed because they were not able to protect their people with machetes against the superior war machines of the occupying forces that landed in their territory, as if from another planet. Since the main and most important role and goal of the state is to protect its people, the African tribes and kingdoms completely failed to fulfill their basic role when they were overwhelmed by the waves of Arab traders on camels and colonial merchants on sailing ships. That failure cost the continent dearly. Its people were sold into slavery, their continent essentially taken away from them, and even many of those not shipped to other lands to be sold as merchandise often became slaves in their own territory and not given much attention as human beings.

That chapter in their history has left deep scars in the common consciousness of the African people. It caused both the African leaders and, to some degree also the African people, to look back at their past with some measure of disrespect. In some of their speeches a number of African leaders clearly convey the impression that "they/we are/were indeed primitive." This was one of the reasons the reforms planned by the professional teams at the World Bank and the IMF were based primarily on the economic knowledge, models, and experience from the Western countries and paid little attention to the social structure and heritage of African societies themselves. The design of the reforms, from the "Washington Consensus" to institutional reforms, did not much involve the African people (although they involved African professionals). Nor was there, to the best of my knowledge, any attempt to take the social system of the tribe as the starting point for designing its social reforms.

I raise these issues at this point, when most African countries are making a transition to democracy. How will Western-style democracy relate to the social traditions, rules, order and institutions of the African people? In the African tradition, the social order is governed at the level of the tribe, maintained by the tribe's elders, and all decisions are made in the context of tribal authority and structure. In Western civilization the social order is governed at the level of the nation-state and maintained by the institutions of the nation-state, but decisions are made at the level of the individual, although ethnic and sectarian affiliations can have a significant influence on the individual's decisions. In the parts of the book that discuss this process and its potential impact on the leadership of African countries, I considered the possibility of using this process of democratization as a lever for improving the system of governance, reducing corruption, and increasing the effectiveness of governmental institutions, as the Western donor countries hope. The conclusions that can be drawn from the experience of the countries is that although most elections have been deeply flawed and vote-rigging has been common, this is only the beginning of a process that is bound to be laborious and have many twists and turns in nearly all countries, this process does have a great potential of influencing the social order of the African countries. This change has to come from within, by the African countries themselves, and they cannot wait for Western countries to send their armies to "build the nation" for them. The impact of their system of democracy will depend on the extent to which it is attuned with their tribal system, their allegiance to their heritage, and their respect for tribal elders.

The time period on which the book is focused has clearly been difficult both for the African continent's economy and its society. It has been a transitional period not only for African regimes but also for their social structure and their economies. After a very successful decade of rapid economic growth, African countries were strongly influenced by the upheavals of the world economy, initially by the food crisis, and subsequently by the financial crisis and the global recession. This turmoil is far from being over, and although more African countries are expected to recover from the slump of 2009, this recovery will concentrate on the resource-rich—primarily the oil-exporting countries. Most oil- and food-importing countries may remain stagnant, and their poor populations are bound to bear the brunt of the crisis. In rural areas the high food and oil prices are combining with the extremely adverse effects of climatic change that may become more extreme in the coming decade as an effect of global warming.

My objective in writing this book was to provide a wider vision of the coming decade's prospective developments in Africa—developments that combine the resource-rich continent's far-reaching economic potential (manifested by its miraculous growth during the past decade until the food crisis) with its major social transformation from a rural to an urban society, and with its political change in the transition to democracy. These changes are still evolving and the threats to Africa's economy in the coming decade, as an effect of the prolonged global crisis and ominous climatic changes, may make the entire transformation the continent is undergoing far more difficult.

In writing this book, I have drawn not only on my own African experiences and my research on Africa, but I have also relied on, and greatly benefited from, the rich literature and detailed analyses of the changes in Africa during the past decade, which highlighted the continent's turning point after more than three long decades of stagnation and deepening poverty, and its new road of rapid growth and comprehensive social and political changes that came with the transition of some 40 countries to democracy.

The most thorough reviews and analyses of economic changes in Africa have been published in the various and numerous reports and research papers of the World Bank and IMF that provided the widest perspective, from the remote villages and the nomads to the macroeconomy. Several path-breaking books on Africa have been published in recent years, most notably those of Jeffrey Sachs, Paul Collier, and William Easterley. Several other books concentrated on African society in its difficult, if not tragic, transition from colonial rule to the exploitative rule of self-centered autocrats.

These books had an important role, not only in guiding research on Africa, but also in raising interest in the continent among a much wider audience that, perhaps for the first time, took a more thorough look and found much greater and deeper interest in Africa, thanks to Bono, Bill Clinton, and Bill Gates. Yet, for many people in the West, Africa is still defined by the stereotype that dominates television screens, one that shows the continent through the eyes of a starving child. Those, including this author, who have taken a closer look and come to better know the continent and its people, have found this a captivating experience.

Foreword

When Professor Bigman approached me to contribute a preface for his current work on poverty and democracy, my first thoughts immediately turned to the American experience and that of the individuals initially drawn to settle in the new democratic experiment called the United States. The push of the frontier constantly westward was done by masses of farmers living well below what is now called the poverty line. Their hardships were alleviated by the hope for the future and a belief structure that constantly supported them, even in the most difficult of times. Their experiences were not unlike my own father's, who at the age of five journeyed with his family from Kansas to seek a new and more prosperous life in New Mexico. Arriving in the Pan Handle in 1905, with their goods on a covered wagon, they found a beautiful 640-acre tract and began the homesteading process. They had five years to improve the property, and it was theirs.

Using their own resources, they built a sod house and considered themselves blessed for the grand opportunity. During the first winter, the warm fire of the relatively sheltered home brought out the worms and other insects that had taken refuge in the sod. One of my father's jobs was to collect the creatures that thought spring had come to the prairie to make sure they were safely placed outdoors. It was a surprise, but they coped. However, the beautiful valley they had claimed gradually turned brown, and the rain so critical for the subsistence farmer did not come. Eventually, all the cattle were gone, one of dad's sisters had died, and the crops to sustain life were just not there. It was not climate change, just northern New Mexico. Thus, this family of nine, with no further options, was forced to return to Kansas, where my grandfather had to start all over again. The homestead opportunity could not be realized in this case. I cannot say how many individuals suffered in like manner, but it was certainly not atypical. Frederick Jackson Turner, in his assessment of the spirit of the American frontier, captured the willingness of these individuals to persevere and still keep their belief in democracy. Certainly, they experienced abject poverty, but kept seeking a better life.

In today's fragile and increasingly interdependent world the, perhaps, isolated stories like those of my father's family become all too common. Returning to Kansas is not an option, as the areas to migrate to are as inhospitable as the ones currently used. And, climate change is affecting increasingly broader areas, only making subsistence farming and living more difficult to people already at the end of opportunity.

David Bigman, in this book, examines these kinds of phenomena on the prospects for advancing democracy in the least developed countries. Perhaps "advancing" democracy in these circumstances is too optimistic. Can democracy hold out the promise of a better life for these imperiled masses? If it cannot, what is the future of this grand experiment in political organization? The implications for peace and security, as well as the underlying social and economic issues are causes for concern for all peoples and their governments that do have resources and are interested in insuring some stability in a very interdependent world. The image of desperate people seeking some modicum of hope for life is one we see almost daily on the BBC or CNN. Ultimately, what will be the future of democracy in these conditions?

Professor Bigman, now a colleague at the SolBridge International School of Business of Woosong University in Daejeon, South Korea, contributes skillfully to the consideration of these questions. If this book can become an agenda for action, or in the least raise and focus the world's attention on this critical issue, he will have done a service for us all.

John E. Endicott
President, Woosong University
Daejeon, Republic of Korea

Foreword

The surge in food and energy prices in 2007–08 was not only dramatic for the day-to-day livelihood of the many poor in the world, but it also reminds us how far we are removed from achieving the first and most pressing Millennium Development Goal, halving the number of poor by 2015. According to World Bank revised estimates, the number of poor has actually increased by more than 100 million as an effect of the food crisis. Poverty and hunger have rapidly declined in China, but by far less in India and other Asian countries, while in Africa it is steadily increasing. Recent World Bank research based on new cost-of-living estimates has raised the bottom, chronically poor, hungry, and malnourished people to a staggering 1.4 billion by 2005, even before the food crisis erupted.[1]

Roughly three-quarters of the poor live in rural areas, where agriculture is the dominant activity. In Africa, the poorest continent, two-thirds of the labor force is engaged in agriculture, but it provides them with only one third of all income. As the development experience elsewhere in the world has shown, raising agricultural productivity is key to breaking the poverty trap and alleviating hunger by improving the income (and purchasing power) of all those connected with agriculture and lowering real food prices for rural and urban households alike. Cross-section studies by International Food Policy Research Institute (IFPRI) and World Bank staff confirm that a 1 percent increase in agricultural yields tends to decrease the number of poor by between 0.6 to 1 percent, and a 1 percent rise in agricultural income would benefit the poorest decile of the population by raising their income by an average of 2.5 percent.

In his earlier work, David Bigman has emphasized that the majority of the population within the poor countries, as well as many of the African nations, do not share the benefits of globalization despite its contribution to global growth. In the book *Globalization and the Least Developed Countries* (LDCs), published in 2007, he explains why there is not necessarily a level playing field for all countries and population groups, and how international trade and trade relations between countries have changed since the 1980s. The continued, and virtually unlimited, supply of low-cost labor with the migration from the rural areas to the urban centers maintains the low labor costs of the two giants, India and China. The continuous improvements in their productivity make it exceedingly difficult for the LDCs, most nowadays located in Africa, to catch up in the foreseeable future and

---

1 This new estimate is based on a poverty line of $1.25 (per person in 2000 prices).

build a competitive industrial sector. Moreover, after the failure to reach a multilateral trade agreement on agricultural products at the Doha Round, and with the current multiplication of regional trade agreements, Africa's LDCs may face trade diversion, or even exclusion.

In the current volume, *Poverty, Hunger, and Democracy in Africa*, the plight of Sub-Saharan Africa takes a central focus. Optimism about Africa in the 1960s, when incomes exceeded those in Asia and food imports were rare, turned into feelings of helplessness and desperation in the following three "lost" decades of stagnation, loss of foreign markets, and disappointing international assistance that left Africa behind the rest of the world. Only in the first decade of this century, until 2008, has its growth picked up, thanks to rapidly rising world market prices of oil, minerals, and some of Africa's traditional agricultural exports, but the prospects of new revival and new hope have been dashed by the food crisis and by the series of crises and the global recession that followed. The drop in its growth from over 6 percent before the crisis to less than 1 percent in 2009 again raises concerns about the capacity of Africa to feed its people and get out of the cycle of poverty.

Many other obstacles, however, cast a heavy shadow over Africa's future. Can Africa regain its international competitiveness and start diversifying its exports when the crises are over? Can Africa overcome some of its geographical and climatic challenges that increase its inland high transport costs and essentially make trade prohibitive? The poor roads also undermine improvement in the health of its population and fragment the already thin markets, thus also preventing local trade between the African countries themselves. And, most important, can Africa improve its governance and institutional capacities to make its policies work? The repeated, and often frustrating, efforts to start raising its agricultural productivity vividly illustrate these dilemmas.

Analyzing the earlier successes of high-yielding crop varieties in the Green Revolution in East and South Asia, Goran Djurfeldt and others concluded that the revolution in Asia was a state-driven, market-mediated, and small-farmer based strategy to attain self-sufficiency in food grains, mainly motivated by national and geopolitical factors. These three characteristic ingredients of the successful process of adopting modern varieties in Asia have largely been absent in Africa. Although the technology is available, and has been gradually adapted to the different and heterogeneous agroclimatic conditions in Africa, important institutional reforms are needed to make up and complement the entire package of necessary conditions, which include private and public inputs, infrastructure and marketing, support services, and an enabling environment that will provide adequate incentives and an initial package of resources to farmers so they can adopt new varieties and production methods. In our world, with plentiful of imperfections and all too many constraints on the adoption of new production technologies, understanding these constraints is as important as understanding the production technologies themselves.

Moreover, farm households are highly unequal in terms of their assets and living conditions. Their ability to access knowledge, acquire modern inputs, and obtain credit is vastly different. Even if agricultural intensification promises high returns, off-farm work and migration may be more rewarding as the number of people in rural areas continues to rise and their resources are shrinking. Under high transaction costs in the product markets and imperfectly functioning labor and credit markets, a price hike for cash crops may have little effect on output when the farmer cannot divert family labor out of food crops in order to supply basic needs. This is bound to happen when farm households cannot rely on additional (hired) labor for seasonal work or on the food market to make up for income shortfalls with cyclical variations in output. Intensification and higher productivity would then help, but since that requires more inputs, like fertilizer and fresh seeds that farmers must purchase, or would increase the farmers' risks, the lack of credit and the limited and expensive costs of fertilizers are likely to stall adoption.

It needs to be emphasized that the contribution of yield improvement to poverty reduction is only one among several rural livelihood strategies. Observing degrees of farm income diversification of one-third (for low-income households) to more than one-half (for the more affluent ones), Frank Ellis argues that off-farm labor- and migration-led strategies are puzzling because they are not driven by agricultural success, as conventional theory predicts, but by agricultural failure. Local markets characterized by price instability, declining real output prices, and contradictory (if not antagonistic) agricultural policies that are combined with high market uncertainties and an institutional vacuum—despite the reforms that were supposed to correct earlier state failures—have convinced rural households over the years that a strategy of food self-sufficiency would be best for them, despite its limited potential to increase their income.

Without subscribing to Ellis's involution argument, the 2008 World Development Report on agriculture reflects these considerations by promoting a strategy that consists of productivity enhancing and crop diversification. The need for such a long-term strategy is clearly far greater now. Within Africa, reforms and decentralization, farmer (including women) empowerment, and public–private partnerships are coming up, signaling better prospects for a market-oriented, small-farmer strategy.

Challenging options are emerging: decentralized approaches to plant breeding and varietal selection involving farmers at an early stage can accelerate development and dissemination of new and high-yielding varieties, in from 10–15 to 5–7 years. Commercially viable FM radio services, cell phones, and solar-powered Internet services nowadays convey price and market information that substantially lowers the transaction costs for poor farmers in dealing with traders. Private sector involvement, including NGOs, in extension, rural credit, and technical and marketing advice have in many countries lifted the quality and reduced the timing of service delivery. The rapid development of value chains has opened up export opportunities for farmers who merely two decades ago were only serving local markets.

Professor Bigman's study makes a fascinating contribution to a better understanding of the obstacles, challenges, and possible solutions to the eradication of poverty and hunger in Africa. In doing so, this book develops a comprehensive agenda to travel the long road toward institutional and policy reforms that, with proper assistance, will bring Africa closer to meeting the Millennium Development Goals.

Arie Kuyvenhoven
Professor Emeritus of Development Economics and
Director *ad interim*,
Mansholt Graduate School of Social Sciences,
Wageningen University,
the Netherlands

Part I
Introduction and Background

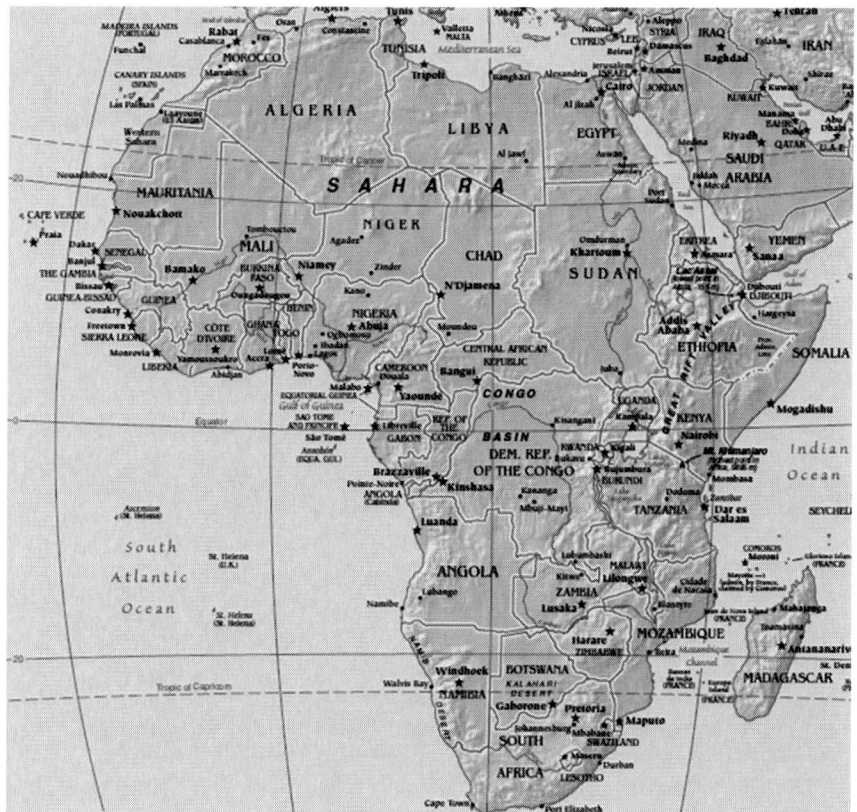

Map 1.1 Africa
Source: CIA, *The World Factbook* (2008).

Introduction

The series of crises since 2008 that have battered the global economy—Zincluding the surge in food and fuel prices, the havoc in the financial markets, and the subsequent global recession—gave rise to doomsday predictions of prolonged global stagnation. If the 1990s was "the age of abundance" and the 2000s (until these crises) was "the age of indulgence," the decade of the 2010s is shaping up to be an "age of scarcity." Not all, however, will be affected by this scarcity—not all countries and not all people; rather, it will affect most people in most countries, but a significant minority will continue to live in abundance. In other words, this is becoming a decade of extreme and growing inequality—between countries, and between people.

During the past decade, until these crises, most African countries had enjoyed the most successful decade of economic growth since their independence. The rapid growth gave Africa, and the world, great hopes that the continent was on its way out of prolonged stagnation to an era of rapid growth, large foreign investments, and a meaningful reduction in poverty. Not all countries in Sub-Saharan Africa (SSA—usually referred to in the book simply as "Africa") took part in the continent's growth, and quite a few are still engaged in civil conflicts and wars. Many countries remained failed states, despite their rich resources, and the vast majority of their populations are extremely poor. The majority of the African countries benefited, however, from a decade of rapid growth after more than three decades of stagnation and rising poverty that made SSA the core of the world's poverty problem. In the mid-2000s, when the clouds of the current crisis were not yet on the horizon, or on the computer screens, the region looked poised to sustain its growth momentum and the reports of the World Bank and the IMF during these years were exuberant ("Africa joined the party").

An important transformation that started already in the early 1990s was the gradual change in the process of economic policy making and economic reforms aimed at restructuring African economies and the institutions of government in charge of the implementation of economic policies. In the wake of the early 1980s debt crisis, the agenda and design of economic reforms in the African countries (aimed at restructuring their economies and economic institutions) was planned and supervised by the international development organization under the so-called "Washington Consensus." These reforms focused on a reorganization of the institutions that implement the fiscal and monetary policies and on the implementation of these countries' macroeconomic policies. The dismal performance of nearly all African countries during the 1990s forced the World Bank and the IMF to restructure these reforms and give greater autonomy and authority to the African countries themselves, while they focused more on helping these countries in the redesign of their institutions and the upgrading of government administration. The end of the prolonged stagnation, toward the end of the decade, was attributed by some to the greater independence African policy makers had in designing their own economic policies and planning their own reforms to suit better their conditions and traditions.

The crises since 2008 exposed the distressing truth that until then was veiled behind a pile of very promising statistical data and under a mountain of very optimistic reports on the continent's renewed growth. In fact, most of that growth was brought about by the commodity boom, and most of the revenues of the resource-rich countries from the export of their natural resources were accumulated by their populations' top percentile, which amassed huge riches, while the rest of the populations benefited very little, and the majority remained poor. According to a World Bank study, more than 80 percent of the revenues of the oil exporting countries was accumulated by the top 1 percent of the population, and even most aid money went to these countries' leading political, economic, and financial elites and the administration in charge of its distribution to the poor. In the urban areas, the majority of the population remained unemployed, and the rural population barely benefited from their countries' rapid growth. The number of poor people continued to rise during the decade, even though their proportion of the population had declined somewhat, but the crises since 2008 reversed even these scanty achievements and raised the incidence of poverty back to its 1990s levels.

The commodity crisis and the subsequent global recession hit the African poor particularly hard due to their paltry assets and low incomes; only a small percentage of the farmers—mostly the large farmers in the vicinity of the urban centers—benefited from the high prices of cereals and other staple foods during the commodity boom, while most others suffered from the rise in production and transport costs with the rise in oil prices and the resulting increase in fertilizers' prices that led to a reduction in their yields, their trade and, thus, also in their real incomes. Even with the bust in commodity prices since mid-2008, food prices remained high and well above their precrisis levels; in the urban centers many people lost their jobs in construction, tourism, mining, and other sectors, which led to a further rise in the already high urban unemployment.

The crash in commodity prices brought also a sharp drop in the growth of the resource-rich countries, from over 6 percent in 2005–07 to less than 1 percent in 2009, as an effect of the steep decline in both the volume and the value of their exports and of the decline in foreign investments. Many rural and urban households also suffered from the decline in remittances they used to receive from family members in the urban centers or in other countries when these individuals lost their jobs in the recession. As a result, within few months the number of the African poor and undernourished population increased by over 100 million people, according to World Bank and FAO estimates.

These and other developments in the African countries during the past decade emphasize that in most of these countries, particularly the resource-rich ones, their rapid growth was largely due to high export revenues from their resources and the flow of foreign investments. This growth benefited mostly the top echelon of these countries' political leaders, army commanders, and economic and financial institutions; it did not much benefit the majority of their people and barely trickled down to the rural areas. For these people, this was another lost decade in which their countries' resources were wasted due to high corruption, reckless spending on arms, and needless civil conflicts and wars. A number of key developments in the coming decade, most notably global warming and the clouds of a global recession, threaten to make it another lost decade that may deepen the poverty and food deficiency of the vast majority of Africa's population. Several other developments, however, may counter these trends, including the rapid recovery of commodity prices, the discovery of vast new natural resources in many countries, and the efforts to settle conflicts and wars peacefully.

The veering economic developments of the past decade constituted only one of three major new trends that started already in the 1990s and are transforming the African continent. The progress of Africa in the coming years will be determined by these three developments and by their combined effects on Africa's countries and people. The first is the capacity of the African countries to sustain their growth and use it more effectively to develop their economies. The second is the comprehensive change of the African society as an effect of the demographic changes generated by the rapid growth of the urban population. The third is the changes in the system of governance and in the relations between the African leaders and their people with spread of democracy.

The demographic change as an effect of the rapid and accelerating flow of migrants from rural areas (and, in some countries, also the flow of migrants from other, poorer countries) is transforming the African continent and African society by dramatically converting a centuries-long rural society and making Africa into an urban continent. That transformation is bound to significantly and comprehensively alter the character of African society: Throughout its history, the vast majority of the African people lived in rural communities to which they were strongly loyal, wholeheartedly supporting their tribes, and admiringly obeying their tribes' elders. In their rural communities "Africa was 'tamed' by its difficult agro-climatic conditions *against great handicaps not generally present in other continents, whether in terms of thin soils, difficult rainfall incidence, a multitude of pests and fevers, and much else that made survival difficult.*"[1] Although the African people did not shy away from aggressive conflict and risked their lives to protect other members of their tribe, their machetes were vastly inferior to the guns of their conquerors. After going through the trauma of the slave trade, they were forced by the eighteenth century to surrender to the rule of the colonial powers and later to the rule of their own autocratic leaders.

An urban Africa will change not only the work and living conditions of its urbanite peoples, but, more fundamentally, their social characteristics, their interactions with each other, and their relations to their traditions. The young generation of Africans now converging to the urban centers is, for example, acquiescing increasingly less to the whims of their leaders, is less submissive and less tolerant to their corruption, far more rebellious in their demands for the accountability of these autocratic leaders, and less willing to accept the dismal share of their countries' resources that these leaders allocate to their people. This new generation is more vocal and more aggressive in demanding fundamental change and radical reforms in their political system and in the form and formation of government.

Their living conditions in the urban areas were, and remain, their greatest frustration: As they arrived to the urban centers they came to realize that the prospects of finding employment were (and still are) very small, their hopes to improve their living conditions not likely to be realized. Instead, they were forced to squeeze into inhabitable shantytowns and do whatever it took to find some food to nourish themselves. Crime, violence, prostitution, and child labor have been their ways of surviving the day, while growing fundamentalism of sectarian groups has been their way of seeking a ray of hope in the next day. Violence was their way of expressing their grievances and frustrations as well as their determination to fight for their rights and change the way in which their government operates—for the benefit of the elite, while cynically neglecting the needs of and its responsibility to the rest of the population.

This broad-brush description of the social impact of urbanization on the new generation of Africans who, with some hope but mostly out of no other choice, had to leave their homes and villages and migrate to urban centers, is obviously a generalization. Its goal is to emphasize that the rural-urban migration has far greater impact on society than what is summarized by the statistical figures of demographic change, and for the African people this has been a traumatic transformation of the social and individual makeup that characterized their society. For the new generation of Africans growing up in the urban centers, this has been a fundamental personal and social metamorphosis, one that has changed ingrained traditions and ways of life and completely disintegrated their social institutions. This subject is discussed in detail in chapters 3.1 and 3.2.

These people will not be "tame" or timid, nor will they remain passive accomplices if they do not have the freedom to determine their fate; they will react to these changes and act to shape their new way of life; they will loudly express their frustrations, aggressively protest against the government, and demand their leaders take measures to improve living conditions in the urban centers, create employment, and make investments to improve the crumbling infrastructure. They will not waver when it comes to demonstrating against their countries' leaders and the gross injustices of the regimes that rob their countries' resources and rob the people of their hope. They will not hesitate to stand up against the security forces that will try to tame their protests, with brute force disperse their demonstrations, and arrest them; they know full well that they have very little to lose, whereas back in the village their forefathers could have lost their land.

In many countries, such protests are hardly likely to bring anything other than the brutal security forces, but as the number, daring, and violence of the demonstrations is rising, more governments in more countries are likely to take some measures to, at least, calm them down. The violent demonstrations in Nigeria, Zimbabwe, and South Africa forced those governments to make tangible efforts to fight corruption and fraudulence in the elections. The deadly street fighting in Kenya forced the government to write a constitution that recognizes individual rights and establishes restrictions on government actions, and to offer that constitution for a vote by the general population.

The important conclusion from this inevitably brief summary of the changes in Africa as an effect of the process of urbanization is that this has not been merely, and only, a demographic change. As the urban population is rising and living conditions in the cities are deteriorating, the social impact of the demographic changes becomes more dominant, and people react more aggressively to deterioration in their living conditions, particularly conditions due to the high unemployment. Moreover, the political impact of demographic and social changes is also likely to increase over time, and the combined effect of all these changes will determined the impact of the urbanization process.

The spread of democratization in Africa is also likely to affect relations between the people and their governments, although these effects are likely to vary widely among countries. In the early 1990s only three African countries held democratic elections and maintained a regime that had the basic characteristics of a democracy. By the end of first decade of the twenty-first century, 48 African countries held democratic elections. At this stage, one cannot be too excited about this development, since many, if not most, elections were merely a sham, and the same autocratic leaders or ruling parties were elected. In some countries, the transition to democracy was evident; in most others, the process of democratization is bound to be slow and gradual, and its role and potential to bring about significant and authentic changes in their systems of government may become more evident only over time.

These three trends are interrelated, and their combined effects may create difficulty in a statistical, or even in a more elaborate, econometric analysis aimed at extrapolating future trends on the basis of their past developments. This is so for two reasons: First, an extrapolation made on the basis of past data must include a sufficient number of years in order to yield statistically significant results. In Africa, most of these data are therefore based on developments in these countries when the majority of their population still lived in rural areas and, thus, the impact of urbanization will not be taken into account for estimating future trends. The data of the past decade or so that characterize both the demographic trends have too few observations to provide statistically significant estimations and, more importantly, do not yet reflect the social impact of urbanization and people's response to these dramatic changes in their lives. The full effects of urbanization will, therefore, be reflected in the statistical data only after a longer time period.

Similar difficulties are likely to arise in a statistical analysis of the change in political systems as an effect of the spread of democracy. For one, the spread of democratic elections was very gradual, and their legitimacy still significantly varies between countries. Although most of these elections were merely a pretense and did not make any changes in the regime, in some countries they did bring a change in leadership and an authentic effort to fight corruption. Even more important was the impact of the voting process on the attitude of people toward the regime, an impact that was evident in most countries. Even in countries where the actual changes that took place as an effect of the elections have been rather marginal (due to widespread vote-rigging), two principles of democracy have been made more widely accepted: The freedom of expression and the freedom of the media. With today's means of communication through the Internet and the mobile phones that are quite common in Africa, effective control over the formal and informal media in various blogs is limited. Nevertheless, the wide acceptance of freedom of the press, despite some casualties among reporters and cameramen, made the media these countries' most effective watchdogs and informal comptrollers and supervisors over government administration.

The actual benefits from the election process are still quite controversial, however; some scholars even doubt the desirability of holding elections in a multiethnic society, since they are likely to inflame emotions of rivalry and antagonism between tribes; many African leaders openly oppose the transition to a European version of democracy, primarily the term limit on the president, which contradicts the African traditions. Among voters there has been much greater support and enthusiasm, even about the election process itself. One reason was that many people, primarily among minority groups, saw the elections as an opportunity to express their opposition to certain politicians who were either corrupt or highly biased against them. Another reason was the widespread favoritism politicians at least promised to their supporters. In quite a few countries, voters were not willing to accept fraudulent elections: In 2007 Nigerian voters expressed anger at how the ruling People's Democratic Party conducted the charade of an election, and they forced the government to make concessions in the conduct of the next election, in 2011. In Kenya, the elections of 2007 were extremely chaotic, and more than a thousand people died in violent clashes that brought back monstrous memories of past tribal rivalries; three years later, the vote on the constitution was surprisingly calm and orderly, even though it introduced much more comprehensive changes in the political system. Indeed, people learned from, and responded to, their experience. In Zimbabwe, voters refused to accept the open rigging by Robert Mugabe and, after his faked victory in the first round, forced him to hold a second round.

Donors demanded the African countries hold elections to prove their commitment to good governance and to receive legitimacy from their people and the international community. The donors tried to minimize rigging by demanding the presence and supervision of international observers, but in practice many elections were still widely fraudulent. Donors' demands to hold elections as a condition for their aid proved quite effective, and even Sudanese leader al-Bashir was forced to hold elections, although their legitimacy was widely suspected. Some African regional organizations also started to punish member states that did not hold elections or where a coup toppled a democratically elected governments. Partly because of these pressures, the number of successful military coups has declined from 20 in 1980–89, to 17 in 1990–99, to seven in 2000–09.

The spread of democracy was strongly influenced by the increase in Africa's urban populations; this influence was due to the more frequent and intense interaction between people and to the greater coordination between them, which made their demonstrations more influential. The spread of democratic elections, however fraudulent, made people more aware of their rights, less tolerant to corruption in the government, and more willing to use their impact to force their government to meet higher standards of governance. An analysis of the impact of democracy should not, therefore, focus on the voting process as a one-time event, but should take into account the impact of this process on people's behavior, their reaction to the power that elections have given them, and their impact on the government.

These three main trends in African economies and societies are interrelated and reinforce each other. A comprehensive analysis of recent and future developments in Africa must, therefore, include an evaluation of the combined effects of their economic growth, of their urbanization and its demographic-social consequences, and of political developments with the spread of democracy. Since the available time series data that encapsulate these developments are not sufficient for this analysis, the alternative used in this book is a scenario analysis that illustrates alternative trends of future development based on the actual developments in selected African countries or countries in other continents that have a longer experience with these changes.

* * *

The massive use and abuse of Africa's incredibly rich resources started with the colonial powers although they were mostly interested in the natural resources spread above the continent's surface: The treasures hidden in its rainforest, from rubber trees to timber to the unique tropical fruits, as well as in the great potential of the abundant fertile lands, tropical climate, and cheap labor for growing crops like coffee, cocoa, and cotton that were exported very profitably to Europe. Interest in the rich resources under the continent's surface started only in the 1930s, when Nigerian oil became a precious resource, but that interest reached its current near-epidemic dimensions only in the second half of the twentieth century, when large international corporations made huge investments to exploit the continent's oil, minerals, diamonds, and even, more recently, uranium.

These resources, which could have been the continent's greatest blessing and a lever of growth, became a curse under the autocratic leaders of the newly independent African countries. There were several reasons why Africa's resources became a curse, but those reasons differed substantially between countries and time periods. Paul Collier, in his famous book *The Bottom Billion*, emphasized the abundance of natural resources as one of Africa's poverty traps because they encouraged corrupt politicians to seize power in order to divide the spoils, which made their economies vulnerable to see-sawing world commodity prices. In other words, not the resources were the curse, but the corrupt leaders (who, in many countries, were military commanders rather than politicians). The explanation Collier gives is, however, incomplete and to some extent a simplifying generalization.

Botswana is perhaps the most well-known counter example: Although it has the world's largest mines of diamonds, Botswana has also had one of the world's highest rates of economic growth since its independence in 1966. Through fiscal discipline and sound management, Botswana transformed itself from one of the poorest countries in the world to a middle-income country with a 2008 per capita GDP of $14,100, and its diamond mining has fueled much of the expansion. Zambia, to take another example, has rich copper resources. It had multiparty elections already in 1991, but it took another decade for the country to stabilize its democratic regime and, in 2001, elected president Levy Mwanawasa launched a successful campaign against corruption, privatized the copper mines, and accelerated the country's growth to 6 percent, despite the variations in copper prices. Although the country is still very poor and 85 percent of its population lives in rural areas, its copper resources did not "encourage corrupt politicians to seize power," and in the past decade the country had three multiparty elections judged by international observers as free and fair.

These and few other countries are, however, the exceptions. In most other countries, autocratic leaders were not motivated to seize power because of their countries' resources; although their authoritarian rule enabled them to embezzle their countries' coffers to enrich themselves, in many of these countries the resources were not even discovered when the race for leadership started: Robert Mugabe, leader of one of the two armed groups in the struggle for the independence of the country then known as Zimbabwe-Rhodesia, won elections for leadership in 1980, when the country was considered resource-poor; the country's treasures of diamonds and gold were discovered only in the past few years. Omar al-Bashir in Sudan was "elected" president in 1993 after serving as chief of state since 1989, well before the country's oil resources were discovered. Most African leaders were not driven to seize power because of their countries' resources. Moreover, corruption is rampant in both the resource-poor and resource-rich countries, although the administration in the resource-poor can lead to political instability and further exacerbate looting. In fact, many of Africa's more than a hundred military coups took place in countries that were resource poor at the time (primarily the mid-1960s through the 1970s).

In many countries worldwide, important economic reforms have been undertaken during dictatorial regimes. The majority of the emerging economies, including Chile under Pinochet, South Korea under Park, and most other East Asian economies, made significant reforms under undemocratic regimes. Yet political and economic development has varied widely in different continents and regions. In some states, democratic regimes have fallen prey to conflicting interests of competing social groups; these conflicts created a deadlock, and blocked further reforms. However, democracy has also proved to be the a very effective way of building the nation-state and strengthening the communion between people.

The debate on the merits of democracy remains controversial, and empirical studies conducted in recent years have not given clear answers. Huntington (1968) emphasized the pressures of interest groups that lead to excessive private and public consumption at the expense of investment, while in other communities the unity among different groups created by democracy increases the willingness of people to make sacrifices to build their nation for future generations. Democracy also provides better security of property rights and personal safety, while autocratic leaders are not restricted by a system of law and tend to be predatory (see the discussion and references in chapter 5.1).

Chapter 2.1 discusses several other reasons why the resources of so many African countries became a curse, and it highlights the differences among countries. In most countries the problem was not the competition between leaders over the control of their countries' resources in order to enrich themselves, but the competition over power and control between tribes and ethnic or sectarian groups of these multiethnic societies. That control enabled the leading tribe to use the levers of the state to obtain a larger and better share of the country's resources and employment opportunities, ranging from agricultural resources to jobs in government, and to gain heftily when the leader they supported spread lavish favoritism to supporters and members of his tribe in order to cement their support.

Under colonial rule, the tribes had full control over their land and water resources; their leaders had absolute power and jurisdiction over the allocation of resources and settling the relations between people and communities within that territory. Even the colonial powers generally acknowledged and respected the territorial integrity of the tribes and the authority of their leaders to settle conflicts between their tribes' members, although there were indeed cases in which they gave preferential treatment to one tribe at the expense of others in order to secure its support. The colonial boundaries that became the borders of the newly independent states divided the territories of individual tribes between different states and demolished the tribes' territorial integrity, turning the competition over control of the land into a winner-takes-all race for power between the fragments of tribes.

That competition over the control of the state brought to power autocratic, self-centered and onerous leaders who used the levers of the state to gain control over territories that, in the past, were under the jurisdiction of rival tribes, and thus further used and abused their power at the expense of minority tribes. In that callous pursuit of power, the losers often lost everything, including sometimes their lives, and the leader who gained power, at least until the next coup, exploited it to strengthen control and thus became the curse of both the resource-poor and the resource-rich countries. In order to enrich themselves and distribute favoritism to their supporters at the expense of the others, these leaders looted their countries' resources, even their farmers' agricultural produce, through high taxes on their export and control over local trade.

Collier emphasized the negative impact of *bad governance* as one of the four poverty traps. Bad governance and corrupt and autocratic leader was, however, essentially the same thing: The autocratic leader did not allow the establishment of efficient institutions and did not give them real authority that could have restricted his own authority; had they been able to establish good governance with sufficient authority, their institutions would not have allowed an autocratic leader to abuse the rule of law. That was the reason why the institutional reforms the World Bank tried to implement in the late 1980s did not receive more than nominal support from the countries' leaders and had limited impact.

The third poverty trap Collier noted is the trap of *land-locked countries*. This is, in my view, a "statistical trap" that substitutes correlation for causality. Botswana and Uganda, the two fastest growing African countries since the mid-1980s and during the 1990s, are landlocked countries that are obvious counter examples. The limited impact of this trap is discussed in chapter 2.1 and can be summarized as follows: The borders of the African countries determined by the colonial powers in 1885 were administrative boundaries designed to divide the continent's resources among the powers. Their main interest was in the territories that had the resources they needed, and they carved the borders so that countries that had these resources were given access to the coast. King Leopold of Belgium, who chaired the conference of the colonial powers that shaped these boundaries, made sure Congo Kinshasa, which had many natural resources the Belgians who ruled the country used, primarily the rubber trees, would have access to the coast through a narrow strip of land, even though the country was in practice landlocked.

The more remote territories were less desirable, both because they did not have rich resources and because of the lack of inland roads; the exploitation of their resources was therefore far too costly. As a result, in the maps carved in 1885 most areas that were resource-poor and had poor road infrastructure were left as territories without coastal access. In other words, it was not coastal access made countries rich, but their rich resources were the motivation for the colonial powers to give them coastal access; similarly, most landlocked countries did not become poor because they were landlocked, but rather they were left landlocked by the colonial powers because they had neither resources nor fertile lands and were thus less desirable. In the past decade, rich resources were discovered in many of the landlocked countries, including Zambia, Zimbabwe, Chad, Niger, and few others. These resources and the possibility of finding more have attracted many foreign investors. Many countries that have coastal access, both resources-rich countries like Nigeria, Guinea, Guinea Bissau, and Sudan, and resource-poor countries like Eritrea, Somalia, and Kenya on the east coast, and Togo and Mauritania on the west coast, became *failed states*, and the vast majority of their populations is extremely poor.

Collier maintains that landlocked countries will need long-term aid because they are at a huge geographical disadvantage. Remote regions in large coastal countries like Sudan, Tanzania, Kenya, and others are also at a huge geographical disadvantage and remain extremely poor. The main reason for the geographical disadvantage of remote regions, despite their countries' coastal access, is the crumbling condition of rural roads that limit trade and leave them isolated. In Mozambique, the high food prices in 2009 had a strong effect on urban consumers but the country's size, the fractured agricultural markets, and the high inland transport costs restricted trade from the remote inland regions to the urban centers and, thus, also the transmission of the high prices urban centers to the remote rural areas. A USDA study found that imported maize from Argentina was sold in Mozambique's capital, Maputo, at the same price as the local maize from the northern part of the country. Another USDA study found that transport costs of wheat from Chicago to the port of Mombasa in Kenya are equal to the land transport costs from Mombasa to Kampala in Uganda. Kenyan farmers therefore preferred to trade in the local markets or in the markets of the neighboring landlocked countries, Malawi or Zambia, that have similar constraints of poor infrastructure on their trade.

Moreover, the criteria for the allocation of aid should be based not only on the geographical disadvantage of landlocked countries but also on the countries' natural resources that determine their capacity to participate in the costs of building rural roads and making other investments in their geographically disadvantaged remote areas. The revenues of landlocked countries like Zambia, Chad, Zimbabwe, and others give them the resources to invest in their rural areas and raise the standard of living of their extremely poor populations, even without aid. But the highly unequal distribution of their revenues from their resources benefit mostly these countries' elites and much of these revenues are wasted in civil conflicts and wars.

The forth trap Collier mentions is *conflicts*. These conflicts indeed had disastrous effects on African economies, but their inclusion as one of the traps that explains their poverty is essentially tautological: In the past five decades *all* African countries, including South Africa, were engaged in one or more conflicts, military coups, or wars. A more detailed explanation is therefore required to determine whether conflicts were the *reason* for these countries' poverty, or whether poverty was the *reason* for their conflicts. That explanation should evaluate the role and responsibility of autocratic leaders, the impact of the ethnic and sectarian divide, and other causes that can explain the many conflicts that have impoverished the continent despite its rich resources. That wider evaluation is crucial to determining the prospects of bringing these conflicts to an end and thus reducing their devastating exacerbation of poverty. The roots of civil conflicts in Africa, and a more detailed discussion of the experience in selected countries, is given in chapter 4.1.

* * *

The combined effects of the economic, demographic, social, and political changes most African countries are undergoing are deep and fundamental, and jointly these trends represent a significant transformation of African society and economy. The longer-term impact of these trends is less clear, however: Resource-rich countries are likely to benefit from growing competition over natural resources between developed and emerging economies, led by China. Global warming is likely to intensify weather instability and increase the frequency of droughts in some countries and floods in others. The rapidly growing urban population will increase unemployment and poverty and aggravate crime and political instability, but the declining power of many autocratic leaders may reduce the pressure to reduce income inequality. On top of all that, the world economy is undergoing very significant changes that also will ripple to the least developed countries.

Despite the rapid growth of the past decade, nearly half the African countries remained fragile or even failed states, and despite the spread of democracy only four countries, Ghana, Namibia, Botswana, and South Africa, are considered stable democracies, while around a score of countries are still ruled by autocratic and despotic leaders, even though they may have been "democratically" elected. Notwithstanding the significant decline in the number and intensity of wars and conflicts in the past decade, quite a few countries are still embroiled in costly internal conflicts or in wars with neighboring countries, and the number of conflicts may rise in the coming decade as a result of global warming due to more intense competition over the continent's dwindling agricultural land and water resources. The transition to democracy may have positive effects on the accountability of some elected governments, but the election process may intensify the tension between ethnic or sectarian groups and may lead to civil conflicts and possibly even to the fragmentation of countries like Sudan, where the rivalry between population-subgroups reaches the point where compromise is not possible. Further discussion of this subject is given in chapter 4.3.

In quite a few additional countries, including Senegal, Mali, Mozambique, Tanzania, and possibly even Nigeria, the emergence of more stable, more responsible, and more responsive government through democratic elections may be a longer and not always stable process, but it is certainly possible. Already during the past decade the economic policies of many African governments have been more disciplined and, despite their high export revenues, even many resource-rich countries have maintained rather prudent policies that were in sharp contrast to their reckless waste during the commodity boom in the 1970s and the subsequent debt crisis. With the escalation of the global economic crisis in 2008, many countries resorted to controlled fiscal, monetary, and exchange rate policies that kept their fiscal deficits in check, maintained the stability of their financial systems, and prevented the accumulation of large foreign debts. The World Bank report on the Global Economic Prospects of 2010 noted that the improved macroeconomic fundamentals in many African countries at the onset of the crisis meant that its impact was less pronounced than in other regions and relative to previous external shocks.

The change in attitude is also becoming more evident in many countries, such as Madagascar, Zimbabwe, Kenya, Nigeria, Mauritania, and others as people more openly demand their rights and a fair share in their country's resources and are less tolerant of corruption, less willing to accept rigging in elections, and less acquiescent to tyrants who embezzle their countries' resources.

One could see this change and the new determination of the common people in the crowds that protested against the stubborn hold on power of Robert Mugabe, who used his old tactics, but this time without success, in an attempt to deny his rival, Morgan Tsvangirai, his rightful victory in Zimbabwe's elections. One could see it also in the anger of the crowd that gathered in the stadium in Guinea to protest against the country's ruthless dictator despite the threat of his security forces, which stormed into the stadium, killed more than 150 people, and raped dozens of women. One could see it even in Nigeria, one of Africa's most corrupt countries, during the violent demonstrations after the deeply flawed elections in 2007, when people protested vote-rigging and fraudulence. Many were stunned two years later when the "go-slow" and ailing Nigerian president, Umaru Yar'Adua, took uncompromising measures to clean up the financial system; and many in the political establishment were bewildered when, with the backing of the president, the new governor of one of Nigeria's most problematic states in the Niger Delta, invited outside accountants and advisors to audit the state's finances and, to the horror of many other governors, instructed them to expose the use of money that flows from the state's coffers to government authorities.

Several other developments are testimony to changes in Africa: Several prolonged wars and civil conflicts—in Sierra Leone, Angola, Eritrea, and southern Sudan—ended with either peace agreements or negotiated settlements that were fragile but seem to justify the hopes that the settlement of future conflicts will be made in an arbitration process rather than on the battlefield. Tribal and sectarian tensions in Côte d'Ivoire and Kenya abated when all parties came to realize the damage their fighting caused their own country and themselves. An increasing number of countries, from Mali to Mozambique and Malawi, have taken effective measures to improve their economy and their system of governance and to help their poor.

The changes are slow and gradual, however, and bound to encounter many obstacles. The stagnation and poverty that crippled African countries for many decades is of the African leaders' own making, and they cannot continue to blame colonial powers for all their malaise. The ongoing transformation of African economies, societies, and political systems gives them the opportunity and the power to unshackle themselves from the burden of the past and embark on a new road of growth and better living conditions.

The first step in that direction is in the economic domain by making more effective and more equitable use of the African countries' economic resources. The past decade of miraculous growth demonstrates this potential, but in practice that growth has mostly benefited the elites or was largely spent on military conflicts. Despite the trough in commodity prices in mid-2008, the demand for Africa's resources remains strong, and their exports have already started to recover, due both to the renewed global demand that also started to raise prices and to the wave of discoveries during the past decade of new resources, from oil and natural gas to diamonds, gold, and uranium, which made more countries resource-rich and made Africa the "second OPEC."

The discovery of new resources, including in countries like Ghana and Uganda that in the past did not have natural resources, is also likely to renew the flow of foreign direct investments to the region, and China is perhaps the most active country in that regard. The continent's rich resources can be used as lever for the development of other sectors and potentially new industries, but so far this potential has been neglected. In Nigeria, Africa's largest oil producer, for decades the lack of investments (even in the country's refineries) is now forcing it to import gasoline and diesel. Instead of investing its huge revenues to build new refineries and develop new industries based on the many by-products of oil, from fertilizers to synthetic materials, and thus provide employment to the growing urban population, most of the revenues were embezzled by corruption, looted by criminal gangs, or spent on lavish favoritism.

* * *

The major threat to the continent's economy and to the majority of its population is the impact of climate changes and global warming on the agricultural sector and on the rural population. The unstable climatic conditions already affect some regions that suffer from more frequent droughts and floods; in the coming decade climate changes threaten to affect vast semiarid areas much more severely. In many African countries, the agricultural lands are already eroding, and water resources are drying out, thus reducing the continent's capacity to produce enough food for its population, while geneticists, soil scientists, entomologists, hydrologists, and many scientists in related fields are fighting to counter or at least moderate these devastating effects. Their path-breaking success in the "Green Revolution" gives hope that human ingenuity will once again produce suitable crops that are drought-resistant, have higher yields, and enable farmers in semiarid areas to cope with the effects of global warming and prevent once again Malthus's dismal prediction that the rise in food supply will trail behind the rapid rise in the continent's population, and repudiate the fate of imminent widespread hunger. The chapters in part II provide an analysis of the various dimensions of this pending crisis.

In fact, even Malthus's algebraic illustration of the process of deepening poverty and hunger—due to the slow growth of agricultural production that falls short of the rapid growth of the population—missed a central element that economists would predict: Even if per capita food supply declines as the growth of the population outpaces the growth in food production, famine will not spread *equally* across all countries and all population groups. Income inequalities between countries and between people will increase the bias in the distribution of the available food supply against the poor, whereas the more affluent segments of the population will continue to have enough food. The African poor will suffer the most and fall victim to the shrinking food supply, while the affluent will continue to afford the same high quality diet they are used to.

The most devastating effect of global warming and the dwindling agricultural resources in Africa will be to force rural communities in many regions to leave their lands. Today, there are about 12 million Internally Displaced Persons (IDPs) across the continent, and they account for half the world's total IDPs. Sudan, alone, has over 4 million IDPs, Democratic Republic of the Congo (DRC) has another 2 million, Somalia has nearly 1.5 million, and many other African countries, including Uganda, Zimbabwe, and Kenya have hundreds of thousands more IDPs. In addition, there are around 3 million African refugees who crossed an international border into other countries. In the past, most had been displaced by armed conflicts, violence, and human-rights violations, but in the coming decade many more will be displaced by natural disasters related to the climate change predicted to cut rain-fed agriculture in the semiarid regions by nearly 50 percent during the decade.

The young people, particularly men, will go to the urban centers; the others will wander and search for other areas where they can settle and produce the food they need for their own consumption and for feeding their cattle. The Intergovernmental Panel on Climate Change (IPCC) predicts Africa will bear the brunt of the climate change, and in the coming years global warming is likely to become the greatest threat for African economies and for their countries' social and political stability. The more frequent cycles of droughts and floods could uproot millions of people in rural areas from their ancestral lands, forcing many to change their lifestyle, impoverishing most of them, and exposing the remaining rural population to violent attacks of gangs that will not spare their lives as they try to steal their cattle, their seeds, their other assets, and sometimes even their children. The International Organization for Migration estimates that most of the world's 200 million climate-change migrants will be African.

As more farmers and herders are forced to migrate from ancestral homelands in search of water resources and agricultural lands, the more affluent countries are likely to tighten border controls in an effort to prevent these displaced people from crossing into their territories and, thus, to protect their own rural population and agricultural resources. But the desperate search for water and food, and the help some migrants may receive from members of their own tribe who had been separated from them by colonial borders and now live in these other countries, are likely to make these controls increasingly more difficult.

The settlement of border disputes between countries is also likely to become more difficult and more intense due to conflicts over ever-scarcer agricultural resources. The spread of famine and malnutrition already threatens many countries' fragile economies and may destabilize their social balance and their regimes by instigating conflicts and wars. As millions of people are uprooted, conflicts and competition between tribes is bound to intensify and border conflicts are likely to be aggravated by claims and counter-claims over agricultural resources. To contain the damage of global warming as well as the long neglect of the rural sector, proper measures should therefore be taken without delay at least to improve the rural transport system.

In principle, the impending scarcity of agricultural resources should motivate more collaboration between countries in joint water projects or cross-country roads, but political rivalry could disrupt this collaboration if the competition over these resources is perceived as a zero-sum game in which some countries will gain while others are bound to lose from this collaboration. Donor countries and the African Union can have a pivotal role in promoting positive-sum collaboration by providing financial aid and pressuring for agreements between countries in ways that will be beneficial to all of them. Their support will also be necessary to implement multicountry projects already planned, most notably the multicountry collaboration in the Nile project; a decline in the river's water resources may increase pressure on the governments of the participating countries to allocate more water for local irrigation and hydraulic projects. The initiation and coordination of joint projects in other regions, with the support of the donor countries and international development organizations, can strengthen collaboration and prevent the escalation of conflicts between countries and the damage of global warming to their rural populations. They can include water projects, development of drought-resistant crop varieties suitable to the conditions in these regions, cross-country roads, planting trees to stop soil erosion, and ending (with incentives, compensations or legal measures) the widespread practice of cutting trees for fuel or for logging that ruins the rainforests

* * *

The economic, demographic, social, and political developments that affected the African countries are closely interrelated and strongly impinge on each other; plans for future development must therefore also be interrelated and integrated by taking into account the impact of each project and policy on the neighboring countries. Economic development plans should take into account not only their direct economic costs and benefits but also their indirect and longer-term demographic, social, and political effects in the entire region.

The lack of development in rural areas, and of the agricultural sector, will remain the Achilles heel of African countries because they affect the majority of their poor populations. Poverty alleviation programs would, therefore, have to continue to concentrate on the rural population and take into account the aging of that population, the decline in their productivity, the dwindling land and water resources, and the risk of conflict between rural communities over these resources. At the same time, future poverty alleviation programs would also have take into account the growing urban population and the growing number of urban poor. These trends in the distribution of the population and of poverty across rural areas and in urban centers will require African countries to plan changes in their economic and social programs both because the urban poor will have greater political influence and because their dismal living conditions will increase the spread of diseases and cause deterioration in personal safety that drives away private investors.

The costs of poverty alleviation programs in urban centers are much higher than in rural areas, since they require employment programs based on the development of an industrial sector and, thus, need much larger government investments in roads, electricity, water supply, and so forth, together with direct government incentives to attract investors. Poverty alleviation in urban centers would also need large investments to improve living conditions in the slums by improving the sanitation systems, providing basic health services, tightening control over crime, and giving some safety nets to the very young and also to the very old, who may no longer be able to rely on the help of the extended family.

The experience of the past decade, however, gives little hope that these goals will be achieved. Despite their rapid growth, even in the resource-rich counties, from Nigeria, Guinea, Gabon, and Congo to the oil-exporting countries in the Horn of Africa, only a tiny share of the huge wealth amassed during the commodity boom trickled down to the rural areas and to their poor, and only few African countries are likely to achieve the MDG goals of reducing poverty, malnutrition, child mortality, and other like goals. A combination of high corruption, extreme inequality in the distribution of income and wealth, ineffective institutions, and a waste of resources on military conflicts has prevented these countries from improving the living conditions of their populations. The horrendous costs of the civil conflicts and wars in human lives, economic resources, and damage to the continent's infrastructure have prevented even the resource-rich countries from reducing their poverty.

Chapter 4.1 examines the roots of the incessant civil conflicts and wars in Africa dating back to the colonial era, and chapter 4.2 evaluates their longer-term impact on the continent's growth and poverty. These chapters also review the driving forces of civil conflicts and the competition between tribes over their countries' leadership that gave great advantage to the larger tribes, while the minority tribes were largely excluded and grossly discriminated against. The violation of the territorial integrity of most tribes by colonial boundaries that became the borders of newly independent states, and the fervent insistence of autocratic leaders to defend their autonomy, have prevented the settlement of border disputes and retained their bias in favor of the leader's own tribe and against minority tribes. These borders, therefore, infringed upon the territorial integrity of the latter and thus perpetuated and intensified conflicts and rivalries between tribes, the alienation and opposition of the minority tribes to the regime, and the formation of any collaboration between tribes that is essential for the creation of any allegiance to their nation-state.

The autocratic leaders also prevented the establishment of a functioning system and institutions of governance that could have constrained their control and restricted their freedom to allocate the country's resources, to embezzle the treasury's coffers, and to determine the laws without any restrictions or accountability. The civil conflicts and autocratic regimes benefited only the countries' leaders and a small circle of their supporters, but they were highly damaging to the rest of the population, including the leaders' own tribes, due to their devastating effects on the economy and the extreme inequalities they created in the distribution of income and wealth between the top echelon of these countries' political, military, economic, and financial elite and the rest of the population.

* * *

The flow of migrants to the cities is creating huge megalopolises in which unemployment is high and poverty is rising, and it requires therefore fundamental changes in the structure of the African economies. After two decades of growing rural-urban migration, Africa is still a rural continent and the majority of population is still working in agriculture. According to estimates of the US Census Bureau (2008), the African population is growing at an annual rate of 2.3 percent, twice the growth rate in Asia and Latin America, and the population in African urban areas is growing at an annual rate of 3.5 percent. According to UN projections noted earlier, by 2030 the majority of the African population will live in urban areas, although the majority of the poor will still live in the rural areas. In the two most populous African countries, South Africa and Nigeria, at least half the population already lives in urban centers.

Most rural-urban migrants were essentially forced to leave their villages as an effect of the decline in per capita food production and income, partly because the declining size of the plots farmers could allocate to their sons is falling below the size is necessary to produce enough food for living. These migrants are tilting the demographic balance and changing the age distribution between rural and urban populations; as the population in the villages is aging, their productivity is declining, and they increasingly depend on aid and remittances.

By the end of the next decade, several large cities, including Cairo, Lagos, Accra, Dakar, Conakry, Abidjan, Kinshasa, Johannesburg, and others will have a population of around 10 million each and, according to Habitat, the UN Agency for urban development, 80 other cities each will have 1 to 5 million people. The cross-country migration, from famine-stricken rural areas in the poorer countries to the cities in the better-off ones, is likely to be another factor that will intensify tensions between social groups; in South Africa, there have already been violent demonstrations in Johannesburg and Pretoria, and the locals have demanded stopping the flow of migrants who take their jobs and lower their wages. Migration of poor Africans to other countries, particularly in Europe, is becoming a major political problem and a reason for growing social tensions and the spread of crime and violence.

In other regions, most notably East Asia, the urbanization process was combined with an industrial revolution, and rural migrants were therefore able to find employment in the growing industries in the urban centers that, in their turn, could take advantage of the flow of low-wage workers; in Africa the industrial revolution failed to establish roots as far back as the 1980s, for reasons that are discussed in chapter 3.2, and the continent has not recovered since. The high cost of doing business in Africa—due to the decaying infrastructure, the ineffective public institutions that deal with trade, the high corruption at all levels of government, and escalating crime—sharply reduced the competitiveness of local industries despite their abundance of cheap labor. The failure to build even textile manufacturing in Africa despite the abundance of cheap labor raises questions about the potential to build competitive industries in the future. With the exception of South Africa, African countries do not have local industries except for light manufacturing that produce primarily for the local market, use primitive technology, and employ a small number of workers, most of them in the informal market and at very low wages. The majority of the migrants to urban centers are likely therefore to remain unemployed.

The growing and increasingly impoverished urban population is more aggressive, vocal, and violent, and less tolerant of government incompetence and corruption. Having lost all hope to find work, they are more prone to resort to violence, crime, drugs, and prostitution. Out of desperation, many have joined local gangs or militias and survive by looting their country's resources or robbing the well-to-do. In Nigeria, kidnapping has become a serious business, and nabbing prominent Nigerians and foreign oil workers has become widespread. These gangs of unemployed youths seek not only ransom but also an outlet for their grievances and frustrations. Even South Africa is not spared the rise in crime and lawlessness; in several other countries local militias have taken control over large parts of the country. In

Nigeria, Niger, the countries in the Horn of Africa, Congo, and even Uganda the authorities do not control large parts of their countries, and in some the loss of control has been so extreme as to make them failed states. Crime is spreading beyond these countries' borders, inflaming old tribal rivalries, and increasing the efforts of the more affluent countries to close their borders to migrants and to trade.

The people in the shantytowns are less divided by their tribal affiliation, however, since they live together in the same shantytowns, join the same gangs, and share the same frustrations and anger toward the government and the rich. They feel exploited by their countries' elite and victimized by oppressive regimes that remain autocratic even though they hold nominally "democratic" elections. These young people (in a variation of the words of the "International") are willing to "stand unbowed before the armor of the forces of their villain autocratic dictators and defy their guns and shields."

The demographic, social, and economic changes represent far reaching transformation of the African society. The extreme income inequality is deeply dividing the population between the haves and have-nots, on the one hand, and along sectarian lines, on the other hand. In the mainly Muslim northern region of Nigeria, gross inequalities of wealth and the abuse of power by the elite intensified the protest against the government and crime against the rich. In countries that have mixed Christian and Muslim populations, the animosity between these sects is deepening. In quite a few countries, from Sudan to Côte d'Ivoire, Niger, and Nigeria, the struggle between these faiths reflects their perception of deprivation and discrimination that turns into protests and armed conflicts against exploitation. The confrontations between the Muslim and Christian religions have intensified with the radicalization of Islam and its strong support among the young, unemployed, and poor Muslims for whom the adherence to Islam gives hope for better, more just, and less chaotic life in the future. Most northern states in Nigeria, Sudan, Nigeria, and several other Muslim countries or regions adopted *Sharia* law, straining enormously the unity of the population within these countries and instigating violent conflicts between Muslims and Christians.

* * *

Against this background, the political transformation Africa is undergoing with the transition to democracy is bound to be controversial. In the early 1990s, only three African countries had democratic elections and democratically elected governments; today, most African countries have held democratic elections and some already have had two or three rounds of elections, although most were flawed, as discussed earlier. Several elections turned into a struggle between tribes for power and for the favoritism public office provides, and in many others the same leaders or ruling parties were left in power, while in a handful of countries, the democratically elected governments were toppled in military coups shortly after the elections. But the process of building the foundations and institutions of stable democracy is inevitably long and complex, and failings at the early stages of the process were common in other countries as well. With very few exceptions, Africa has never had democratic governments, nor even the institutions, the tradition of civilian rule, and any experience with free, democratic elections. In Europe as well, the transition to democracy was not smooth, and seldom flawless. In France, the voting system was based on property qualifications for half a century until the "universal" right to vote *for men only* was introduced in 1848.

In principle, democracy has the potential of making leaders more accountable and more responsible for their policies and their use of public resources. The process is seldom straightforward, however, and in most African countries that have held democratic elections, their transition to democracy was a sham. The transition to democracy in Africa is clearly at its initial stage, though, and while it may not evolve to become a Western-style democracy, as some Western politicians may have wished, this transition may well develop into a system in which the public will have a greater say about their government's policies and express more forcefully the demand that their leaders be more accountable and less corrupt.

The model of democracy that donor countries are now using to evaluate the system of governance requires Western-style democratic elections in which all persons above a certain age are eligible to vote, and international supervisors monitor the elections and the counting of the votes. These are essentially administrative criteria that are only preconditions and a prelude for a democratic system of governance. Nevertheless, even the elections themselves are often tenuous, and the international supervisors are far too few to prevent fraud and rigging, particularly since the voting is persistently along tribal lines and voters are consistently voting for their "big chief" regardless of his or her qualifications. People's strong allegiance to their tribe and their shared interests with other members of their tribe bring them to vote along tribal lines; their motivation was clearly expressed by a voter who said: "For me, voting for the leader of the other tribe is like voting for the leader of the occupation force." The loyalty to tribe also reflects expectations for various amenities given to the tribal members whose leader won the elections, while the voters for the leader who lost are deprived of these amenities. The government that is elected by the support of the larger tribe will continue to seek the support of the larger tribes, even at the cost of depriving some minority groups of their constitutional rights and freedoms. This "illiberal democracy" (Zakaria, 1997) is an inevitable intermediate stage in the transition to democracy in countries that have little or no experience with democracy, few constitutional constraints on the power of the government, and lack effective ways to secure the basic rights and freedoms of all citizens.

It is necessary, however, to exercise caution before judging the merits of democracy for the African countries on the basis of the first two or three rounds of elections. It took Europe nearly two centuries and many more rounds of elections to form the stable democratic system that most (though not all) European countries now have. The experience of African countries with democracy is far too short (their transition to democracy is only at its initial stage), to draw conclusions about the benefits of democracy in the longer run. Although the democratic system they will create may be different from a Western-style democracy, it is nonetheless likely to evolve into a system in which people are better informed and have greater influence on their government policies, largely due to the greater freedom of the media. The media and the people will exert pressure on their leaders to be more accountable, more responsible for their policies, and less corrupt. Moreover, only the voters themselves, rather than teams of international supervisors, are familiar enough with the intricacies of their system of governance to prevent fraud and vote-rigging, and in several African countries voters have already exercised their rights and demonstrated against fraud. In fact, many non-African countries that have much longer experience with democratic elections would fail the test of Western-style democratic elections that donor countries are demanding in Africa.

Quite a few scholars have expressed doubts, or even dismissed the benefits of, the transition to democracy because in many African countries the elections were merely a sham, did not bring any change in governance, left the same autocratic leaders in power, and had little impact on the current system of autocratic, unregulated, and unaccountable policy-making process. Some African politicians have also expressed doubts whether Western style democracy suits their traditions and needs. Some African intellectuals have argued that in some countries autocracy can be more effective in implementing the necessary policy measures, carrying out the reforms, and managing the government. It is obviously impossible, however, to guarantee that autocratic leaders, no matter how promising and widely supported, will *always* remain benevolent. In fact, the long experience in Africa, and in too many other countries, proves that most will not. Over time, however, as voters gain more knowledge and experience about their rights in a democracy and about the obligations of their democratically elected governments, the leaders themselves will come to realize that they must be more accountable, less corrupt and more committed to their obligations if they want to be re-elected.

A number of African leaders in countries that conducted democratic elections expressed, however, doubts whether Western style democracy, or a requirement for term limits (which is not in fact obligatory in a number of European countries) do indeed suit their multiethnic social structure. Few democratically elected leaders, they argued, will be authoritative enough to implement the conditions required by donor countries, by foreign investors, or by lending institutions. Nevertheless, the democratically elected government that is indeed likely to be less experienced, less authoritative, and less effective is more likely to respect human rights and be more accountable. In today's world where people interact more and more frequently with each other, and where communication spreads more freely, democracy sows the seeds of freedom by raising the awareness of people to their rights and to the restrictions their leaders must abide by. As voters gain more power and influence in democratic elections, they gain also more confidence to demand their leaders meet these standards.

Part III provides a more detailed survey of the experience in a sampling of African countries that held democratic elections and examines the impact both during the elections and the post-election performance of their democratically elected governments. This review highlights both the pitfalls of democracy during the early stages of the transition from an autocratic regime to a democratically elected one that changes very little the autocratic character of the regime, and the longer-term benefits democracy can have and, in some countries, already has had. In the early stages of the transition to democracy, the most important benefit is the significant increase in freedom of speech and freedom of the media. Although in many countries the newly elected democratic regimes remained autocratic and kept an eye and ear on what is being said and written, there are today far greater possibilities to exchange information, write reports and express opinions that are critical of the government, and overtly criticize government officials that enforces some accountability on the government and some restraint on corruption.

Another important indirect benefit is the possibility of minority tribes taking more active part in the political process. Under autocratic regimes, minority tribes were almost always excluded from the political process and grossly discriminated against; as a consequence, they were intensely antagonistic to the regime and to the leading tribe. With the transition to democracy, even though elections are along tribal or sectarian lines, the minority tribes have greater impact on the government through their delegates in the parliament, and the government must take into account their votes, even though they are a minority. Moreover, democratic elections open the way for minority tribes to increase their political clout by joining forces and forming an alliance of several groups that can gain enough votes to have a much stronger power in the parliament, and thus force the government to be more attentive to their demands and needs. The minority groups also discovered the potential of forming alliances with other tribes that give them much greater power in the parliament and even enable them to compete with the ruling party over the control of the parliament and the right to form a government.

Initially, that alliance is more likely to be part of a coalition government together with the ruling party even when it gains the majority of the votes and the right to form a government. The formation of an alliance of minority tribes that may have been rivals in the past is not an easy process, but their common interest to unseat the autocratic leader or the ruling party that consistently discriminated against them can offer sufficient incentive to join forces. This possibility by itself will compel the leader in power, who most often implements policies that favor the larger tribe, to be more attentive to the demands of minority tribes. Although leaders Robert Mugabe in Zimbabwe and Mwai Kibaki in Kenya refused to give up their power, they had to agree to a shared government with the leaders of the opposition Morgan Tsvangirai in Zimbabwe and Raila Odinga in Kenya.

* * *

When I prepared the outline of the book in early 2008, the common perception was that the agenda of most African countries in the coming decade will continue to be dominated by their economic development: More African countries were expected to continue to enjoy rapid growth and be integrated into the global economy; after a moderate and clearly disappointing decline in the incidence of poverty during the past decade, it was hoped and expected that in coming years the continued economic growth would bring a more significant decline in poverty, and that quite a few African countries would manage to achieve the Millennium Development Goals. The developed and emerging economies were expected to increase their investments in Africa and thereby contribute to accelerate its growth, and the continent's economic development was therefore assumed to continue to have the highest priority in order to sustain that growth.

The growing instability in the world economy since mid-2008, the crash of commodity prices, the financial crisis and the global recession have imposed a heavy toll on the African economies despite the resilience of their banking system; the optimistic predictions of the World Bank and the IMF in late 2007 had to be adjusted to the new commodity prices and to the more subdued and less upbeat assessment of the state of the global economy. Nevertheless, the recovery of commodity prices toward the end of the decade, the swelling thirst for these commodities, particularly in China, and the responsible macroeconomic policies most African countries conducted in the preceding years gave room to renewed optimism about the coming decade.

During the past decade it became increasingly more evident, however, that the renewed rise in commodity prices and in Africa's exports is only one dimension that will determine the continent's progress in the coming decade. That progress will be shaped and increasingly influenced by the demographic and social changes that will transform Africa to an urban continent within two decades, by the more evident and more devastating effects of global warming, and by the political instability in a considerable number of African countries that will be influenced by the democratization process. A comprehensive analysis of Africa's development in the coming decade requires, therefore, an integrative analysis of all these factors that will jointly determine the future progress of the continent and the rise in the standard of living of its people.

In conclusion of this introduction chapter, I would like to highlight possible scenarios that will affect this progress. These scenarios are concerned mostly with response of the African *people* to the changes in their socio-economic conditions and in their traditional way of life as an effect of all these trends, and emphasize much less the developments at the aggregate macroeconomic level. These demographic, social, and political developments, which are already taking place and closely influence each other as an effect of people's reactions, have not been given adequate emphasis in most reports in the past, perhaps due to their limited impact so far on the macroeconomic developments. The following scenarios illustrate the impact of all these changes and the significance of integrating them in the analysis of future economic, social, and political developments in the coming decade:

- On the economic front, the anticlimactic conclusion of the past decade that, until the crisis of 2008, seemed to be so highly promising has discouraged many Africans who hoped their countries are finally making a clear departure from their prolonged stagnation in the past and will be able to lift more people out of the abyss of poverty. Despite the economic downturn in the last two years of the decade, there are hopeful signs that many African countries are gradually resuming their growth, in large measure due to increase in the demand for their resources and the renewed rise in their prices in the global markets. The discovery of the treasures of new resources in many countries, including several landlocked countries increased the optimistic assessment that the continent will manage to sustain its growth.
- Several other developments, however, raise grave doubts about the actual benefits of these economic developments for the majority of the African people. It is hard to see a significant increase in the living conditions of the people in the urban areas, but the demographic and social changes marked by rapid urbanization will transform Africa within two decades to an urban continent. These demographic developments will accelerate also the urbanization of poverty and the rising power of the urban poor with the increase in their numbers, even though the larger share of the African poor will still concentrate in rural areas. The rise in the urban population and in urban poverty will be caused by the lack of employment opportunities due to the shoddy industrial base in all the African countries (with the sole exception of South Africa) and their poor and fragmented infrastructure. Without a sizable and competitive industrial sector, the growing urban population will not be able find employment and is doomed to live in dismal poverty in crowded shantytowns.

- The urban poor will not, however, remain mute, submissive and acquiescent subjects of their countries' leaders; they will not passively accede to the rampant corruption and extreme inequalities that they regard as a blatant robbery of their country's resources by the tiny elite. They will violently protest against these extreme inequalities, against the dismal trickle of their countries' revenues from its resources that is reaching them, and against the lack of hope of finding employment in the urban an centers. The regime will use its security forces in an effort to control these violent protests but the gangs in the urban centers are well armed and the clashes will lead to thousands of casualties. The international protest will force democratically elected governments to resign and army commanders will take control. The military coups and the spread of crime in the cities will deter foreign investors, and despite the country's ample resources the excavation industries will come to a halt, making the country a failed state that cannot establish law and order, and bring to a standstill its economic growth.
- The increasing power and influence of the urban population, their assertive demands to improve their living conditions and provide employment will be further frustrated, intensifying the violent protest and may further destabilize the regime. In some countries, violent remonstrations may force the military leaders to meet their demands, partly at the expense of the rural population.
- The extreme, and still rising, income inequalities between and within countries is increasingly dividing the African population into two income classes: A small minority of the leading political, military, and economic elite at the top, while the majority of the population remains hopelessly poor. The middle-income class in these countries will remain very scanty and the deepening divide between the very rich elite and the majority of the population remains hopelessly poor. This may transform the African ethnic and sectarian conflicts into a class war between the extreme rich and the vast poor population. That class war is likely to be intensified by a growing rivalry between extremist Islamic groups and the other groups of the population that include the more moderate Muslims and the other religious groups and may widen the division between the country's religious groups, tribal sects, and economic classes.
- In countries where the division between population groups is along racial or sectarian lines, the gap will deepen and the conflicts will further intensify to an extent that will lead to the country's disintegration. In Sudan, the racial divide could be resolved only after half a century of disastrous fighting between the Arab Muslims in the North and the mostly Christian and animist black Africans in the South. An agreement (yet to be realized) to divide the country between these two racial groups brought a temporary cease fire. The division of Sudan into two separate countries will be the first time in which the territorial boundaries carved by the colonial

powers are broken. The prospect of that division, therefore, is raising great concerns among several neighboring countries in which the population is also divided along sectarian and racial lines—including Côte d'Ivoire, Niger, Congo D.R. (Kinshasa), and even Nigeria—by encouraging rival population groups in to intensify their fighting in order to reach a similar agreement on a "two-state solution."

This may seem like an extreme scenario, but there are enough countries to prove that it is by no means impossible. The main point is to highlight the potential, and even likelihood, of developments that may be affected by the most aggressive reaction of the African people to changes in their living conditions. This reaction many reverse the trends in these countries' economies; and the rising urbanization and the political instability may significantly affect their economic developments despite the very promising conditions. The prediction of a country's overall progress cannot, therefore, be made based on macroeconomic trends alone, and they require an integration of the economic analysis of the demographic, social, and political developments, and the reaction of the population to these developments.

1.1
The Black Man's Burden

The title of this chapter is taken from Basil Davidson's 1992 book *The Black Man's Burden: Africa and the Curse of the Nation-State*. The title takes its origins from a poem by Rudyard Kipling, *The White Man's Burden* (1899), in which he presented his very biased views on imperialism. British journalist Edward Morel drew attention to the abuses of imperialism, most notoriously in Congo Kinshasa, perhaps the most exploitative of the European colonies. Morel claimed it is the Africans who carry the "black man's burden" (1920). Basil Davidson focused, in his book, on the period since Africa emerged from colonial rule in the 1950s, and after three decades of stagnation and poverty that led African scholars to call Africa the "lost continent". The past decade, until 2008, offered a much more optimistic view and gave new hope.

The objective of this chapter is to provide a brief overview of the main developments on the African continent in the past decade, after it managed to end those decades of economic stagnancy and impoverishment. Some subjects will be discussed in more detail in subsequent chapters in connection with their impact on the continent's future developments and policies. This review starts with developments in Africa since the late 1990s, when more countries embarked on a new road of economic development and managed to achieve more rapid growth that, against the background of the past, was outright miraculous. This marked a turning point for Africa, since economic developments were combined with significant social and political developments that are changing the entire landscape of the continent and its human scenery as it makes the transition into the twenty-first century. The review of the main characteristics of this transition is a prelude for analysis of these changes in this book. The review is necessarily short, and its main goal is to highlight the major factors that contributed to the new direction Africa is taking as it enters this century. These changes were marked not only by the new economic trends but also by demographic changes, the growing migration to urban areas that was largely a reaction to rising poverty in rural areas.

Africa is in transition. It must now face major challenges and difficult decisions that may lift its people out of the doldrums of the past to higher ground and a to much more important role in the global economy or may doom its one billion people to continued stagnation and hopeless poverty.

From hopeful independence to stagnation

The early years after liberation from colonial rulers were very different and highly promising. The newly independent African countries—mostly during the 1960s—embarked on their own hopeful journey, led by charismatic and patriotic leaders who had also led their struggle for independence, such as Kwame Nkrumah in Ghana, Jomo Kenyatta in Kenya, Julius Nyerere in Tanzania, and Gamal Abdel Nasser in Egypt. Lifted by a spirit of great optimism that was inspired by these "golden leaders," these newborn states sailed on the waves of great hopes for the future and rapid economic growth fuelled by the increase in agricultural production and by their abundant natural resources.

Their journey lost its momentum, and the post-independence spirit of the African identity lost its unifying power, when many of these leaders, enchanted by idealistic perceptions of socialism, focused their efforts on implementing a socialistic agenda, including confiscation of small farmers' lands for collective farms and forceful settlement of farmers. Many of these leaders were toppled in military coups d'état, and quite a few others became increasingly more autocratic and more despotic. The new independence also unraveled old rivalries between tribes and sectarian groups that disintegrated the sense of unity and started a long series of extremely bloody and devastating civil conflicts, tribal wars, and sectarian animosities.

The political borders of these newly liberated states were inherited from colonial rulers who had determined those boundaries to facilitate dividing the continent's natural resources and fertile lands, or simply for colonial administrative purposes. These arbitrary divisions, carried out without paying any attention to the needs of the local population, created barriers between tribes and villages that would become huge stumbling blocks to African unity.

The debate on this heritage of colonial rule has not abated, and many African leaders and intellectuals blame the African malaise on the colonial powers. Border disputes between countries still continue, and the arbitrary boundaries of territories that had been carved out by colonial powers thrust together a mass of different tribes within them. The lack of unity and the entrenched rivalries between population groups deepened the perception of deprivation, discrimination, and exploitation of tribes and sectarian population groups. This state of affairs, termed the "Black Man's Burden" will be discussed in this book, primarily in Part III, in order to examine strategies and initiatives the African countries and international development organizations have implemented since the 1990s in order to relieve that burden on the continent.

The autocratic leaders were mainly consumed by power struggles for survival and failed to make progress in building new nations—the task the first generation of "golden leaders" saw as their main mission. Nevertheless, in the first decades of independence some 115 leaders were toppled in military coups, and ongoing power struggles destabilized the countries while incessant wars and civil conflicts devastated their economies.

The lack of any tradition and experience in maintaining the structure and building the necessary institutions that make the state work prevented these regimes from fulfilling the basic role of government, enabling their leaders to avoid obligations to protect and secure the safety of their people, maintain law and order, and provide other essential public services. Instead, it gave these leaders a free hand to structure state institutions to meet their needs, determine the country's rule without any restrictions, and embezzle from the national coffers to enrich themselves, strengthen security forces, and engage in wars. The lack of autonomous authority or basic laws that establish constraints on, and demand accountability from, the government, personalized governmental control, permitting these leaders to undermine rather than build functioning state institutions.

This, in a nutshell, was the process that brought nearly all African countries to the abyss of long stagnation, ubiquitous poverty, and incessant conflicts that engulfed practically all of them. These lethal wars and conflicts consumed the lives of many millions, expelled millions more from their lands and ancestral homes, and brought on widespread famine. These conflicts deepened rivalry between tribes that escalated into civil wars and intensified their struggle for control, making it more violent and increasingly more deadly as they replaced their machetes with AK-47s and other modern military equipment. Conflicts and despotic leaders brought about a deep economic crisis that wasted not only their own abundant resources but also the trillions of dollars given to them as aid, bringing most to the brink of bankruptcy.

The external constraints imposed by foreign banks brought these governments to the bottom of their coffer and, unable to obtain additional credit, they were forced to ask for credit from sources they have tried very hard and long to avoid: the World Bank and the International Monetary Fund. These international development organizations provided credit, but only under strict conditions that compelled the countries to take disciplinary measures in implementing policies, building the institutions of the state, and establishing an autonomous central bank and an independent legal system. The depth of the debt crisis and the threat of a complete collapse of the central authority forced the African leaders to acquiesce to the conditions the World Bank and the IMF required and to implement policies the lending institutions have designed. In the early stages, however, these conditions put the carriage before the horse by demanding far-reaching economic reforms that could not be accomplished without effective institutions and without true cooperation from the countries' leaders.

This was the beginning of an arduous, and often turbulent, process that (despite numerous ups and downs) enabled many African countries to gradually lay the foundations of a functioning economy and more disciplined government policies. In many countries these reforms encountered obstacles due to noncooperative regimes and to autocratic leaders who resisted the necessary discipline that restricted their power to carry out their own plans or realize their ambitions. The institutions of governance are, therefore, still weak in many African countries, and in quite a few the central authority abides only sparingly by its commitments to enforce these restrictions and implement these policies. As a result, the structural adjustment, which went through different phases of structural adjustment, had limited success with limited progress.

Nevertheless, efforts to resume the growth process continued, and despite the lack of support from many top leaders, a younger and more educated generation of technocrats increasingly assumed more responsible positions and sought ways to reform their economies—without however losing their own positions or risking their lives. In the mid-1990s, more African countries resumed economic growth, driven in part by changes in the global economy but also by avoiding the reckless policies of the past. At the instigation of the IMF and the World Bank, primarily the Heavily Indebted Poor Countries (HIPC) initiative and the Multilateral Debt Relief Initiative (MDRI), the debt burden of many was reduced in order to enable poorer countries to increase their investments.

From prolonged stagnation to a decade of miraculous growth

This dark chapter in Africa's history and the damage of the three "lost decades" shed light on the extent to which their growth during the past decade has been miraculous.[2] As they entered the twenty-first century, growth accelerated, driven by the rapid rise in commodity prices, primarily oil and minerals, whose effects rippled over to many other countries lacking such assets. The revenues of the resource-rich countries from the export of their resources increased at phenomenal rates during the commodity boom of the 2000s, but unlike similar commodity booms in the past, particularly the one during the 1970s, most African countries have now implemented prudent policies that prevented the accumulation of foreign debt or fiscal deficits.

Africa's growth performance during the past decade was impressive even on objective grounds and clearly extraordinary in the departure it marked from the continent's prolonged stagnation. GDP growth in Sub-Saharan Africa (SSA) increased in real terms by around 4 percent over the entire decade and by over 5 percent during 2005 and 2006, reaching 6.6 percent in 2007—its strongest performance in decades. Figure 1.1 demonstrates that miracle of Africa's growth.

The African oil exporting countries gained the most, both from the rocketing oil prices and from the increase in their oil production that took advantage of the high prices as well as the massive demand by the oil-importing countries. Among the oil exporters, growth was particularly strong in Angola (16.9 percent), Sudan (11.8 percent), and Mauritania (17.9 percent). In Nigeria, the region's second-largest economy and largest oil-exporter, continued conflicts and attacks on the oil infrastructure in the Niger Delta slowed down its exports, as oil production fell by 25 percent during 2006. In a considerable number of countries new oil and/or natural gas resources were discovered, and in the past decade Chad, Ethiopia, and Sudan joined the club of oil-exporting countries. In many other African countries other precious resources were found, including uranium in Niger and Botswana; and many foreign companies, from China to the US, made large investments to search for new resources.

The sharp rise in oil prices has received the bulk of the media attention, but in fact the rise in the prices of metals and minerals has also been very large, and countries with these resources also benefited from high revenues from their export as well as from the major investments by large international corporations, which contributed to strengthening these countries' economies. The strong statistical figures for exports, prudent economic policies, and the robust economic growth of the past decade raised great hopes

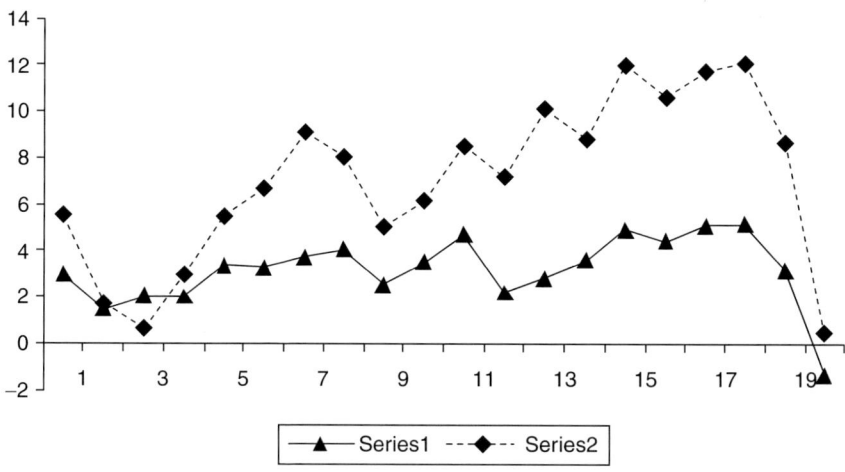

Figure 1.1 Percentage change of real GDP in SSA and in the world

Source: IMF, Regional Economic Outlook (2009).

that Africa had indeed reached a turning point, and this was highlighted in the reports of the World Bank and the IMF (Box 1.1).

> Box 1.1 African emergence from prolonged stagnation
>
> Something decidedly new is on the horizon in Africa, something that began in the mid-1990s. Many African economies appear to have turned the corner and moved to a path of faster and steadier economic growth. Their performance over 1995–2005 reverses the collapses over 1975–85 and the stagnations over 1985–95. And for the first time in three decades, African economies are growing with the rest of the world. Average growth in the Sub-Saharan economies was 5.4 percent in 2005 and 2006....
>
> Since the mid-1990s average incomes in Africa have been rising in tandem with those in other regions. Despite an unanticipated oil shock, growth has remained good.... More than a third of Africans now live in countries that have grown at more than 4 percent a year for 10 years. A group of diversified sustained growers has begun to emerge, and natural resources have gained new importance.
>
> (World Bank, WDR, 2007)
>
> On several other measures, the continent had strong performance. Having successfully stabilized their economies, many sub-Saharan African countries have been increasingly reorienting fiscal policies toward promoting economic growth and poverty reduction.... Domestic investment and productivity have risen in the African countries that have managed to successfully stabilize their economies and see several key reforms through. Externally, strong global demand for commodities, greater flows of capital to Africa, and debt relief have helped increase resources and lift growth across Africa.
>
> On several other measures, the continent had strong performance. Having successfully stabilized their economies, many sub-Saharan African countries have been increasingly reorienting fiscal policies toward promoting economic growth and poverty reduction.... Domestic investment and productivity have risen in the African countries that have managed to successfully stabilize their economies and see several key reforms through. Externally, strong global demand for commodities, greater flows of capital to Africa, and debt relief have helped increase resources and lift growth across Africa.
>
> The region looks well-poised to sustain its growth momentum... The strong growth in the region reflects the institutional improvements, structural reforms, and more rigorous economic policies that have started to bear fruit in many countries.
>
> (IMF, Regional Economic Outlook, 2007)

Not all countries reached this turning point, and even some of the resource-rich countries that had achieved high growth rates due to their high export revenues—including Sudan, Chad, Ethiopia, Gabon, Guinea-Bissau and few others—remained failed states. In those countries that seem to have turned the corner, the change was marked not only by their strong economic performance but even more so by economic policies that were reoriented to promote economic growth and poverty reduction, by their institutional improvements, and by their transition to democracy. The road yet to be travelled is long and arduous, and reverses can happen, but the African people who reached that turning point would not be willing to go back to the old days and old ways of autocratic and onerous regimes that brought upon their countries long "lost decades" of stagnation and decline.

New investment opportunities and capital flows to Africa

One of the interesting chapters of the recovery of the African countries was the large flows of private capital to the continent, in both direct and capital investments. The main reason for these exuberant and risky investments was the massive amount of capital in the world financial markets that intensified their search for high-yield investment opportunities when the stock market in developed countries became bearish. In Africa, only few countries benefited from capital investments, and these were mainly countries that had stable political and security conditions, had improved their economic policies, and accelerated their growth. Intensive competition between investment companies combined with very lax regulations in their countries lured foreign direct investments (FDI), portfolio investment, and private debt flows (Figures 1.2 and 1.3). In 2007 private capital inflows increased almost six-fold from $15 billion in 2000 to $84 billion in 2007 which was double the amount of official development assistance (ODA) to SSA.

Despite these flows of private capital, the World Bank and the IMF continued, and even increased, the debt relief programs. Aid was given also to

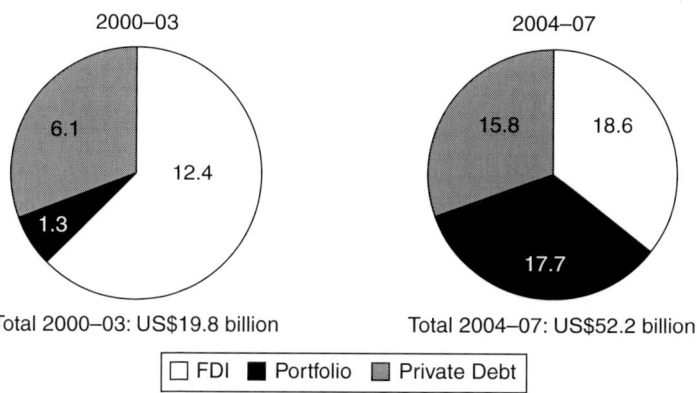

Figure 1.2 Foreign investments in SSA countries

Notes: Total 2000–03: US$19.8 billion; total 2004–07: US$52.2 billion.

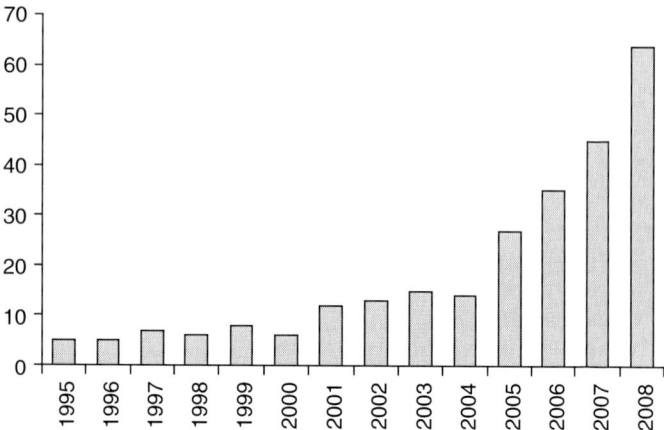

Figure 1.3 Inflows of FDI to the African 33 LDCs (in billions US$)
Source: UNCTAD, FDI/TNC database (www.unctad.org/fdistatistics).

resource-rich countries that had large export revenues and large inflow of private capital. The total Overseas Development Assistance (ODA) totaled $40 billion, and a large portion of that aid was given to oil exporting and other resource-rich countries as well as to countries in which there were large investments of private capital. Large amounts of aid was given even to the well-performing economies that became known as the "Frontier Economies" (Box 1.2, Figure 1.4).

Box 1.2 The "Frontier Economies"

The hectic search of investors for profitable investment opportunities around the globe have saturated the stock markets in the fast growing emerging economies, and another group of developing countries, that came to be known as the "frontiers economies" have become the target of the more daring globetrotting investors. They include countries in Africa, non-EU members in Eastern Europe and the Caribbean. Their stock markets still in their infancy, accounting regulations and reporting standards make the information on local enterprises rather opaque or even dubious, but untapped economic potential in these markets are often very high, in part due to the large changes in commodity prices and in part due to their proximity to the EU or the US markets.

In the decade through the mid-2000s, most of these economies rose at an annual rate of around or sometimes more than 10 percent—compared with an average growth of 8.2 percent of the emerging economies, and in recent years their stock markets, however minor, have outperformed many of the larger and more familiar markets.

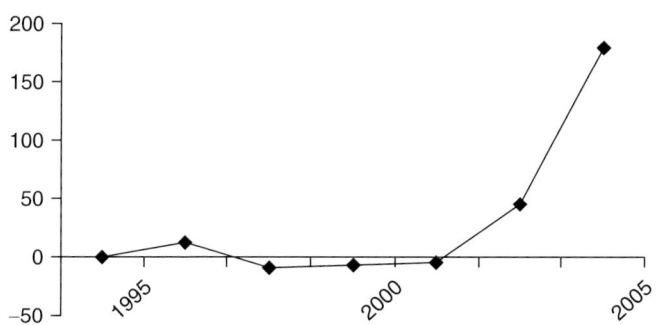

Figure 1.4 Stock Market Index in "New Frontiers" Economies

> Quite a few SSA countries are in this group including Kenya, Ghana, Uganda and Senegal. The main concern of investors in these stock markets is the stability of the exchange rate and the stability of the regime and its macroeconomic policies.
>
> (*International Herald Tribune*, May 20, 2006)

Despite the substantial increase in aid from ODA and donor countries, and their great efforts to improve the targeting of their aid, there are still doubts as to whether this aid actually reached the neediest countries, which could have made effective use of this aid to help their poor people. During all these years, investments in rural areas or in rural roads were very limited; most small farmers benefited very little from this aid, and only a tiny portion of their countries' growing riches, as a result of their rapid growth and large export revenues, trickled down to the rural population. Although the incidence of poverty declined during the decade through 2005, the number of poor continued to rise, and farmers' income was small.

Among western economists there is a long-standing debate, ranging between the preaching of Jeffrey Sachs for more aid that will put an end to poverty and the attacks of William Easterley on *The White Man's Burden* (2006) that explains *Why the West's Efforts to Aid the Rest Have Done So Much Ill and So Little Good*. The debate has not been settled, and various statistically significant variables have been waved to discredit the other's statistically significant variables. In a more recent contribution, Dambisa Moyo, a Zambian-born economist, declared in a controversial book entitled *Dead Aid* (2009) that "aid is not working" and should be cut because it is only compounding Africa's problems. Moyo argues that governments that receive aid are accountable to no one and, therefore, most of the aid is wasted. Paul Kagame, the president of Rwanda, recognized that the cycle of aid and poverty has a self-perpetuating dynamic: As long as poor nations are focused on receiving aid, they will not work to improve their economies. But Kagame also claimed: "We know the road to prosperity is a long one. We will travel it with the help of a new school of development thinkers and entrepreneurs, with those who demonstrate they have not just a heart, but also a mind for the poor" (*Financial Times*, May 7, 2009).

Will the commodity crisis and the global recession end Africa's recovery?

During the first half of the last decade, prices of agricultural products trailed behind those of oil, minerals, and metals, and despite the rise in agricultural prices by 35 percent in real terms in the first half of the decade, this rise took place in the aftermath of their cyclical low levels in 2001, while the rise in the prices of oil and fertilizers increased farmers' production costs and the mounting inflation in all countries eroded the terms of trade of agricultural products and reduced the purchasing power of small farmers. As a result, small farmers in Africa and other less developed countries (LDCs) benefited very little from the rise in food prices, and as they cut their use of fertilizers their yields have declined. Many farmers had to abandon the production of high-value crops for export due to the sharp rise in air transport costs, and the increase in food prices forced them to switch back to the production of food for their own consumption.

The sharp rise in oil prices was the main driving force for a hectic search in the US and the EU for alternative sources of energy that are more environmentally friendly. Part of that search concentrated on alternative sources of fuel for motor vehicles, primarily biofuel. In the US the main biofuel is ethanol, made from corn, and in the EU the main biofuel is biodiesel, made from oil seeds like soybeans and sesame. The leading economic powers coordinated their policies to reduce the use of fossil fuel and increase their energy independence, but their program since 2005 contributed to an increase in the demand for and price of all cereals and, thus, contributed to the food crisis in 2007–08. Part IV examines the factors that led to the food crisis, and the contribution of the programs for the production of biofuel, and evaluates the possibilities for another round of escalating food crises.

The series of crises since 2007 thrashed the global economy and sharply slowed down the economic recovery of Sub-Saharan Africa. The African population was hurt very severely by the food crisis that doubled and even tripled the prices of staple foods, primarily grains, and it was then beaten down by the global recession that brought to an abrupt end the continent's miraculous growth. Despite, since 2008, the crash in oil prices and the prices of most other commodities, food prices declined at a relatively low rate and remained high. The global recession reduced the demand for Africa's oil and other primary resources, and these prices fell sharply in the second half of 2008. As a result, the growth of African economies has slowed down very sharply, and estimates of the IMF show that after record growth rates of over 6 percent in 2006 and 2007, the GDP growth rate in 2009 will fall to less than 1 percent, but is likely to recover in subsequent years.

Global trade may be one of the main victims of this series of crises: Corporations are likely to rely less on trade and more on safer supply of their inputs and more predictable demand for their output; countries will increase their efforts to become more energy independent and more self sufficient in several other key commodities, primarily staple foods. One of the casualties of this trend is the Doha Round that, after prolonged negotiations, failed to reach a multinational agreement on agricultural trade. Another outcome of these crises is likely to be more prudent and more restrictive economic policies and the implementation of measures to prevent the threat of either an inflationary or a deflationary spiral.

The statistical figures, dry as they are, reveal other dimensions of Africa's strong performance in the past decade: Historically, the region's dependence on exports of natural resources made it vulnerable to commodity price swings and demand shocks in the global economy. As a result, many growth episodes of the African countries ended with a dramatic collapse in output and income. This time, though, many resource-rich countries that have benefited handsomely from high commodity prices have, as they improved their policies, also saved more of their windfall profits. The statistical figures summarize the significant improvement in the management of African countries' economies, more disciplined and responsible economic policies that many have implemented, and the greater responsibility their governments have assumed in the conduct of fiscal and monetary policies. The governments in these countries could also intervene to put inflation under control, and in 2007 and 2008, when food and fuel prices shot up, quite a few were able to take measures to moderate the negative impact on their populations, particularly the poor, with food subsidies or a reduction in tariffs on food imports.

Table 1.1 presents a set of data that encapsulates the changes in the economic policies of most African countries during the high growth years. These policies were implemented in only two-thirds of the African countries, whereas many of the others remained failed states that lacked a disciplined central regime. The table summarizes, however, the data for the entire continent; hence the changes in the countries that did implement disciplined and responsible policies were even more impressive. The detailed figures for individual countries show the commodity and financial meltdown increased the trade deficit, reduced the government revenues, and increased the fiscal deficit in many (though not all) of the countries that until the crisis had rapid growth during the decade, but at a much slower rate than in previous crises.

Comparison of these data with data after the commodity boom of the 1970s highlights the fundamental changes in the mode of operation of

Table 1.1 Sub-Saharan Africa: selected macroeconomic indicators (*as percent of GDP*)

	2005	2006	2007	2008	2009
Exports of goods and services	36.5	37.9	38.9	40.8	32.1
Imports of goods and services	33.6	34.4	37.3	38.5	38.0
Gross domestic saving	22.8	24.7	23.6	24.5	17.6
Gross domestic investment	19.9	21.3	22.2	22.4	23.7
Fiscal balance (incl. grants)	1.9	4.9	1.0	2.1	-4.8

Source: IMF Regional Economic Outlook SSA, 2009.

many African governments and their more prudent policies in the recent crisis. In the 1970s, autocratic leaders were not much restricted by growing fiscal and balance of payments deficits, and had no hesitation to transfer part of the revenues from the commodity boom to their private accounts in foreign banks. When the boom turned into a bust, these leaders continued careless spending that emptied their treasury's coffers and created a huge fiscal deficit and large foreign debts. These debts and deficits eventually led to the calamitous debt crisis of the 1980s and forced them to seek emergency loans from the IMF and the World Bank.

In 2007, with the surge in food and fuel prices, the IMF reported that many African countries used fiscal policy to respond to it; by December nearly three-fourths of the countries took some fiscal measure, including a reduction in food taxes and fuel taxes; several countries introduced or increased subsidies on food, fuel, and agricultural products; some expanded their fertilizer subsidy programs, and some food exporting countries banned the export of agricultural products to prop up domestic supply (IMF, *Regional Economic Outlook*, 2009). In many countries, these policies followed massive demonstrations that demanded government action to reduce food prices, sentiments that echoed the demands of the people at the time of the French Revolution: "We the people demand the food we need at prices we can afford, and you the government has an obligation to make sure that we and our children will not starve."

Despite the continent's growth and the more prudent economic policies, poverty continues to rise

In spite of the decade-long impressive growth, hunger and malnutrition are still widely prevalent in Africa, and the number of chronically poor people continued to rise even during the period of rapid economic growth. Although Africa accounts for only 13 percent of the population of the world's developing countries, it accounts for 25 percent of the world's undernourished.

In 2001–03, the prevalence of food energy deficiency varied from around 40 percent in Tanzania, Kenya, and Uganda to over 70 percent in Ethiopia, Burundi, Malawi, Zambia, and Rwanda (FAO, 2007).

Africa is the only continent where the number of malnourished children continues to increase; the proportion of undernourished children increased from around 27 percent in the 1970s to over 33 percent in the early 2000s (IFPRI, 2005). This record was in stark contrast to the trends in all other regions and in the majority of the developing countries where poverty and malnutrition remains a major problem—these countries made significant strides in combating malnutrition, particularly among children. The food crisis of 2007–08 aggravated Africa's grim record and deepened poverty and hunger. According to World Bank estimates, the crisis has reversed the achievements many countries had made in the past two decades in combating poverty: Their incidence of poverty had declined from 47 percent in the mid-1990s to 41 percent in 2005. According to these estimates, the number of people who live in chronic poverty has increased by over 100 million as an effect of the food crisis, and some two-thirds are in Africa. These effects of the food crisis are discussed in Part IV. Figure 1.5 shows the changes in the share of the main regions in the world's poverty.

Several factors contributed to the continued rise in poverty and child malnutrition. The poor population concentrates in the rural areas and the rise in their poverty is attributed to low yields that are largely due to the failure to adopt the food production methods of the "Green Revolution"; to the limited trade, even with the urban centers, that prevented farmers from specializing in specific crops according to their comparative advantages; to the

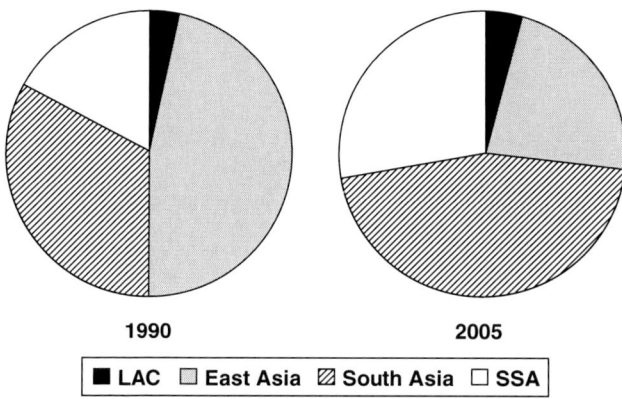

Figure 1.5 The share of main regions in the world's poor population (not including Eastern Europe)

Sources: World Bank, Ravallion and Chen (2008); US Census: World Population Statistics (2008).

declining real prices of cereals until the early 2000s, and the slow growth in all other economic sectors. High child malnutrition is also attributed to the large number of children in rural households, where women typically have five or six children, a birth rate that remained largely unchanged, whereas in all other regions that rate has declined to less than three. The high birth rate contributed to the rapid growth of population in Africa, an annual rate of 2.3 percent compared to less than 1.2 percent in the other continents (Table 1.2), and the poor health services in rural areas.

The large number of children is attributed to the fact that in most African countries the majority of the population still lives in rural areas where the children are an important work force in the families of small farmers. Perhaps even more important is the effect of the spread of diseases like malaria, and the many civil conflicts that take a heavy toll on the lives of small children, thereby reducing the probability that children delivered and raised in rural areas will survive to adulthood. Although demographers predict the birth rate of African children will gradually decline to between three and four, that reduction may require several decades.

In other developing countries, that reduction was much more rapid due to large migration from the rural areas to urban centers that was driven by the industrial revolution. With the exception of South Africa, Africa's industrial sector remained a cottage or home-based industry or small-scale manufacturing that produce mainly for the local neighborhood; in addition, production is very rudimentary, and very few workers are employed. Although rural-urban migration picked pace in Africa in the past two decades, it is

Table 1.2 The share and growth of the poor population in South Asia and in SSA (*poverty line 2005 PPP and $1.25/day*)

	Poor Population (m)	Annual Growth Rate since 1990 (%)	Total Population (m)	Annual Growth Rate since 1990	Poverty Rate (%)
			2005		
South Asia	595.58	0.2	1476.4	1.8	40.6
SSA	388.38	2.3	762.88	2.6	51.0
			1990		
South Asia	579.2		1120.09	..	51.7
SSA	297.51		516.69	..	57.6

Sources: World Bank WDR, various years.

mostly driven by the limited capacity of small-scale farms to provide enough food and employment to all children; as a result, many are forced to migrate to urban centers even though most migrants are unemployed and must live in shantytowns. Africa's transition from a primarily rural society to more urban society will have large effects on the distribution of poverty between these sectors and is likely to create considerable economic problems to most countries. This subject is discussed in more detail in Part II.

The second key factor that prevented a more rapid reduction in poverty, even in countries with rapid growth in the past decade, is the high inequality in income distribution, both between and within the countries. Figures 1.5 and 1.6 show that despite the reduction by 7–8 percent in the incidence of chronic poverty between 1996 and 2005, the reduction in mild poverty—defined by a poverty line equal to $2.50 per day, was considerably smaller, at around 3 percent. In other words, most of the people who managed to increase their income above the chronic poverty line of $1 per day remained mildly poor. Even in countries that have rich resources and accumulated large windfall profits from the rise in their export earnings, most of the increase in revenues remained in the hands of a very small elite. Table 1.3 shows more data on the incidence of poverty in the mid-2000s. Most of the poor concentrated in rural areas, and even under the favorable conditions of these years, rural poverty remained high and investments in rural areas were meager.

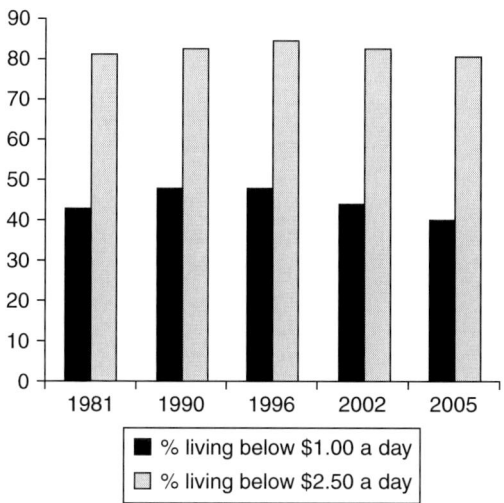

Figure 1.6 Incidence of chronic and moderate poverty in SSA 1990–2005
Source: Ravallion and Chen (2008).

Table 1.3 Poverty rates in selected African countries (*International poverty lines at 2005 prices and exchange rates*)

Poverty Line	Country	Cameroon	Côte d'Ivoire	Ethiopia	Ghana	Kenya	Nigeria	Senegal	Uganda
$1.25	Poverty Rate	32.8	23.3	39.0	30.0	19.7	64.4	33.8	51.5
$2.00		57.5	46.8	77.5	53.6	39.9	83.9	60.3	75.6

Source: World Development Indicators 2008, Poverty Data supplement.

The threat of global warming

According to the projections of the Intergovernmental Panel on Climate Change (IPCC),[3] food security in Africa is likely to be "severely compromised" by climate change, with production expected to be halved by 2020. According to the report, Africa is likely to be the most adversely affected, in large measure because of the increasing aridity in the north (the Sahel) and in southern Africa, the most populous parts of the continent. The most important claim in the report is that global warming could cut rain-fed northern African crop production up to 50 percent by 2020, a remarkably short time for such a dramatic change.

Even if the change is less dramatic, the population in the region, mostly in rural areas, lacks the technology currently available to adapt to environmental change. Over a quarter of Africa's population—nearly 250 million people—do not have easy access to safe drinking water, and their numbers will rise rapidly due both to the rapid population growth—Africa, has by far the highest in the world—and to dwindling water resources. Africa's vulnerability to climate change is particularly high, since over 90 percent of its agriculture depends on rainfall. The report warns, however, that all Africa faces a long-term threat of farmland turning to desert.

Human activity in Africa is also affecting the ecosystem for several reasons: (a) Low-income households in rural areas depend on wood and charcoal for 80–90 percent of their energy needs; (b) fire incidents represent a huge threat to tropical forests; (c) mining of natural resources is causing major damage to the environment; (d) widespread logging for export to developed countries is causing major damage to the rainforest; and (e) with the growing aridity of arable lands, farmers are expanding cultivation to new areas at the expense of the local vegetation.

The IPCC report made several practical suggestions suitable to conditions in Africa: Water harvesting systems to supplement rain-fed farming; weather insurance; national grain reserves; cash transfers, and school nutrition schemes. The report emphasizes the great benefits of biotechnology research in Africa that could lead to drought- and pest-resistant rice, drought-tolerant maize, and insect-resistant millet, sorghum, and cassava. The debate over the adoption of genetically modified crops has, however, not been settled.

The report emphasized that policy reforms must be combined with structural and institutional reforms; otherwise, reforms are likely to be both ineffective and highly biased. In many countries the main thrust of agricultural reforms was to disband marketing boards that were inefficient, highly corrupt, and had a monopolistic status that enabled them to heavily tax farmers. The removal of restrictions on cross-district and cross-country product movements was carried out in recognition of the limited effectiveness of these restrictions and the power they give local officials and corrupt police to increase their profits at the expense of farmers.

Of late, grave concerns have been raised about the accuracy of the report, most notably about the grim prediction regarding climate change in Africa and the extent to which these predictions are based on hard evidence. The doubts about the accuracy of the report will obviously reduce very sharply the incentives to take collaborative global measures to cope with global warming and respond to the specific recommendations made in the report.

The growing gap between countries, and growing inequalities between people

A crucial and threatening development of the past two decades is the growing income gap between countries and people. The gap continued to rise as an effect of the continued and increasing differences in growth rates between countries, ranging from a decline in income of 5.3 percent in the worst performing country to an increase in income of 20.6 percent in the best performing country; eight were near or above the 7 percent threshold needed to sustain poverty reduction. Along this continuum of growth performance, three broad country types have emerged: slow growth economies (36.7 percent of Africa's population), which include many conflict or post-conflict countries; diversified, sustained growth economies (35.6 percent of Africa's population), which have grown at around 4 percent a year for at least ten years; and resource-rich exporters (27.7 percent of Africa's population).

The worldwide increase in income and growth rates was not only between continents, but also between countries within the same continent: Figure 1.7a–c shows the much higher values and the large rise in the coefficient of variation of the real per capita incomes in the three main groups of developing countries. The large rise in the income gap between countries was in SSA, and the large increase in the coefficient of variation of the mean incomes in the African countries reflects the rise in income inequality between countries. That rise was particularly extreme during the commodity boom from 2002 through 2008, as an effect of the sharp increase in the revenues of the resource-rich countries, primarily the oil-exporting countries, whereas the per capita incomes in the resource-poor countries changed very little.

Among those countries where natural resources are less abundant, per capita income in Mozambique increased by 62 percent during these years, thanks to its exports of natural gas and titanium. Ghana, considered a resource-poor country until natural gas was discovered off its shores toward the end of the decade, achieved a relatively high increase in income per person due to its stable conditions, whereas Kenya had high growth until

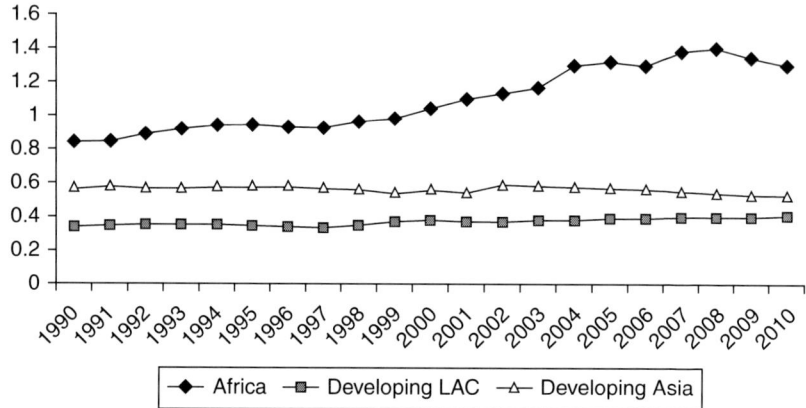

Figure 1.7a Coefficient of variation of mean per capita incomes in main country groups*

* Coefficient of variation of real mean per capita income, in 2000 prices and exchange rates.
Source: Author's calculation based on data of the IMF, Regional Economic Outlook (2009).

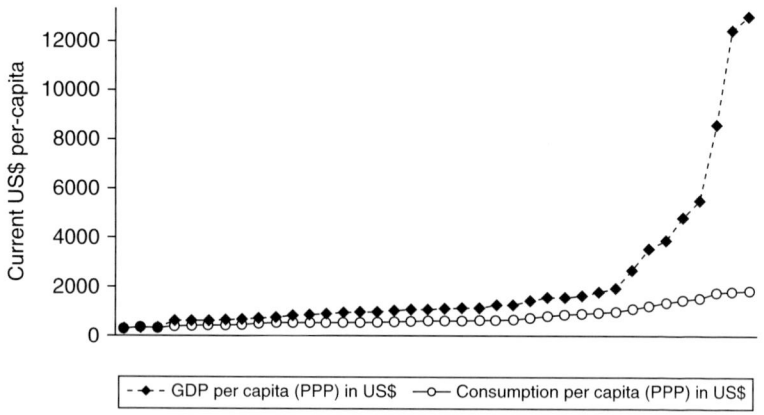

Figure 1.7b GDP and consumption per capita in the SSA countries, 2005
Source: World Bank Data of 35 SSA countries.

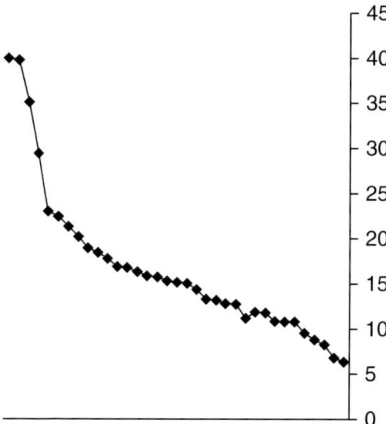

Figure 1.7c The ratio between income per capita of the top and the bottom income deciles in 35 SSA countries, 2005
Source: World Bank Data of 35 SSA countries.

the civil unrest and demonstrations following the elections of 2007. Since then, Kenya has deteriorated, and large amounts of foreign capital have left the country. Income per capita also remained low in Cote d'Ivoire, which together with Kenya was one of Africa's most prosperous countries until military coups and civil wars since 1999, which left it a fragile state.

Many of Africa's more successfully growing economies share several common characteristics: They managed to integrate into the world economy through trade, especially exports; they managed to attract foreign investments, and their productivity is on the rise. Not all these countries achieved their high growth due to rich resources, and in quite a few large foreign investments in a frenetic search for new resources contributed to their productivity and accelerated their growth. Stable political conditions, effective protection of property rights, and well-functioning institutions, primarily financial institutions, have proven to be important factors that contributed to growth. Some countries became Africa's "frontier economies" that also attracted foreign capital investment.

Foreign investment was obviously lured to African countries that had natural resources, but foreign companies expanded their search to other countries, often with considerable success in finding oil and minerals. On the other hand, resource-rich countries, like Nigeria and those in the Horn in Africa, barely managed to keep their foreign investors due to continued wars. In Niger, foreign companies were unable to gain access to the country's newly found uranium due to the ongoing civil war, and in war-torn Congo D. R. (Congo Kinshasa), only the armies of neighboring countries and hoards of armed militias were able to exploit the country's resources. African countries that did benefit from foreign investments benefited also from advanced technologies, trained personnel, and training programs for their own workers that increased the productivity of their labor force.

Interestingly, resources, including oil, did not guarantee high income and rapid growth; even during the past decade, there were large differences in income per capita between the main oil-exporting countries (Figure 1.8). Ethiopia and Chad wasted their revenues from oil on prolonged wars against neighboring countries, even though their populations are among the poorest in Africa. Nigeria is the largest oil exporting country in Africa, but around half its population in chronically poor. Nigeria has long been hobbled by political instability, corruption, inadequate infrastructure, and poor macroeconomic management. Nigeria failed to diversify its economy away from its overdependence on the capital-intensive oil sector (which provides 95 percent of foreign exchange earnings and about 80 percent of budgetary revenues), and failed to meet the spending and exchange rate targets of an IMF program in 2002. Freedom House, an organization that monitors the spread of democracy and free speech, noted that after the elections of 2007 Nigeria was one of the most disheartening examples of "political stagnation, democratic backsliding, and state failure."

Because of civil conflicts and wars as well as the misrule of autocratic leaders, the slow growth economies are now significantly poorer than they

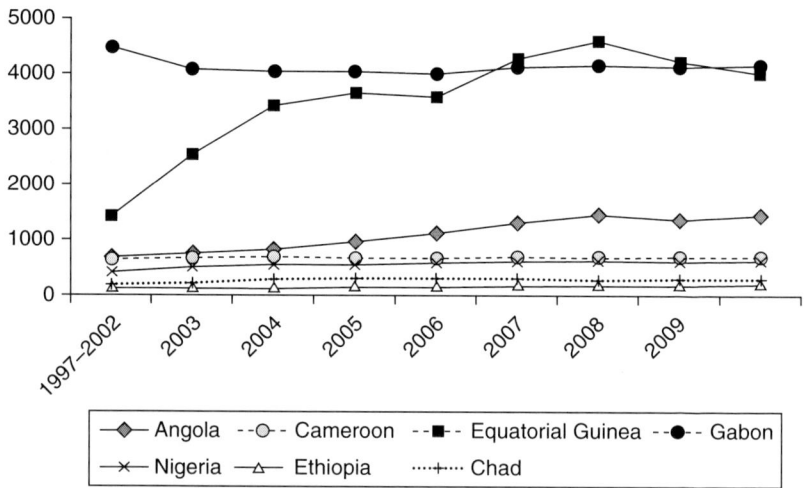

Figure 1.8 Trends of real GDP per capita of the oil exporting countries (US$ at 2000 prices and exchange rates)

Source: IMF, Regional Economic Outlook (2009).

had been at independence. They include also several resource-rich countries that wasted their potential to achieve and sustain higher growth (including the lawless and anarchic countries in the Horn of Africa as well as Nigeria, Niger, Congo, and Zimbabwe).

Jeffrey Sachs and Paul Collier, among others, emphasized the geographic disadvantages of many slow growth economies, particularly the at least 15 landlocked countries. These countries failed to enter into global markets due to their geographic disadvantages and could not be competitive in the export of crops. Their rural populations must therefore depend on low-productivity agriculture, mostly for self-consumption. As noted in the introduction, their main obstacle is the decaying road infrastructure and high transport costs; this, however, was also an obstacle in the more remote regions in countries that do have access to the sea. Chapter 2.1 discusses the paralyzing effects of crumbling rural roads due to the meager investments these countries have made in rural infrastructure.

In the past decade, however, rich resources, from oil to uranium, were found in many landlocked countries, and multinational corporations have made large investments to exploit them. These newly resource-rich countries, and several other landlocked countries where foreign corporations are searching for more treasures, benefited also from large foreign investments that contributed to an increase in employment.

Africa's agenda in the coming decade

Today, Africa is the world's least urbanized continent, with only one third of the population living in cities and the rest in rural areas and heavily dependent on agriculture. But, in the past two decades the rural-urban migration has accelerated, and the continent now has the world's highest rates of rural-urban migration. Since, in most countries, even the largest urban centers cannot offer much employment, most of the migrants (mainly young men) remain unemployed and forced to live in very dreary conditions.

The rural-urban migration presents a difficult dilemma for the African countries and will require significant shifts in policies in the coming decade: On the one hand, the exploding urban population and their high unemployment require large investments in the urban centers; on the other hand, the eroding of agricultural resources due to the climatic changes and the aging rural population as the young people migrate to urban centers, will lead to a decline in food production and a rise in rural poverty, and will require large investments in the rural periphery, particularly in the more remote and isolated areas. How should African countries allocate their limited resources to cope with these two challenges and reduce poverty? How will they be able to provide enough food to their growing populations, especially if droughts will be more frequent or if another food crisis occurs? How can the global community help the African countries cope with this dual dilemma and secure their food requirements?

The following is a more detailed description of these two crucial issues and their implications for the future agenda of the continent, for donor countries, and for the international development organizations:

The rural dilemma

Around three-quarters of Africa's poor live in rural areas and depend on agriculture for their livelihoods. In the coming several years most development efforts will, therefore, be concentrated on the rural sector, and large investments will be needed to increase agricultural production and build rural roads (after years of gross neglect). Rural development is the most rapid and most effective way of reducing poverty and malnutrition in Africa. Although the urban population is expected to double between 2000 and 2030, and the majority of the African population will live in urban areas by 2030, rural poverty will remain high and the effects of climate changes may increase both the number of the rural poor and their proportion of the population. Furthermore, if climate changes will be as drastic as has been predicted, many people in semiarid rural areas will be forced in the next decade to move to other regions and other countries—in Africa or elsewhere— since they will not be able to live on agriculture in their current place of residence. The migration across regions and countries in search of land and water resources will contribute to heightened ethnic tensions, and African countries must design collaborative strategies to cope with their problems, increase food production, and prevent an escalation of tribal conflicts.

Possible measures

The main strategies to reducing rural poverty will have to include:

- Increasing agricultural productivity, possibly by introducing GM crops.
- Preventing a reduction in yields in semiarid areas by developing drought-resistant crops and supporting local extension services to introduce these crops in all rural areas.
- Building the rural road infrastructure so farmers can trade with urban centers and buy fertilizers, seeds, and other needed agricultural inputs.
- Securing the supply of food to farmers in the event of droughts, which may occur more frequently, and in the event of a sharp rise in food prices.
- Diversify income sources in the rural areas both by diversifying agricultural production and by introducing other forms of employment, like processing or even light manufacturing.
- Design a government supported insurance program that will secure the supply of food and seeds to farmers in the event of a drought to increase their incentive to remain in their villages despite adverse climatic changes.

The urban dilemma

By 2030, Africa will be an urban continent. However, since the urban areas are practically stagnant, local industries cannot be developed, the lack of resources will prevent local investors from developing competitive industries able to export to global markets, and unemployment will remain high. Moreover, the pressures of unemployment and foreign migration are likely to force many countries to restrict trade in order to secure their local employment. African countries do not have the resources or the expertise to develop competitive industries, and most of the current 70% unemployed in Africa's urban population will remain so. Health problems may worsen, crime spread, the family structure be likely to fragment, and the growing number of single mothers will have greater difficulties raising their children.

This is not just an African problem: An estimated one billion people in Latin America, Asia, Africa, and the Middle East live in slums or shantytowns that are not even legally recognized and do not receive any public services. In Africa, the main problem of the urban population is unemployment, and this problem will worsen with the rise in the number of migrants. As described above, the lack of employment will life in the cities increasingly intolerable.

In the coming years, the rate of urbanization in Africa will accelerate, according to UN estimates, and some 40 percent of the population in West Africa will move to the coastal cities; by 2020, the entire coastline between Accra and the Niger Delta will become a continuous urban megalopolis, with more than 50 million people, and five other cities will have more than ten million inhabitants.

The large and growing flow of migrants to the urban centers will continue despite the lack of any chance to find employment and the dismal living conditions in the slums, and this will lead to the urbanization of poverty. Although poverty will still concentrate in rural areas for at least another generation, the growing number of poor in urban centers will force governments to change their development policies. The urban poor are more likely to resort to crime, join armed militias, and seek whatever assets they can loot in order to survive.

Possible measures

The growing pressure on the urban centers will force most African governments to change their priorities in very fundamental ways:

- More resources will have to be invested in the urban centers.
- Government programs will have to include the provision of basic services to the urban poor, including water supply, health, and more adequate shelter.

- Since most urban poor will still be unemployed, the first priority will have to be the supply of food.
- The threat of lawlessness, growing crime, and spread of gang wars will require a large increase in the security forces.
- The major effort will have to concentrate on the development of competitive industries and on construction projects that can provide employment for the unskilled labor. The intensification of global competition will make the development of competitive industries far more difficult, but the African countries may be able to take advantage of both the continent's rich natural resources and the abundance of cheap labor and find an appropriate niche in the global market.

The economic, demographic and social challenges ought to be formulated as a comprehensive agenda, possibly and preferably a well-designed Africa-wide growth and poverty alleviation strategy. The rising inequality between countries will make this pan-African collaboration more difficult, however, since it is likely to vastly increase the cross-border movement of people. The better-off countries will try to fence their borders and limit migration, and that may exacerbate border disputes. Nevertheless, the solution to all these problems requires collaboration between the countries, and this must be recognized by African leaders. The African Union can have a leading role in promoting this collaboration and has already taken some measures in that direction. The potential benefits from collaboration and the dangers of competition are discussed in Part V of this book, since this is the greatest but also the most difficult challenge the African countries are likely to face in the coming years.

Notes

1. Davidson, *Black Man's Burden: Africa and the Curse of the Nation-State*, 1992.
2. The World Bank World Development Report of 1993 used the term "miraculous" to describe East Asia's economic growth.
3. Intergovernmental Panel on Climate Change (IPCC, UNEP, September 2007).

Part II
Coping with Escalating Food Insecurity

Africa's unique climatic conditions made it the greenhouse and the incubator of an infinite number of distinctive living species and vegetation, not to mention the human species, as well as of exceptional fruits, vegetables, trees and, in fact, all forms of life. But for the people who live in Africa today, the continent's climatic conditions and the threat of global warming (even if it may not be as soon as has been predicted) may become major obstacles that can prevent the African countries from sustaining their economic growth and could risk the lives of the majority of the African population, which lives in rural areas. The main concern of this part is whether Africa will be able to feed its growing population.

2.1
The Threat of Climate Changes

The fourth *Global Environment Outlook* of the UN's *Environment for Development* (2007) and the report of the Intergovernmental Panel on Climate Change (IPCC) presented in 2008 found water, land, air, plants, animals, and fish are all in "inexorable decline" and food security in Africa is likely to be "severely compromised" by climate change. Over 95 percent of Africa's agriculture depends on rainfall. Based on elaborate agroclimatic models, the Food and Agriculture Organization of the United Nations (FAO) predicts that, while the 80,000 sq km of agricultural land in SSA currently deemed constrained will improve as a result of climate change, 600,000 sq km currently classified as moderately constrained will become severely limited. Malthus's prediction, made 220 years ago, that "the amount of resources needed to sustain it exceeds what is available" seems more threatening than ever (Box 2.1).

Box 2.1 Chronicles of food emergencies: an ominous look into the future

A study of the World Food Program (WFP) published in September 2007 came to the following main conclusions on the most vulnerable regions of East and Central Africa:

- Widespread flooding in Uganda is worsening road access to key regions in the north; in some places, air deliveries are the only option to feed 300,000 flood victims until March. In total, WFP estimates that 1.7 million people are in need of assistance in Uganda, including flood victims, refugees and others displaced by conflict or civil strife.
- As people's food supplies run out, and as the threat of malaria and waterborne diseases rise in flooded areas, it is vital to reach these people with food aid and to keep helicopters in the air to ferry other aid to people in villages cut off by floodwater.
- WFP teams have reached almost 74,000 people in flooded areas with some 1,051 tons of food.

- Over the past few days, rains have been reported across much of Uganda, including areas north of Soroti in Lira District and in the Northeast in Karamoja region. Floods have cut WFP's road access to 27 camps for displaced people surrounding the towns of Pader and Kitgum. There is no road access to Katakwi—one of the two worst-affected districts. WFP warns that a major crisis could develop in Uganda.
- In Sudan, WFP is preparing to start emergency air drops to feed 43,800 people in three flood-affected states in southern Sudan—in addition to 89,000 flood-affected people already receiving food assistance in other parts of South and East Sudan.
- The one-month air drop operation will start in October to drop 1,440 tons of food assistance in Jonglei, Upper Nile and Lakes states where roads are impassable.
- Since the beginning of July, torrential rains have caused flash floods in eastern and southern Sudan, which many local people say are the worst in living memory. Some 500,000 people have been directly affected by floods, and at least 200,000 are homeless.
- In Ethiopia, seasonal floods have occurred in Amhara, Afar and Tigray in northern Ethiopia, in Gambella in the West, in SNNP in the South, and in the Somali region, affecting 226,000 people. A total of 71,000 people have been displaced.
- Government food aid was sent to assist more than 60,000 people in Ethiopia.
- In Rwanda, torrential rainfall combined with the effects of deforestation in the Northwest has left 2,500 people homeless. The government has distributed food to flood victims.

(Based on various reports, primarily in the *New York Times*)

The large share of agriculture in the African economies is likely to increase the difficulties for their rural population to adjust to these changes. In the medium and long run, rapid technological changes are expected to develop drought-resistant crop varieties that would offset the reduction in agricultural yields as an effect of the climate change, but the African countries are generally slower in adopting new technologies, and they have difficulties coping with the growing frequency of extreme weather, such as droughts and floods.

Human activity in Africa is also affecting ecosystems: Low-income households in rural areas depend on wood and charcoal for 80–90 percent of their energy needs. Fire incidents also create a huge risk for the tropical forests in Africa. The most disastrous effects of climate change will be on the African rural population. In recent years, there has already been an increase in the frequency of natural disasters, droughts and floods.

Already in 1972 the famous study, *Limits to Growth*, published by the Club of Rome suggested it would be necessary for all nations to reach a common agreement and collaborative measures to achieve sustainable global growth and jointly bear the sacrifices in order to reach that goal. The main difficulty of achieving a collaborative agreement is that different countries have different limits on their capacity to grow; another difficulty is that some countries will be affected by the environmental degradation much later than others. The environmental and ecological conditions require countries to make painful sacrifices and restrain their growth. The less (or later) a country is affected by climatic changes, the less it is willing to accept restraints on its growth and the greater, therefore, are the difficulties of achieving common agreement required to maintain global ecological and economic stability. Moreover, an agreement that requires all nations to restrict their growth will perpetuate existing income inequalities, since the more developed countries have already achieved much higher standards of living and higher levels of industrialization.

The haunting Malthusian predicament: the water crisis

The UN *Global Environment Outlook* (October 2007) cautions that global warming creates considerable risks to all resources used for the production of food; primarily water and land are at risk. There are also worries about the destabilizing effects of water scarcity, including the possibility it could trigger wars in the Middle East and Africa. In these regions, the local population is rapidly reaching the stage where the amount of resources needed to sustain their population will exceed the amount of resources available for their food production.

The fact that these warnings are necessary shows that in the past 35 years since the publication of *Limits to Growth*, the world has ignored the risks of "continuing unchanged the growth trends in world population, industrialization, pollution, food production, and resource depletion." An absolute trust in the power of science and in the capacity of humans led most countries and peoples to expect mankind will never encounter limits that will require restrictions on growth. Lester Brown, in his famous book, *Seeds of Change* (1970), had an upbeat assessment of the longer-term prospects of increasing agricultural productivity and food supply—an assessment he saw as proof the Malthusian prediction of inevitable cycles of hunger is no longer valid.

The UN World Water Report, "*Water in a Changing World*" (March 2009), warns: "Water scarcity may limit food production and supply, putting pressure on food prices and increasing countries' dependence on food imports. The number of countries and regions without enough water to produce their food is rising as populations increase" (p. 6). The forces at work are the combined consequence of the behavior of all countries, but the effects are likely to concentrate in more limited areas in the form of prolonged droughts or destructive floods. Water scarcity will increase the danger of political conflicts that may intensify as the shortage deepens, and may even ignite wars or civil conflicts between tribes that claim ownership over water resources in certain regions, or among farmers, herders, and local communities. The danger is aggravated by decaying infrastructure, poor water management, pollution, and waste, and by the difficulties in coordinating collaborative policies and designing common projects that would ameliorate the shortage.

Ecologists and demographers remained pessimistic, however, and in his monograph, *The Population Bomb* (1970), Paul Ehrlich still predicted massive and long-lasting famines. A quarter of a century after the publication of his book, Lester Brown was also more cautious in his book, *Who Will Feed China?* (1995), even though at that time thousands of seeds of change were already blooming. Brown predicted that, in order to secure the minimum food needs of the 1.2 billion Chinese, "China may soon have to import so much grain that this action could trigger unprecedented rises in world food prices." In the subsequent years, China itself gave a resounding reply to the dilemma Brown had presented: China managed to feed itself, and with much better food. Paradoxically, Brown's doomsday prediction came back with a vengeance in 2007, with the unprecedented rise in world food prices, but only part of that rise was due to China's growing demand for food.

In the debate during the 1970s, the document published by The Club of Rome (Meadows et al. 1972) had the greatest impact and was the first in a series of studies that applied global simulation models to estimate the interrelation of population growth, global food demand and supply, and the degradation of natural resources. That study was the first to highlight the environmental problems and the degradation of natural resources. The study presented very succinctly the dilemma the global economy is still facing due to dwindling land and water resources and the effects of climate changes that impose increasingly more severe constraints on global food production and economic growth. Box 2.2 emphasizes that these constraints may require mankind to make a very harsh choice between the two alternatives the limits to growth may demand in the coming years:

Box 2.2 The limits to growth

1. If the present growth trends in world population, industrialization, pollution, food production, and resource depletion continue unchanged, the limits to growth on this planet will be reached sometime within the next one hundred years. The most probable result will be a rather sudden and uncontrollable decline in both population and industrial capacity.
2. It is possible to alter these growth trends and establish conditions of ecological and economic stability that is sustainable far into the future. The state of global equilibrium could be designed so that the basic material needs of each person on earth are satisfied and each person has an equal opportunity to realize his individual human potential.

If the world's people decide to strive for this second outcome rather than the first, the sooner they begin working to attain it, the greater will be their chances of success.

D. Gale Johnson was another leading economist who proposed a more optimistic vision. In his book, *World Food Problems and Prospects* (1975), he argued that the world is capable of increasing agricultural production fast enough to permanently remove the Malthusian "misery" of imminent shortages and famines. Johnson saw no reason to doubt human ingenuity and the capacity to find new ways to increase food supply, and his answer to the doomsday predictions was that people's ingenuity and inventiveness is the inexhaustible resource that can remove the limits to growth.

How relevant are Malthus's "principles of production and population"?

In his 1789 "Essay on the Principle of Population," demographer Thomas Malthus expressed his key question as follows: "The great question now at issue is whether man shall henceforth start forwards with accelerated velocity toward illimitable and hitherto in-conceived improvement, or will he be destined to perpetual oscillations between happiness and misery?" To prevent the misery, he claimed, there must be "a strong and constantly operating check on population." In that essay, though, he was referring to the population of the lower classes and that their excessive procreation makes hunger imminent.

One critical missing factor that must be added to complement his claim is that the extent of people's misery depends not only on the amount of food that can be produced and supplied and the number of people that must be fed, but also on the *distribution* of the available food supply among people. Equal distribution of the available food to all people seems at first sight to be the solution Malthus had in mind, since only with equal distribution could the global food supply ever lag behind the food needs of the entire population and his warning be realized. In fact, Malthus had a very different solution that was in some respects the exact opposite, as we shall see later on.

If, however, food supply is distributed *unequally* and people with higher incomes or wealth can afford to buy more food than can others, then the affluent will be able to have enough while others are doomed to perish. At some point in time, the available food supply will be enough to meet the needs of the rich, and the world will reach a stable state. This seems unfair and unjust, but in fact equal distribution is neither the most just nor the most desirable from the point of view of the entire society. The reason is that people differ from one another in their talents and in their capacity to contribute to production. Those who can will make greater efforts and contribute more to production if they receive more in return. With equal distribution of food for consumption, people will receive equal quantities of food for their consumption regardless of their actual contribution to production. The more talented will not have incentives to make a greater effort and contribute more to production and, as a result, society will produce less food and everybody will lose.

In the capitalistic world, each person contributes to production according to her capacity and receives (food) according to her actual contribution to food production. In this world, the people with the lowest capacity will receive the least and, if the quantity they produce according to their talent does not suffice to feed them, then they will die first. The people with higher capacity will receive more food and many, if not most of them, are likely to survive.

In our more altruistic world, we recognize the need to help the poor and this can be done only by allocating then some of the "excess" food supply from the more productive and non-poor individuals to the poor individuals. That distribution can be achieved by means of a progressive income tax that takes transfers resources from the more productive (or "rich") individuals and transfer them to the less productive (or "poor") individuals. The progressive tax also reduces the incentives of the more productive individuals who consume and produce less food.

Even if we accept the principle that some income transfers from the rich to the poor are necessary in the poorer ones to prevent hunger, there is still a dilemma about the degree of progressivity of the tax, given the inevitable losses of the entire society as an effect of the reduction in the incentives for the more productive rich to work when their net income is reduced. This, of course, is a dilemma each person, each political party, and each country must decide by itself. The underlying trade-off in this decision is between the amount of "justice" that can be gained (measured, for example, by the reduction in the number of the poor or the reduction in their poverty gap) and the loss in food production as an effect of these income transfers. The degree of progressivity is decided by the leading coalition as part of the budget legislation, and is therefore a law that must be observed and enforced.

The difficulty of coordinating an egalitarian solution must have been in Malthus's mind when he advocated the *least* egalitarian solution and was even in favor of abolishing *any* form of social welfare. His formal argument was: given the little gains that can be achieved with a subsidy for the poor at the expense of the well-to-do, and given the poor's higher fertility and therefore the inevitable larger increase in the world's population, that subsidy can only bring greater misery. In his view, any effort to redress inequality or mitigate poverty would be counterproductive because poor people multiply at a more rapid pace and any law that forces the community to take care of the poor would only aggravate their scarcity. This was his warning and his strategy to prevent communities or nations from falling into the trap of reaching the limit of their capacity to produce enough food.

In a second edition of his book, published in 1803, Malthus softened his original harsh message by introducing the idea of moral restraint on food consumption. In the words of Mahatma Gandhi, there are no limits to greed, but there are limits to their need. Hence, he would argue, what we need is a moral restraint on greed.

Today, the growing risk that some regions and population groups will not be able to avoid the Malthusian trap, even though global food supply is sufficient to meet all needs, is evidence that mankind has not managed to avoid the excess of greed. Since Malthus's time, the world's population has increased by a factor of more than six; nevertheless, the global average per capita food consumption has nearly doubled to around 3,000 calories today. Since the 1950s, the area under cultivation in the world has increased by roughly 11 percent, while yields per hectare have increased by 120 percent.

The Neo-Malthusian vision of the limits to growth

The apocalyptic scenario that Malthus envisaged for finding a solution for the food crisis rests upon an extreme nonegalitarian solution that would restrict the rapid growth rate of the poor, and he was even in favor of abolishing *any* form of social welfare. By contrast, the Neo-Malthusians saw ethical and humanitarian merits in social welfare programs and mutual help. Their basic approach was, therefore, not to discriminate between people in social welfare programs and, instead, to focus on the demographic threat and on population control programs. The spread of contraceptives in many developing countries (but not, for example, in China) has been much slower (and more cautious) partly due to religious restrictions and partly due to a lack of necessary information.

A renewed warning of mass starvation due to overpopulation, one that echoed Malthus's original prediction was given in Ehrlich's *The Population Bomb*. Ehrlich called for strict and immediate measures to limit population growth; although he maintained at the outset that "The battle to feed all of humanity is over," he predicted that within less than a generation, millions of people would starve to death. That alarming prediction did not come to pass and was countered in the subsequent decades—well after Ehrlich's D-Day for the explosion of the "population bomb" (in 1985)—by the huge increase in food supply made possible due to the "Green Revolution" and the more recent increase in food production due to the highly promising, though still controversial, Genetically Modified (GM) crops revolution. Ehrlich warned, though, that the developed countries have a much greater negative impact on the global environment and on food supply, even though the poor countries will suffer the most.

The increase in the standard of living in many developing countries brought to a sharp reduction in the growth rate of their population. In the African countries, however, the population continues to grow at a much faster rate than on all other continents, even though in the past two decades there also has been a noticeable decline in their population growth rate. Malthus's original prediction, and Ehrlich's later warning, anticipated a world that becomes increasingly overpopulated while its resources are depleting. This bleak vision has not been realized, and food supply continues to grow faster than the global population. Technological innovations in agricultural production and more efficient use of water resources give credence to the prediction of D. Gale Johnson that the world can increase agricultural production fast enough to permanently remove the specter of Malthusian misery. On the other hand, while global food production has increased at a rapid rate, making it possible to feed all mankind and remove any existential threat, great threats still threaten some regions, particularly in South Asia and SSA. In addition, the poor people in these and other regions continue to face the risk of periodic food shortages due to droughts and major floods. Despite the stunning growth in global food production, over a billion people are undernourished.

2.2
Can Africa Feed Its People?

For half a century food was abundant and food prices continuously declined while industrialization proliferated and the global economy grew at an unprecedented rate, though very unequally. Since the 1960s, the Green Revolution boosted food production, and by reaching the poor underdeveloped countries, it pulled millions of people out of poverty. Today, the "Gene Revolution" promises another miracle of expanding food supply by adjusting the conditions of food production to the changing agroclimatic conditions. As a result, during most of the twentieth century, the miraculous growth of the global economy and the increasing food supply put the threatening predictions of *The Limits to Growth* at the bottom of the public agenda.

Does this optimistic belief in human ingenuity suggest Malthus is as wrong today as he was two centuries ago?[1] Although there are more reasons today to discard the dismal prospects Malthus foresaw and that he defined as "vice," in certain large regions there is also reason to be concerned about spreading malnutrition and hunger that will not be prevented despite the ample food supply. Although the flood of new discoveries and scientific innovations seemed to promise that sufficient food supply will be available in the foreseeable future, nearly one-fifth of the world population is malnourished.

The Millennium Development Goals: can they end hunger?

In September 2000, the largest-ever gathering of world leaders adopted the UN Millennium Declaration that committed their nations to a global partnership to reduce poverty, improve health, and promote peace, human rights, gender equality, and environmental sustainability. The Millennium Development Goals (MDGs) declared by all the UN member states and signed by 147 heads of state and governments during the summit were meant to achieve a drastic reduction in poverty by 2015 (Box 2.3).

> *Box 2.3* Millennium development goals
>
> Goal 1: Halving between 1990 and 2015 the proportion of people that suffer from hunger.
> *Target 1*: Between 1990 and 2015, halve the proportion of people whose income is less than $1 a day.
> *Target 2*: Between 1990 and 2015 halve the proportion of people who suffer from hunger.
> Goal 2: Achieve universal primary education by 2015.
> *Target*: Ensure that by 2015, children everywhere, boys and girls alike, will be able to complete a full course of primary schooling.
> Goal 3: Eliminating gender disparity in primary and secondary education and empower women.
> *Target*: Eliminate gender disparity in primary and secondary education no later than 2015.
> Goal 4: Reducing by two thirds the mortality rate of children under 5.
> *Target*: Reduce by two thirds, between 1990 and 2015, the under five mortality rate.
> Goal 5: Halving the proportion of people without access to safe drinking water.
> Goal 6: Combat HIV/AIDS, malaria and other diseases. Halting the spread of HIV/AIDS by 2015.
> Goal 7: Improving by 50 percent the level of adult literacy.
>
> (*Source*: United Nations)

In March 2002, world leaders met at the International Conference on Financing for Development in Monterrey, Mexico, establishing a landmark framework for a global development partnership in which developed and developing countries agreed to take joint action for poverty reduction. Later that same year, UN member states gathered at the World Summit on Sustainable Development in Johannesburg, South Africa, where they reaffirmed the goals as the world's time-bound development targets.

The MDGs represent a unique commitment of all 181 members of the UN General Assembly to contribute jointly to the collaborative effort to bring about a reduction of poverty and improve the disgracefully low standards of living of the large share of world population still suffering from hunger. Differing from previous commitments, this UN declaration was truly historic because it defined specific quantitative and measurable targets for the following goals: eradication of extreme poverty and hunger; achieving universal primary education; promoting gender equality and empowering women; reducing child mortality; improving maternal health; combating HIV/AIDS, malaria, and other diseases; ensuring environmental sustainability; and building a global partnership for development. Each goal has a specific quantitative target, except for the first goal, which has two separate targets, eradicating poverty and achieving food security. The analysis in this chapter concentrates on the first goal of the

MDGs that came to represent the central commitment: reducing poverty and hunger.

Halfway to 2015, the World Bank and the IMF published the "Global Monitoring Report" for 2008 which provides an assessment of the progress made thus far toward achieving the MDGs. In view of the slow progress, the report describes the measures that must be taken in the remaining years in order to achieve the goals, but it also warns that a large number of countries, particularly in SSA, are likely to fall short of achieving the MDGs. Although the report was published in early April 2008, when the dimensions of the food crisis became more evident, its assessments were still based on developments during the period 2000–05, when the majority of the developing countries benefited from unprecedented growth.

Already in 2007, Jeffrey Sachs argued (*The Guardian*, May 24, 2007) that despite substantive progress in several important social indicators included in the MDGs, there was little cause for celebration. The actual progress in the key areas since the signing of the Millennium Declaration was far below the UN plan. One reason for this disappointing performance is that very few donor countries met their obligations and provided the aid they had pledged to the African countries. The other, and undoubtedly more important, reason is the failure of the African countries themselves to implement adequate measures that would lead to a reduction of poverty and a significant acceleration of their economic growth, even though quite a few countries actually reached growth rates that should have enabled them to reduce their poverty and undernutrition and achieve the MDG even without external aid.

Robust growth in the first half of the decade reduced the number of people in developing regions living on less than $1.25 a day from 1.8 billion in 1990 to 1.4 billion in 2005, while the poverty rate dropped from 46 percent to 27 percent (Figure 2.1a). The global economic and financial crisis since

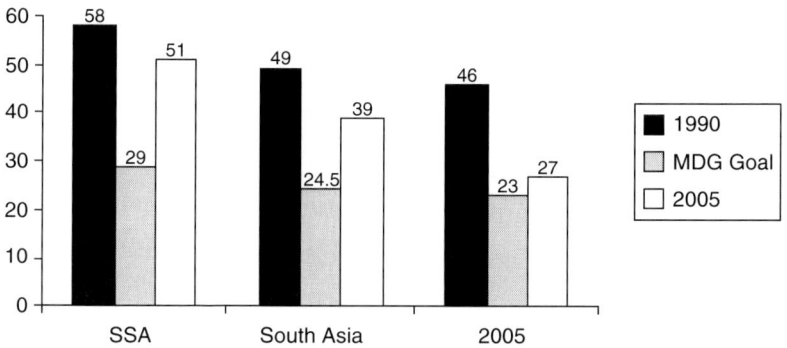

Figure 2.1a   Proportion of people living on less than $1.25 a day: 1990 and 2005 (%)
Source: Millennium Development Goals Report 2010, based on Ravallion and Chen (2008).

mid-2008, however, reduced trade and investment, slowing growth in developing countries—although the momentum of their economic growth is robust enough, and likely to sustain their progress and bring a reduction in poverty to 15 percent by 2015, in line with the MDG goal. In Africa, however, poverty may remain high and well above the goal of 24.5 percent.

Since 1990, there has been slow progress toward the MDG target of halving the proportion of malnourished, and their share of the population in the developing countries decreased from 20 percent in 1990–92 to 16 percent in 2005–07. The reduction in their share has stalled since the late 1990s due to the diminishing effects of the Green Revolution in South Asia and Latin America, and the number of malnourished people has declined from 817 to 805 million during the years 1990–92 to 2000–02 (Figure 2.1b).

As food prices spiked in 2008 due to the food crisis, and incomes have declined due to the spreading global recession, the number of hungry people shot up above 1 billion in 2009 (Figure 2.2). Although food supply was sufficient, despite the food crisis, to provide every person with 3,500 calories per day, the FAO estimates the number of chronically malnourished people increased by over 100 million in 2009, and millions of small children die every year from hunger. As the FAO emphasized, these high and rising numbers of hungry people "are particularly unsettling as undernourishment is not a result of limited international food supplies. Recent figures of the FAO Food Outlook indicate a strong world cereal production in 2009, which will only modestly fall short of last year's record output level. Clearly, the world can produce enough food to eliminate hunger" (FAO Policy Brief September 2009).

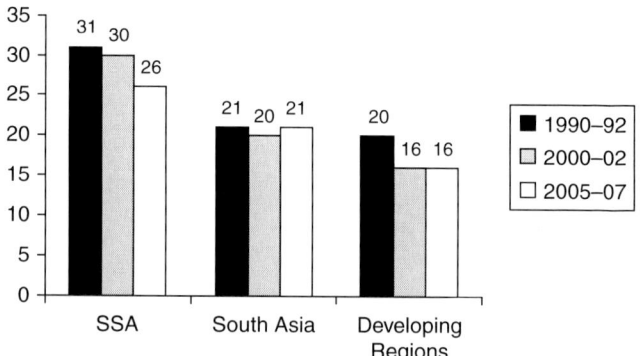

Figure 2.1b The proportion of undernourished people in the developing regions (%)
Source: Millennium Development Goals Report, 2010, and FAO.

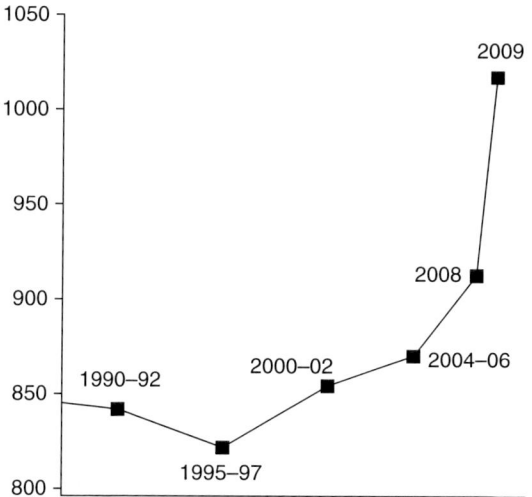

Figure 2.2 The number of hungry people in the world (00 thousands)
Source: FAO Policy Brief (September 2009).

Although enough food is *available* in the world, it is distributed extremely unequally between countries and between income groups within countries. During the three-year period 2007–09, cereal production was high, reaching a record level in 2008, but food prices rose sharply to levels that were far beyond the reach of a large number of people. While the rich countries produce large surpluses, many developing countries do not have enough food to secure their citizens' the supply needed for good and healthy nutrition. Moreover, only one-fourth of the world's cereal production is currently used directly for human consumption. A larger share of agricultural production is used to feed animals in order to satisfy the desire for better food, particularly meat.

Is Africa reaching limits to growth?

During the four decades since the publication of *Limits to Growth*, food production has continued to increase and productive technologies in agriculture have been invented. At the end of the twentieth century, grain prices were at a hundred-year low, stocks were mounting, and the world experienced unprecedented economic growth. Massive famines were no longer an unavoidable fate, and while many of the least developed countries, particularly in Africa, still experienced cycles of hunger and malnutrition, in a world that has ample food production, it could and should have been possible to put an end to hunger.

The World Bank's *WDR 2008* underscored the achievements in the past, noting the progress that had been made:

> A big question at the time of the last *World Development Report* on agriculture in 1982 was whether agriculture would be able to provide enough food for the world's growing population. Twenty-five years later it is clear that world agriculture has met the global demand for food and fiber. Increasing per capita production, rising productivity, and declining commodity prices all attest to this success.
>
> From 1980 to 2004, the GDP of agriculture expanded globally by an average of 2.0 percent a year, more than the population growth of 1.6 percent a year. This growth, driven by increasing productivity, pushed down the real price of grains in world markets by about 1.8 percent a year over the same period.
>
> Developing countries achieved much faster agricultural growth (2.6 percent a year) than the industrial countries (0.9 percent a year) in 1980–2004. Indeed, developing countries accounted for an impressive 79 percent of overall agricultural growth during this period and their share of world agricultural GDP rose from 56 percent in 1980 to 65 percent in 2004. (*WDR* 2008, pp. 50–53)

And yet, malnutrition has not diminished as was planned and hoped for in the MDGs, and the number of chronically poor people has not declined. Sub-Saharan Africa, in particular did not share in these achievements. Cereal yields in SSA have declined or stagnated since the 1970s, and in the mid-2000s were roughly one-third of those in South Asia, according to the World Bank. In the late 1960s, most Sub-Saharan countries were net food exporters; in 2002, Sub-Saharan Africa became a net importer, importing nearly 20 million tons of food in that year. The food crisis was most devastating for the world's poor, most of whom are already the vulnerable populations that, as the *World Disasters Report 2007* noted,[2] suffered the most during previous climatic disasters and will suffer the most in subsequent ones.

The rate of population growth has declined from 2.2 percent annually in the early 1960s to about 1.2 percent today, but it remained over 2.3 percent in SSA. The United Nations expects the world's population to exceed 9 billion by 2050, and the share of Africa in both the world's population and, even more so, in the world's poor, will significantly increase. Nevertheless, there is little doubt food production in the world at large will keep pace with the increase of the world's population, despite the effects of global warming. New arable lands in Ukraine, Russia, and Central Asia will be added to the world pool, and new agricultural production technologies will continue to increase yields.

There are grave doubts, however, whether this increase will reach the bottom 1.3 billion chronically poor people in the world (according to new

World Bank estimates; see also Box 2.4). Plant physiologists estimate that with the current land under cultivation, we would have to increase yields from the current three tons per hectare to four tons to support that population. In the coming decade, high food prices will give strong incentives to increase the area under cultivation, and with further improvements in GM technology the yields will continue to rise. Moreover, with the development of a second generation of crops that can be used for more efficient production of biofuel and the development of other technologies and sources for

---

Box 2.4 The human face of the food crisis in the horn of Africa

DAGAARI, Somalia—The global food crisis has arrived at Safia Ali's hut. She cannot afford rice or wheat or powdered milk anymore. At the same time, a drought has decimated her family's herd of goats, turning their sole livelihood into a pile of bleached bones and papery skin. The result is that Ms. Safia, a 25-year-old mother of five, has not eaten in a week. Her 1-year-old son is starving too.

Even before commodity prices started to shoot up, civil war, displacement and imperiled aid operations had pushed many people here to the brink of famine. But now with food costs spiraling out of reach and people's livestock dropping dead, villagers across this sun-blasted landscape say hundreds of people are dying of hunger and thirst. This is what happens when the global food crisis meets local chaos.

There has been a collision of troubles throughout the region: skimpy rainfall, disastrous harvests, soaring food prices, dying livestock, escalating violence, out-of-control inflation, and shrinking food aid that falls far short of the growing needs. In Darfur, the United Nations has had to cut food rations because of a rise in banditry that endangers aid deliveries. In Kenya, a combination of drought, higher fertilizer and fuel costs and post-election violence displaced thousands of farmers and worsened food scarcities.

The United Nations has declared a wide swath of central Somalia a humanitarian emergency, the final stage before a full-blown famine. Many people already consider Somalia a catastrophe. Even in a good year, this area has some of the highest malnutrition rates anywhere in the world. The collapse of the central government in 1991 plunged Somalia into a spiral of clan-driven bloodshed and a famine that killed hundreds of thousands of people.

Whether Somalia slips into yet another famine depends on whether aid arrives on time and in adequate quantities. That does not look likely. Eleven aid workers have been killed this year, and Somalia became too complicated and dangerous. On top of the warlord and clan fighting, there is now a conflict with Western aid workers. The Bush administration has said that terrorists with Al Qaeda ties are hiding in Somalia, sheltered by local Islamists, and a recent American attack on an Islamist leader in Dusa Marreb, a town in the center of the drought zone, has spawned a wave of revenge threats against Western aid workers. The UN and private aid organizations say it is now too dangerous to expand their life-saving work in Dusa Marreb.

(*Source*: Based on various reports, primarily in the *New York Times*)

energy production, the diversion of corn and rapeseed from the food supply to the production of biofuel will come to an end.

The role of government

The concentration of the majority of the African population and most of the poor in rural areas makes it imperative to make significant reforms in the agricultural sector by increasing production and farmers' productivity. The fundamental changes the agricultural sector is going through with the introduction of advanced production technologies and the GM revolution, the new reality of high food prices and high production costs despite the decline in oil prices and the price of fertilizers in 2009, and the climatic changes and dwindling water resources require far-reaching reforms in order to prevent food scarcities and periodic hunger.

African governments have allocated very meager resources to the agriculture sector since the 1980s. Some governments allocated less than 1 percent of their national budgets to the sector, even though their revenues from export taxes on agricultural products were much higher. Some reasons for the scanty support of the agricultural sector by most African governments were the austere macroeconomic programs under the conditionalities of the IMF and the World Bank, the weak political power of the farmers, and the efforts of some governments to build an industrial base. The main reason, however, was the grossly unequal distribution of these countries' incomes and the huge wealth amassed by their elites.

In July 2003, members of the African Union (AU) pledged to devote at least 10 percent of their government budgets to agriculture programs over the next five years. As of 2008, only Rwanda and Zambia had actually executed the plan. Even the resource-rich countries that had large revenues during the commodity boom allocated very little to the agricultural sector or to rural infrastructure.

The contribution of the government is clearly essential. As the World Bank's *World Development Report 2008* emphasized, "Markets will not work without addressing the massive infrastructure deficit." Without comprehensive efforts of government to provide these public goods by building the necessary components of the rural infrastructure, most farmers will be essentially locked in their villages and unable to develop trade with urban centers, even though this is the only way to increase their agricultural production and their incomes.

The World Bank's report recommends making investments in order to support the private sector. Many economists question the capacity of the private sector to operate efficiently in African economies. In 2005, Malawi attracted attention due to its decision to ignore the free-market policy prescriptions of the World Bank and initiate a governmental fertilizer-subsidy program. In the following three years, crop yields were significantly higher. In 2006, maize production in the country doubled, and in 2007, it almost tripled, allowing the country to export over 300,000 tons of maize to Zimbabwe that year.

Can the government replace the private sector in agriculture? Can the government sustain its policy after a season of bad weather? Can farmers trust the government's commitment to maintain these subsidies? These are some of the questions economists raise when they debate the successful three-year experience in Malawi. The private sector has often failed to maintain effective trade of agricultural inputs and outputs, and in many countries and regions private traders assume monopolistic power over local markets and extract most of the profits from trade. But how effective government can be in replacing the private sector still remains an open question.

The debate over the policy of the government of Malawi reflects the different opinions of those who favor state intervention and those who champion the free market. Both camps, however, are optimistic about the long-term prospects for increasing agricultural yields in Africa. In May 2008, Kofi Annan predicted that within five to ten years the food production of African farmers could be doubled or tripled. Other experts, such as the University of London's Harrigan, suggest a ten- to 20-year time frame is more realistic, because even when the technology is available, it usually takes farmers a long time to have confidence and adopt the technology. In addition, there must simultaneously be significant developments in the market system.

Another problem is the serious shortage of skilled workers. Experts have emphasized the need to train many more African scientists—plant breeders, soil scientists, and agricultural economists—to carry out local research. To accomplish training, technology development, and market strengthening, the region's governments will need long-term assistance from international donors. They also, however, need to make much larger contributions to these reforms. Before the outbreak of the global recession, experts were cautiously optimistic about the World Bank and G-8 pledges to double agricultural aid to Africa. But thus far neither the G-8 nor the donor countries met their pledges. The global recession and high unemployment in the developed countries has made many scholars, primarily in Africa, more pessimistic about the potential to mobilize the necessary resources to make the necessary reforms.

Drawing on the successful experience of Asian countries with the Green Revolution, Paarlberg suggested the Indian, Chinese, and South Korean governments could offer technical assistance to African governments. Others have emphasized the need to reform the US aid program to allow food to be purchased within Africa, instead of shipping it from the United States, and many nongovernmental organizations have demanded a reduction in the huge subsidies given by the US and EU to their farmers.

Africa's obstacles are aggravated by unstable, ineffective, and highly corrupt governments that invest little in education, health, and infrastructure;

to make matters worse, many countries have experienced a complete breakdown of law and order, and civil conflicts remain widespread. Africa is widely regarded by investment-rating services as the world's most risky region, and even the few more stable countries, like Uganda, Ghana, and Senegal, are still rated as risky for foreign investors.

Special efforts were made to bring the poorest and most highly indebted countries (referred to as the HIPC) into the world economy by substantially reducing their debts and implementing economic reforms targeting poverty reduction. Despite these efforts and the loads of money given to these countries in the form of various aid programs, their overall situation has not changed much, and many are still essentially left out of the global economy. As a result, most expert reports conclude that African countries are not likely to attain the Millennium Development Goals (MDG) by 2015, or even by a decade later.

In response to the global food crisis, in mid-2008 the World Bank designed a program that drew lessons from the experience with earlier programs (Box 2.5).

Box 2.5 Lingering African perceptions of structural adjustment programs

I was in Washington last year. At the World Bank the first question they asked me was "how did you fail?" I responded that we took over a country with 85 per cent of its adult population illiterate. The British ruled us for 43 years. When they left, there were 2 trained engineers and 12 doctors. This is the country we inherited. When I stepped down, there was 91-per-cent literacy and nearly every child was in school. We trained thousands of engineers and doctors and teachers.

In 1988, Tanzania's per-capita income was $280. Now, in 1998, it is $140. So I asked the World Bank people: "what went wrong?" Because for the last ten years Tanzania has been signing on the dotted line and doing everything the IMF and the World Bank wanted. Enrollment in school has plummeted to 63 per cent and conditions in health and other social services have deteriorated. I asked them again: "what went wrong?"

(Julius Nyerere in an interview for the magazine
The Heart of Africa, January–February 1999)

Three of the five pillars of the program most relevant in this context are:

- Support governments in the design of sustainable policies;
- Support broad-based growth in productivity and market participation in agriculture;
- Provide a comprehensive menu of possible actions and investments, but countries can select measures most relevant to their individual situations.

The experience of the early reforms designed by the IMF and World Bank to restructure government policies along the lines of neoclassical principles was not effective, since African countries did not have the basic institutions necessary to implement policies that required fiscal discipline and an effective central bank. The later reforms succeeded in educating a cadre of mid-level officials in government institutions, but they had mixed success in improving the mode of operation of the central government because corruption at the top trickled down to lower levels. In the past decade, many of the more educated mid-level officials rose to the rank of high-level officials, either in the government or the private sector, but corruption remained rampant and the effectiveness of government remained low. The main weakness of African governments is at the leadership level, since the majority of the leaders are still autocrats, even though many took office after nominally democratic elections.

Can African farmers produce enough food?

In his book *A Farewell to Alms*, Gregory Clark[3] maintained that the Malthusian trap indeed dominated the English economy at the time Malthus wrote his book, but this trap remained only until the Industrial Revolution. With the major increase in productivity as an effect of the Industrial Revolution, the English and most other European economies managed to achieve amazing affluence. The vastly higher efficiency in production accelerated economic growth that outpaced population growth and raised per capita incomes, thus helping them escape the Malthusian trap. Another outcome of the Industrial Revolution, however, was an increase in the gap in living standards between the richest and the poorest countries, from a wealth disparity of about four to one in 1800 to more than 50 to one today.

Clark claimed, therefore, that nations that do not adapt their economies by making the transition from an agricultural-based economy to an industrial-based economy will not be able to achieve the same production efficiencies and will remain trapped in poverty. In other words, countries that will not remove the constraints of the agrarian economy will be shackled by these constraints. As the populations in these countries increase and their economies remain primarily agrarian they are bound to have greater difficulties supplying the food needs of their peoples.

How can Africa make the transition to an industrial-based economy? Can the African countries draw on the experience, and follow in the footsteps, of the Asian countries in their process of industrial revolution? Many scholars on the developing countries have pointed to the failure of political and social institutions in these countries as the reason why the African countries, with the exception of South Africa, remained poor and underdeveloped. But, according to Clark, the proposed medicine of institutional reform "has failed repeatedly to cure the patient." He likened the "cult centers" of the World Bank and the IMF to "pre-scientific physicians who prescribed bloodletting for ailments they did not understand." The next chapter discusses the prospects of developing an industrial sector in the African countries and brings ample evidence to show the main impediments to the development of a competitive industrial sector in Africa has been the failure of government institutions to provide the necessary conditions for the operation of local industries. These conditions include not only having the basic infrastructure, but also maintaining law and order, including the protection of property rights, and enforcement of contracts, etc., necessary to any business.

The *World Development Report* of 2008 was more optimistic and claimed to disprove this uncomplimentary thesis by emphasizing:

> [In SSA] the growth rate of agricultural GDP per capita and of the rural population in the region was close to zero during the early 1970s and negative through the 1980s and early 1990s. But with positive growth rates in the last 10 years, this trend has been reversed, suggesting that the stagnation in Sub-Saharan African agriculture may be over. (*WDR* 2008, p. 53)

The hopeful diagnosis of the *WDR* was only partially correct, however; the main reason for the positive growth rates in the last ten years was largely the increase in their population, whereas food production per capita still remained stagnant. Agricultural productivity also remained unchanged or even declined and the Green Revolution has failed so far to be adopted by the African farmers. There was some increase in the production of Africa's traditional agricultural produce, primarily coffee, cocoa, and cotton, as an effect of the rise in world prices, but in only a few countries; the standard of living of the rural population remained low, and only a tiny share of their countries' large revenues from the exports of natural resources trickled down to the rural population. Even in the rapidly growing economies, the rate of growth of GDP rose to 5 and 6 percent during 2005–07, while the growth of agriculture was only between 2 to 3 percent, roughly equal to the growth of their population.

The rural sector of African countries remained largely stagnant during most of the decade; agricultural production was suppressed by the rise in the costs of food production and by intensive competition from the developed countries that exported grains to their market at prices that were lower in the urban markets than the prices of locally produced grains. This was possible partly due to the high subsidies farmers in these countries received, to their higher efficiency, and the economies of scale in production, and also partly due to the poor rural roads that increased the costs of the local farmers in bringing their produce to urban markets. African farmers not able to compete with imported grain (particularly those in remote areas) were therefore forced to produce mostly for their own consumption. As a result, the share of SSA in the world's undernourished population increased very steeply, from 19 percent in 1990 to 31 percent in 2004. During these years, a food crisis in the African countries was avoided, however, due to a continuous flow of food aid and the imports of grains at low prices from the EU and the US. Yet, local extreme food shortages erupted very frequently in various regions as a result of droughts or internal conflicts.

The cheap food imports reached chiefly the urban population, but this was very damaging to local farmers unable to sell their produce in the urban market because they could not compete with highly subsidized imported grains. Few of these farmers were able to change the structure of their production and make the transition to exportable agricultural produce due to the poor infrastructure that did not enable them to trade in high-value crops.

The gradual rise in food prices since 2005 and the food crisis in 2007–08 had a devastating impact on African countries: The steep rise in food prices and the rather abrupt decline in food aid led to an excruciating rise in food prices in urban areas and caused severe food shortages. In rural areas, the population suffered less from food shortages, but the extreme rise in food prices in urban areas did not increase farmers' incomes by much, partly due to the sharp rise in the costs of fertilizers and transport, which soaked up much of their profits, and partly because the rise in food prices was so abrupt that farmers were not able to adjust their production to the new market conditions. In mid-2008, the collapse in the world prices of oil and fertilizers reached the developing countries only gradually and partially and did not bring immediate relief. Even the sharp fall in oil prices did not bring a significant decline in the cost of fertilizers.

The prolonged stagnation and the rapidly growing population worsened the poverty problems in Africa during the past two decades, even before the food crisis, and reduced the capacity of local farmers to meet the food needs of the continent's growing population. Africa continues to have the largest proportion of people living in extreme poverty, with more than 40 percent of its population living on less than $1 a day.[4] The continent's political, environmental, epidemiological, and economic obstacles—including poor governance, frequent internal conflicts, low-productivity in agriculture, high prevalence of deadly diseases, and crumbling infrastructure—render African countries most vulnerable to persistent food shortages.

The gravity of the malnutrition problem is highlighted in the following figures:[5]

- Sub-Saharan Africa has the highest rate of undernourishment in the world, with one-third of the population below the minimum level of nourishment.

- At least one million people in Africa die from malaria each year. Child malnutrition remains extremely high. According to estimates of UNICEF (2005) over one-third of children under 5 years old are stunted (are significantly shorter than normal children in their age group), and 15 percent of the children are chronically underweight.
- A woman living in Sub-Saharan Africa has a 1 in 16 chance of dying in pregnancy. This compares with a 1 in 3,800 chance for a woman from North America.
- More than 50 percent of Africans suffer from water-related diseases such as cholera and infant diarrhea.
- In one out of four African countries, half the children enrolled in the last year of primary school do not continue their studies the following year.

Despite the impressive growth in many African countries since the late 1990s, most of the rural population remains trapped in economic stagnation, and their spatial isolation deprives them of the most basic services in health and education. The rural population in the resource-rich African countries benefits very little from their country's export revenues, and even during the decade of rapid growth that brought a sharp increase in their countries' export revenue, only a small fraction of these revenues trickled down to the rural population.

The slow increase in food production and the continued population growth turned Africa from a food exporter into a food importer. Although Africa is far from exhausting many of its nonrenewable natural resources and far from reaching its limit to grow, the failure of African countries to develop a solid industrial base is bound to slow future growth. Indeed, the majority of Africa's population continued to work in agriculture and, according to the International Food Policy Research Institute (IFPRI), some two thirds of the continent's population still live in rural areas.

The failure of African countries, with the exception of South Africa, to make the transition from agricultural-based to industrial-based economies may have led pessimistic observers to conclude that Africa is likely to fall into the Malthusian trap and will not be able, by itself, to produce enough food for its consumption unless it receives a continuous flow of food aid from the developed countries. The damaging impact on Africa's rural population of the surge in food prices that culminated in mid-2008 raises fears that the era of chronic shortages, high food prices, and declining capacity to meet the needs of their growing population is far from over.

The efforts to alleviate malnutrition in Africa by developing the agricultural sector alone are complicated by the fact that Africa is the region predicted to be the most severely affected by global warming; already in the coming decade, according to the projections of the IPCC and the WMO, agricultural production in SSA may fall to half its current level and will be affected by more frequent droughts. The economic decline in Africa after a decade of promising growth is, therefore, likely to contribute to the

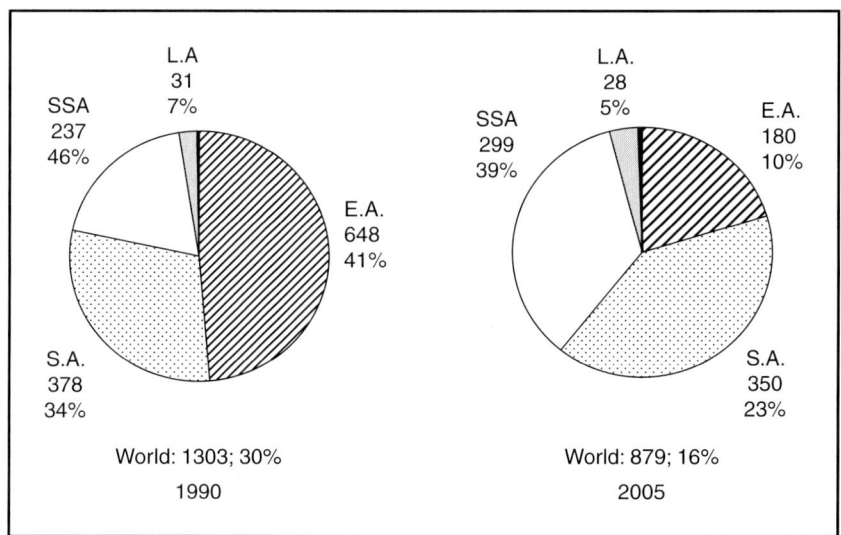

Figure 2.3 The change in the distribution of chronic proverty: 1990–2005 Number in (Millions) and proverty Incidence (%) (poverty line $1 per day in 2005 prices and exchange rate)
Source: World Bank, 2008; IFPRI, 2007.

rise in chronic poverty and malnutrition that prevails mostly in the rural areas.

Figure 2.3 highlights the large shifts, between 1990 and 2005, in the distribution of the poor population across regions. The most important changes were (a) the decline by nearly 280 million in the total number of chronically poor people; (b) the sharp decline in poverty in China that also explains most of the decline in the world's poverty, and (c) the rise in the number of the poor in SSA.

Small farms and low productivity

Africa's small-scale farmers—most of whom are women—face major obstacles that start in the field and extend across the entire agricultural value chain. African small farmers can neither access nor afford basic farm inputs. High quality seeds, organic and mineral fertilizers needed to replenish depleted soils, and simple water management systems that allow farmers to deal with erratic rains are largely beyond their reach. Good roads are scarce; government investments are meager and totally arbitrary. The urban markets are far away, and access to markets is often blocked when roads are washed away by floods, and finance systems are at best lacking and mostly nonexistent.

Another problem is that many of the small farmers in Africa whose land holdings are shrinking with the increase in the population must cultivate more marginal and less productive lands, often without being able to afford expensive fertilizers, fresh seeds, and other inputs that would allow them to increase their productivity. According to the FAO, African farmers add less than ten kilograms of fertilizer per hectare of land, while Asian farmers employ 144 kilograms. As a result of inadequate inputs, productivity remains low and farmers may fail even to produce enough food for their own consumption; in addition, cyclical shortfalls in food supply and rising food prices must be borne first and foremost by those who can afford it the least.

The decline in food production in Africa's arid areas is, paradoxically, not due to a scarcity of water. More than 95 percent of agricultural production is rain-fed, while in Asia a considerable share of the agricultural lands are irrigated; this leaves the African farmers more vulnerable to deteriorating and increasingly unstable climatic conditions. With rain-fed agriculture, farmers are using less than 10 percent of the water resources available in their area. More extensive use of the water with irrigation, projects to collect flood water with dams, and projects to treat the water used in urban areas can very significantly increase the water resources available to farmers. However, all these projects require large public investment, and most African countries do not have the necessary resources.

Hence, even for the population in the arid and semiarid areas, trapped in an abyss of deepening food scarcity and for whom Malthus's dim vision seems to remain relevant, the specter of growing hunger and malnutrition is no longer nature's law or an algebraic inevitability as Malthus thought, but an outcome of people's choices about the distribution of resources that are available in the world but must be allocated from the haves to the have-nots.

Obstacles to agricultural exports and local trade

The low prices farmers receive for traditional export crops are notoriously exploitative, largely due to the monopolistic power of the transnational corporations that control the trade, processing, and storage of these commodities. In the developed countries, business in these commodities is booming and retail prices have risen sharply. More than 50 percent of the world coffee supply is produced by small-scale farmers, but 40 percent of global trade is controlled by four companies. Despite the rise in retail prices, small producers of many traditional crops in the developing countries have suffered a sharp price decline and high volatility. Thus, for example, in the early 1990s, earnings of coffee-producing countries (export prices f.o.b.) were some $10–12 billion, while the value of the retail sales in the importing countries was about $30 billion; ten years later, the value of retail sales jumped to $70 billion, but producers received only $5.5 billion. Coffee prices on the world markets fell from about $1.20 per pound in the early 1980s to around 55 cents in the early 2000s, reaching their lowest levels in real terms in 2002. The increase in the share of the importing countries' wholesalers and retailers in the incomes from the sales of coffee, cocoa, and tea at the retail level took place along the entire supply chain and met little resistance from producers or producing countries because there is very little coordination between farmers or farmers' organizations. Local trade is highly fragmented due to the dissolution of the marketing boards, often in response to external pressures, which prevents farmers from exerting pressure to increase their share.

For farmers who produce for export, the revenues are determined by the price of the products in the export markets, measured in local currency. Part of the volatility of the export revenues is therefore due to the volatility of the exchange rates, which have risen sharply in recent years. Farmers' *real* income, or purchasing power, depends not only on the prices they receive for their crops but also on the prices of the food products they must buy. The rise in the prices of staple foods, therefore, reduced the real income of these farmers and motivated many of them to switch back from the production of export crops to food crops. Farmers who still produce for the export markets must cope with many uncertainties that are only partly related to the weather cycles; instead, most are related to government policies. These factors include trade policy, changes in exchange rates, price stabilization schemes in their own country or in the importing country, and so forth. Farmers are also affected by the trade and exchange rate policies of the countries that import their products, and of the countries that export similar products and are therefore competitors in the same importing countries.

The failure to reach a trade agreement on agricultural commodities in the Doha Round resulted in the continuation of the high subsidies of around 30 percent that the United States and European Union give their farmers, and the high tariffs India and other countries impose to protect their farmers, thus leaving world prices of agricultural products highly distorted. The failure to reach a multilateral trade agreement also gave incentive to forming other trade organizations within the framework regional trade agreements that proliferated in the past decade and are discriminating against nonmember countries. In most regional trade agreements, the less developed countries (LDCs) no longer benefit from any special arrangements or favorable conditions they used to have in the WTO agreements. Moreover, their small market reduced the incentives to include the LDCs in regional agreements and most trade agreements are biased against their interests and needs.

The *WDR* 2008 argued that trade can be a more effective way of stabilizing both food availability and access to food, since "today, with deeper international markets, lower real prices, and more countries with convertible exchange rates, trade can stabilize food availability and prices for most countries. And most countries have diversified their export base, increasing their capacity to import." The experience of the food crisis and the failure to establish the principles of free trade in the world's agricultural markets restricts these effects of international trade, and an increasing number of countries prefer the strategy of "decoupling" by which they rely less on free trade and increase the share of their local producers with various incentives or the share of countries with which they have a trade agreement in order to secure more reliable sources of supply.

African farmers who sell their produce in the local markets also encounter great difficulties, in part due to the poor road infrastructure and in part due to the undeveloped supply chain. For most, the distance to the urban market is too large, the roads are run-down and transportation is infrequent, unreliable, and expensive. Many farmers still prefer to go to the local market and sell their crops by themselves. For farmers in more remote villages, the traders are the only channel through which they can deliver their produce to the market, and they also depend on traders to bring them the necessary inputs during the season.

Traders usually pay farmers in cash and sometimes give farmers some credit and a supply of seeds and fertilizers during the season in exchange for a certain share of the output at harvest time. Nevertheless, farmers tend to be very suspicious about the local traders, who often cheat, abuse, and take advantage of the farmers' lack of information. For the farmers, these traders are associated with "manipulation," "exploitation," and "speculation."[6] Traders do, indeed, take advantage of their monopolistic position vis à vis the uninformed farmers, but traders also encounter great risks since prices are highly volatile, demand is unstable, crops may be damaged, and in most African countries travel on the rural roads is risky. The *WDR 2008* noted that "trade in food staples even within the country or the region is often hampered by poor infrastructure, inadequate support services, and weak institutions, pushing up transaction costs and price volatility" (p. 118). As a result, farmers cannot specialize in certain crops in which they have a comparative advantage, and most of their production is for self-consumption.

In some villages or groups of villages, the farmers form farmers' organizations that provide these services and avoid the traders altogether. These organizations can be effective in enforcing the trade contract, ensuring payments, and getting reliable information on demand and prices in the markets (particularly with the extensive use of cell phones). These organizations, therefore, represent their members' interests and support their trade, although they are not necessarily more efficient. In most African countries, however, these organizations are weak and not very effective, due in large measure to the fact that farmers live dispersed across large and often isolated areas.

In the structural adjustments during the 1990s, African governments were pressured to privatize the marketing boards and leave the market to private businesses. The markets were seldom "free," however, and large segments of the trade, particularly in inputs and in export products, are dominated by a few large traders. Traders are still heavily taxed, however, when they move goods from one district or region to another and even more so across international borders, and governments often fail to provide the public means necessary for trade, such as supervising and enforcing contracts or monitoring quality standards. More trading and marketing activities, therefore, moved from the formal to the informal markets, where payments are also "informal" and involve costly bribes. This change reduced the power of farmers' organizations and their share in trade.

How can African farmers increase their yields?

> In the 21st century, agriculture continues to be a fundamental instrument for sustainable development and poverty reduction.
> (*WDR* 2008, p. 1)

The low productivity of small-scale farmers, their rudimentary technologies, and the inefficient organization of agricultural production and trade make the implementation of far-reaching reforms in the agricultural sector necessary and urgent in order to raise farmers' income and achieve greater food security. The World Bank's *World Development Report* of 2008, devoted to the agricultural sector, advocated a series of reforms designed to restructure production and organize both the supply of seeds and fertilizers to rural areas and the transport of agricultural produce to urban centers and for export. Drawing on examples from other countries, particularly India, the report claims the division of cultivated lands into smaller parcels need not, in itself, be a reason for low productivity in the agricultural sector, nor does it explain the inability of African farmers to adopt the production methods of the Green Revolution. The success of small farmers in India in adopting (and reaping high benefits from) this technology indicates there were other reasons for the failure of African farmers to adopt the more advanced and more productive technologies.

The main barriers that prevented the penetration of Green Revolution technology in Africa were poor infrastructure, the lack of access to credit, the costs to farmers due to the trade policies in many African countries that imposed high tariffs on agricultural exports to finance budget expenses, and the competition of cheap imports of food grains from the United States and the European Union that reduced the competitiveness of African farmers even in their own urban markets. Farming is, therefore, mostly for self-consumption, in small plots of land, with traditional farming methods using hand-hoes, scythes, shovels (and prayers), and it is mainly women's work.

Agricultural reforms under the existing resource constraints involve difficult choices for both the farmers and their governments: Should they concentrate on the production of staple foods for the local market and self-consumption or should they invest in the production of high-value crops for export? Should they use mainly their traditional methods or should they make the necessary investments to adopt more advanced production methods? The production of staple foods using traditional methods for self-consumption or for sale in local markets restricts the capacity of farmers to increase their income and improve their standards of living, essentially dooming them to continued stagnation. The production of high-value crops for export, in contrast, promises more rapid growth but requires considerable investment both by the farmers and by the public sector. The farmers must buy more fertilizers and better seeds and the government must invest in R&D, in the development of extension services, and in an effective organization of the marketing system, particularly to export markets. The very limited investments African governments have made in agriculture and rural sector prevented these developments, and most small farmers remain too poor to adopt the more advanced production methods. Table 2.1 shows that despite their shrinking output per agricultural worker and their growing population, the share of the least developed countries, in general, and of the SSA countries, in particular, of total world trade in most staple foods, was tiny.

Another alternative is to increase the value-added aspect of agricultural products through processing, which can provide employment to the rural population and contribute to increasing farmers' income. It requires, however, a careful selection of the crops farmers produce and of the processing methods, according to the country's conditions and its competitive advantage—primarily the low labor costs and the potential to grow unique crops—and according to the demand in the world market. Again, active involvement of the public sector is indispensable, but under the current conditions it is virtually impossible. In several African countries, foreign entrepreneurs have developed very successful farms for the production of agricultural products for export, and the successful export of cut flowers from Kenya proves these investments can be profitable. Likewise, the

Table 2.1 World trade in staple foods—average 2007–09

	World Market	OECD	Developing Countries	Least Developed Countries
Wheat	121,483	25,874	97,233	12,244
Coarse Grains	118,329	56,908	81,184	2,430
Rice	31,325	5,150	26,130	6,557
Oilseeds	92,647	34,625	65,840	290
Protein Meals	66297	41,252	27,517	409

Source: FAO Database 2010.

development of new varieties of fruits and vegetables that have a longer shelf-life and higher quality, and the unique fruits and vegetable that can be grown in Africa and have high demand in Europe, suggest that such investments have considerable potential.

The reform plans for the agricultural sector in Africa changed, however, in the wake of the food crisis. One of the lessons of that crisis was that dependence on trade for the supply of staple foods to the local population makes a country more vulnerable to the instability of food prices and to shortages in supply. The instability of foreign supply is likely to grow in the coming years due to more volatile weather conditions, to less predictable and less reliable supply, and to higher risks of policy changes in the exporting countries. The failure in the Doha Round to achieve an agricultural trade agreement that would have secured more predictable and regulated trade in agricultural commodities exposed the food-importing countries to higher risks of local shortages. The food crisis in 2007–08 was partly driven by self-centered policies of many food-exporting countries, which led to a two-to-three fold increase in key food prices within a few short months and triggered food riots in many food-importing countries. This subject will be discussed in more detail in part IV. Already in 2006, however, the United States introduced high tariffs on imports of ethanol, and both the European Union and United States greatly increased their support to local farmers by strengthening their incentives to grow crops for biofuel.

The various reform programs suggested in the past decade by different organizations for the agricultural sector in Africa are based on the assumption that agriculture-led growth is the most effective strategy to achieve the Millennium Development Goals in Africa. In contrast, a report prepared in 2002 for the New Partnership for Africa's Development (NEPAD) concluded that "Africa, most of whose people are farmers, is unable to feed itself and has been in this situation for many decades now."

The worsening climatic conditions and growing water scarcity indeed have eroded the capacity of Africa to meet its food needs and it will be more difficult for many African countries to mobilize the resources necessary to build an irrigation system, make the transition to drought-resistant crops, or improve the rural infrastructure. It is by no means impossible, however. The production technologies are available and, with affordable investments, countries can make much more effective use of their water resources and reduce the incidence of droughts; moreover, crop varieties resistant to drought and pests can increase yields and food production. At least half the African countries, from Sudan, Ethiopia and Chad to Sierra Leon, Angola, and Nigeria have the resources to make the required investments and prevent the chronic poverty and hunger to which more than half of their population is exposed.

The only thing missing is a sense of responsibility in the leaders of these countries. In the name of national sovereignty, these African leaders have often resisted external pressures and avoided taking responsibility, and many wasted their resources in armed conflicts and corruption. The international community cannot do much to force these leaders to take responsibility for their citizens, but for the AU and NEPAD to come up with the conclusion that "Africa cannot feed itself" despite the continent's plentiful natural resources is nothing to be proud of.

The analysis in the *WDR* 2008, summarized in Box 2.6, was characteristic of the approach of most international organizations: In the introduction it is claimed that in "much of Sub-Saharan Africa, agriculture is a strong option for spurring growth, overcoming poverty, and enhancing food security" (see also chapter 4 in the report). The section on food security stated: "In the future, agriculture will continue to...be the primary means to generate income for the poor, securing their access to food" (pp. 94–95). These two conclusions are not identical, however. The statement that agriculture will continue to be the main source of income and food for the poor is self-evident and essentially a truism even if agricultural production remains stagnant, since the rural poor will have no other source of income. The first statement promises more: Agriculture can spur growth, help overcome poverty, and enhance food security. In the past four decades, however,

---

Box 2.6 Guidelines for the agricultural development program in SSA

1. Improve market access and establish efficient value chains.
   - Policy interventions to facilitate value-chain development and forming strategic public-private partnerships.
2. Enhance smallholder competitiveness and facilitate market entry.
   - Smallholders can be competitive and innovative with sufficient asset endowments. Policy interventions include trade reforms for greater market access, improved infrastructure, better technology, adequate financial services and inputs, and effective producer organizations to gain access to services, markets, and policy making.
   - Inducing a transition from subsistence to the market by increasing access to assets, particularly to land, entrepreneurial skills, and social capital.
   - Infrastructure to open up regions with agricultural potential but poor market access, and mechanisms to manage risk.
3. Improve livelihoods in subsistence agriculture and low-skilled rural occupations.
   - First: Increase land productivity (for higher yields in small plots) and labor productivity.
   - Second: Reduce risk and food insecurity.
   - Third: diversify income in agricultural labor markets and the rural non-farm economy.
4. Increase employment opportunities in rural labor markets and enhance skills.

(*Source*: WDR, 2008)

agriculture did not play this role and did not meet these expectations, and rural poverty has only worsened.

The key questions are therefore *how* will agriculture help achieve these goals? *What* must still be done so that agriculture will spur growth and enhance food security? The second group of questions is far more difficult: *Can* agriculture achieve these goals in view of current predictions that in the next decade climate change will lead to a reduction in yields from rain-fed agriculture by up to 50 percent? *Who* should do what needs to be done in order to achieve the stated goals? *Who* should provide the necessary resources? *What* should be the role, the responsibility, and the share of the African governments? *Who* will monitor and ensure that those who are currently food-insecure and malnourished will indeed receive the help they need?

The answers to these questions will not be determined on the drawing boards or in the computer models of agronomists and agricultural economists; instead, the institutions in charge of implementing the necessary reforms and the governments that should be responsible for carrying them out will have to make the efforts required if any improvements are to be achieved.

IFPRI's *2020 Vision for Food, Agriculture, and the Environment* (2007)[7] is primarily addressing the poverty problem, the design of pro–poor-growth policies that would promote agricultural growth, and the application of social security measures to protect the most vulnerable groups among the poor. In the section on Africa, the report emphasized four main areas in which action must be taken: markets, infrastructure, health, and education. Specific actions (to which I added few comments/questions in italics) include:

- Marketing: Increase the efficiency and reduce the costs of operating the input and output markets in order to provide better opportunities to the poor to improve their income and livelihoods; (*The role of the government and the share of the private sectors are, however, unclear*).
- Infrastructure: Invest in well-placed infrastructure to increase the income-earning opportunities of the rural poor by facilitating their access to the markets; (*What are the risks of increasing the regional inequalities with these investments?*)
- Health: Tackling disease is important both in itself and as part of poverty reduction strategies.
- Education: Investments in education are crucial for the future of these countries; (*What should be the criteria for determining the priorities between these investments and how should they be monitored?*)

The IFPRI report recognized, though, that given these countries' limited resources, the criterion of maximizing the reduction in poverty per dollar of investment is on the one hand more effective but, on the other hand, will increase the exclusion and isolation of the remote villages that are already excluded (moreover, in most African countries the choice of the target areas is often a manifestation of favoritism influenced by political considerations).

As food prices escalated, IFPRI suggested a *resilience package* (May 2008) which would include a comprehensive social protection initiative to address the risks facing the poor who cannot afford high food prices—comprising, among other measures, conditional cash transfers and employment programs. Perhaps the most important part of the initiative is a call for joint pledges from the main grain-producing countries to hold grain reserves and to coordinate the release of the grains from storage in order to meet regional emergencies when prices increase excessively. The recent report of the FAO–Organization for Economic Cooperation and Development OECD on Agricultural Outlook in the coming decade, briefly summarized in Box 2.7, is somewhat more

---

Box 2.7 FAO–OECD: concerns about food security will remain high

The pressure on food supply is expected to rise in the coming decades. World population is expected to grow by 2.3 billion people between 2009 and 2050 and nearly all this growth will take place in the developing countries. The population in sub-Saharan Africa is expected to grow at the fastest rate and more than double during these years. The population growth together with the accelerating migration to the urban center will increase the urban population at a much faster rate.

The demand for food will also rise as a result of the growing middle class in Africa and the much faster growth and rising incomes of the higher income classes in the emerging and the developed countries. Demand for cereals for food and feed is projected to rise by one-third to 3 Bt by 2050, and possibly higher due to a growing liquid biofuel market. Part of the rise is also due to the change in the diet of the growing middle class that will increase its demand for meat that requires much more cereals.

Production in the developing countries would need to double to meet that demand. Improved technology and the adoption of more advanced production methods and more efficient machines are like to increase the yields and reduce the output losses from disease, pests, storage etc. and the food waste during processing, transportation and consumption. These estimates are inevitably inaccurate due to the great uncertainty about the impact of global warming both on the long-term trend in food supply in different regions and the fluctuations in food supply.

The projections of the FAO and the OECD *Outlook* indicate that global production growth is likely to meet the longer term food requirements. Nearly all developing count5ries are likely to become net importers of food and net cereal imports into these countries is estimated to increase almost three-fold to nearly 300 Mt by 2050. That imports would supply only around 15 percent of their total cereal consumption and would thus leave them vulnerable to fluctuations in local production and in the world prices.

(*Source*: OECD-FAO 2010 Agricultural Outlook, 2010–2019)

optimistic but expresses concerns about the future outlook of food security due to the many unknown that these projections involved:

The Comprehensive Africa Agriculture Development Program

The AU initiated the Comprehensive Africa Agriculture Development Program (CAADP) as a collaborative program that focuses on agriculture and involves wider participation of representatives of the national governments, of the private sector, and of the farmers themselves. To implement the program of agriculture-led growth, the CAADP set specific rules that commit each of the participating countries. The main rules are listed in Box 2.8. The two main objectives of the program are:

Box 2.8 Comprehensive Africa Agricultural Development Program (CAADP): general guidelines

- The main goal of the program is to raise the annual agricultural growth rate of the agricultural sector in each and every participating country to 6 percent per annum.
- The program determines the basic guidelines of the policy and the investment decisions of each of the participating countries and plans the development assistance agenda for each country so that it can meet the target growth rate.
- The program will establish guidelines for public-private partnerships and for business-to-business alliances in order to make the necessary investments in the agribusiness and the farming sectors.
- To achieve the growth target, each government is committed to allocate 10 percent of the national budgets to the agricultural sector (compared with 4 percent thus far)
- The commitments of the individual countries will be carried out under the supervision and coordination of the regional economic communities and facilitated by the *NEPAD* secretariat.

(*Source*: NEPAD secretariat 2005, 2006)

- Give farmers access to improved inputs that include high quality seeds, organic and mineral fertilizer, and systems of reliable water management.
- Facilitate farmers' access to the output markets—including the installation of storage facilities, arrangements to process agricultural produce in order to increase the value-added and marketability; transport, and credit programs that would enable small-scale farmers to buy the necessary inputs and sell their harvests. The guiding principles of CAAPD determined the broad objectives and the rules of the action plan of the Alliance for a Green Revolution in Africa (AGRA).

The Alliance was launched in 2006 and is chaired by Kofi Annan. It is aimed at implementing the African Union's program by finding an

Africa-specific strategy and designing a series of actions to help small farmers increase their output and their incomes. The specific action planned by the Alliance was launched in 2007 and was implemented in the subsequent three years. It focuses on the development of new varieties of staple foods that are the most common in Africa. Within this framework, AGRA is working with African farmers and agricultural scientists to breed new varieties of maize, cassava, rice, beans, sorghum, and other major crops to offer better resistance to disease and pests, and which are suitable for the local environment in the different regions. Their goal is to produce 100 new crop varieties over five years, and to ensure farmers have access to these seeds by creating a wider network of local seed distributors and agrodealers that will provide better and less expensive services to remote rural areas (Box 2.9).

AGRA has already introduced new varieties of at least ten staple crops that have higher yields and is planning to improve the availability and variety of seeds that can produce higher and more stable yields. The main focus is on the development of local and adapted solutions that can reach small farmers and offer more productive and resilient varieties of Africa's major food crops. AGRA also plans a water management initiative to provide low-cost and efficient water management systems, and improvements for crop storage. Other plans include the Program for Africa's Seeds Systems (PASS) aimed at developing seeds that improve crop varieties for small farmers. In ten years, the program plans to introduce more than a thousand new varieties of at least ten staple crops that would increase the productivity of small farmers and thus improve seeds on 20–30 percent of the cultivated lands. The seed

---

Box 2.9 Alliance for a Green Revolution in Africa (AGRA)

The CAADP vision specifically calls for "agricultural knowledge systems delivering profitable and sustainable technologies that are widely adopted by farmers resulting in sustained agricultural growth."

African heads of state promised concrete steps to provide farmers not just with soil nutrients but also with better transport, credit, seeds, irrigation facilities, extension services, and market information.

The work begins in the fields alongside small-scale farmers, to understand their problems and the potential solutions. Individual farmers, women's associations, and farmer unions are key partners.

The work seeks to address challenges involving access to farmer inputs: high quality seeds, organic and mineral fertilizer, and systems of reliable water management. They also involve access to "output" markets—to the crop storage, processing, transport, and finance that ultimately allow small-scale farmers to sell their harvests and make a profit.

AGRA provides locally developed and adapted solutions that can reach the small farmers who would benefit from them.

(*Source*: AGRA Action Plan)

system includes direct seed production and distribution channels as well as market and policy institutions, extension, training, and supportive policy. Seeds of the improved varieties will reach small farmers through public distribution systems or through private seed companies. Today, more than 75 percent of the seeds used by African farmers are obtained through informal channels of exchange, community seed production, and the farmer's own reserved seed.

Coping with hunger: a global imperative

In a World Bank report entitled *The Growth Report: Strategies for Sustained Growth and Inclusive Development* (July 2008), the main focus was on the forces that have driven global economic growth and on ways to accelerate this growth in all developing countries, rather than on the need to find a fair way to establish limits to growth. The report listed a number of questions it sought to analyze in order to gain a better understanding—questions concerned with strategies for sustained growth in all countries. Some key questions are:

- Why have only 13 developing world economies achieved sustained, high growth since World War II?
- Why is engagement with the global economy necessary to achieve high growth?
- Why have many developing countries, blessed with natural resource wealth, failed to achieve high growth?
- Why do some economies lose momentum while others keep on growing?
- Why has no country ever sustained long-term growth without urbanizing?

In the context of this book, two other questions should be added:

- Why have all other continents made impressive gains in reducing poverty while Africa continues to suffer from high poverty rates?
- Why have all other continents managed to raise a large percentage of their population to the middle class while Africa's middle class is only a tiny fraction of its population?

The earlier discussion highlights the stark difference between the sharp decline in the share of the poor in the total population of all developing countries (including SSA) and the obstinately high incidence in SSA of chronic poverty that remained above 50 percent of the continent's population even during the decade in which the continent enjoyed high growth. The series of crises in 2007–09 and the slow recovery have increased the number of the poor by 100–150 million people, according to World Bank estimates, and brought the incidence of poverty to the high levels of nearly 60 percent seen already in the mid-1990s. The food crisis also made clear that the majority of the African countries are unlikely to reach the MDGs, despite the promising growth.[8]

The chapter in the World Bank *Growth Report* on Sub-Saharan Africa noted both the fast growth the region has enjoyed since the late 1990s, and the low standard of living of most African people, who benefited very little from this growth. Some countries in the region made impressive progress, however, and managed to improve their education and health systems, and effectively fought malaria and AIDS; but in the region as a whole, progress was much slower; in some countries, living conditions even worsened due to protracted conflicts and war, and many countries are still facing immense challenges. The main reason for the lack of progress in tackling these challenges is the failure of African countries to translate economic growth into higher standards of living, less poverty, better public services, improved infrastructure, and more effective governance. This failure reflects not so much the failure of the reform programs implemented by some countries, but mostly the highly biased priorities of their governments in the allocation of resources and in determining income distribution. Despite the achievements of quite a few countries in making the transition to democracy, the needs of the people continued to have low priority. Even in countries like Senegal and Ghana, which have stable governments, have not been entangled in wars or civil conflicts for many years, and managed to nearly double their real income per capita from 1996 through 2008, the share of the lower income groups in their countries' income remained very low.

Table 2.2 provides some estimates of the extent of the inequality in income distribution. These estimates are based on the poverty data of the World Bank's World Economic indicators (WDI) and were calculated on the basis of the poverty gap and the poverty line income, which jointly determine the average income of the poor. The WDI provides estimates of chronic poverty and mild poverty (for an international poverty line of $1.25 day and $2 day respectively), and the aim of the table is to emphasize the huge difference between the incomes of the two thirds to three quarters poor population and the higher income population. All data are calculated for 2005. The countries selected in the table, with the exception of Nigeria, all have stable governments regarded as the most attentive to needs of the poor. The estimates of income inequality are indicated by the ratio between the median and the mean incomes. This estimate thus concentrates on the lower half of the country's income distribution and on the share of poor. The lower this ratio, the higher the income inequality and the lower the share in the country's income of the bottom 50 percent of the population. The very low ratio for Nigeria confirms this is one of the least equal countries in Africa. Among the other more stable countries, Senegal is considerably less equal than the others. The high incidence of chronic and mild poverty in Uganda is largely

Table 2.2 Measures of chronic and mild poverty and indicators of income inequality in selected African countries (*estimates for 2005; income per capita in 2000 prices and exchange rates*)

Country	Mean Income per-capita	Incidence of chronic poverty (<$1.25 day)	Income of the chronically poor as % of mean income	Incidence of mild poverty (<$2.0 day)	Income of the mild poor as % of mean income	Median income as % of mean income*
Ghana	1251	30.0	0.33	53.6	0.45	.42
Kenya	1436	19.7	0.30	39.9	0.43	.48
Nigeria	1795	64.4	0.18	83.9	0.22	.13
Uganda	897	51.5	0.41	75.6	0.52	.41
Senegal	1565	33.6	0.26	60.3	0.35	.30

* Estimate. *Data Sources*: IMF WEO 2009; WB World Development Indicators 2008 Poverty Data Supplement.

due to the country's level of mean income, which is around 60 percent of the mean income in Senegal, but the higher ratio of the median-to-mean incomes reflects the higher share of Uganda's poor.

The chapter in the World Bank report on Sub-Saharan Africa noted the fast growth the region has enjoyed since the late 1990s, thanks largely to higher commodity prices, better macroeconomic management, continued flow of aid, and more efficient and responsible leadership in many countries. Nevertheless, Africa's standard of living still falls short of most other developing continents, and only a small share of its growth in the past decade has trickled down to the poor population. Many countries in the region have made impressive progress during the past decade, including improvements in their education system and considerable achievements in fighting malaria and AIDS. Nevertheless, the region is still facing immense challenges in delivering public services, building infrastructure, improving governance, and reducing poverty. The food crisis also showed most African countries are unlikely to reach the MDGs, despite the promising growth.

Most resource-rich African countries were able to accelerate their growth by riding on the wave of the steeply rising commodity prices, but only a tiny flow of the windfall in revenues was used to diversify their economies, reduce dependence on their natural resources, and lower their vulnerability to the high instability of commodity prices. Nearly all African countries failed to develop an adequate capacity to secure their supply in the event of food shortages or high food prices, and they most likely will face more difficult conditions in the coming decades as an effect of rising global instability and climate change. Botswana is the most successful African country that achieved sustained high growth. South Africa, Rwanda, Ghana, Uganda, and Madagascar were also successful in achieving macroeconomic stability. Several other countries were among the "frontier economies" that benefited from capital inflows, primarily due to foreign investments in their natural resources. But only a handful of countries have become more food-secure, while the others have not managed to secure a stable and sustained food supply for their population and are still facing a highly uncertain future.

The report emphasizes that for African countries, the key to achieving sustained improvements in the standard of living and to accelerate economic growth is to reduce their dependence on the agricultural sector and build a more solid industrial base. That conclusion differs significantly from the one quoted earlier from the *WDR 2008*, which described agriculture as the most essential pillar of the African countries' economies, and their main means for spurring growth. However, the new recommendation seems to ignore the past experience of several initiatives to promote industrialization and diversify the African economies—initiatives that have largely failed.

The report calls on the industrial nations to grant African countries time-bound trade preferences to build local industries of manufactured exports, and to help them improve the quality of their education and allocate more resources to secondary and tertiary education. The recommended preferential treatment has been given in the past to African exporters to support the development of a textile industry, but these efforts failed. Future efforts to develop an industrial base, or even to develop secondary and tertiary education, may encounter similar difficulties, partly due to the massive brain drain that is bleeding Africa of its most precious resources: skilled labor, which is in short supply due to shortsightedness of governments that failed to provide adequate and rewarding employment opportunities for their skilled, educated, and well-trained workers in order to keep them from migrating to developed countries.

Another development is important to emphasize whenever sweeping recommendations for Africa are offered: While nearly half the African countries have made significant strides in developing their economies, improving their system of governance, and making progress in the transition to democracy, around one-third of them remain entangled in civil conflicts and wars, and are still controlled by autocratic and extremely self-centered rulers and regimes that care very little about their people. It is perhaps time to emphasize this distinction and to avoid lumping all African countries together, both in the analysis and in the measures that are taken to provide aid and a host of preferences. There is no reason, and no justification, for giving aid or preferential treatment to rich oil-exporting countries like Nigeria, Sudan, and many others. The successive leaders of Nigeria, President Olusegun Obasanjo (until 2007) and now President Umaru Musa Yar'adua, openly rigged the elections and used their country's rich resources without restraint; the Sudanese leader cynically used aid to further enrich himself and strengthen his military forces. Obviously, the people of these countries, particularly the poor, are the ones hurt if aid to their countries is stopped or restricted. But they benefit very little if aid continues to flow. On the other hand, quite a few other countries have made real progress, and their leaders have demonstrated sincere intentions to work for the benefit of their people. If no distinction is made between these two groups of countries, then the resources the developing countries send are necessarily spread too thinly and do not much benefit even the people in countries that are more responsible and accountable.

Can Africa sustain its growth?

The World Bank's *Strategies for Sustained Growth* seems only moderately concerned with the need to limit growth, despite the dire warning of the Intergovernmental Panel on Climate Change (IPCC) report that "it may be too late at this time to avoid all the effects of climate change. If carbon emission is not restricted now then global warming will raise the average temperatures well above two degrees Celsius." Instead, the World Bank study argues:

> To take the extreme case, if the whole world grew to advanced country incomes and converged on the German levels of emissions per capita, then to be safe from a warming standpoint, emissions per capita would need to decline by a factor of four. Reductions of this magnitude with existing technology are either not possible or so costly as to be certain of slowing global and developing country growth.... What these calculations make clear is that technology is the key to accommodating developing countries and global growth. We need to lower the costs of mitigation. Put differently, we need to build more economic value on top of a limited energy base, for that we need new knowledge. (*Strategies for Sustained Growth*, p. 86)

New technology and new knowledge take years to develop, however, and it would certainly be too late for the poor in most African countries that are likely to face the devastating effects of global warming in the coming decade. On the other hand, the slowdown in global growth is bound to be extremely costly, both in terms of the output foregone and of the resources necessary to reduce the carbon emissions and other negative effects of industrialization on the environment. That reduction is essential, however, to decelerate global warming. The key question is how to divide the cost of investment and the losses between the developed and developing countries and between individual countries in a fair and just way.

The developing countries, particularly the least developed ones, claim that deliberate measures to slow down global growth at its current levels would perpetuate utterly unjust income distribution between developed

Table 2.3 Correlation coefficients between key per-person indicators

	Expenditures per-capita	Poverty Incidence	Gini Measure
Expenditures per-capita	..	−0.775	0.42
Income per capita	0.75	−0.429	0.63
Poverty Incidence	−0.775	..	−0.262

Source: Author's calculations based on World Bank POVCAL data.

and developing countries. Such measures are principally unfair, since the rapid industrialization of the developed countries and the highly polluting industrialization in the emerging economies are the main causes of global warming. The least developed countries should not be punished for that outcome, which is not their fault (Table 2.3).

Unless all countries find a widely accepted formula for fair distribution of the costs of establishing limits on global growth, many countries will not agree to participate in that initiative, will not restrict their growth, and will not make the investment to reduce their carbon emission. Given the administrative, technical, and political obstacles that would have to be overcome in order to achieve common agreement, it is hard to be optimistic about the prospects of global collaboration—despite the urgent need for an agreement and for a modus operandi of collaboration. Otherwise, the ominous prognosis of *Limits to Growth*, after four decades of avoiding the warnings, is far more likely to be realized.

Deteriorating agroclimatic conditions increase the risks to the semiarid zones in Africa, the Middle East, South Asia, and Latin America as soon as in the coming decade. Consultative Group on International Agricultural Research (CGIAR) research (2006)[9] found the projected rise in temperatures and shifts in rainfall patterns are likely to shorten the growing periods in SSA by more than 20 percent, putting some of the world's poorest nations in East and Central Africa at the greatest risk. Among the dire predictions is the expectation that harvest time in India's Punjab state, the country's breadbasket, is likely to be impacted and wheat production likely to fall. Production may drop by as much as 50 percent by 2050 and put nearly 200 million people at great risk of hunger or periodic food shortages.

Climate change will shift grain production closer to the North and South poles, thus increasing food production in new areas as food production in the traditional areas is declining. The growing global economic and political polarization will, therefore, change the distribution of food production and, in the arid areas, mostly in developing countries, farmers are likely to bear the brunt of climate change and suffer most from its negative consequences.

Global warming threatens also to deplete the ozone layer that protects the Earth against the sun's heat. As this layer thins, and large holes open up, global warming threatens to desertify much larger areas of land, accelerate the depletion of water resources, and further endanger food production in the semiarid areas. The world will still be able to produce enough food, but the distribution of food production will be highly uneven, leaving many more countries and peoples with inadequate capacity to produce or purchase the food they need.

With these developments, the world is now going through a transition period that presents many conflicting demands:

- Energy and raw materials for industrial production are being rapidly depleted;
- Global warming is reducing the available lands suitable for cultivation and depleting available water resources;
- The demand for food crops continues to rise, partly for the production of biofuel to supplement the deteriorating energy supply, and partly to meet the growing demand of the more affluent populations;
- The growing pressures on the world's resources are likely to intensify the competition between countries and reduce their willingness to cooperate.

This transition is bound to be painful, and the associated burdens are never distributed equally among countries and peoples. However, over time, this transition may be ameliorated due to new inventions and developments, including better energy sources, drought-tolerant crops to provide farmers greater yield-stability, and declining global population growth.

Overcoming obstacles to growth: the need for multinational collaboration

The question whether the slow growth in African countries can be explained by geographical or climatic obstacles, such as landlocked countries, poor and unstable weather conditions, or similar obstacles that slow down growth due to harsh natural conditions, or whether the slow growth is due to poor governance, autocratic leaders, and tribalism, has been hotly debated and a wide variety of different, and often conflicting, views have been put forward. But this question cannot be adequately answered by means of econometric analysis alone, however sophisticated and complex it may be. This analysis must be based on data over a long period of time, during which conditions have changed dramatically, but at a different pace in different countries, and because, however prudent the analysis endeavors to be, it cannot really distinguish between causality and correlation. In fact, Africa's natural conditions are not exceptionally more difficult than in other continents, and a long list of ambitious projects that came to be regarded as milestones in world history, from the Egyptian pyramids to the Suez Canal, proved that even formidable obstacles can be overcome.

It is clear, however, that these obstacles were overcome through major collaborative efforts that brought together many nations and people. But, in Africa the interaction between nature and people has been different from the experience in Europe or in Asia, resembling instead more the conditions in Central and South America: A relatively sparse population spread over large areas blessed with plenty of food but covered with jungles that made it difficult to establish trade and other forms of interaction. Populations in different parts of Sub-Saharan Africa had little interaction and little communication due to the heavy tropical forests and other natural obstacles, but since nature was generous, the population sparse, and food plentiful, there was little need for collaboration in order to overcome obstacles. Even under colonial rule, it was perhaps only in the wars for liberation that collaboration on a large scale, involving thousands of people and several tribes, was necessary for success.

In the modern state, where interactions are frequent and communication is necessary, collaboration becomes a vital necessity. Public assets such as roads, electricity, and even water must be provided by the state, an effort that requires collaboration and the help of a central government, which necessarily represents several tribes that had very little in common for most of their history. The twenty-first century also requires interaction and cooperation on an even much larger scale: Between people of neighboring tribes, but also between neighboring countries and countries elsewhere, even on different continents.

If climate change comes as fast as the IPCC estimates suggest, the only way to meet the food needs of the poor in Africa and Asia would be to share the ample food that can be produced in those countries that have enough water and adequate climatic conditions—primarily Russia, Canada, and some of their neighboring countries—with the countries that will be desertified by the warmer climate. Some of these countries will be able to offer something in return, primarily with their natural resources; many other countries may not be able to offer much in return, either because they are resource-poor or because their resources have already been depleted. These countries will be at the mercy of those that have the water resources and the capacity to produce food.

This is the world Malthus would have seen had he lived today. The "law of insufficient food supply" would no longer apply to the entire world. Instead, the world is likely to be divided into two separate parts: One unable to produce the food it needs for survival, and one that can produce enough food for the entire world, but may have to do so altruistically, since it will not receive much materially in return.

However, the politics of sharing and collaboration is not necessarily driven by altruism, but by give-and-take. Even in the aftermath of the catastrophic food crisis, despite all the promises and declarations, not much has been achieved, and the 2005 promises of the G-8 to achieve the MDGs remain still just promises that are not likely to be realized at a time when the donor countries are struggling with their own economic downturns. To be sure, also in the more distant past, arrangements based on charity, altruism and goodwill were not very reliable. These are reasons for great concern about the answers the world can give to the questions raised by Malthus. In his time, these were questions about mankind's technological ingenuity; in the coming years of our time, these will be questions about mankind's humanity and generosity.

But as cynical as it may seem, the rich world also has a solid self-interest to face up to the fact that, as people are forced to leave lands that cannot provide sustenance, more and more of them will try to reach the countries where food and employment are plentiful. In the developed countries, many will see this as a threat that needs to be countered, and in this sense, concern about the world's hungry and destitute may well be seen as part of a coldly calculated realpolitik.

2.3
Is Africa Doomed to Permanent Food Crises?

Many articles and research projects have analyzed the global food crisis of 2007–08 that was unprecedented in its dimensions and its impact (Figure 2.4). This chapter will, therefore, summarize very briefly some of the main characteristics of the food crisis and concentrate on two main issues highlighted by the unusual combination of events that turned a predicament that for several years did not seem so highly unusual into a calamity that, within a few months, crossed all borders and affected all countries: First, the interconnectedness between markets and not only between commodity markets as an effect of globalization; second, the lessons that can be drawn from that experience about the possibility that another food crisis will happen in the coming years.

The focus of the chapter is on the impact of the food crisis on the LDCs, primarily in Africa, but before turning to this analysis it should be noted that for the majority of the population the food crisis is by no means over. According to recent estimates of the FAO (2009), 20 African countries are still in crisis and will therefore need external assistance. Out of these 20 countries only five would need this assistance due to adverse weather conditions, whereas the other countries will need assistance due to conflicts or war related damage. The problem of the majority of the population in these, and quite a few other, countries is that world prices remained high also in 2009 and were not likely to decline in 2010. The number of undernourished people as an effect of the global crises continues to increase, and the majority of the population in the African countries regressed within two years to their dismal conditions during the "lost decades" of stagnation, despite the very successful decade, until the crisis, in which most of them had record growth rates.

Some lessons from the food crisis of 2007–08

In the mid-2000s, at the early stages of the food crisis, the rise in food prices was triggered by the changes in the "fundamentals"—the changes in food

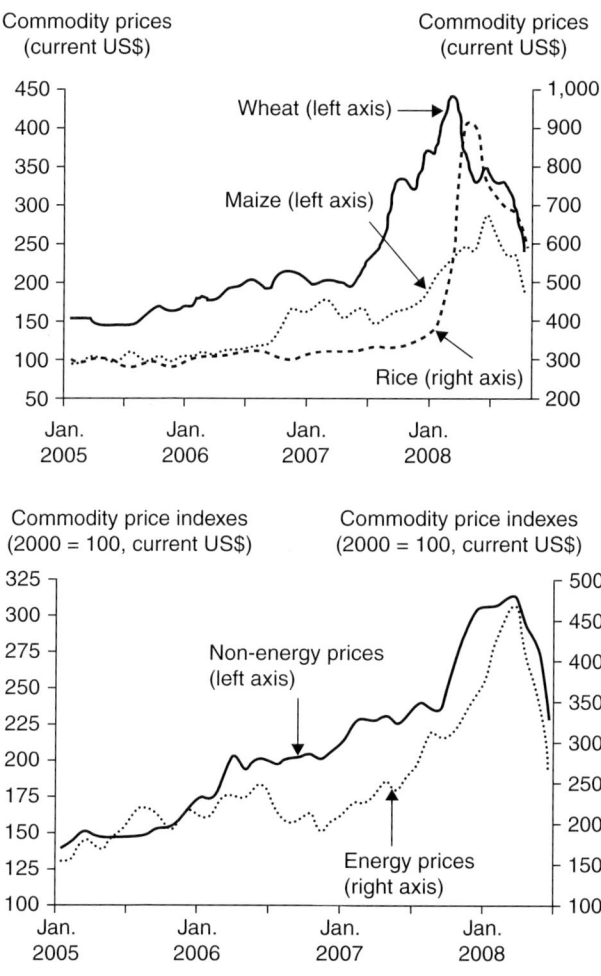

Figure 2.4 The commodity boom and bust: 2005–08
Source: World Economic Outlook (2009), based on World Bank data.

demand and supply in world markets. The increase in the demand for food in world markets was partly due to the growing demand for more and better food in China, India, and other emerging economies as an effect of their rapid growth and the resulting rise in their standard of living, and partly due to the rise in the world population. The demand-pressures in world grain markets further increased due to the demand for grains for the production of ethanol and biodiesel when the United States and the European Union embarked in 2005 on their joint program to find new sources of energy as an alternative to fossil fuel.

Initially, that program affected mostly the price of corn in the United States which was used for the production of ethanol, and the price of other cereal started to rise in the following year thanks to the hefty subsidies given by the United States and the European Union to their farmers as incentives to motivate them to switch to the production of bio-crops. The United States and the European Union announced their plan already in 2002, but started production only in 2005 but increased their production gradually in order to prevent an abrupt impact on food supply.

The global supply of cereals did not contribute to the rise in food prices: In 2008, world cereal production rose, in fact, to record levels after rising by about 8 percent from its level in 2007. Even in the African countries cereal production increased by over 10 percent in 2008, mostly in western Africa.

The impact of these structural factors was well known to market traders and analysts and was taken into account by the common models that focus on the market fundamentals of global food supply and demand in forecasting the changes in food prices. In themselves, these changes did not have a significant role in triggering the sharp rise in food prices in 2007/08 that created the food crisis. The common models for analyzing the trends the food markets and forecasting the changes in food prices are partial equilibrium models.[10]

These models are designed to estimate the impact of the "known unknowns"—the changes in demand, supply for various food products, in the price of the main inputs in food production, including fertilizers and oil, and in consumers' income in the main markets. If there are changes in any of these variables, the models can estimate their impact on food prices, although these changes are subject to uncertainty due, for instance, to weather variations. These models cannot predict, however, the impact of "unknown unknowns"—as Donald Rumsfeld famously said and which refer here to unexpected changes in government policies or unpredicted changes in *other* markets, most notably the financial markets, which have an indirect effect on food prices but are not included in the partial equilibrium models. These "unexpected" and unpredictable changes were the main driving forces of the sharp escalation in food prices that reached crisis dimensions in 2007 and 2008 when the prices of most food and feed grains doubled and the price of rice even tripled; nor could these models predict the equally sharp fall in commodity prices in the second half of 2008, when the financial markets crashed, commodity future prices collapsed, oil prices dropped within few months to one-third of their peak price levels and grain prices fell sharply. These effects of the financial markets are discussed in the next section.

The impact of the financial markets

Since the early 2000s, the financial markets in the United States, and consequently also in the other developed countries, were flooded with liquid assets due to low interest rates in the United States and the rather lax supervision of the Federal Reserve over the banking system and investment funds that enabled them to take higher risks by increasing their speculative lending and investments. The investment funds entered into fierce competition over the savings and investments of customers who took advantage of the low interest rates to increase their investments, in part by taking higher mortgages, in search of more profitable investment opportunities.

When the investment opportunities in the local markets of the developed countries were nearly exhausted by the stalemate in housing prices and the bear stock market, more investment funds started to flow to the more risky markets of the developing countries. Initially, large investments started to flow to the more prosperous and more stable emerging economies. By early 2007, capital flows to the emerging economies in Asia reached over $620 billion, and the equity market index in the region more than tripled between 2002 and mid-2007, while in China and India, the index more than quadrupled.

Their export prices remained stable, however, due to large-scale interventions of their governments and central banks in the foreign exchange markets in order to prevent an appreciation of their exchange rates and thereby protect their exports. These investments brought, however, too steep a rise in asset prices in many emerging economies. During 2002–06, residential property prices rose in real terms at an annual rate of over 8 percent in China and 10 percent in India, increasing the attractiveness of investments in residential property to investors from developed countries (IMF 2007b).

The search for more profitable investment opportunities brought some speculative investment to the more risky less developed countries, though they concentrated primarily in the relatively more stable "frontier economies" like Kenya, Ghana, and Senegal. Still other foreign investments flew to the global oil and commodity markets. In these markets, the developments in the financial markets and their impact on commodity prices were the main "unknown unknowns" that triggered the sharp rise in oil and food prices. With the continued rise in oil and cereal prices these markets became an attractive option for financial investments that sought to profit from the price increases over time.

Commodity futures became attractive because their price increase was inversely related to equity prices, and financial consultants advised investors to "buy and hold" commodities futures, just like stocks and bonds. To reduce their risks they distributed their funds in 25 key commodities and, as their prices continued to rise at accelerated rates, these investment funds poured more money into the commodities futures markets, increasing the assets usually invested in these markets from $13 billion at the end of 2003 to $260 billion by March 2008.

For the spot market, commodities futures prices serve as a benchmark to determine their current price, in part due to increased purchases of the commodities for stocks. As a result, the rise in the spot prices of oil and cereals increased by an average rate of 183 percent in those five years, and most of the increase took place in 2007–08. That rise took place despite the increase in world supply of food and feed grains, and their prices rose also as an effect of the rise in their production costs due to sharp rise in oil prices that raised transport costs and the price of fertilizers. The sharp rise in oil price was also due to the flow of investments of institutional investors to the commodities futures markets in 2006–08.

The accelerated rise in the spot prices of oil and food and feed grains in the world markets increased the inflationary pressures in most countries, developed and developing. However, the depreciation of the dollar against the euro and the yen during these years moderated the rise in oil and commodity prices in Europe and Japan, since the prices of these commodities are denominated in US dollars in the commodity markets. The dollar plummeted against the euro and yen since 2002 and, from 2006 to 2008, the dollar-euro rate dropped from around $1.2 per euro to 1.6 by mid-2008.

Demand for futures contracts of "traditional" speculators, namely speculators who eventually sell their stocks in the spot market, has always been part of the commodity markets, but the spectacular increases in the demand of investment funds increased by far the investments in the commodities futures markets and dominated the market of several key commodities (Tables 2.4 and 2.5). The total value of the demand of investment funds for commodities futures in 2004 amounted to about $180 billion. This was a tiny fraction of the worldwide equity markets, which totaled $44 trillion, but by pouring investments equal to 14 percent of the total commodity futures markets, they added a significant new demand that was translated to a considerable increase in their spot prices.

One unique aspect of these speculative investments in commodity futures is that their demand is actually increasing the larger the rise in commodity prices, since the higher the yield, the higher the risk they are willing to take, thus further accelerating the rise in the prices of

Table 2.4 The annual rise in commodity prices

Annual percentage change	2000M-1– 2003M-4	2003 M-5– 2007 M-7
Crude oil	5.5	30.3
Nonfuel Commodities	0.4	17.9
Agric. Raw Materials	0.8	6.2
Food	3.4	9.3

Source: IMF, *International Financial Statistics 2008*.

Table 2.5 Commodity futures price increases (March 2003–March 2008)

Agricultural	Cocoa	+ 34%
	Coffee	+ 167%
	Corn	+ 134%
	Cotton	+ 40%
	Soybean Oil	+ 199%
	Soybeans	+ 143%
	Sugar	+ 69%
	Wheat	+ 314%
	Wheat KC	+ 276%
Livestock	Feed Cattle	+ 34%
	Lean Hogs	+ 10%
	Live Cattle	+ 23%
Energy	Brent Crude Oil	+ 213%
	WTI Crude Oil	+ 191%
	Gasoil	+ 192%
	Heating Oil	+ 192%
	Gasoline	+ 145%
	Natural Gas	+ 71%
Base Metals	Aluminum	+ 120%
	Lead	+ 564%
	Nickel	+ 282%
	Zinc	+ 225%
	Copper	+ 413%
Precious Metals	Gold	+ 183%

Source: Testimony of Michael W. Masters http://hsgac.senate.gov/public/index.cfm.

commodity futures—and thus also of spot—prices. In other words, their profit-motivated demand for futures profits is the inverse of the behavior of price-sensitive consumers, and the higher the rise in futures prices the larger the incentive of investment funds to increase their investments in commodity futures.

These price increases renewed the debate over whether speculative trading in futures markets creates a "bubble" in which market prices far exceed their "fundamental values," the values determined by supply and demand for the commodities. Time and again, proposals have been made to limit speculations in the markets for commodity futures by, among other things, requiring larger margins on futures contracts, even though there is no historical evidence that the limits on futures trading have indeed lowered or stabilized the commodity price level.

When commodity markets are booming they are highly attractive to these investors, since "hard" or "real" assets like oil and commodities seem to offer a safe haven against inflation. In 2007–08 double-digit gains were no longer possible in the markets for stocks, bonds, and real estate. The high and rising volatility of food grains prices did not deter the large funds and rich individual investors, and they sent a torrent of cash into this arcane market. In 2008, commodity prices became a roller coaster with sometimes record daily fluctuations that were far larger than typical movements in stocks. Nevertheless, in the bear stock market, investors were seeking the higher profits that the rise in commodity prices seemed to offer.

For investment funds the commodities futures markets offered an attractive alternative to increase their yields. These funds are not selling or buying the commodities for delivery at a given date in the future, but they buy and sell futures contracts which give them the "option" to realize the contract and actually receive the commodities or "roll" the contract from one time period to the next as long as they expect that prices will continue to rise and then sell the contract closer to the delivery date to traders (wholesalers or retailers) who buy the contract and on the delivery date receive the commodity and sell it in the commodity market. In principle, speculators are not trading in the commodity market, and they therefore do not have a direct effect on the fundamentals of the demand and supply for the commodity. Figure 2.5 shows the dominating role of the Index Speculators in the Commodity Futures market in 2008. The share of their investments in commodities futures in their overall investments in the capital markets remained very tiny, however.

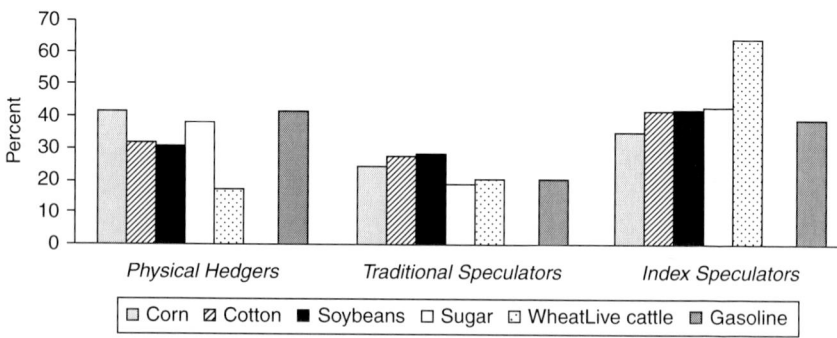

Figure 2.5 The share of investors in the commodity Future Markets, 2008
Source: US Commodities Futures Trading Commission.

The impact of the crisis on political stability and on trade policies

The sharp price escalation during the crisis of 2007–08 was followed in many developing countries by violent public protests, such as those that toppled governments in Haiti and Madagascar. The strong pressure of the local populations forced many governments to take active measures to stem the rise in food prices with subsidies, tariff reductions on imported food, and export restrictions to secure adequate food supply to the local market. Box 2.10 lists the main measures selected countries took in order to ease the food shortages and prevent an escalation of food prices, and thereby reduce the public pressure and prevent violent demonstrations. Many countries, including several African countries, imposed a ban on food exports in order to secure the supply to their own consumers. The trade restrictions had an immediate effect on the reliability of their trade agreements that nearly all African countries have with their neighboring countries.

Box 2.10 Countries' price stabilization policy measures

Russia: Export duties on grain exports introduced in November 2007 and were increased in January 2008. Temporary agreement was reached between the government and the large food retailers and producers in October 2007 to freeze prices on selected types of bread, cheese, milk, eggs, and vegetables.

Ukraine: Export quotas and export licensing for selected categories of grains since autumn 2006. Limits on profit margins of bread sold by local authorities ("social bread") through price controls.

Kazakhstan: Licensing to control exports of wheat introduced in autumn 2007.

European Union: Suspended import duties on some cereals.

Argentina: Increased export levies on corn and wheat. Stopped maize export permits.

China: Introduced export levies on wheat, barley and oats of 10 percent. Increased export levies on wheat flour and starch, maize, sorghum, millet and soybeans. Introduced export quotas on flour made of wheat, maize and rice.

India: Restrictions on exports of rice; eliminated tariffs on wheat and wheat flour; banned exports of vegetable oil.

Mexico: Restrictions on exports of maize.

African Countries:

Western Africa: in Senegal, the government subsidized the purchase of wheat flour by 40 percent, waived tariffs and imposed price controls. In Liberia, the government suspended the tax levied on rice. In Côte d'Ivoire, following social unrest the government temporarily suspended import duties on essential foodstuffs.

Southern Africa: in Zambia, in spite of export surpluses of maize in 2007/08, the government reinstated the export ban which had been in place most of the previous marketing season. It also implemented large input subsidy schemes to foster cereal production in 2008/09. In Malawi, the government continued with the large scheme to subsidize fertilizers and quality seed. In South Africa, the government announced an increase of disability and old age payments from April 2008, and adjusted the amounts paid in social grants to the poor. In Zimbabwe, the government continues to control imports of maize, wheat and sorghum which are sold at subsidized prices.

Eastern Africa: In Ethiopia, the government has recently cancelled the value-added and turnover taxes on food grains and flour, as well as all taxes on cooking oil, and surtax on soap. Earlier, the government took actions to stabilize cereal prices and to increase the purchasing power of the poor, including expenditures of US$38 million to subsidize wheat, and US$366 million to subsidize fuel. The monthly distribution of 25 kg of wheat, edible oil and other products to 800,000 low-income urban dwellers introduced in March 2007 was maintained. The government has also announced the import of a large quantity of sugar, wheat and cooking oil. In the United Republic of Tanzania, the government has authorized duty-free imports of some 300,000 tons of maize, and banned exports of agricultural commodities.

(*Source*: EBRD Office of the Chief Economist and FAAO)

The failure of the Doha Round that negotiated an agricultural trade agreement was partly due to disagreements over the right of countries to impose trade restrictions in order to protect their consumers when food prices escalate and threaten to exacerbate food shortages. There were also disagreements over the right of countries to protect their producers against competing imports in the event of a sharp fall in import prices, particularly when this decline was due to subsidies given by a country to its own producers that affected their trade, like the measures taken by the United States and the European Union to promote the production of crops for biofuel.

After the commodity boom of 2007–08 turned into a bust in mid-2008, and the world prices of cereals fell rather steeply since mid-2008, in most low-income food deficit countries food prices did not decline by much and they are still much higher today than the prices in mid-2006. In part, prices remained high because part of the food supply was used to replenish both private and public stocks and many countries and private traders increased their stocks above their normal levels as an extra precaution. Although many small African farmers refrained from taking the risk of going back to the production of high-value crops for exports and preferred to switch back to the production of staple foods, their output in the subsequent one or two seasons remained low. One reason was that many small farmers were left without enough seed to sow since, during the crisis period, these farmers were forced to use some of their own reserves of seed and other resources to provide food to their families. Another reason was that the few resources these farmers still had did not enable them to buy enough fertilizer.

How can the African countries cope with local food shortages?

In the coming years, the demand for food will continue to be affected by the decision of the United States and the European Union to continue the production of biofuel and by the demand for higher quality and more nutritious and healthy food in the emerging economies and the developed countries. The supply of food will remain robust and, according to FAO forecasts, there would be only a marginal decline in world food production in 2009 and 2010 from the record levels of 2008. Food supply in the African countries is endangered, however, by climatic changes, by shrinking water resources, and by the decline in the growth rates of yields of major grains. Future growth in food output can be renewed, however, by technological innovation, most notably by more extensive use of GM crops and the development of drought-resistant crops. Climate change due to global warming will have very negative effects on food production in semiarid areas, primarily in Africa and the Middle East, but food production is expected to increase in Eastern Europe and Central Asia, most notably in Ukraine and Russia.

The changes in the distribution of food production across continents and the failure to reach a multilateral agricultural trade agreement leave many poor food-importing countries more vulnerable to unilateral measures of the food-exporting countries and to unexpected events in other sectors that will have indirect effects on global food production and trade. The recession of 2009 has been less calamitous than many feared due to intensive and coordinated fiscal and monetary measures the developed countries have taken, but their unemployment remains high and their financial sector remains fragile. It is hard to predict the impact of these developments on food supply to developing countries, but there are concerns that fiscal tightening will force the United States and the European Union to reduce the subsidies to their agricultural producers and thus raise the price of food in the global markets. A renewed rise in oil prices that is an inevitable byproduct of the economic recovery may lead to a further increase in food prices.

Although these likely developments may raise the price of food, they are not likely to create large-scale shortages or lead to another global food crisis. The predicted climatic changes are also likely to be damaging to the least developed countries in the semiarid regions, but will not reduce the global food supply. Despite some doubts that have recently been cast on the predictions of the Intergovernmental Panel on Climate Change, the effects of climate change have already become evident in the semiarid areas with the increase in weather instability and the more frequent cycles of droughts and floods.

Although local shortfalls in food production, a rise in oil prices, or other foreseeable developments are not likely by themselves to escalate to a global food crisis of the magnitude of the crisis of 2007–08, they will be detrimental to the poor countries and to their poor population, particularly in the rural areas that are more vulnerable to droughts or floods, where their farmers are less able to cope with a rise in the price of fertilizers. The oil-producing African countries will actually benefit from a rise in oil prices, but the experience of the past decade shows that only a small fraction of those revenues will actually be used to help their farmers or ameliorate the impact of higher food prices on their poor.

A range of measures can and should be taken without delay in order to enable populations in the vulnerable countries to cope with these contingencies, and these measures should be taken both by the countries in these regions and by the international development organization. These measures must be taken in several directions: First, develop crop varieties and more advanced production methods that will enable small farmers in the developing countries to cope with the more frequent droughts and dwindling water resources expected in the next decade. Second, take measures to make more effective use of available water resources, and third, design adequate safety nets that will secure the food supply to the poor in the event of food scarcities or high food prices.

Measures to cope with the effects of droughts and dwindling water resources require both local and large-scale projects in a wide variety of areas that include:

- Development of drought-resistant crop varieties and distributing to farmers also in the more remote areas;
- Building canals to bring water from the available resource in rivers or lakes to more remote areas;
- Building dams to collect the water from floods;
- Developing and training farmers to use cost effective irrigation technologies;
- Building the infrastructure necessary to be able to use water for irrigation and for drinking water, including electricity for water pumps, water treatment, and rural roads, etc.

The development of new, more productive and drought-resistant crop varieties cannot be made by the individual developing countries by themselves, for two reasons: First, a great deal of research in this area has already been done in many countries and this research must be the basis of further research that may be needed to adjust the crops to specific conditions in certain regions. Most LDCs do not have access to scientific studies that have been conducted or have the scientists and research facilities to conduct their own research. Second, this research has large externalities, since it benefits all countries in the same region and they must all be both able to benefit and to share the costs of this research. In practice, the coordination of this collaboration is a major undertaking, but the initiative of the Africa Agriculture Development Program (CAADP) under the umbrella of the AU is proof that this initiative is possible and can be very effective. The most familiar global initiative is the CGIAR Alliance of 15 international research centers in developing countries that join forces to enhance the impact of their research through collective actions that increase efficiency and spread their inventions to the developing countries.

Country initiatives to develop rural infrastructure and plan social safety nets have been widely and generously supported by the World Bank, by the Regional Development Banks, and by donor countries. But, in all too many countries the participation of their own governments was much smaller than their needs and their capacities. Much foreign aid has been wasted, and its contribution to improve the standard of living of their populations has been quite meager. Despite the more prudent supervision of donor countries and international development organizations over the implementation of the various aid programs, and more careful evaluation of the actual effects of development projects and programs, the participation in these programs of the countries themselves, particularly the resource-rich African countries, fell far short of their actual capacities. The contribution of most countries to establishing viable social safety nets and securing an emergency food supply is still well below actual needs, and in the event of food shortages populations must depend on emergency foreign aid.

Adverse weather conditions are only part of the reason for food shortages that sometimes reach extreme levels. In many African countries, from the Horn of Africa to the Great Lakes region, civil conflicts and wars are far more detrimental to local food production and to the distribution of emergency food supply. In many other regions the HIV/AIDS pandemic, malaria, and other diseases are deadly for the population and highly damaging for their capacity to produce their own food.

The impact on world trade

The food crisis and the myriad policies governments have implemented to protect their consumers and producers, the failure to reach a multilateral agricultural trade agreement, and decisions of many countries to restrict their trade, even when that is in violation of the regional trade agreements in which they participated, are bound to have significant effects on world trade in agricultural products in the coming years.

The rising tide of trade in the process of globalization has been beneficial to most countries as long as trade was free and the market forces determined the direction of trade according to the countries' comparative advantages. In countries that opened their markets to trade, the farmers who produced crops in which their country had a comparative *dis*advantage had to change their production and switch to crops in which their country had a comparative advantage in order to be able to sell these crops at competitive prices in the domestic market or for exports. This was the case of many small African farmers that produced wheat, sorghum, and other grains but could not compete with the cheaper grains imported from the United States or Australia. In several of these countries many farmers switched to the production of high-value crops and could benefit from trade. Most farmers, primarily in landlocked countries or in remote regions, could not make this transition, either due to the short shelf-life of these crops or to the poor road infrastructure that prevented them from getting these crops to the export market fast enough; farmers in areas that did not have enough rain and did not have access to water resources could not grow crops that had to be irrigated.

The many regional trade agreements among African countries also did not bring many benefits to the farmers: Since most countries in the same region have very similar climatic conditions, nearly all had droughts and food shortages at the same time and thus could not import the food they needed from their neighboring countries. The few member countries in these agreements that did not have a drought tended to close their borders in order to prevent the export of their relatively cheaper food to their neighboring countries, where food prices were much higher as an effect of the drought. In a year of ample food production in the region, food prices were low in all member countries and there were no profitable trade opportunities within the region.

Moreover, another important consideration is the income difference between countries and between population groups within countries. When most or all countries in the region are affected by a drought, prices in all countries are rising above their trend level, but the more affluent people are still able to buy the food they need, either in their own country or in a neighboring country. As a result, the market prices for all other segments of the population are rising to even higher levels, and the poorer people suffer from an even larger food shortage.

The main threat to global free trade is the growing opposition in many countries to the trade agreements and to free trade in general. Both right-wing and left-wing political parties in many countries, developed and developing, are demanding rolling back or putting restrictions on foreign trade, since it leaves them more vulnerable to arguably unfair competition from other countries, most notably China, that harms their own industries and takes away their jobs. In the wake of the food crisis of 2007–08, they also argue that the high instability in the global market leaves them more vulnerable to the vagaries of trade policies of other countries that seek to protect their own interests. Many political parties, and also some scholars, are demanding reassessment of the merits of globalization and of benefits from multilateral trade agreements; although it is generally agreed that globalization spreads benefits from trade and economic growth in the good times, it is argued that when bad times hit some countries globalization and free trade are spreading the hardships to all.

Most scholars emphasize the benefits of collaboration in multilateral trade agreements but recognize these agreements are beneficial only provided all countries meet their obligations to the agreement and do not implement trade policies that violate the agreement even if they find it necessary to take these measures in order to protect their consumers. These unilateral measures are likely to trigger the same response in other countries and thus lead to the collapse of the entire agreement. As a result, world markets will be less stable and production far less efficient, to the detriment of all.

There is no dispute that without free trade agreements and free trade, countries will not be able to specialize in products or sectors in which they have a comparative advantage, and their production will therefore be less efficient. Although these principles of international trade are known to all, quite a few countries find it very difficult to agree on a collaborative course of action; this is so out of suspicion that some countries are taking, or will take, a free ride by implementing unilateral measures that violate the agreement. The role of the WTO is to prevent these violations and punish countries that take such unilateral measures, but there are many gray areas in which violations do occur. The lack of a trade agreement in agricultural products gave a free hand to countries to take measures they saw necessary for their interests and invited other countries to take similar measures. These trade wars, even when limited to few products, reduce the general trust in open trade and prompt more countries to take more wide-ranging measures to protect themselves against these eventualities by restricting their trade and increasing local production for local markets even though it is less efficient and more expensive. The food crisis gave strong incentives to many countries to resort to policies of food self-sufficiency and in some cases to rent land in other countries where they can produce food for their own consumption.

The series of agreements reached under GATT, including the creation of the WTO, were the main reason for the proliferation of globalization that benefited all countries. The failure to reach an agreement in the Doha Round raises doubts about the possibility of reaching an agreement on agricultural trade in the foreseeable future and is therefore forcing all countries to take measures to protect their food supplies without relying on trade. Moreover, this failure also raises doubts about the solid foundations of other trade agreements. These doubts increase the tendency of countries to "decouple" their trade and keep their hands on the shut-off valve when they open their markets to trade.

Can the food crisis happen again?

Beside the threat of trade restrictions on food supply and price, the most "expected unexpected" threat is another energy crisis and another massive rise in oil prices. Despite large investments to save energy, find economically efficient substitutes, and search for new sources of fossil fuel, it will take at least another decade before reliable, safe, and cost-effective alternative energy sources are available. In the meantime, the demand for fossil fuel and natural gas will remain high and continue to rise: In the first quarter of 2009, oil prices increased by more than 50 percent above their level in the last quarter of 2008.

When oil prices crashed to less than one-fourth of their peak level, from over $140 per bbl in mid-2008 to around $40 a few months later, it was clear these new prices were too low and below the production and transport costs of many oil-producing countries. It did not take long for venture capitalists and investment companies to spread announcements inviting savers and investors to buy oil futures, claiming oil prices are bound to rise. By mid-2009 oil prices rose to nearly $80 per bbl and according to the IMF's *World Economic Outlook* of 2009, they may continue to rise and remain highly unstable. As a result, the costs of fertilizers and transport will remain high and also will keep food prices at high levels.

Preparing for the worst, consumers and producers are making efforts to find effective and affordable substitutes, from hybrid cars to the use of sun and wind energy. Researchers work intensively on the development of GM crops that require less fertilizers and pesticides and are more drought-resistant, and on the development of second-generation crops like Jatropha and palm oil for more efficient and less expensive production of biofuel; countries build large projects to use the energy of waterfalls and the sun for the production of electricity; innovators and start-up companies are working hardest in search of the magic formula and ultimate solution to the production of affordable energy; perhaps, one of them dared predict, by building in space huge mirrors the size of Arizona and Texas that will concentrate the sun's energy. In the long run, a solution will undoubtedly be found, mainly because the world will run out of existing resources, but the road to that happy end, while it may not be that long is bound to be difficult and expensive.

For the time being, the two main immediate concerns are still the volatility of energy supply and prices and the fragility of the global financial system. The supply of oil and natural gas from most African countries, including Sudan, Chad, Ethiopia, Gabon, Nigeria, Angola, and Cameroon, is highly unreliable. Oil supply from Venezuela and Iran has become a political weapon and is equally unreliable. Even oil supply from the Gulf states is less secured as an effect of the rise of Islamic fundamentalism. The supply of oil and natural gas from Russia is also openly used as a political weapon, and the Western countries would therefore prefer to reduce their dependence on Russian oil. For all these reasons, stable and reliable supply of fossil fuel is by no means guaranteed, and the risk of another food crisis, possibly as part of a larger crisis, cannot be ruled out. There are also concerns about the use of oil as a powerful political weapon, as happened in the oil crisis of the 1970s.

A rise in oil prices is in itself not likely to create a global food crisis, however. The commodity boom of 2007–08 and the subsequent dramatic economic bust in the second half of 2008 were the result of a combination of events in different global markets that, at the outset, did seem to threaten the global food market. Indeed, all studies on the food crisis until mid-2008 focused on the impact of the fundamentals, and they blamed primarily the collaborative program of the United States and the European Union to buy corn in order to produce biofuel. Only when the financial markets crashed and many investment companies went bust did the risks they took in their reckless investments in commodity markets become evident, and the connection between the commodity crisis and the financial crisis became clearer. The financial markets today remain fragile, but all the precautions, monitoring, and supervision that have been put in place to prevent risky investments—and the growing risk aversion of individual savers and investors—are likely to make traders and investors in these markets show more restraint.

There are other dangers and other markets that are likely to have indirect effects on food prices. Even the doubts recently expressed about the actual impact on global warming of the extensive release into the atmosphere of CO_2 from the use of coal and fossil fuel may slow down the search for alternative energy sources and keep oil prices high. But the greatest risk is the possible impact of political events in the Middle East on the supply of oil from the Gulf countries, Iraq and Iran. The war in this region is far from ending, and the confrontation between the West and Iran seems to escalate. The greater involvement of China in the world oil market and its direct contracts with several key oil-exporting countries, from Angola to Iran to Venezuela, further increase uncertainty about future oil prices. If the threat of these developments on the supply of oil increases, a rise in oil prices will become more likely and even some investment companies may bypass their caution and increase investment in oil futures, further pushing up the spot prices of oil. All these developments may bring oil and gas prices back to their peak levels in 2008 and, among other effects, this is likely to raise the cost of food production and food prices. Even if these developments do not escalate to the extent that they create another global commodity crisis, they are bound to be extremely detrimental to the food prices in the least developed countries and extremely damaging to their poor consumers.

The fragility of the global financial system seems even more threatening in the coming one or two years, and some analysts (for lack of better word) volunteered all sorts of doomsday predictions. Now, not only financial institutions face difficulties paying their debts, but even solid countries have difficulties. If the public loses confidence in the ability of countries to pay their debts, it may indeed become a major crisis.

These risks are announced daily in the news media. The lingering effect of the commodity crisis of 2008 is the decline of the trust in world trade. In 2009, for the first time since the 1930s, there was a slight decline in the volume of world trade. This, however, was mainly due to the decline in consumers' expenses due to the global recession. If countries lose their trust in world trade, then their main concern will be whether they will be able to buy, in the world markets, essential goods such as oil, food, and possibly even medications. Although trade would remain a positive-sum game, as Ricardo had predicted, specialization of a country like South Korea in industrial goods may locally raise concerns about global food shortages despite all predictions that there is ample food supply. The response of Korea and many other countries would be to build up larger food stocks, and that response itself will raise the world food crisis. Will that develop into a global crisis? Since expectations play a key role in this eventuality it is impossible to predict.

As trust in international trade is eroding, more countries prefer to decouple their trade and form an alliance with countries they trust. These alliances would reduce the volume of trade in world markets and that, in turn, would increase the vulnerability of countries left out of these agreements to a potential increase and growing volatility in food prices.

The poor countries will have greater difficulties taking most precautionary measures. For one thing, it will be too costly for them to prepare larger food reserves when world food prices are, and may continue, rising; for another, they have limited possibilities to increase local food production by increasing subsidies to farmers, because, with the many obstacles small farmers have, from poor infrastructure to outmoded, low-yield production technologies, their capacity to respond to incentives is very limited. This will increase their vulnerability to external events that raise food prices. Although this range of possibilities belongs to the realm of "unknown unknowns," there are more reasons today to worry about higher food prices and possible food shortages, which—that even if they do not evolve into a global food crisis—may increase costs and aggravate local food shortages in the poorer countries and their poor people.

Notes

1. This, for example, was the conclusion of *The Economist,* May, 15, 2008.
2. *World Disasters Report 2007* (http://www.ifrc.org/publicat/wdr2007/index.asp)
3. Clark, Gregory. *A Farewell to Alms.* Princeton: Princeton University Press, 2007. See also "Malthus, the false prophet," *The Economist,* May 15, 2008.
4. It should be noted, however, that this estimate is based on the "old" estimates of the World Bank and the previous poverty line, even though the debate on the proper poverty line has not yet been settled, nor is there an agreement on the meaning of a uniform poverty line that applies to all countries even after making all the adjustments on the purchasing power parity and the real price changes. See Chen and Ravallion 2007.

5. Source: Various reports of the *Millennium Development Program*.
6. See KIT and IIRR. "Trading up: Building cooperation between farmers and traders in Africa." 2008.
7. The report is largely based on IFPRI's 2005 report, and it is summed up in a synopsis entitled: *Taking Action for the World's Poor and Hungry People* (IFPRI 2007).
8. At the time the report was written, it was still hoped that half of the countries in SSA would reach the MDGs.
9. *Climate Change Increases Food Security Concerns* (http://www.ens-newswire.com/ens/dec2006/2006-12-05-01.asp)
10. Some of these models include, however, a large number of food products and analyze the interrelations between them as well as the impact of the expected changes in income.

Part III
Africa's Poverty Traps and Obstacles to Growth

Africa has many advantages, along with many constraints, due to its location and unique geographic and agroclimatic conditions. The Suez Canal is an essential waterway for the seaborne transport of oil, raw materials, and cargo. Africa's unique climatic conditions made it the greenhouse and the incubator of an infinite number of distinctive living species and vegetation, not to mention the human species, as well as exceptional fruits, vegetables, trees and, in fact, all forms of life.

But in the past the continent's climatic conditions as well as several other geographical and agroclimatic characteristics have had a negative effect on economic growth and development and, for the people who live in Africa today, will remain considerable obstacles for the efforts of the countries to pursue growth. Some obstacles are manmade and could be altered as Africa changes the structure of its regimes and the relations between states. Other obstacles are the product of changes in the agroclimatic conditions. Still other obstacles are evolving as an effect of the changes in the spatial distribution of people across the continent that have resulted in a growing, and increasingly more destructive, wave of rural–urban migration as well as migration across states. This migration is largely the product of the changes in climatic conditions, the shrinking agricultural resources, and the deteriorating living conditions in rural areas; but this human wave itself is likely to worsen demographic conditions and make them even more formidable obstacles.

This part of the book concentrates on the spatial and agroclimatic obstacles that may become major obstacles for Africa's potential to sustain its economic growth. The two obstacles that have received great attention in the economic literature of recent years, particularly since Paul Collier's landmark book, *The Bottom Billion*, are the problems of landlocked countries and the "resource curse." The latter is arguably not only an obstacle created by the spatial characteristics of a country, but is also the product of a country's regime and the policies of its leaders. Since the spatial obstacles of landlocked countries are not likely to change, and the "resource curse" requires fundamental changes in the social and political conditions of affected countries, these obstacles will impact Africa's growth for many years, or even decades.

Jeffrey Sachs and Paul Collier emphasized two specific obstacles that are the product of the countries' geographical conditions and their locations, which became major traps limiting the capacity of the countries to reduce their poverty. The first is the trap of the landlocked country. Both Sachs and Collier considered the conditions of landlocked countries to be major obstacles that slow down their growth and increase their poverty. Collier emphasized that a landlocked country is especially damaged if it has unproductive or "bad" neighbors. Jeffrey Sachs focused in his book, *End of Poverty*,[1] on the traps at the household and village levels, and emphasized the effect of their spatial isolation, the burden of disease, the climate, and the quality of their soil.

The second, and seemingly paradoxical, trap that has affected the growth of these countries is the "resource curse" that turned their boon—an abundance of natural resources—into a bane. Collier gave the example of countries that have oil, copper, or diamond resources, but instead of increasing their capacity to raise the standard of living, these resources encouraged corrupt politicians or army commanders to seize power in order to control this wealth and enrich themselves. In the analysis of Sachs, one example of a related obstacle in this category is the tragic neglect of malaria, which became a curse for the rural population but can be prevented if the right measures are taken.

Africa's declining food security and the increase in the frequency of droughts and floods as an effect of climate change are likely to force millions to leave their lands and migrate either to the urban centers or to other countries. Many developed and developing countries are already contemplating measures to control this wave of migration that threatens to devastate the quality of life in their own cities and limit their capacity to control crime or the spread of diseases. In Egypt, the government is making plans to build no less than 45 new cities along the Nile in order to prevent mass migration to Cairo. In SSA (Sub Saharan Africa), by contrast, not much is being done to deal with the torrent of rural migrants already converging on urban centers. The region between Accra and Lagos is rapidly becoming the largest megacity in the world, and the crowded slums and shantytowns are an immense camp of the poor and destitute. These trends are rapidly creating the two most difficult obstacles that will reduce the capacity of African countries to control their poverty. Food scarcity and urbanization are two of the five main problems that will lead to a large and escalating increase in poverty in SSA in the coming years.

3.1
The Geographical and Man-Made Obstacles

The World Bank *World Development Report* (*WDR* 2009) on *Spatial Disparities and Development Policy* is devoted to an analysis of the imbalance in economic growth that is due to spatial factors. Income disparities between people are often related to and explained by their place of residence. The *WDR* focuses its analysis on the human-induced change of the spatial characteristic of a region, but it does not analyze the complementary aspect that requires more focused and deeper research on the spatial-induced change of the human characteristics or, in the words of the report, "the social and environmental effects of a changing economic geography" (p. 34).

Spatial causes for disparities in income between regions are often attributed to a wide variety of factors: Proximity to urban centers, to an agglomeration of industrial centers, or to the coast attracts enterprises in search of locations that will reduce transport costs, whether to other enterprises, to the port, or to the source of raw materials. As more enterprises converge on an industrial center, more industries follow, until land prices become too high. As more industries come to the center, more employees or employment seekers follow, until the area becomes too polluted, or apartments too expensive.

More affluent people are attracted to regions where they can find a quiet environment or natural attractions, like a river or a lake. But these same features may also lure crowds of tourists with all that entails: restaurants, hotels, entertainment spots, and staff for all these facilities—and what initially attracted people to the area may quickly be spoiled. Sometimes, a place of residence is considered desirable because the people already living in that neighborhood are regarded as an elite, or because they form a community of individuals from the same country of origin or the same tribe.

In rural areas, a high population density usually deters people because they must compete for the shrinking resources of water and land; in the urban center, high density attracts more people, mostly new arrivals from the rural areas or from other countries, who hope to find work.

The *WDR* emphasized in its overview that the term "location" has several dimensions:

1. The *place* in which the country or the region is situated and its natural endowments;
2. Its *distance* to the coastal outlet, the urban center, or the main transport road;
3. The *conditions* in that location refer not only to the agroclimatic conditions or the availability of natural resources, but also to:
   - The political conditions and policy-related barriers on the movements of commodities and people;
   - The characteristics of the population in the country or region, including their ethnic characteristics.

Migration is the change in the location of people or industries motivated by the attributes of the location they are going to—at least relative to the attributes of the location they are coming from. Migration, therefore, changes the spatial distribution of the population, and these changes in turn are changing both the people and the space.

The obstacles to cross-country trade

The arbitrary borders Africa's colonial powers established, and which became the borders of countries when they gained independence, had a major effect on the continent's economic and political geography. These borders made Africa unique in both its physical and its human geography: It has the largest number of countries per square mile of any developing region, and each country shares borders with, on average, four other countries. A large proportion of the population lives in countries with highly detrimental geographic and economic conditions for development. About 40 percent of the population lives in landlocked countries, compared with 23 percent in the landlocked countries of Eastern Europe and the former Soviet Union. In the past two decades, many of landlocked African countries discovered rich resources, while many of the coastal countries have been known to have rich resources since colonial times (Table 3.1).

The colonial powers shaped these borders in order to divide Africa's rich resources among themselves. But despite the depletion of many existing resources (especially in the past two decades), the discovery of massive amounts of new resources has increased the number of resource-rich countries and brought considerable wealth. In the sands of Sudan, Chad, and Eritrea, large quantities of oil was discovered. In Niger and Botswana, uranium was found. For the purpose of analysis in this chapter, the region's 48 countries have been grouped into four main categories: coastal, landlocked, resource-poor, and resource-rich.

Table 3.1 Natural resources and access to the coast in the African countries

Resource-Rich		Resource-Poor	
Oil &Natural gas	Minerals/metals/oil	Coastal	Landlocked
Angola	**Botswana** Diamonds, **Recent discovery of Uranium**	Benin	Burkina Faso
Cameroon	**Namibia** Diamonds	Cape Verde Developed tourism.	Lesotho
Gabon	**South Africa** (platinum, gold, chromium, iron); Oil	Ghana **Recent discovery of off-shore oil**	Mali
	Zambia Copper, **Recent discovery of Uranium**	Malawi	Rwanda
		Mauritius Mozambique **Recent discovery of oil**	**Swaziland** Tanzania
		Senegal **recent discovery of natural gas**	Uganda **Recent discovery of oil**
Fragile Countries[1]			
Chad	Côte d'Ivoire (Oil ,Timber) **Recent discovery of additional oil**	Comoros	Burundi
Rep. of Congo (Brazzaville)	Congo, Dem. Rep. (Kinshasa) (diamonds, gold, cobalt, coltan); oil	The Gambia	Central African Rep. Some gold and diamonds mining
Equatorial-Guinea	Guinea (Bauxite, gold, diamonds, iron)	Kenya	Ethiopia
Guinea-Bissau	Liberia Timber, Diamonds	Madagascar	Niger *Recent discovery of uranium*
Nigeria	Mauritania (iron ore); oil	São Tomé & Príncipe **Signs of large oil reserves**	Zimbabwe **Recent discovery of Diamonds and gold**
Sudan	Togo (Phosphates) Sierra-Leone Diamonds	Tanzania	

Comments: Landlocked; Coastal; Middle Income Countries; [1]**Fragile or Failed State:** *according to OEDC-DEC; WEO* and *Foreign Policy*. The countries marked by grey color are fragile economies also according to the IMF criteria which emphasizes their economic conditions. The other countries in this category have fragile political conditions or civil conflicts.

Sources: CIA, World Factbook; The Economist; IMF Regional Economic Outlook (2009).

Sachs (2005, 2008) and Collier (2007) emphasized the difficulties landlocked countries must cope with, especially if they have uncooperative neighbors. Their difficulties obtaining secure access to the coast increase the costs of trade and pose considerable obstacles for their integration into the global economy. For a resource-poor country, coastal access offers some benefits by lowering the price of its imports and preventing arbitrary restrictions on its access to a port. Several of these countries export traditional agricultural products, primarily coffee, cocoa, and cotton, and proximity to the port reduces transport costs. Their industrial sector is rudimentary, however, producing mainly for the local market. The *WDR* (2009) noted that this is one of the reasons why spatial development in the continent has not conformed to global patterns and urbanization has come without growth.

Coastal access by itself is of much less advantage to the African countries than to Asian countries due to the poor inland road infrastructure and the time consuming administrative costs at the ports. The shipment of products from Nairobi to Mombasa, for example, is very unattractive, even though the cross-country road is paved. The port in Mombasa is inefficient, the administrative procedures cumbersome, and corruption is rampant. Even sea transport from Mombasa has become less attractive and more expensive due to the threat from pirates. However, this has not reduced the attractiveness of Nairobi itself as a trade center; this is partly due to the high volume of air transport and partly because the city is a large central market and financial center, hosting the commerce of local trade and trade with neighboring countries. In fact, most of the eastern coast of SSA is barely accessible, as are large parts of the western coast, particularly in the countries devastated by war and that did not manage to build reasonable port facilities.

Landlocked countries are usually less attractive to industries due to their distance from the coast, to the poor and barely accessible roads, and to the higher transport costs for people and freight. Moreover, only a minor share of the products of local industries in the landlocked African countries is exported. Nevertheless, the distance to the coast in many landlocked countries has been compensated for by their rich resources.

It is important to note that Africa's poor infrastructure makes the distance from the coast and coastal access incomplete criteria by themselves. Transport costs depend mostly on the availability and quality of roads. In the villages the roads are in even worse conditions and continuously decaying; few roads are paved and many villages are cut off during the rainy season, when the roads are flooded. Villages in the interior of countries that have coastal access are just as isolated and unable to trade as are regions in landlocked countries.

In one of the first studies on the impact of spatial location on development, Radelet and Sachs (1998) found the growth rates of landlocked countries were lower by around 1.5 percentage points: Using the CIF/FOB (cost plus insurance plus freight/cost-free on board) margin, they found that cost of freight and insurance for landlocked African countries was, on average, 50 percent higher than for costal economies. For consumers or manufacturers who buy imported products, the purchase price also includes administrative costs and various transaction costs traders must pay. Trading of food products across national boundaries is essential for both producers and consumers, and cross-border trade may sometimes be crucial for food security.

Nevertheless, many barriers limit the extent and efficiency of this trade in Africa and increase its cost. These include laws prohibiting trucks that cross a border from bringing back merchandise; excessive paperwork and "informal taxation" at various trading points, mostly to pay bribes; long queues; and incompetent border staff. These additions to transport costs are indicated by the World Bank report on the ease of doing business, and the subsequent discussion on regional trade agreements examines ways of overcoming these impediments for Africa-to-Africa trade.

In the *New Economic Geography* (2006) Paul Krugman explained this process as follows:

> A dozen years ago, it seemed to some of us that we were facing a stark choice of world visions. One vision was the traditional vision of international trade theory, in which countries were discrete economic points, whose location in space is irrelevant. Another was the pure geography vision, in which location in space is all and borders are irrelevant. ... What seems to have emerged from the empirical work of the past dozen years is a compromise vision. Distance matters a lot, though possibly less than it did before telecommunications. Borders also matter a lot, though possibly less than they did before free trade agreements.

With globalization, the vision went through another metamorphosis: Trade no longer means only the movement of commodities, but increasingly also movement of capital and labor. With the movement of capital and improvements in information and communication technologies, distance and borders mean less in some countries and regions that have developed trade in services, or where labor can move relatively freely between countries. In other countries, distance means less and it is merely one component of the costs, but borders mean a lot, perhaps even much more than before.

On the movement of commodities and capital, the General Agreement on Tariffs and Trade (GATT), and later the WTO, aimed at reducing the importance of borders by reducing tariffs and facilitating trade by removing trade barriers. Yet, trade barriers remained; the failure to reach a trade agreement in the Doha Round, the export restrictions imposed by many countries during the food crisis, and the tendency of "decoupling" all illustrate that trade barriers are still imposed to stop the flow of commodities across borders.

Borders matter even more for the flow of migrants who endeavor to leave poor countries and cross into the more affluent countries. In fact, many of the relatively better-off countries have built high barriers at their borders, with both physical barriers, like the fence between the United States and Mexico, and administrative barriers that restrict visa applications.

Sachs (2005) emphasized that Africans who live in the interior of the continent have enormous transport costs in shipping their goods to and from coastal ports. Problems of isolation are compounded by the small market size in the nearby urban center of all countries with the exception of South Africa and Nigeria, despite the rapid growth in the number of people in these centers. In countries with relatively large markets in urban centers that serve several countries, the growth prospects are better, but their access to the coast plays a rather limited role if they do not have an adequate port and access roads.

Added to the burden of transport costs is the burden of a multitude of regulations, high administrative costs, and "side payments" for border crossing that raise the overall transport costs of cross-country trade. In the ports, all traders face high charges and a long waiting time, but these charges are even higher for traders from other countries. In the cross-country trade in Africa, these charges are particularly high since each country has an average of four neighbors, whereas in Latin America, the average is 2.3. The World Bank's annual reports on the *Ease of Doing Business* evaluate administrative costs and waiting time of the various regulations that affect business activities. The report on Africa shows the difficulties of cross-border trading are, on average, 40 percent higher in landlocked countries than in countries that have coastal access; landlocked countries encounter considerably higher costs for border crossings, which increase their costs of exports and imports; it takes traders much longer in the border crossing or at the port, and their "side payments" are much higher.

The low density of population in rural areas raises internal transport costs and traders usually have to go through more road crossings that are often established arbitrarily by security forces in order to collect "something to eat." All these obstacles reduce the profitability of Africa-to-Africa trade and divert a larger share of trade either to the local market or abroad. Moreover, the small size of the industrial sector and its very limited diversity restricts intraindustry trade and leaves local enterprises highly dependent on trade with enterprises in developed and emerging economies.

In the past decade, the high growth rates of most African countries were mainly due to their export of primary resources, which benefited both the coastal and landlocked resource-rich countries. The proliferation of regional trade agreements between African countries reduced cross-border costs and simplified the administrative process for members of trade agreements, thus reducing the disadvantage of landlocked countries. The goal of the African Union (AU) is to achieve similar reductions for all Africa-to-Africa trade.

The myth of a poverty trap in landlocked countries

Collier emphasized "landlocked countries" as one of four "poverty traps" the bottom billion is unable to escape without help, since these countries are at a huge spatial disadvantage, especially when their neighboring countries are also poor. As the preceding section suggests, this spatial disadvantage is primarily a function of the distance of the village or region to the port and the quality of the inland road, and it is less affected by the fact that this village or region is in a country that has access to the coast. Moreover, most coasts, especially along the eastern shores, are barely accessible and the ports inefficient and decaying. In quite a few countries along the western shores, including Angola, the Democratic Republic of Congo, and the Republic of Congo, the ports were ruined in by wars and are barely useable. In countries referred to as "fragile" or "failed" states, where the government does not provide security and safety to its own citizens, let alone to their traders, cross-country trade is not possible regardless of whether the country is landlocked or has coastal access.

Collier (2006) found that globally, on average, if a country's neighbors grow at an additional one percentage point, then the country itself would grow by an additional 0.4 percent. Outside Africa, the landlocked, resource-scarce economies gain on average a larger spillover of 0.7 percent, and these countries are often consciously orienting their economies toward making the most of these growth spillovers. In Africa, the growth spillover for the landlocked, resource-scarce economies is a mere 0.2 percent. This is primarily due to the lack of diversification of Africa's economies, which restricts Africa-to-Africa trade and concentrates their exports on primary resources and a small selection of agricultural products like coffee, cocoa, and cotton; since these products are produced almost only for export, they are not much affected by economic growth in neighboring countries, nor are they affected much by a rise in transport costs for these exports.

For producers and traders from either the landlocked or the coastal countries, the main considerations are the transport costs to the nearest functioning port, the ease of dealing with the port administration and, in some products, the storage costs. Exporters in Mozambique find it more advantageous to export or import merchandise through one of the ports in South Africa, even though Mozambique is, itself, a coastal country.

The advantage of a coastal country is frequently also political. Coastal countries often use their control of the road to the port and of the port itself to block access for their landlocked neighbors or to subject them to higher administrative costs in order to obstruct their trade and reduce their capacity to compete with their own traders. With free trade agreements, these practices have been reduced, although they are still common by means of various regulations against traders from neighboring countries, particularly if these are landlocked countries. The more prevalent are these agreements and the tighter their enforcement, the smaller is the advantage of a coastal country and the more important is the criterion of transport costs, which also affect the more remote regions in the countries with coastal access but poor inland roads.

Collier argues that for "countries lucky enough to be on the coast, with a large workforce, governance doesn't matter too much; as long as the state doesn't get in the way, export growth can take off." As attractive as it may seem and as relevant (up to a limit) as it has been in East Asia, in the context of Africa this pro–free trade statement is hardly relevant, however. Even in East Asian countries, the government did not "get out of the way," but instead built industrial zones close to the ports in which enterprises agglomerated and thus were able to attract an adequate workforce. The industries in export zones received considerable concessions, like free land, tax reductions, and even tariff reduction. The concentration of a large number of enterprises also gave them benefits of scale and boosted these industries. This is still the case, not only in China and Malaysia, but also in South Korea. The proximity of the industrial zone to the coast was not a matter of good fortune, but a product of a deliberate policy aimed at lowering the costs to entrepreneurs. As we now know, government and governance do matter—a lot—not only in the promotion of industries, but also in supervision over the operation of well-established enterprises that are the symbol of free spirit and the victory of free markets—the US banking system.

In Africa, this sweeping statement is even more problematic, not only because country governments are already heavily involved in all business activities, ranging from construction permits, registering property, protecting investors, paying taxes, trading across borders, to enforcing (or ignoring) contracts. According to the World Bank report on *The Ease of Doing Business* in 2009, of the 30 countries (20 of them African) ranked at the bottom of the list of 181 countries according to their overall performance, only 13 countries were at the bottom due to difficulties they impose on employing workers, and 23 were at the bottom because of the difficulty of (or lack of) getting credit, which is not only highly regulated by the government but also highly biased in favor of some industries and against others. Governance is, therefore, critical to how enterprises are doing, and should do, business, and government is essential to provide basic public assets, such as road infrastructure, port facilities, electricity, and safe drinking water.

The World Bank's report *Doing Business 2007: How to Reform* ranks 175 countries according to the ease of doing business; the average rank of the SSA countries was 131. In practically all the SSA countries, there are obstacles in all private sector activities: licensing, employment, credit, and transactions with the government are all tedious, and time- and paper-consuming activities. Payments made "under the table" can slightly ease or speed up the process, but the costs are high and the process still extremely cumbersome. For instance, it takes an average of 11 procedures to start a business in a SSA country, compared to an average of 8 procedures in a South Asian country; this process takes two months in SSA compared with one month in South Asia; running a private business in an African country costs three times as much in terms of income per capita, partly due to administrative complexities, corruption, and awkward legal systems, and partly due to high expenses of such essential business services as telecommunications and energy.

This discussion, important as it certainly is, takes us away from the main subject of this section: the impediments of landlocked countries and their difficulties easing poverty. In this discussion, the main categories of countries, according to the IMF *Regional Economic Outlook* (2009) were: (a) Resource-rich countries (divided into oil producers and others); (b) resource-poor coastal countries, and (c) resource-poor landlocked countries. It should be noted, though, that in the first decade of the twenty-first century new resources have been found that should be taken into account in evaluating growth potential. They include natural gas in Ethiopia and Ghana, oil in Sudan, and Uranium in Niger and Botswana. With these adjustments, there are only eight resource-poor, landlocked countries: Burkina Faso, Lesotho; Malawi; Mali; Swaziland, and Uganda.

However, these categories provide a very partial characterization of the countries' spatial attributes, which influenced their development in the past and will influence their capacity to reduce poverty in the future. The reason is that in Africa, the fact that a country is landlocked is not the *cause* of its limited growth prospects and its inability to reduce its poverty. Instead, the country's spatial characteristics were the reason that motivated the colonial powers to determine borders that left these countries landlocked. At the time, their reasoning was that these countries did not have the resources colonizing countries were looking for, and in order to reach the hinterland, the colonial power had to make large investments to build sturdy roads through heavy jungles—roads that would survive the rain or cross through vast desert areas—as well as to maintain a military force to establish control. With few exceptions, they developed only trade centers along the main North–South railroad, established in urban areas like Nairobi, and in Cote d'Ivoire where the French developed a trade and financial center. Otherwise, the colonial powers had little interest and made only minor investments in the landlocked countries at the center of the continent.

Another group of countries in which the colonial powers had little interest were those in the Horn of Africa. Until the Suez Canal was opened in 1869, they had no interest even in the coastal areas in this region, where land is plentiful but water resources are scarce and the climatic conditions are highly unstable. Today, many of these countries have rich resources, primarily oil and natural gas, but at the time there was nothing in their soil that could have been of interest to the British Empire, and when the colonial rulers started to leave the continent, they were just as happy to take with them their small contingency force and the small administration there mainly to serve the British military.

In many places, coastal access had been a huge advantage during colonial times, particularly along the shores of the Atlantic Ocean, where most countries now have huge oil resources. Most landlocked countries were deserted, both because at the time they had far less resources and because access to the hinterland was uneconomical or infeasible. Since independence, however, many coastal states, including resource-rich countries along the western shores, have failed disastrously due to prolonged wars that bled their people and wasted their resources. Coastal countries from the Horn of Africa in the East to the two Congo republics, Angola, Côte d'Ivoire, Liberia, and Sierra Leone in the West became war zones, and some still are. Many other coastal countries lack basic port facilities and adequate road infrastructure. Coastal access is a huge advantage to the pirates in Somalia, but it does not help the other inhabitants much, and many had to flee civil strife as fast as they could to the interior of the country to save their lives. The coastal areas in Nigeria and Ghana benefited more from the better ports in Lagos and Accra, but even this entire region is flooded by millions of migrants that turn these cities into monstrous metropolitan areas where millions squeeze together to eke out a meager existence.

The limited impact of coastal access on the countries' economies becomes more evident when the African countries are divided into two other groups: the "fragile" and "nonfragile" states. The World Bank list also includes, however, countries still actively engaged in war as well as countries where a democratically elected government was toppled up to two years after the election by a military coup, and this regime is still in power. The World Bank list includes countries engaged in wars in the previous five years that are still recovering. In many other evaluations, quite a few of these countries are included among the fragile or frail states.

This list is very disquieting: Half the 42 countries in the World Economic Outlook (WEO) list of SSA countries are "fragile" or "frail." The fragile states include practically all the countries in the Horn of Africa, including the coastal countries of Somalia, Sudan, and Eritrea. Their access to the coast did not much help them to develop their economies because most of their trade is in arms. All these countries were engaged in an incessant series of wars and atrocities, including the massacres in Darfur. If the countries of Niger and the Central African Republic, which participated in some of the wars and are engaged in their own internal civil conflicts, are added to this list, then this entire group of countries consists of fragile states, and they account for half of Africa's 20 fragile states. The list of coastal countries on the western coast is even more telling: With the exception of four countries (Senegal, Benin, Nigeria and Cameroon) *all* the other 11 countries on the western coast, from Comoros to Angola, are "fragile" states. Angola and Sierra Leone are the only countries in this list that, after a long and gruelling war, have reached a peace agreement and started to build up democratic regimes, and thanks to their oil and other resources, they seem to have a chance to be dropped from this list.

The large variance in the distribution of Africa's population across the continent did not change much since their independence, despite the discovery of rich resources in some countries. Two main reasons explain this insistence of people to hang on to their lands and territory: First, agriculture remains the main source of income and employment in all countries except for South Africa. The work in agriculture requires people to stay in their villages and on their ancestral lands. Despite meager resources and shrinking landholdings, people still managed to feed themselves. Global warming and dwindling water resources are now prompting more people to move to urban areas, even though they have no chance to find employment and are forced to seek shelter in barely habitable quarters. Second, despite very large differences in the average per-capita income among African countries, income inequality is extreme and at least half the population in the resource-rich countries lives in chronic poverty. Since migrants expect to have the same fate, they are not attracted to the "rich" countries like Nigeria and Cameroon, where they will be worse off. Also, in these countries they are regarded as foreigners, outsiders, or infidels and are despised by the local population. Many would have liked to go to South Africa and have tried to do so, but the authorities in South Africa are making equally strenuous efforts to prevent this migration.

Since living conditions are deteriorating at an alarming rate, more people are forced to migrate. In neighboring rural areas the population faces similar conditions, and tribal differences make them more hostile. The only places rural migrants can head to are the urban centers. Until now, cross-country migration has been minimal, since no improvement in the standard of living was expected and ethnic differences made migrants extremely unwelcome. This may change in the coming years, simply because more people will have less choice and no alternative than to go to the massive and rapidly growing urban centers in Nigeria, Ghana, and Senegal, because in these crowded areas, ethnic and tribal differences may be less important. Tribal rivalries may also change their character in the rapidly growing urban centers and turn into religiously motivated tensions. This has been the process in Lagos, but it may be too early to predict the process in other urban centers.

Finally, it should be noted that most countries along the coasts of Africa have not been very successful economically, and with the new resources in landlocked countries, coastal countries are no longer better off, even on the basis of this criterion. Most coasts are not accessible to trade, and the main occupation of their inhabitants is incessant armed conflicts. Whereas in most developing countries the coastal areas attract people and economic activities, in Africa the coastal areas in the Horn of Africa and in Angola and the two Congo republics have been plagued by decades of incessant wars that claimed millions of lives. Only in the coastal areas of Nigeria and Ghana could the more traditional patterns of spatial distribution of population prevail, but these coastal areas are now flooded by millions of migrants from the rural hinterlands or other countries.

The potential strategy for landlocked countries—regional trade agreements

The economies of the African countries, with the exception of South Africa, are too small, undeveloped and poor to provide local producers sufficiently large markets to enable them to reach adequate economies of scale for efficient production and profitable investment. Fifteen countries are landlocked and their exports prohibitively costly. In all countries, the road infrastructure is terrible and still deteriorating and all other components of the infrastructure, from power grids to electricity generators, railway systems, and telecommunications, barely function. Given the small scale of their economies, investments of the private sector in local or cross-country infrastructure cannot be profitable and therefore needs the support of the public sector (Table 3.2).

Regional integration will enable producers in the different countries to increase the scale of their production and thus increase also its cost-effectiveness. Regional trade agreements can also give incentives to governments to enhance their collaboration in carrying out joint projects and sharing the costs of cross-country infrastructure projects; for the 15 landlocked countries, agreements with neighboring countries that would give them access to the coast can be particularly beneficial.

Table 3.2 Costs of trade across borders

	Sub-Saharan Africa	East Asia and Pacific	South Asia
Export documents (#)	8.2	6.9	8.1
Time to export (days)	40	23.9	34.4
Cost to export (US$ per container)	1,561	885	1,236
Import documents (#)	12.2	9.3	12.5
Time to import (days)	51.5	25.9	41.5
Cost to import (US$ per container)	1,947	1,037	1,495

Source: World Bank, Doing Business 2007.

Regional cooperation between enterprises in different countries or between countries requires reliable and binding agreements for designing projects, carrying them out, and dividing costs and benefits. A necessary step in that direction is to maintain open economies between countries that will allow free trade and free movement of commodities, so both consumers and producers can benefit from cooperation.

More than 300 preferential and free-trade agreements between subgroups of SSA countries have already been concluded since 1990; by giving incentives for greater integration of national markets into subregional markets and opening their markets to trade, they will also increase the profitability of intraregional trade, spur producers to increase the scale of production and its efficiency, and promote collaborative investments in regional infrastructure.

All SSA countries belong to at least one regional trade agreement, and many are members of several agreements. In principle, Preferential Trade Agreements (PTAs) can bring significant benefits to member states, but, with only a few exceptions—such as the Southern African Customs Union and the West African Economic and Monetary Union—Africa's PTAs have been quite ineffective. Most agreements deal only with tariffs; many agreements are subject to a wide range of exemptions; and concerns about the loss of fiscal revenues led governments to delay the reduction in tariffs and prolong transition periods; and member states that are in several PTAs often found it difficult to fulfill their multiple, and sometimes conflicting, obligations.

As a result, the PTAs between the SSA countries did not contribute much to expanding the share of regional trade relative to their overall trade. In the early 2000s, intracontinental trade was only about 12 percent of the countries' total exports, up from 8 percent a decade earlier (*UN Economic*

Report on Africa 2003). During the initial phase, the PTAs primarily had the effect of diverting trade to member states rather than generating new trade between them, largely because their Most Favored Nation (MFN) tariffs were still relatively high and lower tariffs under the agreement gave incentives to trade diversion by allowing local producers and traders to lower prices to consumers in member states via their trade with each other, rather than searching for more competitive prices in other countries or in the world market. The limited intraregional trade reflects high barriers still maintained by these countries on the trade between member states despite preferential trade agreements.

The reason for the limited impact on trade creation was the similarity in factor endowments that limited potential to diversify the production of different countries. These countries have rather limited incentive to trade, and most do not complement each other in their production and consumption needs. Africa's heavy concentration in commodity trade further hinders intraregional trade and gives these countries fewer opportunities for product differentiation and trade. Over time, the PTAs are likely to augment trade creation by forcing producers in regional markets to produce more efficiently and specialize in production of products in which their natural conditions and resources give them a comparative advantage. The pressures of competition, the economies of scale in production, and the potential limitations on trade will force enterprises to diversify production and engage in more intraregional trade. Both trade creation and trade diversion reduce prices to consumers, but trade creation contributes to increasing efficiency in production, while trade diversion reduces economic efficiency by preventing imports from more efficient producers in the world market.

One problem with Africa's regional trading agreements is the number of overlapping agreements that are often internally inconsistent. These regional agreements (including the Common Market for Eastern and Southern Africa, the Cross-Border Initiative for Eastern and Southern Africa, the Southern African Development Community, and the Southern African Customs Union) may require their member states to meet incompatible and sometimes conflicting obligations, rules, and administrative strategies.

As a result, the complexity of many agreements reduces the gains from regional collaboration and undermines incentives for joint investments. The internal inconsistencies and conflicting regulations in these agreements also hinder the creation of a larger market. Under East African Community (EAC) transition arrangements, for example, Uganda and Tanzania may charge higher tariffs on goods imported from Kenya than they can charge on the same goods when sourced from other member countries of the Common Market for Eastern and Southern Africa (COMESA). Ineffective and uncoordinated regional trade policies and agreements reduce the drive countries need in order to make policy reforms that will open them to regional trade;

instead, they foster preferential treatment of local interests trade liberalization and trade agreements are supposed to dissipate.

Africa-to-Africa trade

It is not only the small size of the African economies, with the exception of South Africa, that reduces the capacity to obtain significant economies of scale in production and keep the gains from regional integration rather limited. Other, perhaps more important, factors are the poor road infrastructure, the multitude of trade barriers, and onerous regulations. The main effect of various administrative trade barriers and high import tariffs is to raise the costs importers must pay as bribes in the border crossing, which in turn raises the price to consumers. It has been estimated that effective trade liberalization within SSA could increase intraregional trade by over 50 percent.

At present, though, intraregional trade in Africa is much smaller than in other regions despite the large number of trade agreements. Lack of sustained political commitment, erratic economic policies, and political instability complicate efforts to extend collaboration between countries and integration of their policies. While the share of intraregional trade in the total exports of African countries is rather small, the large and rapidly growing share of the intraregional trade of East Asian countries is mainly due to the growing share of segments of production that have been outsourced to countries within that region as they have increasingly specialized in production according to their comparative advantage. The segmentation of production and the outsourcing of separate segments to different countries in the region has increased the complementarities and their growing specialization in production.

During the past decade, African countries have recognized the benefits of regional collaboration and intraregional trade as an effect of consolidating subregional markets, increasing efficiency in production, and coordinating their trade policies. The coordination of regional trade policies has become more significant in the multilateral trade negotiations under the WTO and due to the growing significance of regional and interregional trade agreements.

Regional cooperation between African countries to improve their crumbling infrastructure in the areas of transportation, water, electricity, and communications is another example of the mutual benefits of cooperation, which include lowering the costs of these investments and lowering the costs of producers in different countries, facilitating their cooperation, and providing incentives for their integration. The costs to neighboring countries of joint investments in infrastructure can be reduced not by the economies of scale in road, electricity, and water projects, but by avoiding expenses their current borders are enforcing. This, however, is also an obstacle to cooperation as long as countries do not have complete trust in their neighbors. The most obvious examples of the huge potential of multicountry cooperation are large projects such as the West African Pipeline for gas transportation and trade, the Nile Basin Initiative for water resource management, and the Southern African Power Pool that provides electricity to neighboring countries in southern Africa. Peter Watson (2004) argued that the selection of infrastructure projects must be based on economic, not political, considerations. However, the large-scale multicountry projects and several others illustrate the critical impact political considerations have played and will continue to play, both when it comes to cooperation in these projects and to avoiding cooperation due to entrenched suspicions and past rivalries, or even wars.

The longer-term objective of SSA countries is to establish a common market of all countries in the region, which would allow traders and people to move and work freely across borders, establish unified procedures and common institutions for trade and trade policies, and increase competitiveness by enabling producers to benefit from the larger scale and greater specialization in production, and by promoting more diversified production across the subcontinent to increase value-added exports and the competitiveness of producers in world markets. The African Economic Community (AEC) established the foundation for a common market and common procedures and institutions for trade and trade policies of all the SSA countries. The current efforts of the AEC focus on strengthening economic collaboration between African countries in order to reach a free trade agreement and a customs union. In parallel to these efforts, the AEC is trying to reach an agreement on a common monetary policy of a joint central bank that will gradually lead to a monetary union of the entire region.

The progress thus far has been quite limited, however. Even PTAs were only marginally effective and failed to reach most of their goals. Thus, for example, the tariff rates of COMESA member countries decreased from an average rate of 11.3 percent in 1994 to an average rate of 5.5 percent in 2003; during that period, MFN tariff rates were reduced even more than the preferential tariff rates (from 17.9 percentage points in 1994 to 10.2 percentage points in 2003), but these tariffs were on average higher than preferential tariff rates in both 1994 and 2003.

Several factors slowed down the process of achieving greater coordination in regional trade agreements and increasing the share of Africa's intraregional trade: An important inhibiting factor was the failure of countries in some PTAs to ensure their enterprises abide by the rules of the agreement, as well as the failure to implement the agreed reductions in trade barriers; there were also problems with the required adjustments of existing economic ties with countries that are not members of the agreement. For similar reasons African countries did not manage to reach effective agreements on the structure and sharing of costs and the gains of cross-country projects; given the high inequality among countries, these are indeed difficult issues.

In many countries, major factors also included continued dependence on trade taxes as a source of revenues for the governments of member states; lack of sustained political commitment due to erratic economic policies, and political instability.

The potential of south-to-south trade

China, India, and the other emerging economies have had a significant impact on the trade of the SSA countries and, in particular, on prospects to increase their exports of industrial products to the developed countries. This short review concentrates on the impact of China and India, but the effects of most other emerging economies are quite similar. The effects of China and India on the trade of the SSA countries have several dimensions.

First, there has been a considerable increase in exports from SSA countries to China and India. Exports of SSA countries as a proportion of their exports to the industrialized countries rose gradually from only 1.8 percent in 1990 to 5.8 percent in 1997, 8.5 percent in 2001, and 10.5 percent in 2004. These exports consisted mostly of oil, iron ore, diamonds, timber, and cotton. There has been a similar increase in imports of the SSA countries from China and India, mostly in capital goods and cheap consumer goods.

The direct trade links between China and SSA give African countries access to a cheap supply of consumer and capital goods. But these imports have had a negative impact on domestically produced clothing and furniture manufactures in Ghana, South Africa, and other African countries, displaced by imports from China. In Ethiopia, for example, competition from Chinese shoe imports bankrupted 28 percent of local producers and forced 32 percent to downsize their activity (Kaplinsky and Morris 2006).

At the same time, the more important effect of these links is on the exports of SSA countries to the global markets to which China is also exporting, even though in most products they are not competing with each other. Most export products from China are manufactured, and the most significant export of manufactured products from SSA is in clothing and textile. Until the end of 2004, textile and clothing exports from SSA countries benefited from preferences by the United States under the Multi-Fiber Arrangement (MFA). When the MFA ended in January 2005, African garment producers could no longer compete in the US market, and the impact on their industries was devastating, forcing them to reduce production and exports. Their relatively small scale of production, poor infrastructure, and bureaucratic obstacles prevent African clothing producers to compete in the US market with Chinese and Indian producers.

Despite the relatively low educational standards of African workers, a World Bank study showed that on the factory floor, African textile and garment firms are almost as productive as the Chinese; indeed, African workers can clearly be very productive when their skills, however rudimentary, are used effectively. Nevertheless, total factor productivity of

Chinese firms is much higher when all other components of production, including management, purchasing, selling, and other activities of the firm are taken into account, and the total productivity differences can be as high as 10 to 1. As a result, few African textile enterprises managed to be competitive in the export markets, even though they have low-wage workers and the cotton produced in the francophone countries is of high quality and very inexpensive.

The limited experience of Africa's local entrepreneurs, and low productivity that is partly also due to the low skills of local workers, reduces their capacity to develop the manufacturing sector, which was initially built on textiles and apparel. The reduction in local production in manufacturing was damaging not only for the current textile workers who had to be laid off, but also for the capacity to provide employment to migrants from rural areas, who found the prospects of getting employment far more difficult, but were not able to return to their villages where land and water was becoming ever more scarce. Most of the jobs lost in the textile industry employed women, and the impact on their families was severe since their prospects of finding alternative employment were very limited. In the future, African producers could try to occupy niche markets, for example garments with African design, but a considerable decline in production is inevitable for quite some time.

The existing trade-agreements between African countries can, in principle, provide incentives to strengthen the African Economic Community and make progress toward the establishment of an African common market. These measures may also have additional political benefits by contributing over time to stabilization of political relations between countries. Moreover, it has been estimated that effective trade liberalization within SSA could increase intraregional trade by over 50 percent. But while the expected economic gains from regional trade agreements led to their proliferation, since the early 1990s, to more than 300 agreements by the mid-2000s, most of the agreements were formed between neighboring countries.

Africa's most crippling obstacle: decaying infrastructure

For the impoverished rural population in Africa, the main problem is the low productivity of agricultural workers. The major factors in this low productivity include dependence on irregular rainfall that restricts the choice of crops and their yields, and the limited use of fertilizers, even though most fields are infertile due to weathered soils or because they are in mountainous and degraded lands. Jeffrey Sachs has described these factors as major obstacles that affect most farmers in tropical Africa and lock them in a poverty trap by preventing them from increasing their productivity. Their cereal yields are one third or less of the yields in most other developing countries, and they suffer from frequent crop failures due to droughts or floods. Small farmers cannot afford the expenses involved in using more fertilizers. The soil is further depleted by the pressures of a growing population; overfishing is depleting lakes and streams; and in the ocean close to the shores people see their daily catch of fish reduced by foreign competitors.

A study of IFPRI (2006) shows the majority of the rural population concentrates in areas relatively close to the urban centers; in all four countries included in that study, the population in the more remote areas was relatively small, even where the share of cropland in the more remote areas was much larger (Table 3.3). Bigman et al. (2000) showed in a study in Burkina Faso that the incidence of poverty in villages located 6–8 kilometers from the main road is two to three times higher than in villages located 2–3 kilometers from the main road. The poor infrastructure is extremely harmful for the development of local industries that could otherwise take advantage of low labor costs. Presently, the costs of production on top of labor costs, including the costs of electricity, water, and transportation as well as access to the bank, are much higher in Africa than in Asian countries.

Investments in infrastructure can remove the economic isolation of rural areas. Improving communication capacity can include paving all-weather roads, providing wider cellular phone coverage, extending the power grids to rural areas, and extending broadband Internet services through fiber-optic cables and satellite connections. Connecting remote villages to regional and world markets would enable them to increase earnings by selling agricultural produce, or processed goods such as textiles, at higher prices. An analysis of the impact of Africa's poor road infrastructure by Collier and Gunning (1999, pp. 71–72) showed these roads are in much worse condition than the main roads in most other developing countries; thus, for example, the density of the rural road network is only 55 kilometers per thousand square kilometers, compared to over 800 kilometers in India (Table 3.4).

However, African villages or entire regions located far from the urban center or from the main road so far have remained rather isolated and, therefore, have very limited prospects to develop trade or diversify crops. High cross-country transport costs and cumbersome administration also limit trade between neighboring countries, thus isolating many by reducing their potential to export produce and by raising the costs of their imports. The corruption that thrives due to complex administration required for transporting goods abroad always includes demands for "something to eat," but the result is that all people, especially in rural areas, have less to eat, less opportunities to plan better alternatives for their production, and less prospects to gain from specialization or economies of scale.

The poor infrastructure includes erratic access to electricity and safe drinking water, and frequent power failures, common even in large cities. Nevertheless, new communication technologies, primarily the mobile phone and the Internet, are becoming widespread and reduce the isolation

Table 3.3 Distribution of cropland and rural population by market access zones (*in percent*)

Access to towns > 5(1,000 (hours)	Burundi		Eritrea		Ethiopia		Kenya	
	Rural population	Cropland	Rural population	Cropland	Rural population	Cropland	Rural population	Cropland
<2	58	49	38	9	18	16	37	17
2–4	34	39	29	29	31	26	38	25
4–6	8	8	15	34	24	29	19	25
6–8	1	3	10	20	13	17	6	16

Source: IFPRI (Strategic priorities, 2006).

Table 3.4 Infrastructure of personal services in developing countries

	African Countries*	Developing world
Paved roads per person, km	0.01	4.49
Electricity consumption per person, KwH	118.5	1227.9
Public health spending per person, $	6.2	87.5
Public education: pupil-teacher ratio	44.7	27.6

* Ethiopia, Ghana, Kenya Senegal, Tanzania and Uganda.
Source: World Bank, World Development Indicators.

even in rural areas, helping the development of trade, especially within the country. In more remote areas, where farmers are more vulnerable to weather vagaries, droughts and floods, poor infrastructure makes life more risky, since floods can easily cut roads, making it more difficult to deliver emergency food supplies. In 2007, many regions across Africa were hit by floods that, in some places, were the worst in decades. Protracted torrential rains caused widespread and devastating flooding in 14 countries in central Africa, affecting over two million people; thousands of acres of crops were destroyed, and many dams and bridges badly damaged. Air deliveries of food and medications were the only way to bring emergency supplies, and in some places it took more than ten days before help could reach them, while the lack of medicines increased the spread of malaria and waterborne diseases.

The burden of disease is particularly debilitating in Africa's tropical regions, where the population is exposed to lethal diseases, such as malaria and worm infections, that are borne by water or insect vectors. These tropical diseases, especially malaria and other water-borne and insect-borne diseases, are readily preventable and often completely treatable. What the countries in this region need is an effective and timely supply of vital medicines, availability of primary health units in rural areas, and trained health workers. The results can be dramatic by sharply reducing child mortality and upgrading family planning.

Malaria is one of the most devastating diseases in SSA and, despite all efforts, has not yet been controlled. In 2000, a world health conference in Abuja, Nigeria, set a goal that by 2005, 60 percent of African children would sleep under nets. By 2005, only 3 percent were doing so. Wide distribution through the so-called social marketing of mosquito nets at subsidized prices of around $1 for insecticide-impregnated nets that normally cost $5 to $7, with donors underwriting the cost, was hoped to be the answer. However, only part of the subsidized costs reached the poor in the rural areas, and widespread corruption at all stages of the dissemination of nets prevented their distribution. Corruption was not only the domain of local traders; it was later revealed, for example, that the United States Agency for International Development (USAID), which distributes foreign aid, was spending 95 percent of its malaria budget on consultants and only 5 percent on goods like nets, drugs, and insecticide. An Asian medicine, artemisinin, came out a few years ago and proved to be highly effective malaria remedy; however the cost of the medicine, between $5 and $8, was a major obstacle to its widespread use. Many people in rural areas are not able to get medicines cheaply through government health clinics because these clinics are often too far away and there are no passable roads. As a result, up to three quarters of the population still buy malaria medications from private suppliers that have the monopoly and can keep consumer prices high and not pass on subsidies to consumers.

The "resource curse"

The study of Sachs and Warner (1995, 2001) on the impact of the African countries' natural resources on their economies concluded that resource-abundant countries may not benefit from their resources and may even grow at a slower rate than resource-scarce countries. This is due not only to the unfavorable variations in the exchange rate that became known as the *"Dutch Disease."* Many African countries with rich resources of oil and/or other natural resources were infected by a *resource curse*: instead of benefiting from their resources by taking advantage of them to improve their standard of living, they suffered income losses for a variety of reasons. This paradoxical effect is, of course, not the fault of the resources but of the way they are being used—or wasted. Paul Collier pointed to the most notorious reason—simply "greed"—why so many resource-rich African countries are lagging behind in development. This section provides a survey of the various reasons that have been suggested to explain the negative impact resources had on many countries' growths:

- The "Dutch Disease" is the original reason given to explain the resource curse. Countries blessed with natural resources suffered from the Dutch Disease: increase in revenues from natural resources will deindustrialize a nation's economy by increasing the value of the country's exchange rate and thereby making the other sectors less competitive; some also emphasize in this context the negative impact of the public sector's involvement in business interests, although this argument lost much of its force after the financial crisis and, in the African countries, had a positive impact in quite a few countries. The term was coined in 1977 by *The Economist* to describe the decline of the manufacturing sector in The Netherlands after the discovery of a large field of natural gas in 1959.

- Related to the impact of the discovery of natural resources is the impact on the country's comparative advantage. Consider, for example, the Heckscher-Ohlin model that explains the country's comparative advantage and its trade by the relative abundance of labor and capital. Suppose that in a labor abundant country that specializes in the production of labor intensive products, for example, agricultural products, there is a discovery of natural resources in which production is capital intensive. The discovery, production, and export of the high-value resources (that may include large value added of domestic capital) will raise the rate of return on capital products and reduce the relative wage rate on labor. The country as a whole will still gain from this discovery, but only after a change in income distribution that will reduce the relative share of labor and will be a "curse" for workers.
- Countries with natural resources that provide enough income for the government have little pressure to implement disciplined fiscal policy or target their investments in sectors that would later provide fiscal revenues. If it is deemed desirable for political reasons, the government would not have budgetary restrictions to make investments in less profitable sectors. One extreme example is Botswana, which has rich resources of diamonds and recently discovered uranium. Since its independence in 1966, Botswana has had one of the world's highest economic growth rates. Through disciplined fiscal policy and prudent management, Botswana used its diamond resources to transform itself from one of the poorest countries in the world to a middle-income country with a per capita GDP of nearly $15,800 in 2008. The transition was difficult for subsistence farmers and herders because the government stopped all its investments in the agricultural sector and people had difficulties finding alternative employment; as a result, the government must deal with high rates of unemployment and poverty. Unemployment officially was 23.8 percent in 2004, but according to unofficial estimates, it was closer to 40 percent. HIV/AIDS infection rates in Botswana are the second highest in the world and this is both the cause and the effect of the country's high unemployment.

    Botswana is a tiny (but well-known) example, even in Africa's proportions; a more serious claim is that the high revenues of many African countries from the sale or export of their natural resources reduced the dependence of their governments on the taxes imposed in the past on agricultural exports in order to obtain income to finance expenditures. When the government had other, richer sources of income, it lost much of its interest in agriculture and cut its investments in that sector as well as in rural roads; the result was a sharp reduction in the investments of many governments in rural infrastructure and the agricultural sector.
- The factor Paul Collier focused on and termed the "resource curse" is known to economists as "rent-seeking" but, strict and simple, it is sheer greed. The measures taken by leaders to exploit their countries'

resources in order to enrich themselves reduced their incentives to make use of these resources for investment in their economies. It is also typical of these leaders to refuse to adjust their expenditures when the commodity boom that enriched them turns into a bust. Instead of reducing their expenses according to the resources available with the new prices, many continued to spend well beyond their countries' means through excessive borrowing. The combination of poor macroeconomic policies, large fiscal and trade deficits, and the lack of institutions that govern the economy's incomes and expenses, prevented even the oil-rich affluent countries from making significant investments in their economy or to use the country's financial resources to prevent hunger and provide better health care to children. The outcome of this curse was that resource-rich countries tend to grow at a slower rate than resource-scarce countries.

This damaging effect of abundant natural resources with which many African countries have been blessed was, for some, a man-made "curse," and it is not exclusive to countries with rich natural resources, or to countries in Africa. Several empirical studies did not concur with Collier's main conclusions, including Deaton and Miller (1996), who estimated the impact of commodity price fluctuations on African countries, and Raddatz, (2007) who analyzed these effects in a wider sample. Raddatz found that during the period 1965–97 the volatility of low income countries (measured by the standard deviation of output growth) is two-times larger than in high income countries, and the frequency of negative shocks (large *drops* in real GDP) in low-income countries is five times larger than in high-income countries. This larger volatility and prevalence of negative shocks are particularly burdensome for the poor. In a thorough analysis, Raddatz also demonstrated that although external shocks have an economically meaningful effect on real activity, especially when compared with the average economic performance of low-income countries, they account for only a small fraction of the volatility of these countries' real GDP. Thus, he concluded, "from a policy perspective, our results suggest that the emphasis on external shocks as a source of economic instability in low-income countries is probably misplaced."

The problem with a statistical context-specific analysis is that it tends to average out the impact of price fluctuations across countries and time periods. The most striking difference is found between the commodity boom of the 1970s, when spiking oil prices brought huge fortunes to the resource-rich countries (most of it looted by their leaders), and the commodity boom of the 2000s, which varied widely between countries (reflecting the extent and manner of their democratization process), but accelerated the growth of most resource-rich countries. The discussion in subsequent chapters, particularly on the commodity boom and bust in 2008, highlights some of these differences between countries.

The assessment of the curse, which was due to greed, had to be adjusted when these resource-rich countries made the transition to democracy. However, in some countries, these changes did not have positive effects. Collier noted in an interview that even democratic governments, particularly in small countries, that are menaced by threats of coups and rebellions can be entangled in great difficulties and will try to secure their position by increasing their military spending—"buying the coup off." If, on top of this, the regime is corrupt, there may also be efforts to secure the hold on power by rigging elections or changing the constitution. Another negative aspect is inefficient redistribution in return for political support.

But one cannot ignore the growing consensus about the central role of good governance and democracy in meeting Africa's daunting developmental challenges. In quite a few countries, the emerging leadership is moving boldly forward with reforms, improving management capacity, making the government more accountable, and ensuring that institutions are performing more responsibly. In these countries, corruption and other curses of rich resources cannot disappear overnight, but they are noticeably less damaging, and the resources are used for significantly more beneficial aims.

- Abundant resources reduce the need of the government to make effective and carefully planned budgetary decisions since it has ample revenues and thus does not have to adjust expenditures to revenues from taxes that are carefully monitored by the taxpayers. Instead, the governments in these countries often make imprudent and ineffective investments and have little restraint to wasting its revenues.
- Conflicts between tribes in the same country or wars between nations are the worst manifestations of the "resource curse." These aspects of the "resource curse" will be discussed in more detail in Part III. In this section, I will only mention the conflicts that are on the verge of wars: One is between northern and southern Sudan over oil resources, which are mainly in the South. Another is between north and south Niger after the discovery of uranium in the South. The bitterest conflict, and one loaded with tribal hatred, is in Congo. In each of these conflicts, there are also other dimensions, including conflicts between tribes and between religious groups. But the main fuel that ignites these conflicts is competition over the country's resources.

The next chapter deals with the worst and most threatening resource curse in the coming decade: water.

Why have Africa's resources become a "curse"?

The "resource curse," also referred to as the "paradox of the plenty," has been a longstanding theme in both the political sciences and in the economic literature. The paradox that countries with rich natural resources tend to have lower economic growth than countries with fewer natural resources has been explained in several ways, some of them listed above. The finding of Sachs and Warner of a negative correlation between the rise in the price of primary commodities and a country's longer term growth, and the findings of Collier and Goderis that commodity booms give incentives to nonproductive activities, primarily government employment, illustrate the impact of this curse in Africa.

In his book, *Untapped: The Scramble for Africa's Oil*, John Ghazvinian provided details on the pathetic reality in oil-rich African countries where, despite an influx of oil drillers and investment in exploration and production activity during the past decade, most Africans are seeing little benefit from these developments. His analysis shows that between 1970 and 1993, countries that have no oil saw their economies grow four times faster than those countries that have oil. One reason he highlighted is that the governments in the oil-producing countries are not dependent on income taxes and, therefore, have little concern for the needs of their citizens.

Some economists chalk up all of Africa's problems to corruption. Nigeria is the most notorious example: Although most of the country's oil resources are in the Niger Delta, the poor, rural inhabitants there live in utterly miserable conditions. The region is the world's most polluted area due to frequent oil spills and careless practices of the oil companies; the locals are squeezed in stick huts built on little islands in the mangrove swamps, and their schools and hospitals are crumbling due to lack of government support. This enormous gap between the region's riches and the people's poverty contributes to civil unrest and lawlessness; thousands of people are killed each year in guerilla warfare, and the gangs finance themselves by drilling holes in the pipelines to suck out hundreds of thousands of barrels of oil a day, though much of the oil is just spilled and further pollutes the area. Ghazvinian found the same situation in other countries: The booming oil sector is enriching a clique of politically well-connected people, but it is rarely used to provide wider economic benefits or employment for local people. Angola is the second largest oil-producing African country, and its capital city, Luanda, is one of the most expensive cities in Africa for the mostly foreign employees who work in the oil sector and reside in extravagant apartments in the city's luxury high-rises, while the majority of the population lives in extreme poverty. Another example is Gabon, which has been the world's largest importer of champagne per capita.

Political scientists explain the paradox of plenty with the devastating effects of civil conflicts and wars triggered when minority groups or tribes have grievances, like government oppression, marginalization, and often exclusion from government positions as well as gross unfairness in the distribution of the country's resources. Collier's studies of civil conflicts and rebellions led him to conclude that these are not protest movements, but a manifestation of organized crime motivated by *greed*. Collier also found cross-section evidence between the "resource curse" and the curse of bad governance, highlighting the main reason for the "curse":[2] Bad governance, corrupt institutions and self-centered and omnipotent leaders who made even the transition to democracy a transition to "a new law of the jungle of electoral competition...the survival of the fattest." In his book, *The Bottom Billion*, the "resource curse" is listed as one of the four traps that increase poverty.

The different explanations of political scientists and economists for the "resource curse" reflect, in part, the focus of political scientists on the forces that drive the *community*—the tribe, the religious group, or the nation—whereas economists focus on the forces that drive rational *individuals* who seek to enrich themselves.

The resource curse is not a preordained fate, however, and a country need not be cursed with lower rates of growth just because it has rich resources. In my view, this is a stage in the social and political development process of African countries, and countries with more effective institutions have been able to avoid or minimize the impact of this curse. In countries with autocratic and corrupt leaders, where government administration and the institutions of the legal system are subject to their command, and where corruption is the only way for people in these administrations and institutions to survive, the "curse" was unavoidable in all countries. The main difference between resource-rich and resource-poor countries was the volume and value of their embezzlement.

In some countries, the transition to democracy may over time play a more positive role by forcing the democratically elected governments to be more accountable to their parliaments and to restrain corruption. During the commodity boom, there were some encouraging signs in this direction, which were reflected in the more prudent and disciplined economic policies of many African countries compared with the rather reckless policies in the previous commodity booms, particularly in the 1970s (although the pressure of the international development organizations had a significant impact on that discipline). But in all too many African countries, the abundance of natural resources has not been an economic boon. Greed and corruption, wasteful government policies, civil conflicts, and wars made these resources a bane that harmed the development of many resource-rich countries. Abundance of oil, copper, aluminum, uranium, gold, diamonds, and many others resources offers immense wealth to leaders who control these resources, and thus increases competition for leadership positions, encouraging corrupt politicians or army commanders to engage in a bloody race to seize power, and increasing the rivalry between competing clans, tribes, and countries. The wealth many leaders accumulated from these resources (mostly from bribes by the companies that excavated the resources or produced the oil) were also often used to sabotage the transition to democracy through large-scale vote rigging and by allocating money to supporters who falsified the election results and made the transition to democracy in these countries a sham. Box 2.2 describes Nigeria's experience and provides an illustration of the resource curse.

Nigeria's resource curse

With a population of 130 million people, Nigeria is Africa's most populous country, but this population is divided into a huge number of ethnic groups with different tribal structures, leaderships, and heritage, and around 250 languages (Box 3.1). Nigeria is also Africa's largest oil producer and the continent's second most affluent country, behind South Africa. Nigeria's ex-president, Olusegun Obasanjo ,has allied his country closely with the United States in the war on terrorism, and has taken a leading role in efforts to end the civil wars in Liberia and Sierra Leone.

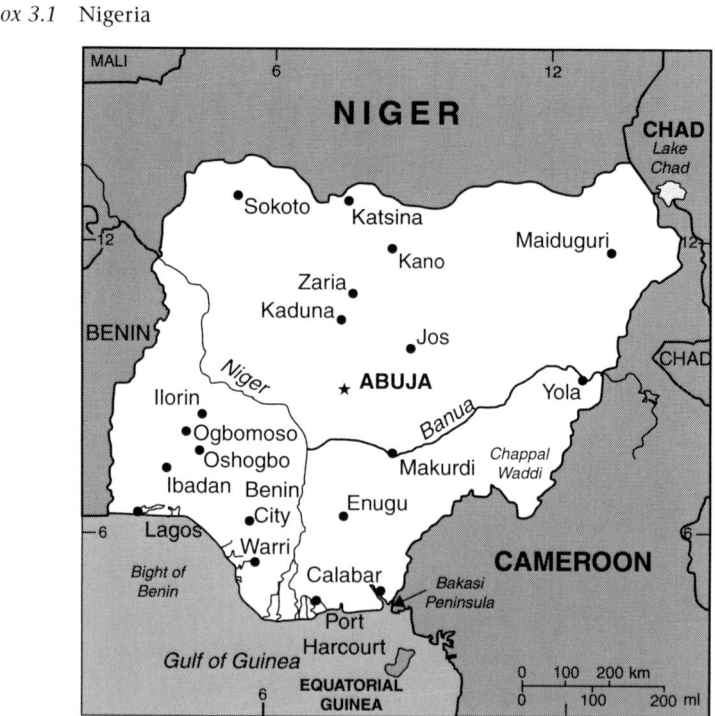

Map 3.1 Nigeria
Source: CIA, The World Factbook (2008)

- Coastal length: 853 km.
- Population: 149 million; Fertility rate: 4.9 children born per woman.
- Population growth rate: 2.0% Infant mortality: 94.35 deaths/1,000 live births.
- Ethnic groups: More than 250 ethnic groups.
- Religious groups: 50% Muslim; 40 Christians; 10% animists.
- Main ethnic groups: Hausa and Fulani 29%, Yoruba 21%.
- Urban population: 48% of total population (2008).
- Rate of urbanization: 3.8%.
- GDP per capita (PPP): US$2,300 (2008).
- Poverty rate: 70% (2008).
- Exports: Petroleum and petroleum products 95%; 2.3 million bbl/day.

In 1999, President Obasanjo initiated a transition to civilian rule and was elected as the country's first president. After decades as a country that since independence knew only military and authoritarian rule, the transition to democracy did not seem to change much and was regarded merely as a different version of despotism. Ethnicity still remained a crucial construct of the power struggle, though Obasanjo made extensive use of favoritism to secure his control, both as head of the army and as president. As president, he was the center of power in the party and could remove candidates at will or could have opponents disqualified or harassed by the legal system. Under the Nigerian system, the president remains the autocratic leader and does not delegate or even share power.

During the three decades until the oil boom in the early 2000s, the country's stagnation deepened due to irresponsible fiscal deficits, poor macroeconomic policy, the lack of any effort to establish proper governance, and widespread corruption among government officials and at all levels of the military and police. The oil boom until mid-2008 brought a massive flow of wealth to the country, and the transition to democracy in 1999 enforced some restrictions on the trickle out of funds to "Swiss accounts." However, standards of accountability introduced during these years relied more on shame than on the rule of law as the main deterrent. In that decade Nigeria had, however, high revenues and ample resources that could be invested in the economy.

With its huge oil resources, and to a large degree as a result of these resources, Nigeria has become Africa's epitome of corruption. After the oil boom of the 1970s, and despite the sharp fall in oil prices since then, during the following decades the country's leaders continued to amass huge wealth that they deposited in foreign bank accounts. Most of the oil revenues were wasted by the country's leaders and military commanders to build a massive but largely ineffective military force. Since a large share of these revenues "trickled out" and a large share was spent on the military expenditures, ordinary Nigerians benefited very little from the country's rich resources, and only a tiny fraction trickled down to the rural areas. Nigeria endured three decades of economic stagnation, deteriorating public services and institutions, and rising poverty.

In a recent book entitled *Crude World: The Violent Twilight of Oil* (2009), Peter Haass emphasized that in the oil-rich countries, the leaders and their governments are not the only villains. The worst in this list are the oil companies that bribe the dictators and government officials while extracting most of the revenues. Despite mammoth exports of over 2 million barrels of oil and net revenues of nearly half a billion dollars, even before the commodity boom, 70 percent of the population live in extreme poverty, nine out of 10 Nigerians live on less than $2 a day, infant mortality is nearly 10 percent, and 20 percent of children die before their fifth birthday. At the same time, the World Bank estimates that some 80 percent of Nigeria's oil wealth goes to 1 percent of its population.

According to World Bank Governance and Anti-Corruption indicators, Nigeria was ranked 133 out of the 175 countries included in the study. Among the 75 countries at the bottom of the list, Nigeria had a higher than average value of the index of governance for its economic policies (4.3 compare to an average of 3.5 for the countries in this group), but slightly lower than the average value of the index for its social policies (3.2 compared with an average value of 3.3), particularly in its social protection and labor laws (3.0 compared with an average of 3.5), and lower value for protection of property rights and rule-based governance (2.5 compared with an average of 2.9). In the latter category, Nigeria had the same value of the index as Eritrea, Comoros, Guinea-Bissau, and Togo.

After amassing huge wealth from its oil exports, Nigeria paid in April 2006 the last installment on the $30 billion it owed the Paris Club of donor countries as well as most of its other debts—according to the Paris Club's concessionary terms for restructuring poor countries' external debts. Amazingly, in 2005–06, when Nigeria concluded the buyback of its debts, it was entitled, according to the rules of the Paris Club, to a shocking $18 billion write-off, even though it was flooded with oil revenues. In addition to the disgrace of these concessions to a rich country like Nigeria, the mere fact that, with all its wealth Nigeria was entitled to receive rescue aid through trade credits, which was part of the IMF reform program for poor countries, raises questions about the criteria used in these programs.

Oil was a curse for Nigeria also because of its damaging effect on the environment. In the country's most fertile region, the Niger Delta, the damage caused by oil spills, frequent fires and careless work practices of the oil companies, made the Niger Delta one of the most contaminated regions in the world. Nevertheless, the hundreds of thousands of people who live in this region and grow food crops on their farms are subject to constant health hazards that affect also the people who buy and eat this food.

Obasanjo was re-elected in the subsequent elections in 2003. Nigeria's constitution limits a president to two terms, and accepting this term limit became his most difficult test. Nigeria is not the only African country in which an autocratic leader saw no need to abide by any constitutional law or any other rules that limit his authority. At the same time, Obasanjo himself had initiated the transition to democracy and therefore felt greater pressure to abide by its rules. During his second term (2003–07), President Obasanjo implemented comprehensive economic reforms that included fiscal, structural, institutional, and governance reforms. Obasanjo even launched an anticorruption campaign that implemented an Extractive Industries Transparency Initiative. This initiative, which consists of a set of standards to promote revenue transparency and accountability, had been adopted in 2002 at the Johannesburg World Summit for Sustainable Development. At the end of his second term, supporters of Obasanjo attempted to push through a constitutional amendment that would enable him to serve a third term, but there was a peaceful transfer of power to his protégé Umaru Yar'Adua, one of the country's governors.

The 2007 election represented a true test of the strength of Nigeria's democratic system, and its ability to manage a successful electoral transition, which would have been the first in its history. The previous two elections were marred by serious irregularities, and there were few systemic improvements since then. Therefore, the elections in 2007 did not have credibility, nor the support of significant parts of the population, whose alienation sparked tremendous unrest.

Nigeria is almost evenly divided between Muslims and Christians, and the political tension between them during the 2007 elections was almost explosive. Since Obasanjo is a born-again Christian, there were suspicions among northern Muslims that, perhaps with American encouragement, he would seek to change the constitution and run again or extend his term. However, an attempt to formally ignore and effectively violate the constitution met with a strong backlash from the media, the public, the international community, and even Obasanjo's own party, the People's Democratic Party (PDP), and the amendment was voted down in the Nigerian Senate.

The country's resources and the steep rise in oil resources enabled the Nigerian government implement more balanced macroeconomic policy that constrained spending by transferring oil revenues to the budget in accordance with a reference price, and by imposing a ceiling on the non-oil deficit. At the conclusion of Obasanjo's term and in the 2007 election, the newly elected President Umaru Yar'Adua signed the Fiscal Responsibility Bill that imposed the oil–price-based fiscal rule into law and intensified the battle to improve transparency and tackle corruption, signaling Nigeria's determination to make a clean break with the past by fighting corruption and improving governance. Presidents Obasanjo and Yar'Adua undertook these initiatives in order to boost the country's credibility among donors, financial institutes, and investment companies, which led to sizable increases in foreign direct investment in both the oil and the non-oil sectors. The transition to democracy was also largely aimed at gaining recognition by the international community and particularly the business community.

Although President Yar'Adua himself is not deemed to be personally corrupt, the Economic and Financial Crimes Commission (EFCC), an anticorruption body, has lost its deterrent power under him, and government officials who took a courageous stand against corruption were relieved from their jobs. More recent efforts of President Yar'Adua were aimed at cleaning up the country's financial institutions and many of the country's top financial systems. Gradually, these measures helped reduce the country's corruption and gain greater credibility among foreign investors.

There was considerable resistance to these measures within the government, in government ministries, and in the civil administration. In the oil-rich Delta region, civil strife worsened, and many young men who had given up all hope of finding work joined an insurgency, kidnapping and stealing oil to earn a living. The "resource curse" of Nigeria and most other resource-rich countries was because governance is weak, institutions barely function, and corruption spreads as more money accumulates (Box 3.2). As *The Economist* concluded (Oct. 8, 2008), "Accountability, openness and democracy seem to have diminished in proportion to the increase in oil money flowing into the states' coffers."

Box 3.2 Oil wealth in Nigeria leaves the majority behind

In 2008, with oil prices at record highs and government coffers in Nigeria swollen to extremely high levels, the vast majority of Nigeria's 140 million people lived in no better conditions than their neighbors in West Africa, which is the least developed region in Africa.

In Lagos, a megacity of around 10 million people, the majority of the population lives in slums without water or electricity. Healthcare is virtually nonexistent, the roads are potholed, unemployment and crime are on the rise, and Nigeria suffered from spiraling food prices. Large regions did not have electricity for weeks at a time, and hundreds of factories were forced to close down and to slash millions of jobs. Former President Obasanjo spent $10 billion on the electricity sector during his years in power without raising by much its capacity, which plunged in 2008 to less than 1,000 mW from 3,000 mW in 2007, largely due to the lack of proper maintenance at the power stations; a parliamentary probe showed that millions of dollars had been paid to nonexistent companies.

(*Source*: Based on reports from the *International Herald Tribune*, July 21, 2008)

But the experience of the 1970s offered, nonetheless, an important lesson that just as oil prices rise, they are also likely to fall, sometimes even faster. This indeed is what happened in mid-2008: The heavy dependence of Nigeria on its oil revenues—which accounted in 2007 for more than 95 percent of its exports, 85 percent of government revenues and 52 percent of the GDP—was also a warning not to mismanage the economy recklessly, as had been done in the 1980s; even during the price boom, it is necessary to prepare a contingency plan for the event that oil prices fall.

One reason for the reluctance to criticize Nigeria in various meetings of world leaders was the sectarian rivalries. When democracy was restored in 1999, most northern Muslim states introduced *sharia* law, forcing tens of thousands of local Christians to migrate to the southern states. In the urban centers and border states that have mixed Christian and Muslim populations, it has become increasingly more difficult to live peacefully alongside each other. Frequent tensions and violent confrontations that left thousands dead have been particularly common in the so-called "middle belt" between Nigeria's largely Muslim North and the predominantly Christian South, and clashes there were readily inflamed by fierce animosities between various religious groups.

Despite all these obstacles, elections were held in Nigeria on three occasions and people are accepting them as a necessary norm for good governance. There are still problems in the elections, largely due to urban violence and sectarian confiicts. Even local elections raise tensions, since local officials wield enormous power in Nigeria due to their control over a wide variety of budgetary and administrative decisions that determine the fate and fortune of individuals, businessmen, and politicians. The names of the rival parties in recent local elections in Jos, the largest town in the region, are testimony to the prevalent hypocrisy: The ruling Christian party is called *The People's Democratic Party*, and the local Muslim party is the *All Nigeria People's Party*. In practice, local politicians from all parties openly support criminal syndicates that conduct the "election campaign" for them, and the politicians handsomely reward them.

3.2
The Demographic and Social Changes and the Urbanization of Poverty

The African rural development is handicapped by low population density, long distances between most rural villages, and poor rural infrastructure. The average population density on the continent (77 people per square kilometer) is among the lowest in the world. Africa is still the world's least urbanized continent and only one third of the population live in urban areas; according to the UN's *World Urbanization Prospects*, low density and poor infrastructure are among the main reasons for the slow rural development.

In most developing countries, accelerated urbanization and large-scale rural–urban migration started only in the second half of the twentieth century, driven by large investments to develop local industries. The Green Revolution and rising productivity and income in the rural areas slowed down this process, but it continued and accelerated due to the development of labor-intensive industries, primarily textile and garment production. The new industries also benefited from the agglomeration and concentration of industries in the urban centers, and from declining transport and communication costs.

The growing congestion in urban centers increased crime, health problems, and pollution. This all widened the income gap between urban and rural areas, between regions where industries concentrated and regions that remained mostly rural, and between people in urban areas. Industrial complexes concentrated in the existing urban centers, close to the main ports and highways and in regions that have rich resources; all too often, deliberate and highly biased government policies that favored certain regions also had an important impact.

Rural–urban migration and growing urban population

The exploding population in many African cities has been termed by the UN human settlements agency, UN-Habitat, as "premature urbanization," because industrial development is meager and cannot offer employment to new migrants. The 2007 report of UNFPA, *The State of World Population 2007: Unleashing the Potential of Urban Growth*, estimates that by the end of this decade, more than half the world's population will live in cities and towns, but in the least developed countries the rural inhabitants will still constitute the majority of the population until 2030 (Figure 3.1)

According to the UN report on the *World Urbanization Prospects* (2007), the rural population in many African countries will be forced by changing climatic conditions to migrate either to other rural areas or to urban centers in search of employment and income. With a rural population of nearly 600 million people, Africa has 17.5 percent of the world's rural population, and currently about 38 percent of the continent's population live in urban areas. By 2050, Africa's rural population is expected to increase by 30 percent and reach nearly 800 million, or 27 percent of the world's rural population. A growing share of the rural population will have to move, however, to off- or non-farm livelihoods, either permanently or in certain seasons. The continent has an urbanization rate two times higher than that seen during the West's Industrial Revolution. As mentioned previously, in West Africa by 2020 the entire coastline between Accra and the Niger Delta will become a continuous urban megalopolis.

By 2030, Africa is predicted to be an urban continent (Figure 3.2), and 70 percent of the people will live in slums without basic services, such as access to water, housing, sanitation, education, or healthcare. This is not just an African problem: An estimated one billion people in Latin America, Asia, and Africa live in slums not legally recognized, and do

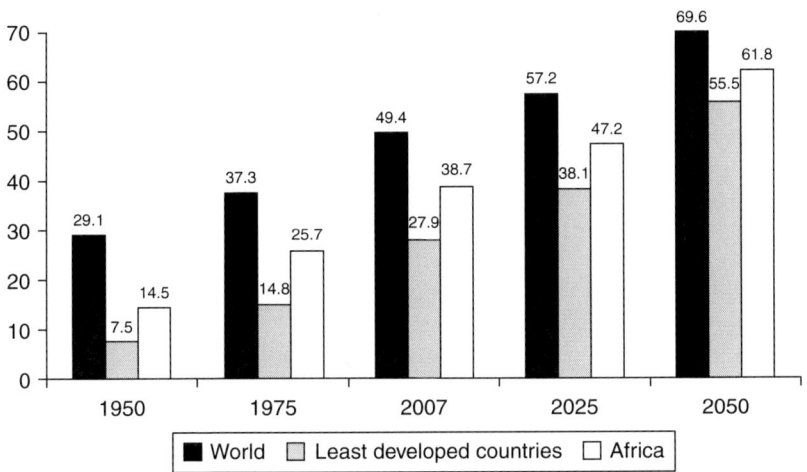

Figure 3.1 The increase in urbanization: 1950–2050

Source: World Urbanization Prospects: The 2007 Revision, United Nations.

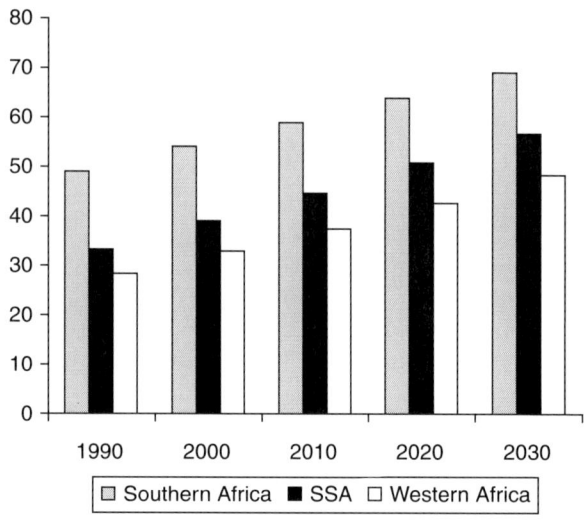

Figure 3.2. The rate of urbanization in SSA (percent of the urban population)
Source: World Urbanization Prospects: The 2007 Revision.

not receive any public services (Table 3.5). In one of the early models of rural–urban migration, Harris and Todaro (1970) provided a thorough explanation of the process often observed in developing countries: Despite high levels of unemployment in urban areas, a large number of people continue to flow to cities. Many newcomers may initially remain unemployed or find work only in the informal sector and barely manage to scrape out a meager existence. In their analysis, however, they expect most of the migrants to find work after some time. In Sub-Saharan Africa, despite its highest rate of rural–urban migration, people who leave their villages and migrate to the cities are usually well aware of the very limited opportunities they can expect. The industrial revolution has basically failed to take hold in SSA, but the threat of hunger is forcing these people to seek refuge in cities, although the prospects there are hardly enticing.

The estimated number of refugees and migrants in Africa varies between 20 and 50 million, depending on the vagaries of the weather, internal conflicts, and wars. In recent years, large numbers of refugees and migrants have fled from, among other countries, Somalia, Eritrea, Ethiopia, Ghana, Senegal, Cape Verde, Liberia, Sierra Leone, Mali, Gambia, and Chad. Recent data show a clear slowdown in the flow of what can be termed "economic refugees," but more migrants are lured by the more rapid economic growth in some African countries, even though they find it harder to cross the borders.

Table 3.5 Demographic trends in the world and in SSA: 1950–2050

	Population in urban areas (millions)					Rate of urban population change (percentage)			
	1950	1975	2007	2025	2050	1950–1975	1975–2007	2007–2025	2025–2050
World	1,798	2,558	3,377	3,426	2,793	1.4	0.9	0.1	-0.8
Least developed countries	185	305	580	734	775	2.0	2.0	1.3	0.2
Africa	192	309	592	736	764	1.9	2.0	1.2	0.1

	Population in urban areas (millions)					Rate of urban population change (percentage)			
World	737	1,519	3,294	4,584	5,398	2.9	2.4	1.8	1.3
Least developed countries	15	53	225	452	967	5.0	4.5	3.9	3.0
Africa	33	107	658	658	1,234	4.8	3.9	3.1	2.5

	Percentage of the population in urban areas					Rate of urbanization (percentage)			
World	29.1	37.3	49.4	57.2	69.6	1.0	0.9	0.8	0.8
Least developed countries	7.5	14.8	27.9	38.1	55.5	2.7	2.0	1.7	1.5
Africa	14.5	25.7	38.7	47.2	61.8	2.3	1.3	1.1	1.1

Source: UN World Urbanization Prospects: The 2007 Revision.

The urbanization of poverty

The large flow of migrants to urban centers will create another, even more ominous, danger: The urbanization of poverty. Thus far, poverty in Africa has mainly been a rural phenomenon and in the early 1990s about three quarters of the African poor concentrated in rural areas. Therefore, most development efforts in Africa concentrated on agricultural development.

Rapid urbanization and high unemployment among new migrants, who make up nearly 70 percent of the population in the largest urban centers, is changing the social composition of the urban population. While rural poverty remains high and is likely to continue rising, Africa will become an urban continent within less than two decades, and the majority of the urban population will be unemployed, dismally poor, and forced to live in debilitating shantytowns that do not qualify as human habitat (Table 3.6).

In a carefully planned study, Ravallion, Chen, and Sangraula (2007) used data from over 200 household surveys in 90 countries to estimate the extent to which poverty has been urbanized in developing countries, taking into account the higher cost of living in urban areas in each of the countries. Their conclusions clearly show urban poverty rates are growing rapidly in Africa, and the rapid rise of the urban population is twice the rate of growth of the rural population. By the end of this decade, nearly half the urban population will be poor.

According to their estimates (Tables 3.6 and 3.7), the number of rural poor increased by 10 percent from 1993 to 2002, while the number of urban poor increased by nearly 35 percent. During these years, the incidence of rural poverty *declined* by 5 percent, while the incidence of urban poverty rose slightly; the share of the urban population in the total population increased by around 15 percent, while the share of the urban poor in the continent's total poor population increased by nearly 25 percent. These estimates are based on a survey from 2002. During the five years from 2002 until the

Table 3.6 Urban and rural poverty in SSA (Poverty line is US$1 a day in1993 international purchasing power parity)

Number of Poor (millions)			Percent below the Poverty Line			Urban share in the poor	Urban share in the population
Urban	Rural	Total	Urban	Rural	Total		
1993							
66	207	273	40.2	53.1	49.2	24.3	29.8
2002							
99	229	328	40.4	50.9	47.2	30.2	35.2

Source: Ravallion et al. (2007).

onset of the food crisis, the rural population in most African countries gained from the higher food prices, while the urban population incurred higher losses. The crisis years 2007–09 were far more devastating for the urban population, which suffered more from the sharp rise in food prices. While these are only preliminary indicators, they suggest urban poverty has worsened.

Paradoxically, however, public investment will still have a larger and more rapid impact on poverty if invested in rural areas because of the lower costs required to reduce poverty there. These investments typically concentrate on raising the productivity of farmers by subsidizing the costs of improved seeds and fertilizers, and helping farmers diversify crops. In urban centers, any initiative to provide employment to unemployed poor migrants must start with a plan to build an industrial base and gradually bring the Industrial Revolution to African countries. Even though some industries could have a considerable advantage in Africa due to cheap labor costs and rich resources, setting them up requires basic infrastructure, from the supply of electricity and water, to access roads and much more to attract private entrepreneurs.

For the more daring individuals, migration to urban centers is only a transition stage in a search for better life in other, more affluent countries. The efforts the better-off countries are making to close their borders and prevent illegal migration from poor countries, demonstrates the potential danger of this migration for them. As migration is increasing, more poor people are willing to take great risks, trying to cross the Mediterranean on dangerous rafts and climbing high walls in order to cross a border to the "promised lands," where employment and better living conditions are possible.

The dilemma: promoting urban industrialization or alleviating rural poverty

Until the 1970s, both SSA and the developing East Asian countries were primarily rural and the majority of their population lived on agriculture. After World War II, a few East Asian countries, initially Japan and later (in the 1950's) the four "Tigers"—Korea, Taiwan, Hong Kong, and Singapore—started an industrialization process. These countries, followed in the 1970s by most other East Asian countries, started their growth process with massive investments to build a solid industrial base. Tight central government controls on the economy enabled these countries to narrowly target the allocation of resources on the new industries, on infrastructure, as well as on public services in health and education that were provided to the entire population.

In the initial stages of their industrialization, the Asian countries developed textile and apparel industries that took advantage of their abundance of unskilled cheap labor to develop these highly labor-intensive industries and could, thus, provide employment to the many workers who converged in the urban centers to form the basis for the development of these industries. The abundance of unskilled labor due to the waves of migrant workers from the rural areas, and their low wages, gave Asian countries considerable advantage over the traditional textile producers in Europe and the United States.

Despite the efforts of donor countries to help the African countries in developing local industries by granting African exporters "special and differential treatment," their industries did not take off, and during the 1990s most production migrated to China, India, Pakistan, and Bangladesh, where the *overall* production costs are lower. Although the francophone African countries produce cheap, high-quality cotton, they could not develop a competitive textile industry, so they ship their cotton to Asia. The development of an effective industrial base and solid infrastructure enabled the Asian countries to gradually move to more advanced industries and benefit from economies of scale that enabled them to further lower their costs and increase the effectiveness of institutions that deal with trade.

Even a "big push" of large investments in infrastructure may not suffice to enable African producers to compete with Asian producers, where labor costs are still low. Although labor costs in Africa are lower than in China or even India, the Asian countries have several other key advantages that make their overall production costs much lower and their value-added much higher. Among the most damaging obstacles to local industries in Africa are the unstable and inefficient public institutions, and the unbridled corruption that increase the risks of investments in local industries and deter foreign investors.

The obstacles to Africa's competitiveness

As mentioned previously, the World Bank's report *Doing Business 2007: How to Reform* ranking 175 countries according to the ease of doing business; estimated the average rank of an SSA country as 131 (see Table 4.3 in the next chapter). In practically all the SSA countries, the public institutions create obstacles on private sector activities through cumbersome process of licensing, various and largely unnecessary regulations employment, limited availability of credit, and various other costly and time consuming obstacles that are piled up mostly by public institutions. As a result of these obstacles and endemic corruption, investments in local manufacturing remain low.

Despite the many African economic problems, the accelerated growth of the past decade and the continent's rich resources have made South Africa an important source of investments in some African countries, and investments from China are also picking up. The World Bank's investment climate survey also found that some African countries have begun to reform their business regulations, and according to this survey, two thirds of the African countries made at least one positive reform in 2005–06. Tanzania and Ghana ranked among the top ten reformers in the world, and plans for reforms in other countries would reduce business costs throughout the region. The investment climate is also influenced by the very high business tax rates in Africa, by far higher than in all other world regions, driving companies to the informal sector and thus reducing overall tax receipts. The other way to avoid these practically impossible taxes is with bribes to the officials in charge.

Corruption prevails at all levels of government, from low-level bureaucrats who depend on bribes for their survival, to politicians and ministers who often sign false contracts with government suppliers. Foreign investors, especially in Africa's oil industry, often pay high bribes to politicians to win contracts or the rights to pump. The large oil exporters—Chad, Sudan, Nigeria, Equatorial Guinea, Gambia and Angola—are the most corrupt in Africa, and many local industries are dominated by Western oil firms. In recent years, the public has become increasingly wary of that corruption: In Kenya, the public voted in 2002 to remove the longstanding and corrupt regime of Daniel arap Moi; in 2006, when evidence of high-level corruption of the new government came out, reports that described the corruption at the highest levels of government forced the finance minister to resign. When new evidence of high-level corruption was uncovered after elections in December 2007, a wave of violence and massive street demonstrations erupted and forced the president to resign. Even in South Africa, President Thabo Mbeki sacked his deputy for corruption in 2005, and in 2007, Mbeki himself was forced to resign.

The *Global Competitiveness Report*s of the World Economic Forum provide important assessments of countries' competitiveness and growth potential by examining the main factors that enable national economies to achieve sustained economic growth. The competitiveness analysis is based on the Report's Global Competitiveness Index (GCI), which captures the basic microeconomic and macroeconomic characteristics that determine the level of productivity of a country. The productivity level determines, in turn, the level of income people in these countries can earn and the rates of return to investments, the economy's *growth potential*. In addition to investments in physical capital and infrastructure, the country's growth potential is also determined by its investments in human capital, with education and training. Equally important are macroeconomic stability, good governance, the rule of law, and transparency and functioning of public institutions.

In the report of 2007–08, 19 of the 24 countries from Sub-Saharan Africa included in the survey were ranked among the 25 weakest performers, including Angola, Burkina Faso, Burundi, Cameroon, Lesotho, Mauritania, and Zambia. In Nigeria, the analysis shows weak and deteriorating institutions—including serious security problems. The country also had low ranks in infrastructure, basic health, and education, and the report highlighted a very significant change for the worse in macroeconomic management. Despite the country's huge revenues from record-high oil prices, the large majority of the population remains very poor and without access to basic health care and education. Tanzania and Uganda, two of the region's larger economies, have not improved their competitiveness and had low overall rankings, even lower ranking in health and primary education that are likely to continue to limit their growth prospects.

The financial sector in African countries is the Achilles heel of the private sector: In the 1990s, the financial sectors suffered from chronically weak banks (most of them publicly owned), inadequate interest-rate controls, high government-directed lending rates, and weak compliance with international financial standards. Many of these impediments have been corrected in recent years, but on standard indicators of financial depth African countries still lag far behind other developing countries. For example, bank deposits as a share of GDP in the low-income African countries are half the level of other developing regions, in part because Africans do not have much trust in the banking system and prefer to be more cash (or dollar) intensive. Quite a few African banks still persistently violate international banking regulations, especially those that pertain to diversification of risk. Interest rates on loans are very high, in part because banks are reluctant to expand their domestic lending portfolios and prefer instead to accumulate substantial holdings of bonds, loans to large corporations, and foreign assets, despite their low returns due to their much lower risks. It should be noted, though, that for these reasons African banks floated on the wave of the global financial crisis without much damage. In rural areas the coverage of the formal banking sector is extremely poor; in recent years, informal financial institutes have been cautiously expanding, but their interest rates are very high.

Public institutions are also very weak: More than any other region, Africa is handicapped by its inability to implement economic policies due to weak public institutions. Any future effort to support these countries' development must therefore focus on strengthening its institutions by providing training and technical assistance to build local capacity, tightening supervision, and establishing a reliable process of auditing. The IMF has contributed to this effort by establishing regional technical assistance centers (AFRITACS).

A broad definition of economic institutions refers to the set of laws, rules, and other practices that govern property rights, secure law and order, and protect people's safety. Bad economic institutions fail to secure property rights for most people, prevent arbitrary and illegal expropriation by the state, fail to enforce contracts and prevent corruption. A *"failed state"* is one with bad economic institutions and also one that fails to secure human rights, freedom of speech, equality before the law, and other laws of the country's constitution.

According to Hernando de Soto (2000), one reason the weak, inefficient and corrupt public institutions are so highly damaging is due to the obstacles they place on obtaining formal, officially registered rights of ownership of the assets poor people own. The inefficient and corrupt organization of property rights deprives poor people of their legal ownership of their assets and, in the absence of these legal instruments, a poor person cannot sell, exchange, bequeath or lend his assets, nor use assets as collateral for a loan. As a result, these assets cannot be used for savings or an accumulation of capital. They become, in de Soto's words, "dead capital."

Doing business in Africa

Table 3.7 provides another perspective of the results presented earlier from the World Bank study of the *Ease of Doing Business*. In this analysis the emphasis is on one component that affects the competitiveness of African industries: The costs of starting a business. These costs include an evaluation of the bureaucratic and legal hurdles entrepreneurs must overcome to register a new firm, including the number of procedures, the time, and the cost involved in launching a commercial or industrial firm with up to 50 employees, and the required start-up capital.

The following quote from an article published in the *NYT* provides a vivid description of obstacles a textile manufacturer has to cope with in Kano, Nigeria, a region once a vibrant manufacturing center:

> I was forced to shut down because I couldn't pay for private generator power to spin the knitters and pump water. Here, each household must

Table 3.7 The costs of starting a business

Region	Procedures (number)	Duration (days)	Cost (% GNI per capita)	Paid in Min. Capital (% of GNI per capita)
East Asia & Pacific	8.6	44.2	32.3	37.3
Eastern Europe & Central Asia	7.7	22.6	8.6	36.0
Latin America & Caribbean	9.7	64.5	39.1	3.4
Middle East & North Africa	8.4	23.5	41.0	331.4
OECD	5.8	13.4	4.9	19.7
South Asia	7.4	32.5	31.9	0.6
Sub-Saharan Africa	10.2	47.8	111.2	173.4

Source: Doing a Business, The World Bank.

have its own power and water company, since the electric company provides light just a few hours a day. I was thus unable to compete with cheap imports flooding the country in the wake of trade liberalization. The country's dilapidated condition lay with its leaders and corrupt officials. We are not a poor country: we have oil, we have resources. But it is the management of those resources that has been lacking. (Nicholas Kristof, NYT, April, 24, 07)

In a paper by Sachs et al. (2003), the authors argued that Africa's "development challenges" could be overcome once the problems were properly understood: "The standard diagnosis of Sub-Saharan Africa is that it is suffering from a governance crisis. This is too simplistic. Many parts of Africa are well governed considering the income levels and extent of poverty, yet are caught in a poverty trap" (p. 121). The approach suggested in the paper envisaged "a big push in public investments to overcome the high transport costs, the small markets, the low productivity in agriculture, the adverse agroclimatic conditions, the high disease burden, and the slow diffusion of technology from abroad" (Ibid, p.121). Attractive as this solution may sound due to its relative simplicity; it does not square with the diagnoses of other studies on conditions in SSA, most notably with the studies of Easterly on the large sums siphoned off by corruption in ineffective government institutions.

Improvements in the business climate are essential and can be made only by the public sector. Nevertheless, indicators of the business climate and governance in most African countries have shown little improvement during the past decade, in part due to civil conflicts and wars. Progress in the dismantling of regulatory barriers that impede the diffusion of new technologies in the urban and rural sectors has also been slow. Restrictions on labor mobility between countries, and regulations aimed to protect local workers, create additional barriers for foreign corporations that want to employ their own skilled workers in certain tasks.

The limited effectiveness of contract enforcement and the high level of corruption also deter foreign investors. Necessary conditions for domestic and foreign investments in new technologies require the public sector to strengthen the regulatory framework, enforce law and order, secure property rights, and establish effective regulations and supervision of financial markets. Some SSA countries, including Ghana and Senegal, have made considerable progress in that direction, but in the majority the business environment still deters foreign investors.

Introducing new technologies

Technological progress also requires improvements in the quality of the labor force beyond the formal education systems. Joint training programs with private enterprise can make an important contribution to raising productivity, facilitating the adoption of more advanced technologies, and increasing the technology spillover from Foreign Direct Investments (FDI). Although most new technologies have been transferred from the developed countries, it is still necessary to also develop local R&D in order to adjust these technologies to local conditions to ensure their successful adoption by local producers.

Open trade policies played an important role in promoting technological progress in countries that developed an industrial sector and managed to attract foreign investors. By exposing local industries to foreign technologies and attracting foreign investors that brought advanced methods of production and the necessary machinery, these countries accelerated their technological progress. The capacity to absorb new technologies varied widely between countries, however, in large measure due to the quality of the local labor force, the availability of skilled workers, and the many formal and informal regulations that often suffocate local industries.

Some countries built industrial parks, designed by and for foreign manufacturers, which provided better services and infrastructure. These parks were mainly designed for large-scale industries, whereas small and medium-size enterprises are spread throughout the country and use simpler industries that do not require skilled workers or extensive training. Many of these industries work in the informal economy in order to avoid government regulations.

In the rural sector, investments were aimed at acquiring simple tools to help farmers in adopting more advanced cultivation methods, constructing rainwater collection systems that improve access to clean drinking water, and so forth. Government support to facilitate the adoption of these methods was necessary to support the dissemination channels, provide credit or financial assistance, and support local R&D to adjust methods to local conditions. Government support is equally important in building local infrastructure, primarily roads and electricity that are particularly essential in more remote regions. Africa's poor infrastructure is perhaps the main reason why Green Revolution methods were not adopted by local farmers and why the textile industry failed to compete with the East Asian textile producers.

The World Bank survey *Doing Business* (2005) noted the business environment in Africa is influenced by the nexus of policies, institutions, and physical constraints that come on top of spatial obstacles. Poor and erratic policies, unstable regimes, and weak private and public institutions are the main constraints (Eifert and Ramachandran 2004). In addition, African firms incur heavy costs for transport, logistics, telecom, water, electricity, buildings, marketing, accounting, security, bribes, and so forth, which make their doing business nearly impossible.

The proliferation of trade agreements in Africa, and the longer dream of consolidating these agreements to a continent-wide trade agreement within the framework of New Partnership for Africa's Development (NEPAD), offers new possibilities for investors—possibilities that also may benefit plans to develop export processing zones (EPZs) that are institutionally exterritorial and, thus, much less affected by the low efficiency of local institutions, and which can benefit also from better supporting services and from the preferences regional trade agreements and developed countries would give to local producers.

Using Africa's resources to develop new industries

Another, perhaps more promising, direction for the development of local industries in SSA is based on their comparative advantage due to local resources, including oil, minerals, and agricultural products, in addition to cheap labor. These industries can increase the value-added and their revenues from their exports. However, they require considerable investment since they are usually highly capital-intensive, and they also require skilled labor. Moreover, these industries would have to use imported technologies and thus require the participation of foreign investors. Although these industries may not contribute much to increasing local employment, they can attract foreign investors and create the basis for the development of local industry.

Local agricultural products also offer advantages for the development of local industries, ranging from processing of tropical fruits and vegetables in high demand in developed countries to the production from sugar cane of ethanol, a biofuel product that has become all the rage for industrial development. The development of local industries based on agricultural products also seems an effective way of promoting the development of rural areas and increasing the income of the rural population. The poor road infrastructure, however, creates high and, in some areas, insurmountable obstacles, and the wave of young migrants to the urban centers empties the villages of their productive workers.

The allocation of resources for development presents a difficult dilemma regarding the selection of industries in which the country can have a comparative advantage and to which more benefits and subsidies should be given at the infancy stage; the regions that should be given more government support; and the division of resources between regions, industries, and between urban and rural development.

The promotion of local industries also presents major organizational and administrative challenges to strengthen weak contract enforcement and reduce corruption. These are major obstacles on a continent where 16 of the world's 20 countries with the most difficult business conditions are located. The change in economic environment, and in the political climate, that is reflected in the NEPAD presents a vision of Africa that currently may seem messianic, but close partnership with international donors and the strong demand for employment of people in the urban centers will increase the pressure on governments to take greater responsibility and be more accountable in implementing development programs. To help improve the countries' systems of governance, *NEPAD* adopted the African Peer Review Mechanism, which measures progress in terms of political, economic, and corporate governance.

The contribution of peace and economic stability to economic growth is reflected in accelerating annual per capita growth in more than a dozen countries that are home to more than one fourth of the continent's population. The more prudent macroeconomic policies that brought fiscal deficits under better control, reduced inflation, and brought down foreign debt were also necessary steps in that direction.

Integrating African manufacturers into the outsourcing network

In the classical (Heckscher-Ohlin) model of international trade, countries export those goods in which they gain a comparative advantage by making more intensive use of their more abundant and relatively less expensive factor of production. With trade, the production of labor-intensive goods is therefore shifting to countries that have abundance of labor and relatively low wages, while the production of capital-intensive goods is shifting to the capital-abundant countries.

The structure of production and trade may change, however, if it is technically feasible and economically profitable to divide a vertically integrated production process into several segments. This division gives firms in the developed countries the option of outsourcing production of some parts to producers in countries that have cheaper labor costs. These parts are intermediate inputs in the production process and are assembled into the final product then shipped to consumers in the final stage of that process. Today's intense competition, rapid technological progress, and sharp reduction in transport and communication costs pressure firms to divide their production process into separate segments and outsource the production of many parts to external suppliers, where they can be produced at lower costs.

For example, the production of a car requires nearly 10,000 different parts. In "made in the United States" cars, approximately 30 percent of the car's value originates in Korea, 17.5 percent in Japan, another 15.5 percent in Germany, Taiwan, Singapore, the United Kingdom, Ireland, and Barbados, and only 37 percent in the United States. Outsourcing to developing countries the supply of components in which production is labor-intensive has become increasingly more attractive to the transnational corporations (TNCs) given the large wage differential. Intense competition worldwide is forcing corporations to outsource offshore larger segments of their production, or push local suppliers to do the outsourcing for them by subcontracting certain functions to suppliers abroad.

Along with the reduction in communication and transportation costs, the immense improvement in quality, the standardization of software packages, and other technological innovations make it possible to outsource many more business functions, including certain customer services, telemarketing, and document management that affect many white-collar professions, including services like tax preparation and financial services that previously seemed, like flipping hamburgers, to be country-specific. Corporations benefit from outsourcing these segments of production (and jobs) because setup costs have become relatively low and the wage differentials in these professions is very high. The publisher of this book is located in the UK, aspects of the editorial work were done in the United States, Canada, and India, and the book itself was written in The Netherlands, Israel, and Korea.

The process of outsourcing has become two-directional: As firms in developed countries outsource the supply of parts in which production is labor-intensive to producers in developing countries, many firms in developing countries are now outsourcing the supply of parts in which production requires specialized machinery and/or skilled labor to the United States, the European Union, and increasingly to China. Outsourcing has become a major contributor to the rise in international trade during the past two decades, promoting trade in intermediate inputs.

Outsourcing has also contributed to a rapid increase in productivity due to the specialization of companies in all countries in segments of production in which they are most efficient and have a competitive edge, and to the transfer of more advanced technologies from developed to developing countries. Lucas noted that, until the early 1990s, the flow of capital was meager from the rich and capital-intensive countries to poor countries where labor is abundant and wages low. One reason is that the developed countries continue to produce the capital intensive parts of the final product and outsource the production of the labor-intensive products to the poor countries. Another reason is the high cost of doing business in many poor countries. A third reason is the growing supply of cheap labor in the developed countries due to migration of workers from the poor countries. Another possible reason that is particularly relevant to Africa is the high risk of investing in many African countries and the low enforcement of contracts and of property rights.

While wages in African countries are very low, the costs of doing business are higher due to all these other costs and, in addition, the high corruption and high crime rates deter foreign investors, except for investors in the continent's rich resources. The attraction of the low wages of the African workers is therefore far outweighed by the high costs of all the other processes that are part of production. As a result, most African countries are less competitive and less attractive to foreign investors despite the many unique advantages they could offer. The growing share of outsourcing in global trade is, therefore, reducing the share of African producers, and reducing their potential to be integrated into the global trade. Even revenues from the export of most natural resources, including oil, were limited to contractual arrangements according to which the foreign corporations searched for, excavated, and exported the raw material without any processing in African countries, themselves, and even used their own (or Chinese) workers.

This situation extends even to agricultural products, from cotton to tropical fruits to tobacco. A person can buy jeans made in the United States, but the actual production work is carried out in Vietnam, and the cotton is grown in Mali. Coffee everywhere is sold by Starbucks at exorbitant prices from coffee beans grown in Kenya or Ethiopia, and local farmers receive only a pittance of the cost of a cup of espresso in New York or Amsterdam.

One "big push" of investments in African countries might contribute to removing some obstacles, such as the poor infrastructure (if the aid money is indeed properly used). But as long as all the other obstacles that are somewhat mysteriously hidden in the concept of "governance" are not improved, such an investment push will not increase Africa's share in global trade or the employment of African workers. To achieve that, African leaders must design their policies with a time horizon that spans beyond the time they expect to serve or survive as their countries' leaders.

Notes

1. Sachs, Jeffrey D. (2005). *The End of Poverty: Economic Possibilities for Our Time*. New York: Penguin Books.
2. See for example Paul Collier and Benedikt Goderis: "Commodity Prices, Growth, and the Natural Resource Curse: Reconciling a Conundrum," University of Oxford, August, 2007. The division made by Collier and Stephen A. O'Connell in "Opportunities and Choices" should be complemented by the discoveries of oil, uranium, and other resources in a considerable number of African countries categorized in their Table as resource-poor. The numbers in brackets are the rankings of countries according to the World Bank ranking on the *Ease of Doing Business* 2007–08.

Part IV
Civil Conflicts, Wars and Democracy: Will Democracy Inflame or Help to Settle Civil Conflicts?

> Africa is fundamentally communocractic. The collective life and social solidarity give it a basis of humanism which many people will envy. These human qualities also mean that an individual cannot imagine organizing his life outside that of his family, village or clan.
>
> President Sekou Toure of Guinea, in a speech quoted by UNESCO

In past decades, Africa went through a series of prolonged and extremely brutal conflicts that took the life of millions of people, expelled millions from their homes and lands, and wasted their economic resources, notably in Darfur, southern Sudan, Rwanda, Congo, and Sierra Leone. In Rwanda, alone, more than 5.4 million people lost their lives. Reports in the media about the death and destitution caused by these conflicts have contributed to the widespread sense that Africa is a lost case, a continent in perpetual crisis. But, in recent years, the number of wars and violent conflicts has been declining, and several peace agreements signal that greater stability is beginning to take hold in the continent. Among the most encouraging developments has been the spread of democracy, which seems to have become well-established in an increasing number of countries, even though some of Africa's democratic practices may be controversial and rather unique. The question of whether the transition to democracy will indeed lead to more stable and accountable governments is still hotly debated, particularly since many elections were flawed and autocratic regimes remained in power.

The rapid economic developments of the last decade arguably helped spur the spread of democracy. Equally important was the pressure coming from donor countries, the international development organizations, and many NGOs. They promoted democratization in the hope it would lead to more stable governments that would replace the autocratic regimes whose misrule and abuse of power had contributed greatly to Africa's incessant wars and civil conflicts that took millions of lives and brought about three decades of stagnation and an immense increase in poverty.

The transition to democracy was an encouraging development in a continent that just 25 years ago had only three democracies: Botswana, Senegal, and Mauritius, but by 2005 had more than 40 countries holding regular elections, quite a few of them more than once. Although a peaceful transfer of power to the leader of the opposition when he won the elections is still uncommon in Africa, it is becoming increasingly more accepted and even demanded. The African Union (AU) increased the pressure to deepen and spread the transition to democracy by, among other means, declaring it would not recognize governments that seize power illegitimately or through controversial elections not supervised by international observers.

The process of democratization has been praised as a step in the right direction by the UN and all the other international development organizations as well as by the donor countries, which may have regarded this development also as a vindication of the infamous structural adjustment programs. However, as we shall see later, some African leaders have questioned whether the act of election by itself is sufficient to indicate a country has indeed made an authentic transition to democracy. Whether the Western-style democracy the African countries were urged to adopt was a form of democracy suitable to the African heritage and the continent's unique social and political conditions, and whether that form of democracy is the right way to deal with Africa's many challenges.

The hope that democracy will soon bring greater stability to the continent was dampened when several democratically elected governments—in Togo, Guinea-Bissau, and Mauritania—in 2009 were toppled by military coups d'état within few months after the elections, without encountering strong protests of their citizens, who were disillusioned by the flawed elections; in several other countries leaders sought to change the constitutions by extending their rule to three terms, in some countries against strong protests, but in others with the muted acquiescence of their constituents.

The recent series of global economic crises that hurt African economies contributed to disillusions and doubts about the merits of democracy, since people expected democracy would bring significant improvements in their living conditions and, in many countries, they blame the elected government for food shortages and high prices. The AU reacted swiftly to the 2009 military coups that toppled democratically elected governments by issuing forceful condemnations and making plans for prompt interventions to allow for the reinstatement of the elected governments, particularly as more people in these countries became disillusioned, within a short time, as the military regimes failed to provide more effective leadership and resorted to the tactics of "take as much as you can as fast as you can."

4.1
The Roots and Long-Term Effects of Africa's Wars and Civil Conflicts

When the African countries gained independence, the leaders of the new states were more than just heads of state; they were seen as unifying symbols that could create a sense of national identity by representing the ideals that had inspired the fight for independence and brought the country's people together. Houphouët-Boigny of Ivory Coast was known as "The Ram who Defends his People," Jomo Kenyatta of Kenya was "The Flaming Spear of Kenya," and Julius Nyerere of Tanzania was "Mwalimu," the "Teacher." These and other charismatic leaders like Kwame Nkrumah, Ben Bella, Nasser, Lumumba, Kenneth Kaunda were the first ("golden") generation of African political leaders, and they gained enormous popular support as the leaders of the independence movements in the struggle against colonial powers. When they became leaders of the newly independent states Africa's prospects seemed brighter than ever, and there were great hopes and enthusiasm everywhere on the continent that the new leaders would make major improvements in living conditions.

The end of colonial rule, for which the independence movements had fought so tenaciously, left the former colonies and their economies in disarray. These early difficulties made "nation-building"—and the creation of a sense of national identity—all the more challenging, since the countries these African leaders inherited were not nations, but an amalgam of diverse and often antagonistic tribes bundled together within arbitrary borders drawn by the colonial powers according to their own needs.

The cult of personality during the early rule of post-independence leaders reflected the efforts to unite different tribes and groups that made up the citizens of the new African states. However, popular support for these charismatic leaders quickly began to wane when quite a few of them tried to establish socialist regimes, sometimes by collectivizing the lands of small farmers and forcing them to relocate to new collective farms. The results were disastrous: When people strongly protested and refused to work in the collective farms, agricultural production fell sharply, and there was widespread impoverishment. The first leaders became increasingly autocratic and focused on solidifying their control in order to strengthen their power to build a nation and a state.

Some leaders indulged in tyrannizing their countries as they became obsessed with enriching themselves and strengthening their grip on power by spreading various benefits to their supporters, usually members of the leader's tribe. These supporters could expect to gain desirable lands confiscated from other tribes, acquire positions in government or in the army that provided ample opportunities to receive bribes. Huge resources were wasted to build the security forces; civil liberties were systematically suppressed, and discrimination against the minority tribes was common.

Many regimes failed to provide even a minimum of stability and were toppled in military coup d'états that brought army commanders to power. The military leaders in charge of government could initially claim to have popular support from a people disillusioned by the tyranny of some heroic independence leaders, but the military leaders also became tyrannical and looted their countries' riches without inhibition, dashing any hopes for improvement. Since independence, nearly all African countries have been engaged in wars and civil conflicts. Between 1960 and 2008, 115 African leaders were overthrown or toppled in military coups d'état, two-thirds of them assassinated, imprisoned, or forced into exile; two incumbent presidents were voted out of office, and one resigned.

Short-term shock remedies such as overvalued exchange rates, high taxes on exports, and subsidies to food imports only worsened the state of their economies. Despite high revenues during the commodity boom of the 1970s, little investment was made to improve the countries' infrastructures or raise the standards of living in rural areas, and the countries sank deeper into stagnation and poverty. As a result of prolonged stagnation, in 1999 average per capita GDP in SSA was $200 *lower* than in 1974; meanwhile, the rest of the world was *growing* during these years at an average annual rate of 2 percent. SSA was the only region where poverty increased, while in nearly all other developing countries poverty was on the decline, and the economies of many countries, particularly in East Asia, were growing at miraculous rates.

The most devastating effect of all these regimes was the spread of armed conflict that engaged practically all African countries. Most became entangled in at least three wars or violent civil strife that wasted their resources, exacted a horrendous toll on the population, and ruined economies. These conflicts badly damaged the economic prospects of Africa's newly independent states and cost the lives of millions who died in the wars or as result of hunger and deadly diseases; millions more were forced to flee their homes, and massive population displacement separated families and broke up numerous communities (Map 4.1).

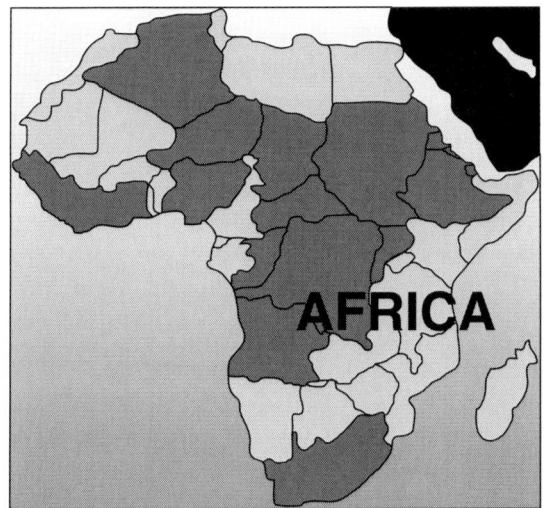

Map 4.1 African Countries in Conflict: 1990–2005 (Dark Areas)
Source: "Africa's Missing Billions," International Action Network on Small Arms; MCT (2007).

As the regimes became more thuggish, wars increased the human toll, and hunger was frequently used as a deliberate weapon in these conflicts. Refugees often had no access to food partly because paramilitary forces—in an effort to starve the populations of their rivals into submission—deliberately cut off their food supply, including the hijacking of food aid sent to civilians. Food shortages were further exacerbated when the fighting prevented farmers from cultivating their lands and cut off their access to fertilizers and seed.

In the past decade, the number of wars in Africa has declined, but in nine African countries continued wars and conflicts have brought the worst humanitarian crises the continent has even experienced: these include the genocides in Darfur, South Sudan, and Rwanda. Despite the high growth rates of the past decade, the scars of these conflicts have not been healed, and in many countries the animosity between tribes or sectarian groups has even deepened.

The tribal roots of civil conflicts

Most conflicts in Africa are rooted in tribal rivalries that often last several generations. Ethnic rivalries and tribal competition triggered civil conflicts that sometimes escalated to all-out wars. In rural areas, tribal rivalries exacerbated the ferocity of fighting fuelled by anger between neighboring tribes that compete for land or water resources. In many cases, the disputed lands were given to the leading tribe by the colonial powers that sought to secure their loyalty; in other cases, Africa's autocratic leaders confiscated the lands of the smaller tribes to give them to members of their own tribe. The tribes that were chased away from their ancestral territories and homes fought whenever they could to regain their lands.

Minority tribes thus blamed inequality and discrimination on members of the larger tribe favored by the country's leader. These kinds of rivalries triggered the atrocious conflicts between, among others, the Lou and the Kikuyu tribes in Kenya, the Tutsi and Hutu in Rwanda, and between the black and the Arab Sudanese. Similar conflicts erupted in nearly all multi-ethnic African states, and the survivors of the fighting and starvation were doomed to extreme poverty and hopelessness.

In some countries, including Sudan, Eritrea, Niger, and Côte d'Ivoire, tribes and sectarian groups have long fought, and continue to fight, against the regime in power that marginalized them and denied their rights. The resulting resentments can even fuel violence in urban areas, where gang wars and civil strife pit rival tribes against each other due to grievances from two or three generations ago. However, in urban areas, poverty and unemployment usually have a much more powerful impact on people's anger against the regime, and demonstrations against the government often become violent. The strong tribal support for a political leader also intensifies rivalries by fuelling resentment against the leading tribe.

Among the tribal conflicts that exemplify the deep roots of civil conflicts plaguing Africa is the strife in Kenya, which goes back to colonial times; the wounds have not healed, and old rivalries erupted like a volcanic force after the elections in 2007, resulting in violence that took place mostly in the capital city, Nairobi. The two leaders who competed in these elections, the incumbent President Mwai Kibaki, an ethnic Kikuyu, and opposition leader Raila Odinga from the rival Lou tribe, were equally strong, but Odinga was backed by a coalition that included some 40 ethnic groups that joined together in order to compete against the powerful Kikuyu. While many Kenyans saw this as a test of multiparty democracy, the confrontation manifested itself along tribal lines, and the main criterion in the election was which of the two leaders would best serve the interests of the voters' tribe.

The power-sharing agreement reached after prolonged negotiations and violent demonstrations remained fragile. In the two years after the election, a series of summit meetings were held for representatives of the three large parties in an effort to form a government, but the ministers could not even agree on the subject of the discussions that would enable them to find common ground. According to *The Economist*, foreign diplomats referred to the squabbling coalition that finally was formed as an "unconsummated marriage." The result was that Kenya still did not have a functioning executive and was run by a temporary alliance of rivals. The parties were also unable to agree on a tribunal to judge those responsible for the post-election mayhem, and Kenyan newspapers came up almost weekly with new revelations of corruption scandals. Since many senior figures from the main parties were members of the government, the interim government had no less than 94 ministers and deputies with hefty salaries, thus effectively making Kenya a one-party state, although the ministers continuously squabbled over pay, protocol, and seniority.

The roots of the resentment of smaller tribes toward the Kikuyu are grounded in the preferential treatment the Kikuyu received during the colonial era. At that time, the fertile lands of the northern Rift Valley were taken from local tribes and given to white settlers (see Box 4.1). When the settlers vacated these lands during the 1960s, after Kenya became independent, these lands were "purchased" by the Kikuyu with the active assistance of Jomo Kenyatta's government, which tried to gain the support of the Kikuyu. The tribes from whom these lands originally had been taken,

Box 4.1   Kenya

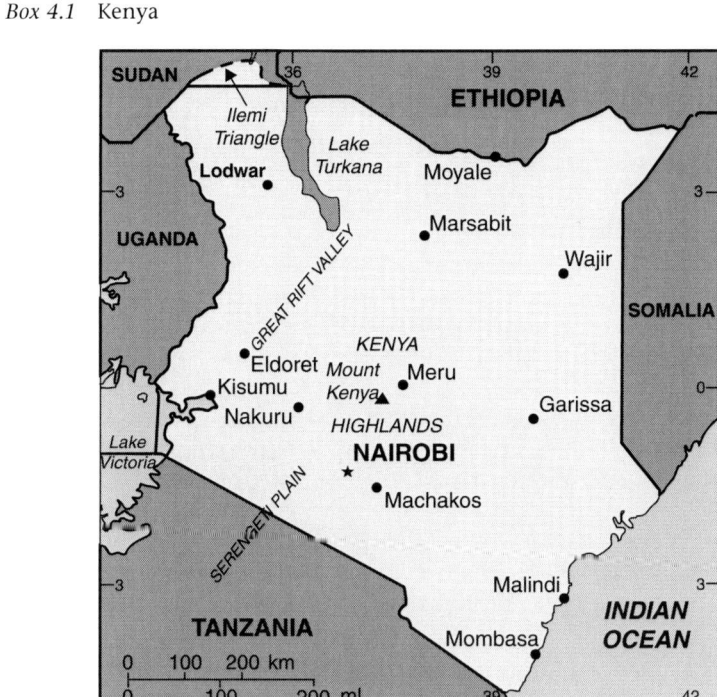

Map 4.2   Kenya
Source: CIA, *The World Factbook* (2008).

- Coastal length: 536 km.
- Population: 39 million (2007), compared with 8 million at independence in 1963.
- Infant mortality: total: 54.7 deaths/1,000 live births.
- Ethnic groups: Kikuyu 22%, Luhya 14%.
- Life expectancy: declined from 62 in 1984 to 52 in 2006, mostly due to AIDS.
- Urban population: 22% (2008).
- Unemployment: 40% (2007).
- GDP per capita: US$1,600 (2008).

primarily the Lou, did not get back any part of these lands, and the resulting resentment continued to simmer for many years. The post-2007 election violence included an extremely angry outburst of violence in the Rift Valley against the Kikuyu inhabitants. Nearly 1,500 people died, and an estimated 250,000, mostly Kikuyu, were displaced from their homes.

It was the rural population that usually suffered most from the fighting, since farmers were frequently unable to cultivate their lands, making them increasingly poorer and vulnerable to periodic food shortages, which further emasculated the rural people and weakened their ability to fight in order to protect their rights. Even when Jomo Kenyatta did not return the lands owned by the Lou during colonial times, the Lou tribesmen did not stage an effective opposition to his decision, although this traumatic event remained an open wound in their collective memory for many years.

Kenyatta remained in power until his death in 1978, when President Daniel arap Moi took power. Despite a strong and violent, but ethnically fractured, opposition, the ruling party of President Moi remained in power for 24 years, even after the country established a nominally democratic regime and conducted elections in 1992. In 2005, a coalition was formed of tribes that opposed the regime and, inspired by the "color-coded" movements that at the time had been successful in Eastern Europe, labeled itself the Orange Democratic Movement. It defeated the government's draft constitution in a popular referendum in 2005 and strongly opposed the reelection of Kibaki in 2007, blaming him for widespread vote-rigging. That protest unleashed two months of violence in which 1,500 people died; eventually, talks sponsored by the UN produced a power-sharing accord that brought Odinga into the government as a prime minister.

Conflicts caused by deprivation and exclusion

In the multiethnic societies of African countries, perceptions of deprivation and exploitation are practically inevitable, regardless of how justified the grievances are. In most countries, there is a leading tribe, and most political leaders either come from that tribe or, like Kenyatta, use favoritism to gain its support. The leading tribe thus benefits from preferential treatment that usually comes at the expense of the others. Perceptions of deprivation and exploitation are thus indeed painfully real and often based on a long experience of discrimination and humiliation. Divisions along sectarian lines can greatly intensify conflicts, as in the case of Sudan between the Christian and animist Sudanese in the South and the Muslim Sudanese in the North, where the rivalry became so intense that it led to a prolonged and ferocious war in which millions lost their lives and millions were expelled from their homes and lands; despite all the misery, the fighting continued. In the social scientist's terminology, the perception of relative deprivation became a reality of absolute deprivation.

In the early post-colonial days, the main conflicts were about cultivated lands and water resources. Many disputes were between tribes that demanded their ancestral lands, taken by the colonial regime, and tribes that had settled in these lands, often because they benefited from the favoritism of the country's leadership. In the past two decades, a number of conflicts erupted when dispossessed tribes demanded a share in newly discovered resources in their ancestral lands.

The previous section reviewed the tribal roots of conflict in Kenya. This section provides a review of more extreme conflicts driven by entrenched enmities between tribes and ethnic groups due to deprivation and exclusion, specifically the conflicts in Niger and Côte d'Ivoire, and the two major conflicts that became the continent's most horrific genocides: the conflicts in Sudan and Rwanda.

Niger

Niger is one of the world's poorest countries. Most of this large, landlocked country is covered by the Sahara desert, and the majority of its population of around 14 million lives along a narrow band of arable land on the southern border. The economy is dominated by agriculture, including livestock, mining (uranium), and informal trading activities. Rain-fed agriculture accounted for nearly half Niger's GDP in 2006, and livestock production accounted for about a third of the value added of that sector.

The country's dominant tribe is the Hausa, concentrated in the South, who make up more than 50 percent of the total population and control the government, armed forces, and police. They have relatively fertile lands and water, and relatively higher standards of living. The minority tribes, such as the Tuareg and the Berbers, live in the northern part of country, which is mostly Sahara, and are mainly herdsmen and considerably poorer. The Hausa have refused to this day to give equal rights to these smaller tribes, which have never accepted their exclusion and resent being left out of the government and treated as second-class citizens. Niger restored a multiparty democracy in 1993, but military coups continued until 1999. Tribal conflicts were aggravated in recent years with the discovery of precious resources. In February 2007 a predominately Tuareg ethnic group established the Nigerien Movement for Justice (MNJ), and attacked several military targets throughout 2007 and 2008. This movement has since evolved into a fledging insurgency.

Despite Niger's poverty, it is blessed with valuable natural resources, particularly uranium, and gold, found in the Sahara, where the security situation is so precarious that it prevents their excavation, and even UN delegates are unsafe. Yet, in the continuing confrontation that punishes all sides, the South refused to give up its power. President Tandja made every effort to ensure his control, violating agreements, dissolving the national assembly and the constitutional court, and attempting to change the constitution to extend his term limit in spite of repeated constitutional court rulings against it. The president ignored massive demonstrations in Niamey, the country's capital, and brought the country to the verge of a civil war. A new agreement between the government and the rebel forces was signed at the end of 2008, under the auspices of Libya, but it remains to be seen whether the president will abide by the agreement.

Côte d'Ivoire

Once the pearl of Africa, Côte d'Ivoire has been plagued by incessant conflicts between Muslims who live in the North and the Akan, the leading tribe in the mostly Christian population in the South (Map 4.3). Houphouët-Boigny, who ruled the country since independence and is considered the "Father of the Nation," established an anti-West alliance between the leading tribe in the South and the Muslim people in the North, but nonetheless openly discriminated against the Muslim majority. The Muslims felt they were not receiving a fair return for their political support and their region was discriminated against in terms of economic development and political appointments. They had endless trouble obtaining national identity cards because the authorities treated them like second-class citizens, or even foreigners. In 1990 the *Front Populaire Ivoirien* (FPI), led by the Bété tribe was founded and the northerners began to express increasing frustration. This was the political expression of frustrations due to discrimination by the government dominated by the Akan, the ethnic group to which belonged Houphouët-Boigny and Konan Bédié, who became president after his death in 1993.

Once he became president, Bédié ruled his political opponent was not a genuine Ivorian and therefore not qualified to run for the presidency. In 1994, regardless of history and geography, an Ivorian nationality clause was added to the constitution, which ruled that any candidate for the presidency in 1995 must be Ivorian by birth and born of parents who were themselves Ivorian by birth. This clause created an immediate conflict. In

Map 4.3 Côte d'Ivoire.
Source: CIA, The World Factbook (2008).

December 1999 Brigadier-General Robert Gueï seized power and immediately suspended the constitution and adopted a one that discriminated even more severely against the North. In a referendum held in July a new, even harsher, constitution was voted in with over 86 percent support across all parties. As a result, politicians of all parties became victims of the controversial clause they themselves supported. The elections in 2000 were grossly rigged and, although Gueï declared himself the winner, massive demonstrations against the flawed elections forced him to step aside and brought Laurent Gbagbo to power. The first decade of the twenty-first century was very stormy and unstable as leaders were frequently replaced, and only in November 2009 was an agreement reached. Several thousand UN troops and several hundred French soldiers remain in Côte d'Ivoire to support the peace process.

The half-century long conflict and genocide in Sudan

Since independence from the British in 1956, Sudan has been embroiled in a prolonged civil war between the largely Arab, Muslim, population in the northern part of the country and the black Christians and animists in the southern part. Military regimes have supported the Islamic governments that dominated national politics. A temporary lull was maintained from 1972 to 1983, until fighting started again, lasting more than 20 years. Two million people, mainly from the South, died in the warfare, and more than four million displaced. After oil was found in southern Sudan about a decade ago, the Sudanese government—eager not to lose control of the territory and its oil revenues—applied all tactics and manipulations to prevent a division of the country (Box 4.2).

Despite Sudan's considerable resources, the country is classified by the FAO as a "Food Deficit Low Income Country" and included among the countries in crisis that require emergency assistance. Yet, there is considerable abuse of aid: it was revealed that the Sudanese government sold some of the food aid to finance its military expenditures; moreover, Sudan's president, Omar al-Bashir, even "rented" large areas of agricultural land in the South to several Gulf countries that sought to buffer their food supply and avoid the high volatility of world food markets.

Box 4.2   Sudan

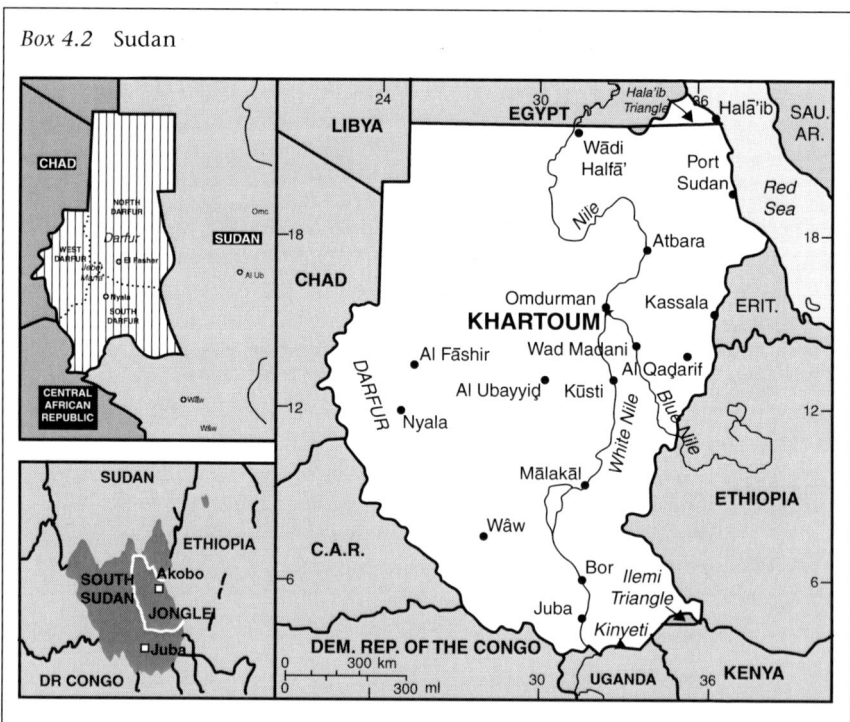

Map 4.4   Sudan
Sources: CIA: *The World Factbook*; World Bank country reports.

- Coastal length: 853km
- Population: 41, million (2009 est.)
- Infant mortality: 82.5 deaths/1,000 live births
- Ethnic groups: 52% Blacks—Christian/Animists; 39% Arabs—Muslims
- Urban population: 43% of total population (2008)
- Government: Military regime
- Natural resources: Oil; 500,000 bbl/day.
- GDP per capita (PPP): US$2,200.
- Civil war in South Sudan: Since 1956 (independence); cease fire: 1972–83
- Peace agreement: 2005.
- Civil war in Darfur: Since 2003; temporary peace settlement: 2008.

In May 2006, the government of Sudan and one faction of the rebel Sudan Liberation Army/Movement (SLA) signed the Darfur Peace Agreement. Since then, the number of displaced civilians has risen from roughly 900,000 to 2.5 million, up to 300,000 more civilians have died, and an untold number of women have been raped.

Violations of Minority Rights by the Government of Sudan:

1. Failure to ensure equitable access to resources, especially land.
2. Political marginalization of minority groups—including the manipulation of political territory arrangements and appointments, partisan support and rewarding of certain groups over others.
3. Socioeconomic underdevelopment—unequal access to, and low level of, social services, and neglect of the region in Sudan's development.
4. Racial and cultural discrimination.
5. Abdication of responsibilities for law, order, and security.

The Sudanese government and its army commanders are motivated to ensure their complete control over the southern territories, and the continued war impoverishes the majority of the population in both the North and the South. The situation is particularly dire in rural areas that were hit very hard by the food crisis in 2008.

What makes matters even worse is that Sudan's government is entangled in yet another devastating conflict in Darfur, its region to the west. The large quantities of oil resources could enable the country to resolve its poverty problems and prevent the misery of the food crisis and the genocide in Darfur. Sudan could also make much more intensive use of the Nile project and, with proper investments, significantly increase its agricultural production. Instead, these resources are divided mainly among the country's elite and the top army commanders, who decide how to allocate the resources and conduct the conflicts.

The backgrounds of Sudan's conflicts are complex, and oil is only one part of the equation. The prolonged civil war in the South is even worse than the conflict between Arab Muslims and black non-Muslims. Sudan has a long and bitter history of fighting between the South and the North, one that includes centuries of slavery and war, and discrimination against the black African Christians and animists by the Arab Muslims. Against this background, the people of southern Sudan have never been willing to pretend some sort of Sudanese "national unity" could erase the bitter memories of their subjugation by the North, which continues to discriminate against them. The lack of a common identity that could hold the country and the people together is not unique to Sudan, and is also a problem in many other African countries, although the hostility in Sudan is perhaps the deepest. Many Sudanese Africans call their country a "colonial nation-state".

The rivalry between northern and southern Sudan was sparked by a deep animosity between the largely nomadic Arab tribes that were not willing to accept claims by the rural population in the South to ownership of the agricultural lands they had farmed for centuries. The Arab tribes have been supported and armed by the Muslim government in the North for its own political purposes. The black mostly Christian Africans were not willing to share the ownership of their agricultural lands with the population that was brought south by the government and settled on their land. This was before oil was found in the region, and the dispute was only over agricultural lands.

After half a century of brutal fighting it became clear that the war in Sudan can only be resolved by dividing the country. The breakup of Sudan, however, would send shock waves across the continent and set a significant precedent, since this would be the first time a colonial boundary is changed to form a new state, which could inflame separatist insurgencies elsewhere.

In 2005, a peace accord ended the fighting, but the peace remained fragile and tensions persist over a number of issues, including the control of the oil-rich region, located between the North and the South. The Comprehensive Peace Agreement (CPA), signed in January 2005, granted the southern rebels autonomy for six years, and scheduled a referendum for independence in 2011. In 2009, an international tribunal redefined the borders of the disputed oil-rich region. The ruling split the contested zone between the two sides. It gave the government control of the region's richest oil fields, but consolidated control of the remaining region under an ethnic group loyal to South Sudan. Both sides accepted the ruling. However, serious problems remain, including the division of grazing lands and other holdings, and renewed violence is possible.

Aggravating the situation further is the help Sudan gives antigovernment rebel forces in neighboring Chad, with arms and refuge. The main motivation of the Sudanese is to counter the support given by the government of Chad to rebel fighters in Darfur. A quarter of a million refugees from Darfur escaped to Chad, and their camps became the base of rebel groups. As a result, Chad, one of Africa's poorest and least stable nations despite its own oil resources, became an active participant in the conflict in Sudan. The refugees from Darfur initially were protected in Chad by a rather ineffectual African Union contingent and later by a UN force, and survived in dreadful conditions on the food distribution of the World Food Program (WFP). Sudanese-backed forces, the Janjaweed militia, attacked the camps inside Chad, killing aid workers and many civilians, and turned the conflict in Sudan into an open war between the two countries.

The rich resources of oil found in Chad gave the country new wealth, but the revenues have not been used for the country's development or to provide food for its starving population. Only a small share of the country's annual oil revenues of more than $1 billion are allocated for poverty reduction, while the main share of its new wealth is siphoned off by corrupt officials—in spite of their pledge to allocate funds to new schools and hospitals, which were not completed.

Despite major efforts of aid workers in the refugee camps, child mortality in Darfur continues to rise, and the area remains the site of a grave humanitarian crisis. Rebel forces in Darfur have been increasingly marginalized by the Sudanese government, and their demands ignored. To assume their position in the negotiations-cum-confrontations, the rebels attacked government forces in 2007, and the Sudanese government responded by arming tribal militias to wipe out the rebels and civilians in the area.

President al-Bashir of Sudan backed away once again from the peace agreement, this time the "Comprehensive Peace Agreement" deal of 2005 intended to bring an end to the war against Chad, and revived the war with the military forces in South Sudan. In the agreement, both sides had accepted the "final and binding" ruling of the Abyei Boundary Commission, but Bashir rejected the findings because they would have meant giving up oil wells. Small-scale armed clashes have broken out since 2007 between South Sudan's armed forces and a large tribe of Arab nomads. It looks increasingly likely that these conflicts will be the prologue to a far bloodier conflict that engulfs all of Sudan.

Despite the worldwide condemnation of the atrocities committed by Sudan's government and its proxy militias in Darfur, the International Criminal Court prosecutor, Luis Moreno-Ocampo, had a grim message for the United Nations Security Council even at the end of 2008: "Genocide continues. Rapes in and around the camps continue. Humanitarian assistance is still hindered. More than 5,000 displaced persons die each month." Yet, the African Union and the Arab League, seeking to protect one of their own, were pressing for a delay of any formal indictment and arrest warrant for Bashir, arguing that it would hurt chances for a negotiated peace.

When the United States sought the deployment of UN peacekeepers in Darfur to replace the ineffective African Union force, Sudan resisted this initiative until President Bush announced in May 2007 that he was imposing new unilateral economic sanctions against Sudan for failing to allow the deployment and end its support for the Janjaweed. Only then did Sudan agree to a deal with the UN, allowing an international force of 20,000 troops to shore up the struggling 7,000-member African Union force. After two years and six rounds of abortive negotiations, a peace deal of sorts to end the conflict in Darfur was finally signed in May 2008. Though only one of the main rebel groups, the Sudan Liberation Army (SLA), signed the agreement with the government, the accord has nonetheless been hailed as a breakthrough.

However, it also has to be acknowledged that at present, there is no such thing as a Sudanese national identity that could hold the country together. The same could be said about many countries in Africa, though the hostility between different groups in most of them is not nearly as deep. Sudan has been engaged in bitter and extremely cruel warfare and in South Sudan, which is rich in oil, its people are poorer than those in Darfur. Their poverty is mostly the result of the civil war that has been raging for two decades. A division of the country may therefore be inevitable.

The tribal wars in the Great Lakes region

One of the most cataclysmic chapters in Africa's post-independence history, and its worst experience with the "resource curse," is the genocide in Rwanda. Several recent books describe the horrors of this incomprehensible and yet little known conflict,[1] and the chronicle of the resulting war that embroiled at least seven countries for nearly a decade and became known as "Africa's World War" portrays the depth and ferocity of the grievances and hostilities that drove entire communities and ethnic groups to a collective suicidal violence and hate that led to the systematic killing of millions.

The root cause of the rivalry was the deep-seated resentment of the Hutu against the domination of the Tutsi, who controlled much of the economy and the government even though they were the minority of the country's population. Strong feelings of deprivation were also the trigger for post-election riots in the ethnically and religiously divided Nigeria, factors that played an important role in most other conflicts mentioned earlier. Africa's rural population is still torn by tribal rivalries encouraged by the "divide-and-rule" strategy of the colonial regimes, and these rivalries became even more pronounced after independence, when many of the newly established central governments pursued policies that discriminated against the rural population in general and against minority tribes in particular.

The genocide in Rwanda: Africa's world war

The region that includes Rwanda and Burundi came under Belgian rule as a League of Nations mandate after World War I, and was known as Ruanda-Urundi. Before the colonial period, Hutus and Tutsis here lived for the most part peacefully as neighbors. The enmity between the two tribes goes back to colonial times, when the colonial powers favored the Tutsi. The Belgian colonial regime (which also controlled a vast colony then known as the Belgian Congo) even developed the myth that the Tutsi have Caucasian ancestry, and were therefore considered "superior" to the Hutus. The Belgian administration issued identity cards that registered ethnic origin and thus institutionalized the racial divide, and the Tutsi were given the power to administer the country and have the political control, even though the Hutu were the majority. This enabled the Tutsi to dominate the economy of the rich North Kivu Province that had tin mines, and large parts of the province's best farming and grazing lands were controlled by a handful of Tutsi owners. Reforms instituted by the Belgians in the 1950s to establish democratic political institutions were resisted by the Tutsi, who saw these measures as a threat to their rule.

In 1957, an extreme Hutu movement actively opposed the monopoly of power held by the Tutsi minority and demanded their share in power. The Tutsi reacted by forming an opposition party in 1959, demanding immediate independence for Ruanda-Urundi that was to be based on the existing Tutsi monarchy. Two years later, the political party of the Hutu won an overwhelming victory in a UN-supervised referendum; the government that was formed following the 1961 election was granted autonomy by Belgium in January 1962, and in June of that year, a UN General Assembly resolution granted full independence to Rwanda and Burundi.

The Republic of Rwanda established by the Hutu party persecuted the Tutsi, forcing thousands to flee to neighboring countries and excluded the Tutsis who remained in Rwanda from any political power. In Burundi, an army-controlled Tutsi government persisted for decades, even though the country also had a Hutu majority. Similar to other African conflicts, the driving force was deeply rooted animosity due to prolonged discrimination against the Hutu, who had been systematically excluded from power, but the scale and ferocity of the resulting carnage were far greater than in many other conflicts in the post-World War II era.

In 1990, a rebel group composed mostly of Tutsi refugees invaded northern Rwanda from neighboring Uganda and started a civil war against the Hutu regime. With support from the African Francophone nations and from France itself, the Hutu regime resisted the invading force, but it also increased the ethnic tensions in the country by claiming the Tutsi intended to enslave the Hutus. A displacement of large numbers of Hutu in the North by the rebels, and ethnic cleansing of Tutsi in the South, increased the pressure on the government and led to a ceasefire in 1993.

In 1994, the assassination of the Hutu president brought an end to the ceasefire and caused agitation among more extreme Hutus. Within three months, around 800,000 people, or 20 percent of the country's population, mostly Rwandan Tutsis and moderate Hutus, were killed. The rebel army of the Tutsis, under the leadership of Paul Kagame, entered Rwanda from Uganda and managed to defeat the government forces in Kigali and install a minority Tutsi regime, forcing some two million Hutus to flee to refugee camps run by the UN in the Republic of Zaire provinces, North and South Kivu (Box 4.3).

Box 4.3   Rwanda and Congo Dem. Rep.

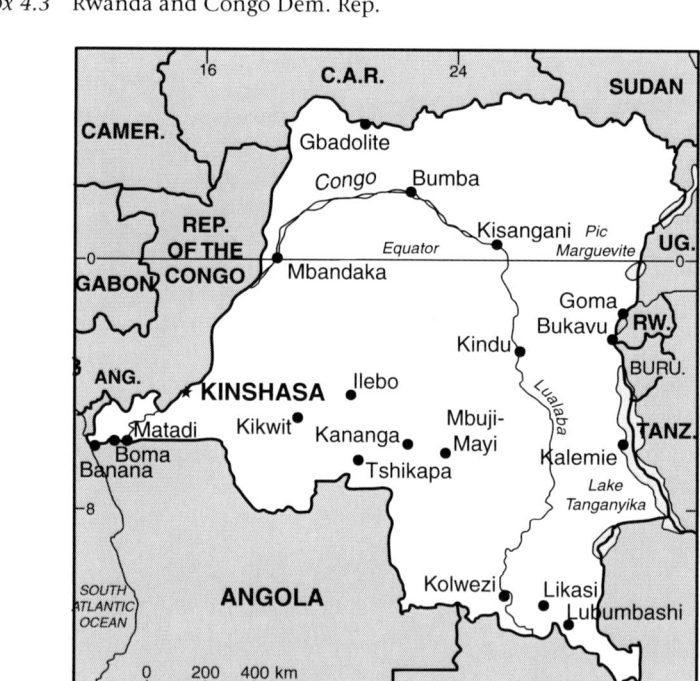

Map 4.5   Congo Democratic Republic
Source: CIA, *The World Factbook* (2009).

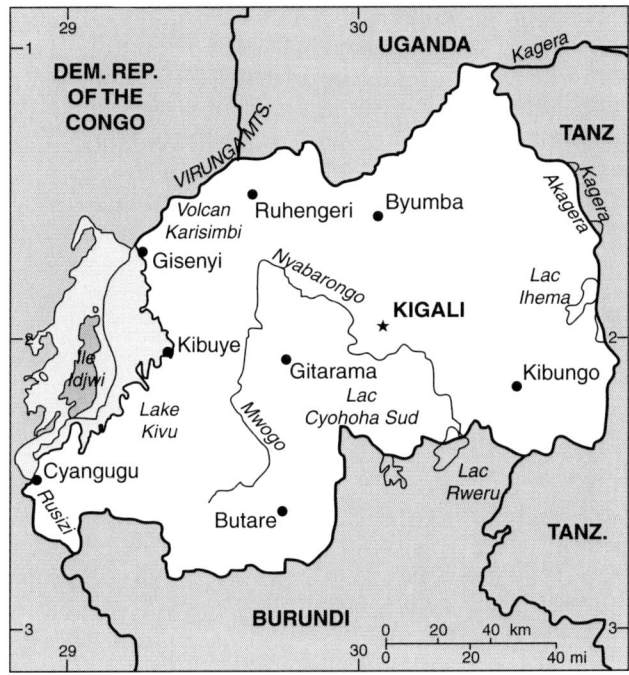

Map 4.6 Rwanda
Source: CIA, *The World Factbook* (2009).

Rwanda

- Population: 10.5 million.
- Pop. growth rate: 2.8%; fertility rate: 5.25 children born/woman.
- Urban pop. 20% of total; rate of urbanization: 4.2%.
- Main ethnic groups: Hutu (84%); Tutsi (14%).
- Economy: Poor rural country; 90% of population works in agriculture.

Congo Dem. Rep.

- Coastal length: 37km.
- Population: 69 million.
- Pop. growth rate: 3.2%; fertility rate: 6.2 children born/woman.
- Urban pop: 38% of total; rate of urbanization: 5.1%.
- Ethnic groups: Over 200 ethnic groups.

The Hutu refugees established a military force, using the camps in eastern Zaire (soon to be renamed the Democratic Republic of Congo) as a basis for incursions against Rwanda. These Hutu militia soon allied with Zairian armed forces to launch a campaign against Congolese ethnic Tutsi. Rwanda's intervention in Congo began in 1996, with the First Congo War, when it joined Uganda in aiding a force of Congolese Tutsis under insurgent leader Laurent Kabila, which entered the Kivu provinces to pursue Hutu militants. Supported by Rwanda, Uganda, and Burundi, Kabila launched an uprising that overthrew Mobutu Sésé Seko, Zaire's dictator of three decades, who had given refuge to leaders of the Hutu extremists. Kabila came to power in 1997 (with the backing of the United States), renamed the country Congo, and took control over the vast mineral resources. This marked the beginning of the five-year multi-nation war in the Democratic Republic of Congo (DRC).

Kabila's efforts to solidify his control turned him against his previous supporters, and in 1998, Hutu rebel forces backed by Rwandan and Ugandan troops started the Second Congo War by attacking the DRC army. Kabila received the support of Southern African Development Community (SADC) members and military forces from Angola, Zimbabwe, and Namibia. This widening war became known as Africa's World War.

While the war was triggered by deeply rooted tribal rivalries, the leaders of the armies had also other reasons for warmaking, including ousting Mobutu and the plundering of Congo's minerals. Tens of thousands of soldiers from several armies participated in the war that became the worst bloodbath in the continent's post-independence era. The war also became a ferocious battle over control of Congo's rich minerals, oil, and other resources, as well as its fertile land and water resources. The leaders of the participating countries also wanted to prevent neighboring countries from entering the fighting in an attempt to share the gains from the region's resources.

The genocide that claimed the lives of some 5.4 million people in Rwanda, Burundi, and Congo has been one of the darkest chapters in Africa's and, indeed, the world's history.[2] Most victims were civilians not involved in the fighting, but who died from the spread of malaria, diarrhea, and pneumonia and from malnutrition. Many victims could have been saved if aid agencies had been able to reach the area to provide food and medical aid. Children accounted for 47 percent of the deaths, although their share in the population was less than 20 percent. Some 1.5 million people remained internally displaced or refugees and tens of thousands of them die each month. Several organizations, including since 2000 Human Rights Watch and Oxfam, have called for international intervention to put an end to this humanitarian disaster, and a subsequent report by Amnesty International in mid-2003 harshly criticized the lack of multinational action.

Rwanda took advantage of the total lack of central control in the DRC to take over the Congolese diamond mines and other mineral mines, and various paramilitary forces have also participated in the looting and the killing. The fighting continued despite a peace agreement signed in 1999 in Lusaka. Teams deployed by the UN supervised the agreement and were supposed to protect civilians, but Amnesty International noted that these forces lacked the necessary equipment, personnel, and the equally necessary international political backing.

Laurent Kabila was assassinated in 2001 and succeeded by his son, Joseph, who called for multilateral peace talks to end the war. In the peace deal that was brokered, foreign troops were supposed to withdraw from Congo, and UN forces arrived in April 2001. The conflict was reignited in January 2002 by ethnic clashes in the Northeast, and a new round of talks between Joseph Kabila and rebel leaders was required to reach a peace accord in which Kabila would share power with former rebels. By June 2003, all foreign armies except those of Rwanda pulled out of Congo. The fighting did not subside, however.

A renewed rebellion in Congo was supported by Rwanda, whose army occupied vast parts of Congo and plundered millions of dollars' worth of minerals. The continued clashes in Eastern Congo, on the border with Rwanda, between the Congolese army and troops of a dissident general exacted a grievous toll on the population already ravaged by a decade of war. In 2005 and 2006, around 400,000 people were forced to flee their homes, thousands of women were raped, and hundreds of children were press-ganged into militias.

Five years after Congo's catastrophic war officially ended, the number of people who die each month as a consequence of the prolonged fighting is still 45,000, about the same number as in 2004, despite major efforts of the UN's largest peacekeeping force and billions of dollars in international aid. The nationwide elections in 2006 did little to mend Congo's many divisions. Even though the country amassed enormous wealth from its oil exports in the past decade, tens of thousands still die from hunger.

In the elections of 2006, Joseph Kabila became Congo's first democratically elected leader in over four decades. The polls, organized by the UN, were regarded as reasonably free and fair. However, the election did not much change the dismal state of this resource-rich country's economy and the prevalence of hunger and disease. In both Rwanda and Congo, ethnic hatreds and devastating conflicts between the rival groups frustrate efforts to establish some form of national unity. The Tutsi in Congo see themselves primarily as Tutsi, with very little affiliation to the Congolese nation.

For President Kabila, whose government is mostly concerned with maintaining control over the country and surviving the next rebellion, the Tutsi are enemies rather than fellow citizens. Congo's government spends most of its oil revenues on strengthening the army, largely by paying high salaries to the soldiers in order to secure their loyalty. Although the African states have formally recognized the borders of the countries in the region in various agreements, Congo's neighbors totally disregarded those borders. Corruption remains rampant, and large sums are used to buy ammunition for paramilitary groups, or end up in the Swiss bank accounts of their leaders. In these conditions, international aid is mostly a waste, since it has no effect on the belligerent forces or on the root cause of the conflict: The division of the population into rival ethnic groups with deep hatreds toward each other is nourished by bitter memories and conflicting interests.

Rwanda remains deeply involved in the struggle in eastern Congo that continues due to the lack of effective leadership by Joseph Kabila. Rwandan forces still operate in the eastern region, supposedly to protect the local Rwandans, even though a large UN peacekeeping mission is present. The Rwandan military is reportedly making more than $30 million a month from mining coltan, and is still exporting diamonds and gold mined in Congo. In the provinces of North and South Kivu, armed groups and the Congolese national army control the trade in precious minerals, including tin ore, gold, and coltan. This piratical mining by these armed gangs prevents the central government from establishing any order, and the paramilitary groups encounter few obstacles in their quest to plunder the rich resources and rob defenseless people. Their unrestricted access to the minerals enables paramilitary groups to maintain highly profitable trading networks that finance arms purchases and the recruitment of soldiers. The minerals are smuggled almost openly from the DRC through Rwanda or Burundi, and government officials in these countries provide access routes to bring the minerals to international markets.

In January 2008, another peace agreement was signed, but it did not take long before fighting started again. Hundreds of thousands of people were once again forced to flee their homes and to endure a new wave of hunger, disease, and the ravages of war perpetrated by brutal armies that killed and raped many thousands of civilians. The complete lack of central control also prevents the AU from mediating between the parties and drawing up an agreement that will be accepted by all parties. The AU lacks the necessary forces and, even with the support of the insufficient UN forces, it cannot intervene militarily, and the leaders of the African countries that determine the mandate of the AU do not seem concerned enough to find a solution to this calamity. The blue-helmeted peacekeepers are not strong enough to be able to put an end to the violence and the continued conflicts between Tutsi rebels and Congo's army.

Can Congo become a viable state?

The situation in Congo presents one of the worst cases of the deep and emotionally loaded division between tribes in Africa. Jeffrey Herbst and

Greg Mills have argued in an article entitled "There is no Congo" (*Foreign Policy* March, 2009) that the very concept of a Congolese state has outlived its usefulness. They suggest it is time for the international community "to recognize a simple, albeit brutal fact: The Democratic Republic of the Congo does not exist. All of the peacekeeping missions, special envoys, interagency processes, and diplomatic initiatives that are predicated on the Congo myth—the notion that one sovereign power is present in this vast country—are doomed to fail." The territory colonial powers carved out that became Congo has none of the characteristics required to make it a viable state: There is no central control and there are no institutions; the government has neither authority nor legitimacy; and it fails to establish the rule of law and prevent complete anarchy mainly because people refuse to cooperate. There are no shared interests that would give people incentives to establish some collaboration or maintain the rule of law; in fact, given the complete anarchy in the country, those who would try to maintain the law are bound to lose.

Although AU forces proved to be ineffective in the difficult situation in Congo, even with support by UN forces, the AU is key to an African solution, since this is the only way to exert pressure on the countries involved to reach an agreement that will not be perceived as foreign intervention. It is also becoming evident that in many regions, ethnic tensions and violence can ultimately only be resolved with agreements to make changes in the national borders that, in their current configuration, perpetuate the hostilities. Congo's rich resources complicate the situation, but they may also provide the means to compensate the countries involved and encourage them to agree to border changes that will prevent future conflicts. External entities, primarily the former colonial powers, will not be welcomed to the negotiations for this solution, but they can use their economic and political influence to convince the parties that they stand to lose if the negotiations fail.

Only the AU can mediate between the parties and design a mutually beneficial solution that will be accepted by all parties and will prevent, or at least minimize, future conflicts. Unfortunately, the AU has so far not proved to be effective enough for the task; the forces it has mobilized to prevent hostilities in this and other regions have been far too weak and disorganized, and the leaders of the African countries that determine the mandate of the AU seem concerned more with their own self-interests (at the national and personal levels) than with any genuine effort to find a solution to the conflicts.

Nonetheless, it is important to acknowledge that the African countries were able to reach an agreement to establish the AU and give it an ambitious mandate that would allow the organization to push for changes in the current divisive national borders in order to seek solutions for Africa's people, regardless of their current location, but with careful consideration to their ethnic affiliation. However, in the case of Congo and Rwanda, a solution could require the rival countries to give up part of their sovereignty and part of their gains from the region's rich resources, which would certainly be difficult to achieve. At this stage, it is hard to foresee a fair division of these resources that would be acceptable to all parties unless they are made to realize that without a compromise, they risk suffering greater losses.

The Namibia "border war"

Even bitter conflict between neighboring countries can have a promising end that leads to collaboration between the fighting armies that will benefit everyone. The conflict in Southern Africa that involved, among other countries, South Africa, Angola, and Namibia, had its roots in World War I, when South Africa invaded Namibia (German South-West Africa) on behalf of the Allied forces. After the war, South Africa was given the mandate by the League of Nations to administer the territory. The South African "Border War" (also known as the Namibian War of Independence) was conducted under the shadow of the cold war and lasted from 1966 to 1989; the two conflicting camps were allied with the two opposing superpowers of the cold war. Only in June 1988, after a long series of wars and an infinite number of skirmishes, the United States and the Soviet Union reached an agreement at a summit meeting between Ronald Reagan and Mikhail Gorbachev that Cuban troops would withdraw from Angola, and South Africa would withdraw from Namibia.

As the "Border War" raged, the countries involved in the fighting realized that the only way to overcome this destructive antagonism was to form an agreement for cooperation. The first step was taken in 1980 with the establishment of the Southern African Development Coordinating Conference (SADCC) that was initially formed as a loose alliance of nine majority-ruled states in southern Africa. The aim was to coordinate development projects in order to lessen the member countries' economic dependence on the existing apartheid regime in South Africa. In 1992, the organization was transformed from a coordinating conference into the Southern African Development Community (SADC) with a declaration and treaty signed at a "Summit of Heads of State and Government" that gave the organization legal status. Today, SADC includes provisions for a Free Trade Area (FTA), thus creating a regional market worth $360 billion, with a total population of 170 million in 15 countries.

The legacy of colonial borders

The history of the continent and its political and economic developments since the frantic "Scramble for Africa" by the leading European powers during the 1880s played a critical role in shaping the relations between the

African countries and in the civil conflicts within these countries since independence. Perhaps the most important and most obstructive legacy of the colonial powers is the borders they carved in the nineteenth century in order to divide Africa's ample resources among themselves. These borders were drawn on the map with little or no regard to the needs, historical heritage, and ethnic divisions of the African people, but these arbitrary lines became the continent's political borders when the African countries became independent.

The process of determining exclusive regions of colonial control in Africa started with a conference, convened in Berlin by European colonial powers in 1884–85, that divided the continent into agreed-upon spheres of influence to be free from encroachment by other colonial powers. The regions were determined by delegates from European countries that had some involvement or territorial claims in Africa. By carving out these regions, the colonial powers defined their respective spheres of influence and divided the continent's natural resources among themselves. Even though specific colonial borders (developed later) nominally separated the continent into different "countries," the local population had a very limited role in drawing up these borders; similarly, the colonial powers determined the regime or the governing authority in each of the colonies according to their own interests, which included not only exploitation of the country's resources, but also the efforts to prevent any opposition by the local population.

After the Berlin Conference, the colonial powers and/or their delegates in the African countries used threats, extortion, forgery, blackmail, murder, and even genocide to acquire "proofs" that the Africans who lived in these territories had given away their lands and their freedom in order to be governed by Europeans. A thumb print or an "X" mark by quill pen on a piece of paper was supposed to document the consent of the local people, who usually were not able to oppose the division of their lands because they lacked a unified authority that could represent the different ethnic groups. "Chiefs" supposedly signed these papers, even though many had no authority to do so and were not even aware of the implications of their signatures. The objective of the thumb prints was to give European trading or mining enterprises an excuse and a formal legitimacy to travel to Africa and then demand military protection from their European nations. In the following decades, most of Africa was divided into different regions under the rule, institutions, and laws of colonial powers.

When the colonial powers carved up Africa, they made no attempt to take into consideration the ethnic characteristics of the population, the differences in their heritage, their social norms, the leadership of tribal elders, and often not even differences in their languages. In some regions, it was not even possible to divide the territory between the tribes due to the large number of different tribes that lived there. In Nigeria, there are more than

400 tribes, and many of are divided between Nigeria and its neighboring states.

Many issues that were so arbitrarily disregarded by the colonial regimes became flashpoints once the colonies became independent states. But while the colonial administrative borders sometimes separated villages of the same tribe, or cut off villages from their agricultural lands and water resources, these borders did not serve as political borders dividing sovereign states, and there were no restrictions on crossing them; people could therefore continue to cultivate their lands and visit family members on both sides of the borders. However, when the African countries gained their independence, borders became international borders that could no longer be crossed without restrictions. All the potential problems created by the arbitrarily drawn colonial borders now came into the open, often resulting in border disputes between tribes that escalated into disputes between countries, violent conflicts, and wars. Similar problems emerged in later years with respect to the distribution of natural resources, particularly when new resources were discovered or when existing resources became more valuable due to a rise in their price. To be sure, similar disputes existed also in many countries in other continents, and some were resolved without armed conflict, through arbitration or negotiations. This also proved possible in some disputes in Africa, but in most cases, African leaders chose to fight for the outcome they preferred and some of the wars were exceedingly brutal and deteriorated into outright genocide.

Since Africa's colonial borders changed only marginally after the end of colonial rule, many tribes and ethnic groups remain divided between several different countries and villages are separated from the community's ancestral lands. At the same time, the population groups and tribes within many countries have very little in common and, in many cases, their only common language is that of the former colonial power. Rival tribes and different ethnic groups thus had to share the same country and, in the absence of a unifying national identity, these borders inevitably sowed the seeds of conflicts and wars that tore the countries apart in the decades after independence.

Yet, the legacy of colonialism does not provide a complete explanation of Africa's incessant civil conflicts and wars. Can the African leaders be exonerated, even though they made few efforts to prevent tribal conflicts and usually failed—for their own real or imaginary reasons—to seek peaceful settlements to border disputes?

For African intellectuals, these are sensitive and difficult questions. On the one hand, the legacy of colonialism remains an open wound in the African psyche and, all too often, is the main explanation African leaders offer for the difficulties their countries encountered after independence and that continue to plague many countries until today. On the other hand, the contribution of African leaders themselves to these conflicts should not be overlooked. Many did not make any effort to seek compromise solutions that could have prevented or mitigated the devastating conflicts, and all too often, these leaders were motivated by self-interest.

There is little dispute that the prolonged wars and the damage they inflicted were among the main reasons for Africa's stagnation and rising poverty. By deepening the hostilities between people, tribes, ethnic, and sectarian groups, these conflicts and wars made it far more difficult, and often downright impossible, to resolve disputes peacefully through negotiations and collaboration that would ultimately benefit all. These conflicts also allowed autocratic leaders to hold on to power and pursue their own self-interests by ruthlessly controlling and embezzling their countries' resources to enrich themselves, and these tyrannical regimes faced few restraints when they embarked on long and brutal wars.

Another critically important factor is the unequal power of the tribes that reflects the differences in their size or their territories. Some tribes gained greater economic power due to resources found in their lands or to their water resources and valuable agricultural lands, and some tribes benefited from preferential treatment under the colonial regime. In many African countries, the larger tribes led the struggle for liberation from colonial rule. The considerable differences between tribes led to rivalries that easily erupted in bitter conflicts when minority and poorer tribes challenged the preferential treatment the dominating tribe often continued to enjoy even after independence.

Mitigating cross-border hostilities

The successful struggle for African liberation had the potential to create a sense of common purpose and thus sow the seeds of national identity, but when they achieved their independence tribal disputes started to emerge over claims to the same land and water resources. The newly established central governments, in order to secure their sovereignty, often repressed these disputes rather than resolving them, even though the disputing tribes had no secessionist tendencies. The disputes and opposing claims were primarily due to arbitrary decisions of the colonial power to reallocate lands and resettle tribes according to their needs, but for newly independent states they created immediate problems that were sometimes described as the "black man's burden." The intense rivalries between tribes that were created by these disputes increased the divide between them and enabled political despots to strengthen their control.

The borders themselves created similar problems because they involved the reallocation of arable lands between the territories determined by the borderlines, and when the African countries became independent these now-international borders often also required either the division or the resettlement of tribes. One proposal to overcome some of the problems created by these arbitrary borders was to limit the power of the states to restrict cross-border movement of goods and people. But that did not appeal to the governments in power because it seemed like an infringement of national sovereignty. Over time, inter-country trade in goods has become much easier in Africa thanks to many trade agreements, but this could not settle disputes over lands that were divided by these borders.

Much remains to be done to settle these disputes, and the only realistic approach is negotiations in which the ruling criterion is quid pro quo. The same approach can be applied to settle border disputes, if the countries' leaders are in agreement. The plan sometimes suggested is to eliminate all obstacles and resolve all disputes in a single step to which all countries will agree, but this may be self-defeating; in practice, this can only be the conclusion of a gradual process of bilateral negotiations that will be beneficial to all and create conditions for more effective economic development.

One example is the settlement of the border dispute between Nigeria and Cameroon over the control of the Bakassi Peninsula. This dispute, settled in 2002 by the World Court (the UN's International Court of Justice in The Hague), had some moments of bitter irony when both countries justified their competing territorial claims (which had brought them to the brinks of war) with copies of yellowing colonial-era documents. Their intense interest in this territory was due to expectations of finding oil there; the irony was that both countries relied on colonial-era documents to make their cases, even though they both in principal opposed these borders. This basis for the settlement only highlights how difficult it would be to change these arbitrarily drawn borders. Although all African countries have disdain for the legacy of colonial rule, they based their competing claims on colonial documents. Following the agreement at the World Court, Nigeria handed control over the Bakassi Peninsula to Cameroon, even though most people in Bakassi indicated they preferred to be part of Nigeria. While Nigeria emphasized that by following the World Court's ruling it was showing its respect for international law, there was little improvement on the ground, because the inevitable result of the unpopular decision was a continuation of guerilla attacks against the central regime of Cameroon.

In another quite similar case, one of the conflicts in the Horn of Africa led to a bloody and very damaging war between Ethiopia and Eritrea from 1998 to 2000. After the war ended, a UN body entitled "Eritrea-Ethiopia Boundary Commission," established with the agreement of the two sides, decided the disputed territory belonged to Eritrea. Nevertheless, as of 2009, the territory is still held by Ethiopia. The question of how to solve border disputes between countries obviously involves many complex issues, but a solution that can be reached either by an agreement or arbitration that requires the agreement of each of the contestants seems infinitely preferable to war. Any solution must take into account the needs and preferences of the people who live in the disputed territory.

One obstacle is that political leaders often view a compromise as doing little to enhance their power. Continued confrontations between tribes in a contested area can make a compromise more difficult and make each tribe more dependent on the government that supports their claim. In Africa, dictators like Mobutu Sésé Seko and Robert Mugabe secured the loyalty of their followers and the subordination of those they ruled by stoking rivalries and conflicts between tribes, thus "rallying the troops" by supporting one side's fight against their perceived enemy.

The unwillingness to compromise, however, incurs high costs in human life and economic resources, and these costs have been intolerably high in Africa. After six decades of brutal wars, millions of victims, and economic stagnation, both the African nations and the international community are desperate to find solutions that will pacify the continent and enable sustainable economic development. While all countries agree there is an urgent need to resolve disputes over borders, territories, and resources, they are also aware of the major difficulties involved. At this stage and in the foreseeable future it is clear that no major changes can be made in the colonial borders, even though the leaders are all in agreement that these borders are highly damaging to the people, and border wars exact an intolerable toll.

The multitude of ethnic groups in Africa and within many African countries makes it impossible to divide countries along ethnic lines. The option of exchanging some territories or finding another arrangement to compensate groups that would be dislocated has not been ruled out, but even that cannot offer a comprehensive settlement given the large number of ethnic groups in many countries.

The African Union can have a central role in these settlements. It can be a widely accepted arbiter that has the trust of the contesting countries, inspires the trust of all the people that will be affected, and its ruling would have the support of most other African countries and peoples. The formal agreement between African countries today is that if two neighboring states declare a territorial dispute, the AU[3] would look into the colonial treaties to determine where the border ran in colonial times—and therefore, where the border ran at the time of independence and should run ever after. In other words, for most African countries, independence still leaves them totally dependent on the original borders of the colonial powers. Nevertheless, commonly agreed settlements can go a long way to easing the tension between tribes and ethnic groups within countries, and by easing internal tensions the sense of national unity could be strengthened, opposition to central authorities could be reduced, and even hostilities between countries could decline.

The only way to provide incentives for enhancing collaboration between countries is to increase the gains all of them will have from such collaboration. In other words, this must be a positive sum game in which the gaining countries will compensate the countries that suffer some losses, or in which an arrangement is made that will benefit each and every participating country. This strategy is quite complex and can be implemented only if countries have trust in each other and can be sure they are not shortchanged by any agreement made between them.

Has poverty been the cause of conflicts and wars in Africa?

In his bestselling book, *The Bottom Billion*,[4] Paul Collier argues that the main explanation for Africa's many wars is poverty: Most people in the bottom billion concentrate in 58 countries, 40 of them in Africa, and nearly three quarters of the poorest have been caught in a civil conflict or a war at one time or another. Seventy percent of the continent's population is below the age of 30, and most of these young people find themselves caught in a trap of hopeless poverty. According to Collier, the spread and depth of poverty in Africa has been, and continues to be, the main reason for incessant conflicts. Poverty, Collier writes, is both the main cause and the effect of wars that can drag on for years with disastrous effects on economies and people's lives.

Several studies have examined how this is possible. In his book, *States, Scarcity, and Civil Strife in the Developing World*, Colin H. Kahl describes the path from extreme poverty combined with scarce resources to violent conflicts, the collapse of law and order and the deterioration into lawlessness and anarchy: Deepening poverty leaves the population desperate, but the government is unable or unwilling to respond and offer any solution; growing desperation gives rise to violent groups determined to seek "self help" by fighting other groups and against government forces over the country's resources.

The question of whether poverty has been the cause or the effect of war, however, requires an analysis that goes beyond statistical analysis of correlation. The World Bank 2003 report, *Breaking the Conflict Trap*, calculated meticulously that aid combined with military action could halve the probability that civil wars would break out in a poor country, from precisely 44 percent to 22 percent,[5] which evokes the old adage about the average depth of the water in a lake in which a champion swimmer has drowned. Collier's conclusion in *The Bottom Billion* is: "The evidence is against...internal solutions[;] breaking the conflict trap and the coup trap are not tasks that these societies can readily accomplish by themselves." It does not require an African intellectual to smell the racist fragrance, even though I cannot imagine Collier had this in mind. Breaking the conflict trap is no easier in Iraq (although the coup trap was broken by Western troops), in Central Asian countries—whether or not they are in Russian or Chinese territories—and in many other "societies."

I also found unconvincing the thesis put forward by Collier, according to which the poorest countries are trapped in a vicious circle of poverty, civil war, military coups, looting of natural resources, and failed states. Obviously, there is no statistical method to prove this is a vicious circle, and correlation does not establish causality. I argued earlier that poverty was the *outcome* of civil conflicts and not their cause, and all the civil wars described in this part of the book were not triggered by poverty, as some erupted well before the countries' natural resources ignited or escalated the conflicts. Even the genocidal conflict between the Hutu and Tutsi was not an outcome of poverty but of deeply rooted feelings of discrimination, exclusion, and deprivation since colonial times that created deep animosities between these tribes. The obsessive looting of Congo's rich natural resources was not instigated by the rival tribes but by the neighboring countries that became involved in this conflict and by warlords who found it an easy way to enrich themselves. This, and the other bloody conflicts, started before the natural resources were discovered or could be exploited. The vicious circle Collier describes was indeed vicious, but it was not a repetitive cycle but rather an ongoing sequence of events that had historical roots that nourished these conflicts and were their driving forces.

Poverty has not been the cause of these conflicts, and the poor were not able to fight against the mighty security forces that guarded the president, were well-equipped and well-nourished, and by and large loyal to their chief who bought their loyalty with hefty rewards. Although since African countries became independent, as noted, some 115 African presidents were toppled in coups, often quite grisly, most were toppled by army commanders and much less were toppled in uprisings caused by tribal rebellions.

The impact of the rural poor

The African poor who live mostly in rural areas did not organize resistance movements or effective oppositions to regimes *because* they were poor, even though they were often exploited by governments that imposed heavy taxes on agricultural exports in order to finance their reckless expenses, and were grossly neglected, without government investment in rural areas. The call for arms against despotic leaders did not reach them because the rural poor could not unite due to their tribal divisions. Even when the rural poor were angry enough to protest against government policies that discriminated against them, they could not muster the power and the arms to form an effective opposition. Their dispersion across large areas and their inability to join forces prevented them from forming a unified front and an effective opposition to the government. In countries where the poor managed to form a united front against the regime—Côte d'Ivoire, Chad, Eritrea, Sudan, and Niger—they were able to unify along tribal, ethnic, or sectarian lines, whereas in countries where the poor are divided into a large number of ethnic groups and tribes—Cameroon and Nigeria—they did not manage to unite, even though the elites looted the countries' riches.

In several meetings of African leaders and leaders of the G-8 developed countries that convened in the wake of the food crisis, it was recognized that the poverty and weakness of the rural population enabled the leaders to practically bypass them in the allocation of resources. As a result, their share in the government budget has been very small, and most African governments have made few investments in rural areas. Even in the past decade, when the resource-rich countries accumulated enormous wealth from their exports, only a minute share trickled down to the rural areas. Despite the rapid growth of these countries the income per capita of their rural population has barely increased, and most remained poor.

Moreover, nearly half the African countries are still failed or fragile states that do not manage to maintain law and order; they continue to be engaged in wars or civil conflicts, or are still recovering from the damages of prolonged war. These countries are still ruled by dictators even though some of leaders were elected in nominally democratic elections. In these countries, the rural population is at an even greater disadvantage since they live in such insecurity, are often robbed either by gangsters or by government forces, and in many conflicts millions of them have had to flee their homes because they were essential unprotected.

Civil conflicts were not triggered or caused by poverty, but by rivalry between tribes that is entrenched in a long history of enmity in the wake of many years of deprivation, discrimination, and exclusion that in many cases goes back to colonial times and in some cases, like the conflicts between North and South Sudan, predates colonial times. Many civil conflicts escalated when these countries became independent, and the leaders deepened the discrimination by favoring their own tribes while minority tribes were excluded. Favoritism and nepotism are still common and often lead to violent demonstrations by minority tribes against their exclusion.

An escalation of civil conflicts into a broader war between states is first and foremost a decision of the countries' leaders. Some wars between states have erupted when a neighboring country became involved in a civil conflict by supporting a rebel tribe's fight against a central regime. That was the reason for the escalation of the civil conflict in Darfur to become a war between Sudan and Chad. As we saw earlier, the support Chad gave to Sudanese rebel forces, giving them shelter and arms, triggered the war between Chad and Sudan. The conflict between the Hutu and the Tutsi escalated to the African World War when Uganda and Rwanda came to the support of the Hutu in Congo and other countries then came to support the Congolese government. In most African countries, though, the poverty of the people in rural areas and the division between them along tribal lines did not constitute a threat to autocratic leaders, and even communities of the minority tribes that were widely discriminated against were in most cases too poor and powerless to form an effective resistance and challenge their country's leadership. These leaders also spent huge resource on building up massive security forces that enabled them to repress any opposition by local tribes.

According to Collier's calculations, low-income countries have a 14 percent chance of being exposed to a civil war in any five-year period. Collier speaks of a vicious circle, in which the poorer the country the more frequently it succumbs to civil war: "halve the...income of the country and you double the risk of a civil war." Once a country has one civil war, the likelihood additional civil wars will follow is higher: "Half of all civil wars are post-conflict relapses."

One civil war indeed increases the likelihood of that additional civil wars will follow, but this was mostly a reflection of the entrenched enmities between tribes, which entangled them in an incessant cycle of wars that indeed impoverished them and exhausted their resources. But the driving force for a new round of civil wars between these tribes was still their old enmity and unsettled past conflicts, and not because they succumbed to a civil war *because* they were poor. Statistical analysis does not distinguish between correlation and causality, but a study of the historical origins of these conflicts unravels old rivalries. One example noted earlier is the civil war between South and North Sudan that has a long history of deep animosity between black Sudanese in the South and Arab Sudanese in the North, exacerbated by the scars of periods of slavery underpinning the stubborn and extremely costly resistance of black Sudanese against Arab Sudanese. The conflict between the Hutu and the Tutsi goes back to the times of the Belgian colonial rule that discriminated against the Hutu on racist grounds.

4.2
The Impact of Wars and Civil Conflicts on Africa's Growth and Poverty

The staggering toll of Africa's wars and civil conflicts in human lives and resources has been aggravated by the devastating impact on its economies. Entire regions have been ruined, communities brought to ashes, and millions have had to flee homes and land, and become refugees. The frequency of countries engaging in wars and conflicts, and the devastation of their economies, has been higher in resource-rich countries, in large measure due to the extremely unequal distribution of their income.

In these countries up to 80 percent of revenues from exports of primary resources were shared by the top 1 percent of population, whereas the majority benefited very little. The countries' leaders and their economic elites had full control over these resources, while the rest of the population was largely left out. That unequal income distribution increased the inequality between tribes and regions and intensified the animosity of the deprived population and their feeling of being exploited. That exclusion and deprivation increased their motivation to fight against the central regime to demand their fair share in the revenues and often also to claim control over lands in which these resources were found if these were their ancestral lands. The central regimes had used excessive power to expel these tribes from their lands by burning villages and killing many. The regimes in Sudan, Niger, Nigeria, Sierra Leone and many other countries refused to give up control over these resources or to share revenues, thus triggering civil conflicts and long wars that ravaged their economies, deterred foreign investors, and reduced revenues. Angola, Africa's second largest oil producer, was unable to export its oil for nearly a decade due to a civil conflict.

William R. Easterly and Ross Eric Levine (1997) coined the term "Africa's Growth Tragedy" to describe the continent's three-decade long stagnation due to wars. They focused on two particularly important factors that caused these wars: The destructive policies of many African leaders, and the ethnic fragmentation of the population in many African countries that led to most conflicts. These factors are not independent from each other, since the destructive policies of the African leaders who did all in their power to maintain their grip on their country and obsessively prevented any potential opposition from challenging for control, with highly biased policies in favor of the leading tribe in order to secure its loyalty, intensified tribal rivalries. In fact, the African country in which the population is the most homogeneous is Somalia.

The ethnic fragmentation of the population was and remains a problem in many other countries, including in Europe. The fragmentation of Yugoslavia into several ministates along ethnic lines occurred after a devastating civil war that cost the lives of hundreds of thousands, and a cease fire was enforced only after the intervention of NATO forces. Civil war in parts of Central Asia is also far from reaching a settlement and, as a consequence, their economies are left behind despite their great potential. In many other economies, ethnic diversity did not lead to extreme rivalry and armed conflicts, as the different ethnic groups came to realize the benefit they can obtain by settling disputes peacefully and thus avoiding rivalry and costly wars, most notably in the ethnically most diverse country, the United States. In Africa, the number of wars that have engulfed the continent, their extremely high costs, and their paralyzing effects on the continent's growth have been devastating, however, and their ruinous effects on the African people and the waste of the continent's resources exceeded all proportions, to the extent that the even the World Bank questioned whether Africa can claim the twenty-first century.

The ethnic fragmentation of African societies is an integral part of their historical heritage and their rich culture, and this of course cannot be changed. The impact of the African leaders on the continent's "Growth Tragedy," however, goes far beyond their destructive policies. The report discussed in the next section noted that in most African countries it was not even possible to conduct any coherent country-wide economic policy. The tyrannical control of these leaders over their countries, the embezzlement of the countries' resources to enrich themselves, their deliberate measures to prevent the establishment of functioning institutions, and their control over the legal system were more damaging to their countries' development. To secure the loyalty and cooperation of the government institutions, all the middle and high level positions in these institutions as well as judges most army commanders were appointed by the country's leader and they were richly rewarded for their loyalty.

The transition of many African countries to democracy in the past two decades was hoped to be a step in the right direction, but so far most elections have been a mere façade and in many of them the same autocratic leaders remained in power. Nevertheless, it is far too early to reach negative conclusions, and this transition is a process still going on; the current leaders are far less free to control their countries without accountability or responsibility. At the same time, though, in the transition to democracy voting patterns were clearly along tribal or religious lines, and all too often exacerbated hostilities and intensified competition between rival ethnic groups, thereby undermining the countries' stability. This change in the political systems raises questions, therefore, about whether this is the correct strategy to bring over time the fundamental changes necessary to reverse their growth tragedy.

Africa's missing billions

Currently, more than thirteen million people in SSA are internally displaced, and more than three million are refugees who live in camps outside their countries. In the conflicts ravaging Africa, the vast majority of victims did not take an active part in the conflict, but died from hunger and disease. The decline in the number of wars in Africa since the early 2000s, however tentative, including in the conflict zones of Angola, Mozambique, Liberia, and Sierra Leone, is testimony to the capacity of the countries themselves, sometimes with the help of other governments and the UN, to bring fighting to an end by exerting pressures on the antagonists involved. Nevertheless, stability in these countries and in other weak African nations remains fragile.

Between 1990 and 2005, 23 African nations were involved in armed conflicts. They included some of the more stable countries such as Ghana, South Africa, and Uganda; in several other countries, conflicts turned flourishing economies into fragile states. All too often, regional or even local conflicts expanded to neighboring countries, prolonging the conflicts and increasing the number of civilian casualties. The civil strife in Darfur has rapidly spread to neighboring Chad, Ethiopia, and the Central African Republic. The fighting in Côte d'Ivoire in 2002 disrupted the economies of Mali, Burkina Faso, and Niger, and the continued genocide and war in Congo and Rwanda, that in the late 1990s became Africa's World War, continues to threaten the stability and economic recovery of the entire region.[6]

A report entitled "Africa's Missing Billions" (2007) prepared by the International Action Network on Small Arms, a London-based international network of NGOs Safer-world and Oxfam International, concluded that during the past 15 years more than $300 billion has been squandered on armed conflicts in Africa. These sums could cover the cost of solving the HIV and AIDS epidemic as well as provide prevention and treatment for tuberculosis and malaria. According to the report, African countries involved in conflicts had, on average, 50 per cent more infant deaths, 15 percent more undernourished people, a decline in food supply per person by 12 per cent, and a decline in average life expectancy by five years. The report also highlights additional costs:

> The indirect costs from lost opportunities are even higher. Economic activity falters or grinds to a halt. Income from valuable natural resources

ended up lining individual pockets or their Swiss bank accounts rather than benefiting the country. As a result it was not possible to conduct any coherent macroeconomic policy or give the Central Bank any power over the money supply or the interest rates. These countries suffered from chronic inflation and mounting debts despite their export earnings and deterred any foreign investment. People suffered from unemployment, lack of public services and major trauma when they were expelled from their homes, their families were killed, women were raped, and they lost hope to build their life. More people, especially women and children, died from the fallout of the conflict than in the conflict itself. (p. 3)

Many local conflicts deteriorated into an open confrontation and civil strife when the government took sides in favor of one of the tribes or ethnic groups and used the state apparatus, often with brute force, to support that side. The Rwandan genocide reached that extremity as a result of a tribal conflict that deteriorated into a regional war. Despite the region's rich resources, the political and economic consequences of the conflict make the prospects for a settlement increasingly bleaker. Violent conflicts have increased poverty and famine and sown the seeds of another more violent conflict that brought about the collapse of the countries that were engaged in war and accelerated their decline into lawlessness and anarchy, further reducing the possibility of resolving the conflict. The ceaseless confrontations in the Horn of Africa, Congo, and Rwanda have lasted well over a decade and, despite the horrific toll in human lives, and a series of fragile peace agreements, there is no end in sight.

The report on "Africa's Missing Billions" emphasized how conflicts impoverish the people in the countries involved and exacerbate hunger and the spread of diseases. The massive waste of resources in these conflicts also raises difficult questions about the actual contribution of international aid to the African countries. Has this aid made any material contribution to saving lives or reducing hunger in countries trapped by the ravages of these wars? Could this aid have in fact contributed to prolonging rather than shortening the wars by reducing the pressure on the rival governments to end the war?

Although the conflicts in Africa have not ended, and despite the waste of billions of dollars, it is essential in many countries and regions to continue with international aid to save the lives of hungry people. The enormous waste of resources emphasizes, however, the need to intensify efforts to bring these conflicts to an end. In some countries, it may be necessary to involve the forces of the UN peacekeeping mission that, together with intense international pressure, would be able to establish a ceasefire that would enable parties to reach an agreement on a more stable modus vivendi.

Unfortunately, the military force of the African Union has been ineffective in the continent's confrontations, though it has to be acknowledged that this is only the first step in the process of creating coalition among the African countries to establish this force. The developed countries can support that process by providing training and equipment to this force. It is equally essential to strengthen the pan-African bodies, most notably the African Union (AU), to apply strong and effective pressure, through sanctions or incentives, on the countries to stop the fighting and abide by international laws.

The threat of rising inequalities

Inequality in Africa has several dimensions and not all of them can be measured along the income scale:

- Inequality between countries that became rich due to their natural resources and countries that are becoming poorer due to rapidly growing population, dwindling resources, and higher prices in the world market for fuel and food imports;
- Inequality between rural and urban populations;
- Inequality between poor urban slum dwellers and the elites, or even the middle classes, in the urban areas that have accumulated, legally or illegally, the riches created by the process of globalization, and
- Inequality between tribes in rural areas.

These inequalities are still increasing, and their explosive potential is growing. Despite economic growth, and perhaps even because of it, these inequalities continued to rise along all these dimensions. With few exceptions (such as Malawi, where the government's pioneering experiment helps the rural population with a free supply of fertilizers), income inequalities continue to rise in most countries due to highly unequal distribution of revenues and the embezzlement of state coffers by the elite.

Although the majority of the poor live in the rural areas, poverty is increasing also in the urban centers. According the UN-HABITAT's global urban indicators, by the mid-2000s more than two-thirds of the urban population in SSA (except for South Africa) lived in shantytowns and most of the rest of the urban population lives in slums. In the resource-rich countries a tiny elite is enjoying their country's riches, a short drive from their well-protected compounds brings you to extremely dismal shantytowns.

Only few countries that benefited from the rapid growth made sincere efforts to allocate more resources to public services in health, education, and infrastructure, and to improving living conditions of the poor in the urban centers. Even in these countries, however, the government's investments combined with investments of donor countries fell far short of the population's needs in order to reach the Millennium Development Goals.

The resource-poor countries incurred high losses due to the rise in oil prices. Some of these countries benefited, however, from large investments of international corporations in a frenetic search for natural resources in their lands. In some countries, including Ghana and Uganda, new oil and natural gas resources were found. In some resource-rich countries, too, new resources were found, including Sierra-Leona (oil) and Botswana (uranium). Several other resource-poor countries benefited from ripples of growth in the resource-rich countries due to their stability and peaceful conditions, and they became "frontier economies" that attracted foreign investors to their capital markets. Most resource-poor countries were further impoverished by the rise in the prices of oil and food, and quite a few of them were hit by drought-related crop failures. Prolonged civil conflicts continued to ruin the economies of the resource-rich countries, and some of them, including Niger, Côte d'Ivoire, and the Democratic Republic of Congo benefited very little from exploitation of their precious resources.

Despite an ample supply of labor and the low wages, the industrial sector remained undeveloped, and only small investments were made in primarily light manufacturing for the local market, since local industries are uncompetitive in world markets. Small government investments left local industries in poor condition, unable to invest in modern production technology or to compete with the East Asian industries, and unable to provide employment to the growing urban population.

The threat of rising inequalities between and within countries has become a security risk, and the civil unrest in Kenya, Nigeria, Côte d'Ivoire, and other countries was largely due to the growing gap between the haves and have-nots. The global recession aggravated income inequalities due to the sharp decline in remittances that had become an essential component of the income of the rural population. As a result, societies are increasingly divided along income classes, particularly in urban areas.

Income inequality between countries

Chapter 1.1 offers several diagrams to highlight the large increase in income inequality between countries in the past decade due to large differences in export revenues of the resource-rich countries and the resulting differences in their growth rates. The threat for the continent of widening income gaps between countries is that incentives of the better-off countries to collaborate with the poor and fragile states are diminishing. The growing divide slows the development of Africa-to-Africa economic intercourse and cooperation and is likely to deter countries from participating in regional initiatives such as water projects, inter-country roads or a railway system. Many of these projects require regional cooperation that may include also the worse-off or fragile states. In some regions inequality between countries may also augment the "bad neighbor" effects due to flows of migrants from the poor to the more developed and stable countries.

The rise in inequality between countries vastly accelerated in the past decade. Until the late 1990s, the impact of globalization on Africa was unfavorable due to the low and declining prices of their natural resources. During the last two decades, the growth in world trade concentrated in the emerging economies and their share has increased sharply. That growth has not yet had an impact on the price of primary commodities, and even oil prices have declining. The demand for consumer goods in the emerging economies was still rather small since their incomes have just started to rise and their production was mostly labor intensive with low wages. During the first phase of globalization, Africa's share in world trade has gradually declined, and the region was increasingly marginalized as global trade rapidly expanded. During the 1990s, the share of African countries in world imports declined from 1.13 percent to 1.02 percent, due in part to its slow growth, whereas the share of the entire group of developing countries increased from 18.7 percent to 25.3 percent.

Income gaps between countries during these years were relatively small, although income inequalities within countries were already very high due to the high and growing earnings differential between the top 5 percent and the rest of the population. The income differences between rural and urban populations were not very extreme and rural–urban migration was still on a small scale. Estimates of the GNI index between individuals in selected countries do not show extreme inequalities, but this was in large part because the top elite did not take part in these surveys.

Figure 4.1 compares the ratio between the mean per-capita income in a country in 1997–2002 (normalized to be 100 in 2002), and the mean per capita income in that country in all the subsequent years until 2009 in a group of 26 African countries. The countries were selected so that they represent 85 percent of the population in SSA, and these are the largest countries in each of five groups of countries that include the oil exporters, the other resource-rich countries, the resource-poor landlocked countries, the resource-poor coastal countries, and the fragile states.

Figure 4.1 shows the trends in these ratios in all 26 countries. The distance between the uppermost line and the bottom line shows the change in the income gap between the most rapidly growing country and the country that grew at the lowest rate. High growth rates were achieved, as expected, by the oil exporting countries. As subsequent figures show, however, not all resource-rich countries achieved high growth rates, mainly because they were bogged down in conflicts and wars. Also, some resource-rich countries had high growth rates, whereas others remained stagnant and poor due to civil conflicts or despotic leaders who embezzled a large share of the countries' revenues. Quite a few countries, like Sierra Leone and Angola, had

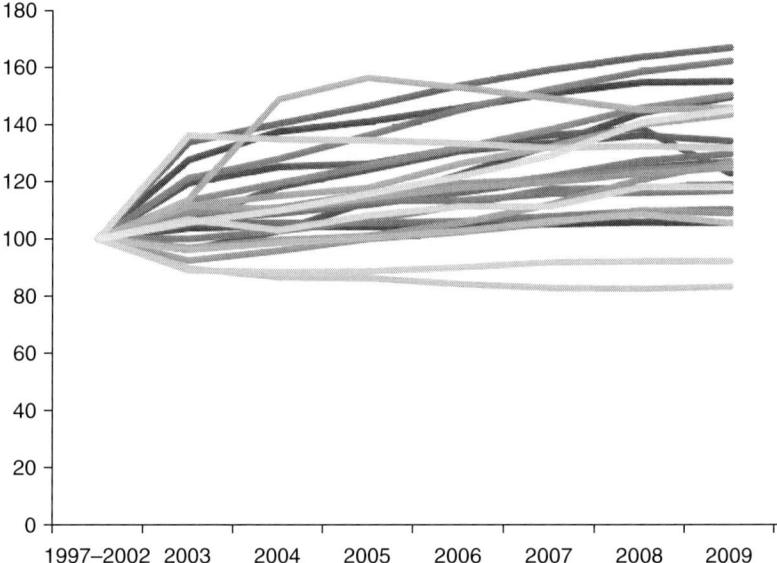

Figure 4.1 Changes in the income gap between the countries of SSA* (Measured in current US$ per capita)

* The income gap is indicated by the distance between the lower and the higher lines which shows the percentage difference between the lower and the higher incomes.

Source: Based on the Regional WEO, 2009, and the author's calculations.

high growth rates when they managed to reach a peace agreement and put an end to the conflicts. Their rapid growth was also due to the very low levels of income in the early 2000s after many years of conflicts. Sierra Leone also reaped high revenues from its exports of highly lucrative titanium ore. In more recent years, oil was discovered there.

The relatively small income gaps between countries made it easy to plan and develop regional projects and strengthen collaboration between countries. Since the economies of African countries (except for South Africa and Nigeria) are too small, only joint projects can have sufficient economy of scale to support profitable investment in regional industries. That development required both the countries and the development organizations to give high priority to subregional and regional integration of both production and markets. Regional projects, like regional infrastructure networks in roads and telecommunications and regional water projects, were designed and promoted by the World Bank and donor countries to give incentives to such collaboration. This also required more open national economies to Africa-to-Africa trade, and there followed a wave of trade agreements between the African countries.

Rising inequality between countries reduced incentives for collaboration. Despite the steep decline in prices of natural resources as an effect of the commodity bust, there is still robust global demand for oil, natural gas, and other resources; their prices have started to rise and the resource-rich countries are likely to have resumed their growth by 2010. The potential gains of the resource-rich countries from regional projects for development of other sectors in industry or agriculture will, therefore, be quite small because the contribution of these sectors to their national economies and to the budget will be much less significant.

This is clearly a shortsighted view, however, because by giving lower priority to the diversification of their economies by developing other sectors, these countries remain dependent on revenues from the export of few natural resources that have unstable prices, which will therefore increase economic instability and dependence on credit in the global financial markets. Equally imported is their limited capacity to increase employment in the urban areas, where the unemployment rate often exceeds 50 percent. The diversification of economies will also increase the incomes of the low income groups and, over time, create a substantial middle class, as it has in the East Asian countries.

Africa's "fragile" and "failed" states

In the past decade, as the number of conflicts in Africa have somewhat subsided and the leading and more stable regional countries, primarily South Africa, Ghana, and Senegal, gained more influence, they increased their efforts to further reduce the continent's conflicts by strengthening regional trade agreements and the African Union (AU). The AU now represents all 53 African countries; with the support of the leading world economies, primarily the G-20, as well as international organizations, the AU now has the potential to play a far more important role in providing leadership for the entire continent and assuming the role of moderator and arbiter in many local conflicts.

Presently, however, many African countries are still fragile and continue to be embroiled in wars and civil conflicts. The eruption of a new war in the Democratic Republic of Congo, the continued crises in Darfur, Ethiopia, and other countries, highlight the fact that the continent is far from being at peace. Efforts to further reduce armed conflicts may face a major challenge due to the growing scarcity of water resources and the erosion of arable lands as an effect of global warming. The current conflicts between government forces and local tribes in fragile states may give a worst-case, but not insurmountable, scenario of the potential damage to the entire continent if these conflicts escalate.

In some fragile states the government has lost control over large parts of its territory; countries like Somalia and Congo D.R. have collapsed into total chaos and lawlessness and even their capital cities are controlled by militias and armed gangs. The loose coalition of Islamic clerics and militia leaders that in 2006 captured several main urban centers in Somalia, including Mogadishu, collapsed in early 2007 with the support of Ethiopian troops that crossed into the country to chase away the remnants of the insurgency. The region's instability spilled to neighboring countries, worsened the refugee crises, and contributed to escalate the clashes between rebel groups backed by the governments of Chad and Sudan.

These and other failed or fragile states offer fertile ground for terrorists, organized crime, and drug trafficking as violent conflicts spread and the country's authorities are unable to maintain law and order. In extreme cases, drug smuggling, arms dealing, and shelter to forces of terrorist organizations like al-Qaeda may create security risks not only to the neighboring countries but to the entire international community. The keen interest of the developed countries in strengthening fragile states, preventing the eruption of new civil conflicts, and restoring government control is therefore an integral part of the strategy to fight terrorism.

The donor countries have also recognized that since government leadership is practically absent, coordination of donors' activities is necessary, but building the capacity of government and public institutions often can be achieved more effectively without formal consultation and coordination with the government.

Many African countries are to some degree fragile states, and only a handful have more stable regimes (Table 4.1). According to the Freedom House Institute's 2006 survey, only seven countries in Sub-Saharan Africa are considered as "free" countries. Despite the large-scale transition to democracy, only about one third of the democratic countries can be characterized as having a legitimate and dependable democracy with timely elections, and an orderly change of power. Nearly half the African countries are included in the various lists of fragile states, and in the past decade many have been engaged, or are still engaged, in violent civil strife and wars. Somalia and Congo D.R. are the most extreme examples of failed states in Africa (even though Congo had free elections in 2006), but they are by no means the only countries in which the central government does not have control over large parts of the country.

According to the World Bank definition, in "fragile" or "weak states" the government's policies and institutions are often unable to deliver even the most basic services to their citizens, including security, protecting life and property, and defending the country against internal or external terrorist groups.

A "failed state" fails to provide physical security or prohibit illegal use of arms; these states fail to provide economic security or basic public services like health and education. A failed states can also endanger neighboring

Table 4.1 List of African fragile states

Country	Av. Ann. Growth rate 2000-2008	IDA Rating
Somalia		N.A.
Liberia*		N.A.
Togo*		2.34
Sudan	7.6	2.39
Zimbabwe		1.34
Chad	7.6	2.42
Dem. Rep. Congo	3.9	2.49
Côte d'Ivoire	0.1	2.59
Cent. African Rep.	0.1	2.46
Angola*		2.59
Eritrea*		2.60
Guinea-Bissau*		2.63
Congo Rep.*		2.69
Burundi*		2.77
Guinea*		2.78
Sierra Leone*		2.91
Ethiopia	7.1	3.35
Uganda	7.5	3.54
Nigeria	8.7	3.15

Source: IDA.
* Not included in the OECD list.
DFID and the OECD-DAC define "fragile states" as states where the government *cannot or will not* deliver food and humanitarian support to the population or prevent epidemics.

Many are in continued stagnation, their leadership is weak or highly autocratic, and their human misery has actually worsened.

According to the OECD, fragile states are "unable to provide physical security, legitimate political institutions, sound economic management and social services for the benefit of its population."

The World Bank's IDA rating is a country performance rating which rates countries on the basis of 16 criteria grouped in four clusters:

(a) Economic management;
(b) Structural policies;
(c) Policies for social inclusion and equity; and
(d) Public sector management and institutions.

states by providing refuge to illegal armed groups that use its territory to reorganize and train their forces. Chauvet, Collier, and Hoeffler (2007) estimated that the total population of failed states makes up only about 7 percent of the world's population, but 15 percent of the world's poor. Wars and civil conflicts absorb huge resources, and Chauvet et al. estimate the direct costs of failed states are $270 billion annually, about 3.5 times total global development aid.

To determine the group of countries classified by the OECD as "fragile states" (OECD *Development Effectiveness in Fragile States, 2007–08*) the organization established a forum of experts to determine principles for "Good International Engagement in Fragile States and Situations," and to define priorities for assistance in state building (Table 4.2). In order to provide practical recommendations for donors, these experts identified the needs of fragile states to help them reach stability. The OECD now monitors the flow of resources to the fragile states in order to assist donors to allocate aid and increase coordination between them. According to OECD definitions, a third of the world's poor live in fragile states.

In the recent OECD list of 20 fragile states, 11 are in SSA and all were included in the 2004 list. The OECD criteria rank 181 countries; the majority of those in the bottom one-third are African. In contrast, several of the African countries that had stable regimes and were not involved in wars are included among the "frontier economies" that attract foreign investors and are growing more rapidly.

Table 4.2 OECD criteria of fragile states

DEMOGRAPHIC PRESSURES
REFUGEES AND DISPLACED PERSONS
GROUP GRIEVANCE
HUMAN FLIGHT
UNEVEN DEVELOPMENT
ECONOMY
DELEGITIMIZATION OF STATE
PUBLIC SERVICES
HUMAN RIGHTS
SECURITY APPARATUS
FACTIONALIZED ELITES
EXTERNAL INTERVENTION

Source: OECD Development Effectiveness in Fragile States.

The ranking of "fragile states" by the OECD is only one of several rankings made annually by various private and public organizations and are also used by foreign investors to decide whether or not to invest in these countries. For these investors, the most important indicators are the stability of the regime, the risk of civil conflicts, and government effectiveness in maintaining law and order. In their rankings the OECD used the criteria in the above table.

DFID-OECD advocated an approach to providing aid to the fragile states which includes small funds for short periods; policy dialogue in addition to, and sometimes as a condition to, aid; direct funding for projects rather than channeling aid through the budget, and giving preference to NGOs rather than to state institutions to carry out projects.

The World Bank's International Development Assistance (IDA) is using two main criteria to determine which countries can access IDA resources:

- Relative poverty: Defined as GNI per capita below an established threshold and updated annually (in fiscal year 2009 the threshold was $1,095).
- Lack of creditworthiness: Countries that cannot borrow on market terms and are therefore in need for concessional resources to finance development programs.

The main factor that determines the allocation of IDA resources is the country's performance in implementing policies that promote economic growth and poverty reduction, as measures by these two above criteria.

Conditions for aid to fragile states

Collier and Dollar (2001) argued that if aid is used more effectively, it could make a greater contribution to reducing poverty in lagging regions. Even more potent than aid are significant policy reforms in these countries. They developed a model for efficient allocation of aid, in which aid is given in response and according to policy reforms that create conditions for a more effective use of aid for poverty reduction. By evaluating different scenarios of policy reforms and their impact on the effectiveness of aid, they sought to identify strategy that would enable the world to cut poverty in half in every major region. Collier further developed this scheme in his book, *Wars, Guns and Votes* (2009), which will be discussed in more detail in the next section.

Their analysis obviously does not include emergency food aid in the case of large-scale famine due to a drought, or health aid to control the spread of disease. Even in these cases, though, the government in many countries takes too little responsibility for helping its own needy population and covers a very small share of the cost of that aid. Since neither the World Food Organization nor the World Health Organization, nor any other organization that provides food or health aid, are going to withhold emergency aid until negotiations with the government reach an agreement, there have been quite a few cases in which the government in some countries effectively withheld its own aid or contributed very little to the costs of emergency aid in anticipation that the international organization would cover the entire costs of this operation.

In the case of nonemergency aid to help failed states build their economies, there is an obvious dilemma in setting conditions or demanding policy reforms as a condition for aid. Incomes of such countries are low and government resources extremely limited. Policy and governance are persistently bad, but this could be because of poverty and lack of resources. How can such countries first make the reforms to qualify for aid if they do not have the resources in the first place? Would it be correct to demand policy reforms as a *pre-condition* for aid that is in fact aimed at helping a country make these reforms?

Clearly, a failed state needs both the resources and the guidance to implement necessary reforms. Institutional reforms that can achieve tangible results in reducing poverty and promoting growth are inevitably difficult and require considerable time, especially in countries that do not have these institutions or cannot establish effective systems of governance. Growth policies can be well designed to be "pro-poor," as they have been under the "Washington Consensus," but their implementation is in the hands of indigenous governmental institutions. For that reason, the later stages of IMF and World Bank reforms emphasize measures for building effective governmental institutions as an integral part of long-term reforms. Under these constraints, a more productive approach than the one suggested by Collier and Dollar is taken by the UK Department for International Development (DFID) and OECD: Their strategy is to give the country the first tranche of aid so its government can use these funds to start building institutions; additional tranches are conditioned on the progress the government makes in improving the system of governance.

The design of policy reforms in a fragile state also must depend on the causes of the state's fragility. These causes determine, in turn, the priorities of policy reforms. The first and highest priority is to build the capacity of the state to give security to its people. In an increasing number of African countries there is deterioration in the security conditions despite the decline in the number of civil conflicts and wars. In large measure, this is due to demographic and social developments, primarily to accelerated urbanization discussed in Part II. If the state is failing to provide security and to control the illegal use of arms, then this should be the first priority, and more aid should be given to assist in building effective and reliable security forces. That aid should be designed, and proper conditions set, to prevent the participation of these forces in any coup d'état in the future, and prevent the sale of arms that escalates internal conflicts and fosters illegal use of arms.

Only after providing security, protecting the life and property of its citizens, and asserting control over the entire country can the government proceed to build functioning civil institutions and recover its economy. Since it takes time and expertise to build an effective, well-trained, and loyal security force, financial aid alone may not be sufficient or adequately used. A country may need the assistance of UN peacekeepers or, at a later stage, AU military personnel in order to build and train its security force. This process will require strict conditions and close supervision to make sure that the funds are properly used, that the security forces and weaponry are under direct governmental command.

The need to guarantee the security force will remain loyal to the central government presents difficult choices, both for aid donors and for the government:

- First, the wave of military coups in Africa still continues, and there is an obvious dilemma in how to build security forces and at the same time prevent the participation of these forces in any future coup attempt. To some extent this risk can be reduced by strengthening the regional or pan-African agreements to include political agreements that would reduce the risks of wars between countries and, on this basis, build and equip security forces of the individual countries to deal only with internal security matters, and thus reduce its warfighting capabilities. This diminishes the risk that security forces operating to maintain law and order within the country and equipped mainly with small arms will be able to carry out a coup d'état. At the same time a regional or a pan-African military force should provide guarantees to intervene and protect the country against an attack by any neighboring country.
- Second, the regimes in most fragile states are highly autocratic, freedom is strictly curtailed, and the leader employs his power to suppress the judiciary system. Obviously, donor countries are not willing to provide aid that strengthens the security forces of despotic leaders. This may create a vicious circle in which development aid cannot be provided due to the lack of internal security, since that would prevent effective use of this aid; but aid to strengthen internal security conditions might be used by the autocratic leader to further tighten control and thus reduce the security of large groups of the population.
    - One way to get out of this conundrum is to provide the aid that is aimed at increasing the country's security under the condition that an external/international force would intervene to compel the government to increase its accountability. This is the strategy suggested by Paul Collier in his book, *Wars, Guns and Votes*, which will be discussed in the next section.
    - Another way that I find more effective and ultimately more feasible is to establish conditions that strengthen the country's democracy. As a

prelude to a more detailed discussion of this subject in the next section, it should be noted that conditions that require the government to accept an external intervention force are bound to reduce the government's own power to assert control over the country and reduce the freedom of the government to implement policies and use the country's resources according to its priorities. Such conditions would certainly be rejected by at least half of fragile states, from Sudan, Chad, and Ethiopia to Nigeria and Guinea, which have ample natural resources and high revenues and, at the same time, very different priorities than the effectiveness of policies for reducing poverty and promoting growth.

Under the current shoddy security conditions in many poor countries, the gangs of young people that roam the streets and destroy property are causing great damage to the economy as well as to poor people by bringing trade to a halt, by robbing the poor's homes, and by stealing their animals. In urban areas, the poor are hurt most by gang violence that takes place mostly in the poor neighborhoods, while the government security forces pays less attention and allocates fewer resources to preventing crime in those neighborhoods. The soldiers, themselves, are often engaged in illegal trade in arms, drugs, and sex.

The most extreme examples are Guinea, Guinea-Bissau, and Niger, among the world's ten poorest countries and whose populations depend on rudimentary farming, fishing, and (in Niger) herding. Yet, these three countries have extremely rich resources of oil and minerals. The dire security situation, numerous coups and prolonged civil conflicts deter foreign investment and prevent the use of resources. Moreover, tyrannical regimes in these three countries leave nearly all people extremely poor even if their resources were exploited since most revenues would go to the ruling elite.

Another condition for aid to a fragile state, one that may be self evident but is not actually demanded, is participation of the government in countries that have the resources, in covering part of the costs of implementing the reforms in institutions and economies. Presently, the list of countries that, according to World Bank criteria, are entitled to concessional funds "due to their very significant needs" include quite a few resource-rich countries that have high revenues and are by no means in a desperate need of aid. For these countries, the more important goal is to leave of the list of fragile states so they can attract foreign investors and search for new resources. Angola is the second largest oil-exporting countries in SSA, and yet it is entitled to "concessional funds" without making any contribution out of its huge revenues to meet its "very significant needs." Quite a few other resource-rich countries are entitled to aid due to their low per capita income, since they are still embroiled in or recovering from long wars and civil conflicts. Their low mean incomes and high poverty rates entitle them to aid without requiring them to take more active parts and some share in the costs of reforms, even though their low mean per capita income is due to the extreme inequality in income distribution.

Many of failed states have never functioned as states. The colonial powers had no use for some of these territories, primarily in the Horn of Africa (Map 4.7), and therefore did not develop local administration, leaving these countries undeveloped. Several other states, like Kenya and Côte d'Ivoire, were Africa's most prosperous states both under colonial rule and for many years after independence. Internal tribal conflicts led to military coups and civil war in Côte d'Ivoire, and in Kenya to violent and deadly confrontations. As a result, the security conditions in these states deteriorated to the extent that they became fragile states. There is no common factor that can explain why certain countries became fragile states while others, like Senegal, Ghana, Uganda, and Zambia (under President Mwanawasa) managed to maintain stability, law and order, and even restrict corruption. The only common explanation can be the sincerity, commitment, and sense of obligation in their leaders.

Map 4.7 The Horn of Africa
Source: CIA, The World Factbook (2009).

Criteria of governance

The distinguishing features of countries that, under both World Bank and OECD definitions, make them fragile states are their failure to maintain law and order and to fight poverty and social inequalities. In principle, these two features address two different problems, but jointly they represent the priorities of the development goals of the international development organizations and donor countries. Senegal is also a poor country, with more than half its population living below the poverty line, unemployment high, and three quarter of its population living in rural areas and working in agriculture. Nevertheless, Senegal remains one of the most stable democracies in Africa. Gabon, in contrast, is one of Africa's most affluent countries, according to its average income per capita (four times higher than the continent's average) but income inequality is so extreme that a large portion of its population remains poor.

The characterization of a state as being fragile is mainly used by the Official Development Assistance (ODA) to recommend whether or not to grant aid to the country. The main guiding principle is to grant aid to those states that have "good governance." To that end, recipient countries must have policies and institutions capable of guaranteeing effective use of aid. That criterion has replaced the complex conditionalities under structural adjustment programs with a set of performance indicators that characterizes the country's system of governance. These performance indicators are used in the World Bank's Country Policy and Institutional Assessment (CPIA). In order to benefit from ODA, a state must be in compliance with these governance indicators and must demonstrate ownership of the poverty reduction objectives. Table 4.3 combines several different criteria of competitiveness and shows the correlation coefficient between the rankings determined by these criteria:

Kaufman and Kraay examine the two options to determine the set of indicators that can be used to characterize the system of governance and provide a measurement that shows whether a given system indeed meets the criteria of good governance: One is a rule-based indicator that lists rules according to which government institutions operate. These can include the rules according to which the staff of these institutions must operate, and the existence of specific institutions, such as auditing, certain legal institutions, and so forth. It is straightforward to define, determine, and measure whether the system of governance meets the rule-based criteria. However, the existence of statutory rules on the books does not guarantee these rules are actually being implemented. It is also not clear whether these rules would actually bring the desired outcomes, nor can it be determined whether the same institution would have been able to achieve the same outcomes with different rules. Outcome-based indicators, such as those listed below, are more

Table 4.3 African countries' indicators of governance global competitiveness (2007–08); ease of doing business (2008); corruption (2008); political stability (2008)

Country	Competitiveness Rank	Competitiveness Score	Ease of doing business (Rank)	Corruption (Rank)	Political Stability[1] (Rank)
Senegal	100	3.61	157	99	43
Gambia, The	102	3.59	140	106	49
Tanzania	104	3.56	131	126	55
Benin	108	3.49	172	106	43
Burkina Faso	112	3.43	147	79	61
Mali	115	3.37	156	111	64
Cameroon	116	3.37	171	146	72
Madagascar	118	3.36	134	99	70
Uganda	120	3.33	112	130	45
Zambia	122	3.29	90	99	81
Ethiopia	123	3.28	107	120	94
Lesotho	124	3.27	130	89	57
Mauritania	125	3.26	166	130	82
Mozambique	128	3.02	135	130	44
Zimbabwe	129	2.88	159	146	91
Burundi	130	2.84	176	168	90
Chad	131	2.78	178	175	96
Correlation coeff. with competitive.			0.032	0.557	0.666

Sources: World Economic Forum; World Bank; Transparency International; Aggregate Governance Indicators 1996–2008.

[1] The ranking is from the most stable–0, to the least stable–100, to correspond to the other rankings.

difficult to assess because these measurements are determined by subjective evaluations.

Kaufman, Kraay, and Mastruzzi (2003) suggested the following indicators that measure six aspects of governance:

1. *Voice and Accountability*—measuring political, civil, and human rights
2. *Political Instability and Violence*—measuring the likelihood of violent threats to, or changes in, government, including terrorism
3. *Government Effectiveness*—measuring the competence of the bureaucracy and the quality of public service delivery

4. *Regulatory Burden*—measuring the incidence of market-unfriendly policies
5. *Rule of Law*—measuring the quality of contract enforcement, the police, and the courts, as well as the likelihood of crime and violence
6. *Control of Corruption*—measuring the exercise of public power for private gain, including both petty and grand corruption and state capture

These criteria offer a comprehensive evaluation of governance that is measured by the *outcomes* good governance aims to achieve. There is an inevitable delay between the time the rules are introduced and the time in which the outcome is achieved, and this delay is different in different countries. The links between indicators are also subject to delays. Since the institutions were established and the rules introduced in different countries at different time periods, the difference between countries in the quality of governance reflects the length of the time periods in which institutions were established, rules enacted, and civil law developed. The comparison between countries must also recognize differences in social norms and traditions between countries. Even control of corruption is not only the outcome of the institutions that were built and the rules that were enacted but, perhaps even more so, of the social norms in different societies.

The outcome-based indicators are very complex and may include dozens of indicators; most of them cannot be quantified and, instead, they are ranked by experts. Moreover, the list and ranking of indicators is highly subjective. In addition, the indicators noted in this list are likely to have different meanings to the different experts who determine the rank, and they certainly have different meaning and different significance to people in different countries. The difficulties of making the right choice of outcome indicators explain why a multitude of models have been developed in recent years. Nevertheless, the basic approach of making decisions, like the allocation of aid or supporting the legitimacy of the government, requires the solid foundations these models can provide.

Figure 4.2 presents the index of public sector ethics for selected African countries. This index measures variables related to public integrity, bribery, and favoritism in the public sector. It ranges between 0 and 100. The average score for the non-OECD countries was 36. South Africa exceeded that score, whereas the score for Ghana was equal to the average, but was considerably higher than the other African countries. Ghana also had a high score in judicial and legal effectiveness (64.4) that was considerably higher than the average score for the non-OECD countries (39.8) and far higher than Nigeria (26.7). The correlation between this indicator of governance and the countries' income per capita was lower than in other world regions for two reasons: First, the per capita income in African countries was strongly affected by their natural resources. Second, although both Ethiopia and Kenya are categorized as failed states, their relatively higher score in public

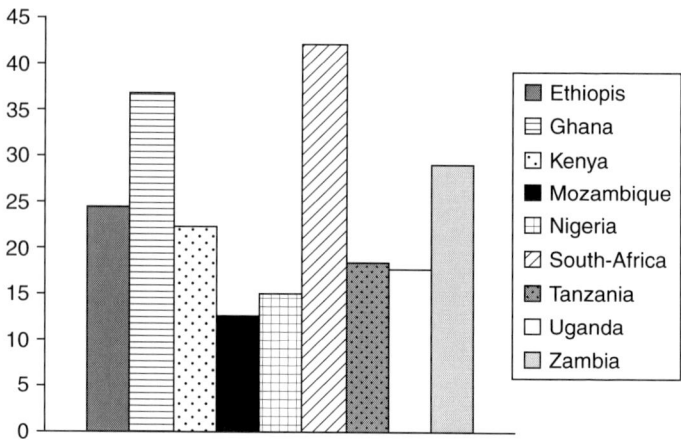

Figure 4.2 Indicators of public sector ethics
Source: Kaufmann (2004).

sector ethics is the heritage of the many years in which they had a relatively well-organized public sector—Ethiopia during the many years under the rule of Emperor Haile Selassie, when the country was independent.

The role of state institutions

> Let us focus on a more practical, more attainable peace, based not on a sudden revolution in human nature but on a gradual evolution in human institutions.
>
> President John F. Kennedy[7]

The unstable, ineffective, and highly corrupt regimes that invested little in education, health, and infrastructure have been a major obstacle in African development. The failed economies experienced a complete breakdown of law and order, particularly in countries that were engaged in a civil conflict or in war. Africa is regarded by investment-rating agencies as the world's most risky region, and even the few more stable African countries, like Uganda and Senegal, are still rated as risky for foreign investors. In an article on "Institution Rule," Rodrik, Subramanian, and Trebbi (2002) demonstrated in a sample of 140 countries that the role of institutions, particularly the role of institutions having to do with property rights and the rule of law, is far more important in determining a country's growth than the role of other factors that used to be considered as the most essential for economic growth. The econometric analysis in their article is indeed convincing, but the results themselves should not come as a surprise: Without the safety of property rights and the rule of law, a country's production, investments, and trade cannot develop. Open trade policy by itself cannot attract private investors as long as investments are not protected, and a country's comparative advantage depends much less on the relative costs of labor and far more on the effectiveness of the country's institutions, the obstacles they load on enterprises conducting business, or what they demand in bribes.

To what extent do government institutions matter for economic growth? The IMF's *World Economic Outlook* of April 2003 estimated (conservatively) that had Sub-Saharan Africa's institutions been raised to OECD quality, average per capita GDP in the region could have risen by 150 percent, at an annual rate that could have been higher by almost 2 percentage points ("Testing the Links," p. 35). Equally important, however, is the distribution of these gains in income. Public institutions have little effect on the rural population and the agricultural sector, except for agricultural production for export. In the urban sector it will not have much effect on the industrial sector, which consists mainly of light manufacturing for the local market and operates mostly in the informal market. The main effect will therefore be on trade and on the production and export of natural resources. The effect on employment will therefore be quite small. The main question is whether more effective institutions would attract more investments in local industries for the export market. This question cannot be answered by partial equilibrium models, but it is clear the low quality of local institutions and the high level of corruption certainly deter foreign investors and reduce the competitiveness of local industries.

The three criteria used by Kaufman, Kraay, and Mastruzzi to measure the quality of public institutions that, in turn, determine the quality of governance, are:

- *Government Effectiveness*—measuring the competence of the bureaucracy and the quality of public service delivery
- *Regulatory Burden*—measuring the incidence of market-unfriendly policies
- *Control of Corruption*—measuring the exercise of public power for private gain, including both petty and grand corruption and state capture

There are three dimensions along which the quality of the public institutions can be improved: First, improving the effectiveness of the staff through training; improvements in the equipment they use, including computers; and a more careful design of their work system in order to eliminate unnecessary tasks. Second, reducing corruption; this can be done by establishing tight supervision, although it can also be argued that corruption can be helpful to reducing the obstacles currently ineffective institutions create. In other words, reducing corruption without improving institutional effectiveness would not contribute much to increasing the overall quality of the institutions. Third, designing a more complete system of institutions;

the current system, inherited from colonial administration, is severely deficient. The regulatory burden can be reduced only within the framework of more comprehensive reform that would determine the role and responsibility of different institutions. I have discussed this point before, so at this stage suffice it to say that important institutions, ranging from auditing to the ombudsman's office, are missing or lacking adequate authority and independence. These institutions are also necessary to establish proper supervision that would reduce corruption.

The question about the importance of state institutions can also be asked about the prescriptions suggested by Paul Collier and Jeffrey Sachs to trigger the process of economic growth after years of stagnation. In *The Bottom Billion*, Collier stated: "Aid is not very effective in inducing a turnaround in a failing state; you have to wait for a political opportunity. When it arises, pour in the technical assistance as quickly as possible to help implement reform. Then, after a few years, start pouring in the money for the government to spend." In a country that has no institutions to secure an orderly process of using this technical assistance, and well-established supervision and auditing, an effective use of aid does not depend on the right political opportunity (meaning what?), but it is a process in which aid is given and is partly used to build the necessary local institutions. If aid is poured "as quickly as possible" it will be mostly wasted.

The World Bank's report, *Sub-Saharan Africa: From Crisis to Sustainable Growth* (1990), mentioned for the first time the lack of proper "governance" and the lack "of political power to manage a nation's affairs" as being among the reasons that have prevented orderly development of the African system of governance. In that report, the bank did not attempt to make the connection between "good governance" and democracy, but noted the need for greater freedom of speech and for transparency in decision making. The *WDR 1997*, devoted to the role of the state, noted: "Researchers have yet to reach a consensus on the precise relationship between growth and democracy[;] states need skill to manage the political transition [to democracy] in such a way that it supports rather than impedes the development agenda" (p. 150).

"Good governance" was not regarded as either necessary or sufficient for democracy, and at the time most African countries had only experienced their first round of elections and did not have the institutions or the independent legal system necessary for effective implementation of democratic reforms. The election process by itself, regardless of how free and fair it may be, is not sufficient to secure a functioning democracy; the report also emphasized the need for an adequate process of conflict resolution in order to guarantee good governance during the transition process. The report also raised the possibilities of regional cooperation for cross-border conflict resolution. The *WDR 1997* made another evaluation of the importance of government institutions in the promotion of economic growth and found that the failure of many African countries to maintain the rule of law and secure efficient, transparent, and noncorrupt government institutions were among the main reasons for the decline in their per-capita GDP during the three "lost decades."

Institutions and regulations proved to be necessary to ensure the effectiveness of the free market system. Even staunch supporters of free market capitalism would agree that the state must set formal rules to establish standards on the interaction between enterprises and to supervise that these standards are met, even though this would limit the freedom of the market. The recent experience in financial markets of the developed countries went a long way to remove doubts about the need for supervision by institutions of the state. Both the free market and the supervising institutions must have two other important assets: trust and reliability. Thus far, however, neither the people nor the entrepreneurs have had much trust in the free market and in the reliability of the state's institutions, because both were not truly free.

In many African countries, the weak and unreliable protection of the law to private property and to contractual agreements between individuals and between enterprises prevented the development of an effective market system and, in particular, of sound and reliable financial and credit institutions. Credit was subject to high risks, partly because banks were exposed to arbitrary rules that did not conform to ordinary banking practices, partly because they did not trust the consistency of government policies or even the stability of currency, but mostly they did not trust the system that was supposed to enforce the law. Banks that sought to preserve minimum standards to protect the savings and investments of their clients could not operate in this environment, and the lack of trust in the financial system limited private savings in local banks; people preferred to put their savings in foreign currency, either in cash or in "Swiss Banks"—a term used to describe all foreign banks.

Many laws were violated due to arbitrary and highly corrupt enforcement of the law by the state institutions, or even by the judiciary system. Thus, for example, according to a recent World Bank report on "Doing Business in 2008," the requirements for starting a business in Nigeria are still governed by rules set almost two decades ago. For those who do not have the right connections, it takes ten procedures and 38 days, and incurs high costs of around 9 percent of the property value just to register that property. Companies that operate in the formal economy must therefore either go through all these procedures and have much higher expenses or try to establish connections with "insiders" who can help accelerate the process and reduce its costs. This is the reason so many small and medium-size enterprises prefer to work in the informal economy. According to "Aggregate Governance Indicators," the effectiveness of the Nigerian government is among the lowest on the continent and there is high insecurity in parts of the country.

In recent years, with the increase in foreign investments and the growing activities of international corporations, the countries that sought to attract foreign investors had to strengthen their institutions, their regulatory quality, and the rule of law. The gains African countries had from these investments were high enough to convince local authorities to adjust their institutions to global standards and to tighten their supervision over the enforcement of rules and regulations.

The spread of regional agreements on open trade and the increase in trade between African countries also contributed to increasing the significance of effective and trustworthy institutions and maintaining the rule of law. The African Union can make an important contribution to achieving these goals by establishing common standards that conform to international standards but which take into account the special conditions and institutional constraints in African countries, and by establishing credible institutions to monitor and regulate the implementation of these rules.

Building the state institutions

The role of state institutions and the significance of effective central government have proved pivotal in raising the standard of living of all citizens and increasing their motivation and their confidence in collaborating with each other. The advantage all of them derive from that collaboration also gives them incentives to be part of the state, and over time their common experience as citizens will further increase their motivation to maintain stability. These are the foundation and building blocks of the state.

In an interview on his book *State-Building* (2004) Francis Fukuyama emphasized that in most SSA countries, the common characteristics of people who live in the same country and their identity as citizens of the state are still quite weak, since they have a much shorter common history as citizens than their heritage and common identity as a tribe. In Africa, the states were created rather abruptly and citizenship determined by the arbitrary colonial borders that brought together tribes with very little in common and often divided tribes between different states.

Fukuyama emphasized that the identity of the state evolves over time, as it has in Europe, and in the African countries the process is still in its early stages since many neighboring tribes have few shared interests and lack common identities to bring them closer together. To build state institutions and establish a central government, these countries must first have the necessary know-how and the basic understanding of the organization of the state institutions that are the basis upon which they would be able over time to build the unifying organization of the state.

The obstacles this process must overcome are not unique to Africa, as we see even today in South and East Asia, from East Timor to Tibet and Kashmir, nor are they unique to countries that had been under colonial rule. The recent failure of French-speaking and Dutch-speaking citizens of Belgium to form a government more than a year after the elections, is an extreme but pointed example of how most countries in all continents have encountered difficulties in building a unified nation-state in a multiethnic or multireligious society.

The process in Africa has been far more complex and far more destructive, for three main reasons: The first and most obvious reason is the monumental diversity of African tribes and sectarian groups. The rather abrupt manner in which the colonial powers left the continent created artificial independent states in territories determined by colonialism according to administrative needs.

Upon independence the tribes became citizens of the same state, although there might be rather deep divisions and entrenched rivalries between them. In many countries, hostility and rivalry between tribes or sectarian communities had been instigated by the colonial regime and, in many of the Francophone countries, predated even the colonial regime.

People from different tribes had little shared history, often not even the same language other than that of the colonial regime, which became the country's official language. In countries in which the population was divided along racial lines, most notably along the borders of the Sahel desert, from Sudan to Mauritania, where the population is divided between black African communities and Arab communities, the animosities have only intensified over the years, particularly after the discovery of rich natural resources in their lands.

These peoples often found it impossible to establish any form of communal life, share the same public institutions, and be the citizens of the same state. They were unable to resolve the differences between their communities and, in many, civil conflicts have only intensified and taken a horrendous toll on their populations while ruining their economies. Although the number of conflicts has declined somewhat in the past decade, the threat exists of intense competition and rivalries between tribes and countries over dwindling water resources and eroding agricultural lands, major dangers for the entire continent.

These countries create a difficult dilemma for the African Union that represents the entire continental community: Is there any advantage to keeping these countries unified within the territory determined by colonial borders, even though there is no national unity among their different communities and many are engaged in incessant armed conflicts? This is the most difficult issue African countries face, and it will be discussed in the concluding section of this chapter.

Another reason for difficulties in the formation of an effective system of governance in African countries is the absence of any prior experience as citizens of an independent state and the lack of knowledge about the structure and role of the different institutions of the state, including of the government itself. In fact the basic structures of the state and the formation of a system of rules and institutions that apply to all the citizens of the state (despite their tribal affiliation) were entirely foreign to them, antagonistic to their traditions, and rivaling their own traditional leaders.

The perhaps most detrimental reason was the little interest leaders had in building an effective system of governance and even in resolving tribal and ethnic conflicts to strengthen the interaction between different tribes—an accomplishment that could endanger their own political power. For them, an effective system of governance and an independent judiciary would restricting their personal control over the country, and until recent years only few leaders had a sincere interest in settling tribal disputes. Without some form of coexistence it was not even possible to build state institutions, and without some structure of modus vivendi that would, over time, reduce the barriers between peoples and give them incentives to increase their interactions and perhaps even their collaboration with other communities, eventually motivating them to become cooperating citizens of the same state.

As more African countries gradually solidify their regimes—stabilize relations with neighboring countries, increase country-to-country trade, foster more peaceful conditions and improve the potential for collaboration among individuals—this will allow their citizens to devote more resources to improving living conditions. This, in turn, will increase the motivation to maintain that stability in the future. Stability, trade, and collaboration require proper state institutions and, over time, also regional institutions. Then they will come to know full well what John F. Kennedy was referring to when he said that the more practical, more attainable, peace will be achieved not by a sudden revolution in human nature, as the golden leaders once dreamed, but by a gradual evolution of human institutions.

The deterioration of the African state institutions

In the first five decades after independence the African countries did not achieve that evolution of human institutions. Much of the decline of the continent and the stagnation of its economies were due to the deterioration of state institutions. In the newly independent African countries state institutions were essentially the those designed by the colonial administration, often not suitable for an independent state. Under colonial rule there was no need, for example, for an independent central bank, since the colonies did not have independent monetary policies. Also, the colonial judicial system had limited autonomy, not designed or authorized to deal with issues of an independent state or relations between the new government and its citizens. In an independent state, the autonomy of the judicial system and its wider authority to obligate the government to abide by the fundamental rules of the state are the basic building blocks of government by the rule of law.

Under the post-independence "golden leaders" captivated by socialist ideals and the Soviet system of government, a judiciary independent of the all-powerful state and with the authority to form independent opinions and issue verdicts that restrict government policy was not conceivable. Thus, for example the decision to collectivize small farmers' lands would not likely have passed the test of an independent judiciary that has the obligation to protect the rights of citizens. Such a judiciary would, however, be considered a detrimental intervention in the implementation of reforms aimed to improve farmers' living conditions.

The next generation of autocratic leaders lacked the idealism and good intentions of the "golden leaders" and further weakened state institutions for their own self-interests, systematically eroding the quality of their staff by nominating their supporters and people from their tribe to key governmental positions. The independence of the judiciary was seen as a nuisance and was first resolved by the leaders personally nominating the judges and then by almost openly encouraging them to accept bribes, thereby eroding what little moral authority they still had.

There were several other reasons for the *deterioration* in the competency of state institutions and of the entire system of governance under these leaders:

- The built-in conflict between the rules of the state and the traditional rules of the tribe. Under the colonial regime this conflict was muted, since the rules of the state were exclusively under the authority of the colonial administration, and, even on matters between the colonial government and private African individuals, there was an understanding that the rules of the government and of its head—the colonial governor—clearly superseded any traditional native hierarchy. On matters related to the private lives of tribal members and their communities, the authority remained in the hands of the tribe's elders. Under autocratic leaders, the conflict between the two systems was intensified mainly because many of the state's rules were determined according to the traditions of the largest and most powerful tribe, in total disregard of the traditional rules of minority tribes. This issue will be further discussed below.
- The extremely fragmented structure of state institutions after independence, and the lack or limited authority of several key institutions that had not existed under the colonial rule, but were essential in an independent state. I mentioned earlier the lack of an independent central bank; the results were experienced most memorably in Zimbabwe, which in 2007–08 had monthly inflation rates in the thousands of percent.

Following are two other examples of institutions designed by colonial powers to suit their objectives but which were entirely inadequate for an independent state.

Tax administration

It has long been recognized that in developing countries taxation systems can be highly supportive of good governance. These systems can contribute, for example, to enhancing accountability. Government that has its own source of revenue and does not need to tax its citizens has little incentive to be publicly accountable, responsive, or efficient. The governments in most resource-rich African countries have high enough revenues from the export of resources so that they do not have effective legal obligations of accountability and responsibility for its expenditures ("no representation without taxation").

When the African countries became independent, the institutions and officials in charge of tax administration and collection, including tariffs, income taxes, and property taxes, were given near-monopoly power and full discretion to make decisions provided they transferred proper amounts to their superiors and to the state's coffer (Mahesh Purohit 2007). The newly independent states did not, however, have the rules, regulations, and institutions to monitor the tax administration and supervise the performance of officials. Typically, tax administrators are allotted a particular geographical area in which they control an entire operation, and for the people in that area the taxation officer is the entire tax administration. This monopoly power, and the lack of regulations and supervision, give tax officers ample opportunity to entice, or even demand, taxpayers to use corrupt practices in managing their tax reports and making their payments. The lack of clearly defined rules, functions, and duties for tax officers, and of an administration to monitor the implementation of these rules, gives tax officers the power to implement those rules as they see fit and abuse their power for their own benefit.

Supreme audit institutions

The role of Supreme Audit Institutions is to report the unauthorized expenditures of a government authority, any waste of public funds, or any abuse of procedures resulting in losses to the public treasury. Under good governance, these institutions have a great deal of independence in order to make unbiased judgments, and by auditing the financial statements of government officials and government agencies they are highly respected for protecting the public against corruption or abuse of public funds. Good financial reporting and auditing is aimed at reducing fraud and assuring that audited financial statements can be trusted.

In most African countries, these institutions either did not exist or were established hastily and unprofessionally, with staff that lacked both the knowledge and experience for this complex duty; many received their jobs as rewards for supporting the president. Most government officials did not welcome or cooperate with government auditors, who came to realize that the only way to keep their jobs, and perhaps get a "piece of the pie" was to avoid any critical report (Kenneth Dye 2007). Lax compliance with laws and regulations related to contract provisions, grant agreements, and so forth in institutions that lack clear rules and regulations, and where supervision is sporadic at best, give ample room for fraud. Although violation of the law starts at the top, the "top" has complete immunity and is essentially outside the authority of the auditors. As a result, fraud is practically impossible to detect, collusion is common, and fraudulent transactions are not recorded. In addition, audit departments are usually underfunded and understaffed, and the auditing staff has little support from superiors. Audit institutions, therefore, played a marginal role in controlling corruption and in most countries were merely a façade.

Another reason for the deterioration in competency of state institutions, and the resulting ineffective system of governance, was the power of the autocratic leaders to control and restructure the institutions according their personal needs and wishes. For these leaders the main function of state institutions was to serve the regime, whereas the rights of individuals, the obligation of government institutions to abide by the rules and regulations nominally set for them and meet minimum standards of competence, were openly violated. The autocratic regime itself showed little interest in setting up a complete system of rules and regulations that would define the roles, obligations, and authority of government institutions that might restrict their own complete freedom.

For all these reasons, the deterioration in the competency of state institutions and in the effectiveness of the system of governance was not a gradual process, but took place within the first few years after independence; government institutions essentially ceased to function and were not able to carry out even the duties they had under colonial rule. The disintegration of the budgetary process left government employees without salaries for months, but fear of unemployment made staff members completely dependent on supervisors and unwilling to do much without explicit instructions.

The damage caused by the collapse of state institutions can be summarized as the failure to meet the IMF definition of governance: "The process by which decisions are made and implemented (or not implemented). Within the government, governance is the process by which the public institutions conduct the public affairs and manage the public resources." Good governance, according to the IMF, is "the management of the government in a manner that is essentially free of abuse and corruption, and with due regard for the rule of law." By failing to perform their duties the state institutions in the newly independent countries made the entire system of governance ineffective, and while serving the short-term needs of autocratic leaders, they increasingly paralyzed their regime.

The deterioration of state institutions and decline of governance made many African countries fragile states. Most fragile states did not improve their institutions in later years, and remained fragile for decades later. A few countries that had performed quite well in the early years, most notably Côte d'Ivoire and Kenya, later became fragile due to civil conflicts that devastated their economies, incapacitated their governments, and prevented the establishment of control over their countries. In a series of studies over nearly a decade, Kaufmann, Kraay, and Mastruzzi showed that, during the eight-year period from 1996 through 2004, there were only minor changes in the effectiveness of the systems of governance in most countries, and in quite a few, including Côte d'Ivoire, Zimbabwe, Sierra Leone, and the Central African Republic, there was considerable deterioration as result of civil conflicts that brought about the collapse of the central regime.

Does the public trust the public institutions?

The transition to democracy represents a significant step forward in gaining approval by the general public of the government's legitimacy, and winning that public trust was the main subject in a survey conducted by Afrobarometer, a research project that measures the social and political atmosphere in Africa on the basis of surveys conducted in selected countries and repeated on a regular basis. The Afrobarometer survey is based on personal, face-to-face interviews; the recent survey, their fourth, was conducted in the second half of 2008 in 18 countries. In the context of this chapter, I highlight the answers to some of their questions in five of the 18 countries, which show the attitude of their citizens toward several key public institutions. The following is brief summary of the results:

Do officials who commit crime go unpunished? Senegal (65–21)
 [Always/often—Rarely/Never]: Nigeria (64–31)
 Mali (62–27)
 Kenya (72–26)
 Ghana (28–66)

Are people treated unequally under the law? Senegal (69–22)
 [Always/often—Rarely/Never]: Nigeria (63–33)
 Mali (71–27)
 Kenya (70–26)
 Ghana (33–62)

How much do you trust the police? Senegal (78–16)
 [A lot—very little/not at all] Nigeria (25–72)
 Mali (50–44)
 Kenya (27–70)
 Ghana (47–51)

How much do you trust the courts of law? [A lot—A little bit]	Senegal (70–23) Nigeria (41–56) Mali (43–53) Kenya (42–55) Ghana (58–38)
How much do you trust traditional leaders? [A lot—A little bit]	Senegal (76–12) Nigeria (45–50) Mali (82–17) Kenya (56–34) Ghana (67–31)

In all five countries, the public has greater trust in traditional leaders than in government officials (Figure 4.3). Only in Nigeria does the majority have little trust in traditional leaders, most likely due to the country's huge ethnic diversity and to the concentration of a relatively larger share of the population in urban areas, where contacts with traditional leaders are much less common. There are large differences among countries in the trust of the public in the institutions that maintain law and order: In countries with predominantly rural populations people seek much more the help and advice of tribal elders and have very limited contact with police or courts. Their trust in these institutions is, most likely, not based on firsthand familiarity. In Nigeria, in contrast, people have much less trust in police and the courts of law.

Lavallée et al. analyzed the survey data of the Afrobarometer survey of 2005, which included 15 African countries. One of the key questions to measure public trust in the president. On average, 38 percent of respondent had little or no trust in the president. The mistrust/disapproval rates varied from

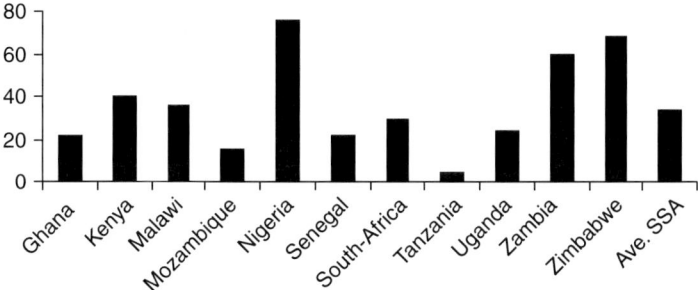

Figure 4.3 Percent of respondents who had little of no trust in the president
Sources: Afrobarometer surveys. Lavallée et al. (2008).

6 percent in Tanzania and 12 percent in South Africa to nearly 70 percent in Zimbabwe and nearly 80 percent in Nigeria (under Obasanjo).

The impediments of the endemic corruption

The experience in Sierra Leone (see below) is but one example of the endemic corruption and the lack of adequate institutions to monitor and establish controls over government accounts. After independence, government ministries and institutions were adjusted very little to meet the needs of the state and changes over time. The main criterion for the division of authority within and between institutions was loyalty to the leading elite. This loyalty was assured from the outset, because functionaries owed their appointments to these positions to the country's leader and his ministers, and many were appointed due to their tribal affiliation. Each institution and each individual was assigned, in principle, a specific role and an area of responsibility, but in practice there were no effective rules that determined these responsibilities, no effective supervision to ensure these institutions and individuals would abide by the rules, and no effective system with the legal authority to enforce rules and monitor the entire process. The result was rampant corruption and a complete lack of accountability.

Nevertheless, when the World Bank and the IMF implemented the reforms to revitalize the stagnant economies of the African countries, they had to rely on existing institutions and implement reforms through existing administrations. In the early years of the structural adjustment program, the focus was on macroeconomic reforms. To pull an economy out of the doldrums of stagnation and high poverty, the textbook solution is to stimulate that economy by increasing government expenditures on labor-intensive projects and thus increase aggregate demand, output, and employment.

In the African countries the projects were designed to provide employment in rural areas where most of the poor live. The most suitable public projects were the repair of crumbling infrastructure, since this could be an effective strategy both to improve the access of farmers to the urban markets and to provide employment to the many unskilled rural workers.

While the projects were designed by the experts of the international development organizations, they had to be implemented by the countries' existing institutions. Funds allocated for this stimulus package to the ministries in charge and then to their regional branches and local municipalities, were siphoned off at each stage of the administrative process. Only a small part actually reached the regional branches, and the remainder, allocated through the bureaucratic maze to local municipalities and the projects themselves, were only a small fraction of what was originally donated.

Foreign investors encountered similar problems in dealing with the government administration. The officials in charge, from the top down, were mostly concerned with their own "piece of the pie" and the interests of their tribes. The only way to "grease the wheels" of the bureaucratic jumble and obtain permits that would otherwise take weeks and months was through bribes. Bribery was an efficient way to reduce red tape, the heavy bureaucratic burden, and long delays.

In some of the writings on the subject of corruption in developing countries, it is not seen as an illegitimate tactic to facilitate the development process with bribery, given the hurdles local and foreign entrepreneurs encountered, while in other writings it has been argued that the red tape and long delays were deliberately created in advance in order to extract bribery payments (e.g., Kaufman and Vincent 2005; Kaufmann 2005; Kaufmann and Kraay 2008).

Another example is the privatization programs that were part of the structural adjustments and the World Bank's sine qua non for economic reforms. In practice the privatization had the effect of transferring control over government enterprises and organizations to the strong private hands of influential individuals at a fraction of their actual value. There was no orderly process, no competitive bidding, and no supervision to ensure the government would recover at least its costs and receive the proper value for the assets of these public enterprises. Many of these privatized enterprises were transferred to the country's economic elite which, through their connections with high government officials, effectively "tailored" the privatization bids and clinched the deal so they could have large profits and acquire high-value assets at a fraction of their cost—after heftily rewarding administration officials. The economic elite that gained control over privatized enterprises gained monopoly power and strengthened its domination of the economy.

The absence of an adequate legal framework and a comprehensive set of laws, and the weak enforcement of existing laws regulating business activities and economic transactions enabled business leaders—those with the right connections to government officials in charge, in part as members of the same tribe who knew which wheels needed "greasing"—to find many loopholes in the existing laws that enabled them to increase their profits. Down payments "under the table" are, in most African countries the norm rather than the exception, and they are common practice in most economic transactions, particularly those in which public institutions are involved.

Only in the past decade, when democratic regimes started to spread to more countries, has the legislative process been more formalized and basic rules became the countries' constitutions. Although a large part of this process has been a sham, and in many countries the rules and constitution, particularly term limits, are frequently changed, the mere formation of a clear structure and a set of rules the government and its institutions must abide by, even though mostly on paper, provides a more solid basis for a slightly more accountable and less arbitrary system of governance. This has been demonstrated in several countries when the strong opposition of the general public and electorate opposed attempts of leaders to change the constitution. Even the omnipotent Obasanjo could not overcome public resistance and remain president for a third term; under public pressure a peaceful transition of government took place.

Corruption and aid

In the past decade, the quality of governance and the prevalence of corruption were given higher priority in development aid. More donors and international development organizations now work with developing countries to help them reduce corruption and increase accountability. The UN convention against corruption, signed in 2003, requires, among other things, repatriation of looted assets held by corrupt leaders abroad. The decision of the G-8 to double aid and debt relief to the poorest countries in Africa emphasized the need to improve governance, and the recent joint report of the Africa Commission explicitly stated: "Good governance is the key.... Unless there are improvements in capacity, accountability, and reducing corruption... other reforms will have only limited impact."

Many writers put at least part of the blame for Africa's "lost decades" on the prevalence of corruption. Corruption, collusion, and nepotism exist in all countries, but their spread in Africa is directly related to the autocratic regimes. The 2003 "Corruption Perception Index" of Transparency International rated eight African countries among the bottom 20 most corrupt countries worldwide. In 2009, ten African countries were rated among the 20 most corrupt countries. Practically all were under autocratic regimes, with or without the democratic veil. In 31 of the 47 African countries surveyed, corruption was perceived as common and widespread by their own experts and businessmen, and the overall picture remains one of serious challenges across the region, particularly in countries that have considerable political instability.

Lavallée et al. analyzed the Afrobarometer data of in round three of the survey conducted in 2005 in 15 countries; one question inquired about the prevalence of bribery by asking whether, in the past year, the respondent had to pay a bribe to a government official in order to get a document or permit, avoid a problem with police, and so forth. On average, 20 percent of the respondents said they had to pay a bribe at least once in the past year, compared to 2 percent in Peru and 6 percent in Ecuador.

The 2005 Global Corruption Barometer survey conducted for Transparency International in eight African countries found that an average 24 percent of the population had personally experienced corruption, compared with only 2 percent in the developed countries. The Afrobarometer survey shows large variations between countries, ranging from 46 percent in Nigeria to 6 percent in Malawi, and 12 percent in South Africa (Figure 4.4).

The "Global Competitiveness Index" of 2006–07 concluded that in terms of competitiveness, the region lagged far behind the rest of the world due to

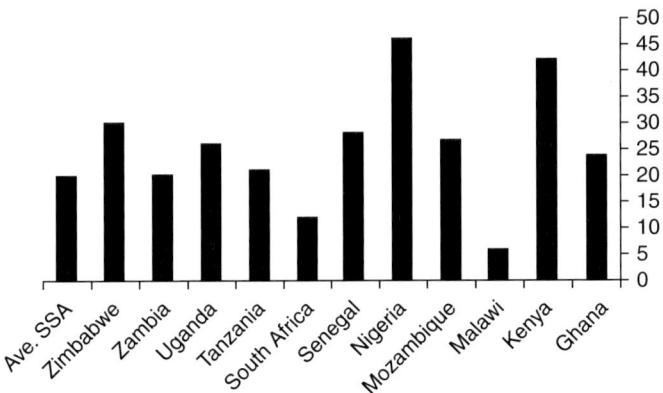

Figure 4.4 Prevalence of bribery in selected countries
Sources: Afrobarometer surveys. Lavallée et al. (2008).

poor governance and weak rule of law. The inefficient, discriminating, and onerous manner in which government institutions function has sometimes gone to the extent that they have prevented the access of certain groups or regions to staple foods, even when enough food was available.

The unlimited power of the ruling political and economic elite has intensified corruption that was common in all government institutions and embezzled not only the countries' resources but also a hefty share of aid funds. This was one of the main reasons why William Easterly, a leading critic of aid programs, argued strongly in his book, *The White Man's Burden*[8] (2008), against the Jeffrey Sachs plan for a "Big Push" of aid to the African countries. Easterly noted the highly unsuccessful past experience of aid programs, emphasizing that the complete lack of accountability at all levels of government and the very limited reliability of government institutions that are supposed to audit the government budget, are bound to fail all aid programs. Only a small part of the aid money is reaching the target population, and some funds are used in ways that intensify tribal rivalries and increase income inequality. The main mistake of the Washington planners (where Easterly himself had worked) was, in his opinion, that their "computer-designed" ideal programs imposed on the local institutions prescribed reforms that ignored the country's cultural, political, and bureaucratic characteristics and traditions.

Zhang (2004) compared the experience of the African countries with the experience of the East Asian countries during the years of their miraculous growth, and highlighted the main reasons for the successful development strategies in the Asian countries: stable political and legal systems, strong institutions, community participation, and firm government control. These principles were pillars of the miracle despite the limited accountability and high-handedness of the central regime. As a result, the governments in the two subcontinents operated very differently: although public expenses were high both in East Asia and Africa, the expenses in the African countries were primarily on government consumption, whereas in the East Asian countries they were mostly on investments, particularly investments on infrastructure, and on the provision of public services. These differences contributed to their rapid development. Whereas in 1970 incomes per capita in much of East Asia, with the exception of Japan and South Korea, were on average considerably *lower* than in Africa, by the end of the 1990s average per capita income in East Asia was more than *five times larger* than in Africa.

To cope with corruption, high standards of accountability are required to deter violations of the rules and to increase trust in public institutions. Proper institutions and auditing procedures to inspect and monitor the accounts of various public institutions have to be established, together with clear standards to secure their implementation. According to an initiative promoted by Paul Collier that is discussed below, accountability may have to be established by international intervention. In *Wars, Guns and Votes*,[9] and in later articles, Collier strongly maintains that accountability should be one of the missions of that intervention force and it must be a condition for aid, since, "The international strengthening of accountability is likely to be seen as more legitimate than the international provision of security." In other words, establishing accountability is an integral part of state building and should therefore be one of the missions of the UN peacekeeping force.

The political reality attaches much lower significance to accountability, and governments in the failed states will certainly resist infringement on their national sovereignty in order to establish accountability, regardless of how important it is considered by donor countries. In fact, most of these governments would not agree that this is even necessary. The cynicism of this *real politique* was demonstrated by African leaders when, out of concern for national sovereignty, they refused to intervene in the catastrophic developments in Zimbabwe. Although Mugabe clearly forged the election results after losing the first round and brought the country to economic collapse—thus dooming thousands to die from starvation and cholera—the principle of national sovereignty was regarded to be more important. Despite the humanitarian disaster, neither neighboring countries nor the UN Security Council could master the resources and the support to use military force in order to remove Mugabe from power; even more timid proposals to impose economic sanctions were blocked in the Security Council by China and Russia.

Collier suggests, therefore: "Given the reluctance to pool sovereignty within neighborhoods, the only alternative is a phase of international assistance in the provision of vital public goods." His reasoning: "[T]he temporary external supply of public goods to the bottom billion raises no issue of principle; it is already fully accepted. For example, many poor countries need a malaria vaccine, but its development requires the big-science available only in the countries of the OECD. As public goods, security and accountability are like that malaria vaccine: those who need them cannot adequately supply them." With all due sympathy to the effort of Collier to mobilize public support to this basic need, his comparison is lopsided if not outright misleading:

The need for international aid has been widely accepted, but the forms of aid needed are highly debated. Aid in the form of financial support to scientists in Lausanne or Bonne to develop malaria vaccine is broadly supported by the public and by private funds in the developed countries, but aid in the form of troops sent to dangerous places for a decade or so to first establish peace and then build state institutions in failed states like Guinea-Bissau or Sudan is not likely to have much support in Europe or the United States. A peacekeeping force to stop massacres in Darfur is likely to be more widely supported, but so far none has been sent; military force to build public institutions and secure the accountability of the governments in these countries will not generate much support.

The strategy Collier suggests is therefore to "develop voluntary standards and codes, which governments can then choose to follow.... Making aid conditional on government actions can also help. But those actions should relate to the accountability of government to citizens rather than to the adoption of economic policies, which was the past practice of donors." Despite the distinction Collier carefully makes, it is hard to avoid the comparison between this proposal and the unsuccessful experience with the conditionalities of the reforms developed in the "Washington Consensus."

The main lesson from that experience was that the IMF and World Bank needed both the active participation of the country's institutions in the implementation of these reforms and a more direct responsibility for, and active contribution of the governments to, the design and execution of reforms. Aid donors try as much as they can to bypass the public administration by allocating the money to public projects. The "big push" Jeffrey Sachs suggests must, however, be implemented by the government and public institutions, and it may therefore have a much smaller impact on the country's development than the models suggest.

4.3
Will Democracy Settle or Intensify Civil Conflicts?

Despite the transition of some 40 African countries to democracy, people remain skeptical and suspicious. One discouraging phenomenon mentioned earlier is the renewed wave of military coups that toppled several duly elected democratic governments without much protest from the electorate due to widespread fraud in the voting for these governments. In these and many other countries people have been deeply disillusioned, distrusting the election results because rigging is common and the autocratic leaders use their power and the power and resources of the state in order to secure their election.

Another reason for disappointment with the democratization process is far too high expectations many people had in the transition to democracy. For them this new regime represents a sea change: Under the tribal system, the elders had absolute authority to set rules and serve as judges. These rules reflected tribal traditions, however, and were therefore accepted by all. Moreover, by giving authority to make the rules and serve as judges to a group of elders, the tribal system prevented any perception of autocracy that is necessarily divisive, and thus strengthened the acceptance of the rules.

Under the colonial regime, the colonial power had complete control over the affairs of the state, but the tribal elders continued to have the authority over issues related to personal and community life. The first generation of autocratic leaders of the independent states made no great efforts to settle the many conflicts between tribes that had erupted when colonial rule ended. Tribes that had been forced by the colonial regime to leave their lands demanded these lands back from the tribes that had settled there with the support of the colonial administration. The leaders of the newly independent states were against attempts to settle these disputes, since it was bound to create new conflicts and thus be detrimental to their efforts to create national unity.

The leaders of the second generation were far less idealistic, and they came to realize that tribal rivalries can, in fact, help them in maintaining their rule by weakening the tribes and preventing them from uniting against the regime, even when leaders used and abused them. Autocratic leaders often deliberately inflamed tribal conflicts and made them more extreme with an aggressive "divide-and-rule" strategy aimed at securing the loyalty of the dominant tribe. These leaders ignored existing state laws and set their own laws according to their needs, often by discriminating against minority tribes. Autocratic leaders and the leading elite embezzled state coffers, even in the poorest countries, and used the money to enrich themselves, increase security forces, and give preferential treatment to supporters, mainly members of their own tribe.

The subsequent transitions to democracy raised hopes for change better forms of governance. These hopes have not been realized, however, since most elections were widely flawed, as autocrats used every means to twist the voting process to secure their elections. These leaders then became democratically elected and therefore legitimate leaders, but in fact they did not want to change the regime in any way that would restrict their power. Nevertheless, they could not prevent some changes widely regarded as an integral part of democracy. These changes included more freedom of the press, whose reports on the misdeeds of government officials made people more aware that the corruption is at their expense, thus making them less tolerant of government follies, incompetence, and corruption. This was the beginning of a process that restricted the autocratic leaders and gave people more power to influence government policies.

The debate over Western-style democracy

As donors and international development organizations became more cognizant of the damage of the inefficient and corrupt public institutions, they made much greater efforts to improve the systems of governance, allocating aid funds for that purpose. In the past decade, donors have put more and stricter conditions on the allocation of aid, one of the more controversial conditions being the demand for Western-style democracy (combined with a demand for term limits, which is not required in many European countries). These demands raised fierce debates in the aid-recipient countries about the merits of Western-style democracy for African countries.

Abdullah Wade, president of Senegal and also president of the Organization of African Unity (OAU), claimed the multiparty system proved to be a failure: "We entered into the phase of mutiny and military coups in the following sequential order: Coups...elections...mutiny [and] having an elected president unable to complete his presidential period due to mutiny movements and we have a lot of examples for such cases: in Ivory Coast we have an elected president who was overthrown, in Guinea-Bissau and Central Africa the elected presidents were also overthrown."

In a speech quoted in Box 4.4, President Abdullah Wade summarizes very succinctly the obstacle African societies face in making the transition to

Box 4.4 Africa's view on western-style democracy

The third phase was the phase of multi party system and elections. Elections didn't differ much from military coups. Instability still prevailed, and every four years a new president was elected and then failed. The elections demonstrated the limitations of constitutions, since the constitution stipulates that the president is entitled to be re-elected only twice. Some presidents claimed, however, that "If the people decided to re-elect the president one, twice or even ten times, the constitution must allow the same. Why should the people be deprived from a serviceable president who has a beneficial program and wants to implement it? Elections provide us no stability and we did not get use thereof, while multiparty system is formal and it is a mere accession to the orders of the west, World Bank, WTO, IMF, EU and USA. They make their aids and loans conditions to set up liberal democracy and multiparty system. We cannot establish multiparty system arbitrarily. No multiplicity was witnessed in America, Britain, Spain or Italy and we have only a single ruling party in these states.

Africa does not know parties, we are tribes and almost closer to people's conferences and committees which suit us better than parties. Our people know neither parties nor elections. For instance Egypt is an independent and ancient country but the fact that when elections were held in the Egyptian countryside, an Egyptian voter was asked for whom he would vote? He replied that he would vote to Saad Zaglul, who passed away in 1920 and who led the 1919 Revolution and who is still latent in the intellects of farmers.

Currently there are numerous mutiny movements such as in the Sudan, Chad, Burundi, Rwanda, and Uganda. Thus elections did not solve the outstanding problems. We badly need stability which shall entail or necessitate firmness in the political leadership...consequently the authority should be handed to the constant and firm people and to the firm and constant people's conferences and committees.

After securing stability, firmness and constancy, there will come the authoritative source that is needed at times of shortcomings and upsets. Authoritative source is too significant in Africa and in some countries you see the example a king or a queen that has nothing to do with the Executive or Legislative Power but he / she is dealt with as a reserve reference to be resorted to at times of disagreements of the said powers in order to finally settle the disputed matter. The already elected nominees shall necessarily require the approval and signature of this king or queen. This reference or authoritative source is missed in Africa. European and other countries worldwide have such references or authoritative sources whether royal or presidential permanent bodies which have no relation with the Executive, Legislative or Judiciary Powers but stand as a reference resourced thereto. Every European country has a legal authoritative source such as the Supreme Court, constitutional court, the state tribunal of which laws are binding. We have no neutral or binding court and we have not yet reached a stage in which we respect the court and its decisions.

(President Abdullah Wade, 2005)

Western-style democracy: "Africa does not know parties, we are tribes and almost closer to people's conferences and committees which suit us better than parties. Our people know neither parties nor elections." He sees no merits in term limits and asks: "If the people decided to re-elect the president once, twice or even ten times, the constitution must allow the same. Why should the people be deprived from a serviceable president who has a beneficial program and wants to implement it?"

The transition to Western-style democracy was perceived in many circles as another "donors' design" reform that is not suitable for African countries. It has been recognized, however, that equal voting rights can mitigate perceptions of deprivation and help reduce the power of autocratic leaders even though elections are still very strongly along tribal lines. Furthermore, although most elections left the autocratic leader or ruling party in power, the effect of giving more freedom to the media to criticize the government or elected officials has made the public more aware, and less tolerant, of incompetence and corruption, thus creating pressure on government officials and institutions to be more accountable. Even in Nigeria, one of Africa's most corrupt countries, strong media criticism of the leading financial institutions forced President Umaru Yar'Adua to sack the CEOs of several leading banks, and he was the first president who declared all his assets upon coming to office.

Nigeria still has a long way to go to clean up the government after decades of unrestricted corruption, but growing pressure from the large urban population in Lagos and other major cities, including the gangs of youngsters no longer willing to accept high-handedness and discrimination by government officials, makes it clear that without public trust the government will not be able to rule. Even the omnipotent President Obasanjo had to succumb to public pressure and did not try to change the constitution and abolish term limits.

But democracy is not a panacea, and may not yet be suitable where the system of governance is still weak and inefficient. In many countries, the election process is merely a pretense, the voting is for one party (or, as in Uganda, for "no party"), and voters remain loyal to tribal leaders regardless of their qualifications (or lack of). Voting along tribal lines is deeply rooted in African tradition, partly motivated by expectations of benefits if their leader wins, and by concerns they will be left out if the other party wins. Voters also have tended to support the sitting president because he is regarded as the "big chief" who represents the country's dominant tribe, and opposing him may also invite problems with the security forces.

Yet traditional acceptance of autocrats out of respect for the "big chief" is waning in many countries, particularly in the urban areas, and people are no longer willing to accept a leader who ignores the rule of law, accepts no obligations or accountability, and pursues arbitrary, self-serving, and corrupt policies. This change of attitude is bound to be a prolonged process, however, and there is an equally strong opposition by those who benefit from the autocratic regime.

In many of the countries that have made the transition to democracy, elections were held well before the necessary institutions of the three branches of government were in place and had the capacity and authority to implement democratic procedures, during and after the elections, by demanding the elected government meet its constitutional and legal obligations. President Wade noted in his speech quoted above:

> Every European country has a legal authoritative source such as the Supreme Court, constitutional court, the state tribunal of which laws are binding. We have no neutral or binding court and we have not yet reached a stage in which we respect the court and its decisions.

Most African countries do not yet have an independent, qualified, and experienced judiciary that can make rulings on the implementation of laws, since most judges owe their nominations to the country's leader. There are too few provisions for creating an independent electoral system that can ensure a functioning legislative process. Without these institutions and regulations, and without prior experience in how a multiparty system works it has been difficult to put in place well-functioning political parties: In Burkina Faso there were no fewer than 62 different parties, mirroring the country's fragmentation, while in many countries the voting is still for a single party that mirrors the country's autocratic rule.

Countries' experiences with the transition to democracy

In Africa, leaders and intellectuals debate the merits of Western-style democracy in countries that are deeply divided along tribal, ethnic, and sectarian lines. The transition to democracy requires major adjustments by both the government and the public, and a clear departure from many traditions and practices of the past. The experience in some countries shows promising developments, while in others the transition has been tumultuous, highlighting serious problems—primarily instigating rather than resolving or mitigating existing conflicts and rivalries. This section provides a very brief overview of the experience of several countries (in addition to ones already reviewed in this book), which manifest different forms of African democracy and the obstacles encountered that, in some countries led to the collapse of their democratic systems.

In all countries the tribal divide in rural areas is deeply entrenched, and the large differences between tribes in their customs, rules, heritage, leadership, and even language have increased their difficulties finding enough common ground and incentives to collaborate, even when for their own benefit. Open wounds due to deeply rooted rivalries or unresolved disputes could not be healed without a commonly agreed compromise, and the country's leaders were the only ones who could bridge the divisions by directly and personally intervening—provided their verdicts would be accepted as fair—or by initiating a formal judiciary process to find a solution.

In the urban areas the divisions along tribal lines have been weakened due to the common fate of people living in the same shantytowns in the same miserable conditions and with high unemployment that unites them in their opposition to the government. They blame the country's leaders for corruption and incompetence that has deprived them of their fair share in the country's resources, and for making practically no effort and no investment to improve their living conditions. In many countries new hostilities have emerged along sectarian lines, mainly due to the radicalization of Islam, and along the poverty lines between the haves and have-nots, the very rich and the hopelessly poor.

Senegal

The country having the longest experience with a democratic system is Senegal, widely hailed as a beacon of democracy in Africa. Its current leader, President Wade, took office in 2000 in a peaceful transition of power after 22 years as the country's main opposition leader. In the past decade, Senegal has been doing rather well, not least because power was transferred twice without revolt. Africa's most stable country, Senegal, has benefited from years of chaos in nearby Côte d'Ivoire, once the financial hub of francophone West Africa, but where the outbreak of civil war has caused many international organizations and banks to leave Abidjan, the Ivorian seat of government, for Senegal's capital, Dakar, bringing rich expatriates and a building boom to the city. Senegal's relatively good communications network brought investment in businesses, such as call centers, challenging francophone North African countries as outsourcing destinations for France. Senegal has also attracted considerable investment from Arab countries, and the Organization of the Islamic Conference (OIC) held its summit there several years ago.

In a quest to gain respect beyond his country's borders, the increasingly haughty President Wade began to adopt the role of continental statesman. He has tried to broker talks to end the crises in Zimbabwe, Darfur, and Chad. Reflecting the president's lofty ambitions, a huge statue symbolizing "Africa's Renaissance" is being erected by North Koreans in a location overlooking Dakar.

Nevertheless, people seem dissatisfied with the country's democratic regime, which has left most of them in chronic poverty and failed to help during the food crisis, despite the sharp rise in prices of staple foods. The Senegalese had higher expectations from democracy, and in the aftermath of the food crisis President Wade faced unprecedented rage and frustration from the population. In 2008, there were violent demonstrations that called for more active measures to tackle the food crisis, and rumors that President Wade is preparing his son to succeed him only intensified these demonstrations. Against this backdrop, Senegal's democratic credentials are being questioned. Rows between the government and press have become frequent. A prominent newspaper publisher was jailed for printing a controversial article about the president and his son, and democracy-minded Africans elsewhere were disappointed when Wade seemed to endorse a military coup in neighboring Guinea late last year, after the death of its longtime president.

Uganda

Ugandan president, Yoweri Museveni, had been in power for six years when, in 1992, he decided—without any constitutional process—to begin the transition to democracy. When he became president a few years after the murderous regime of Idi Amin, Uganda was in ruins and most of the country's economic and intellectual elite, who had Asian roots, had been forced to leave. Museveni successfully managed to rebuild Uganda's tattered economy, attracted back the country's elite, and won widespread praise for his efforts to combat AIDS. He was elected to a second term and remained president until 2002–03. Thanks to his stable domestic policies, Uganda experienced ten years of consistent, strong, and broad-based growth that was the highest in Africa during those years of deep stagnation, and helped reduce poverty although the majority of the population is still chronically poor. Services to the poor also improved, and Uganda achieved the highest net primary school enrollment ratios among low-income countries.

Museveni insisted on maintaining a one-party democracy, arguing that multiparty elections are bad for Africa, because parties divide people along ethnic lines. He rejected Western-style democracy in favor of "African democracy" characterized by one-party rule by a leader devoted to improving living conditions in the country. He even justified the use of authoritarian methods if deemed necessary for the country, and during the second election he imprisoned the main opposition leader and accused him of treason.

When Museveni's second term as the elected president ended, he exerted pressure to have the constitutional limits on his tenure lifted, allowing him to run for another term. Despite Museveni's promise of orderly succession at the end of his second term, Uganda's constitution was amended to allow him to remain in office. Nevertheless, Museveni's "African democracy" has not been a complete oxymoron, since he tolerated a critical press and refrained from making dissent illegal. He remained adamantly opposed to multiparty elections, even though his "no-party democracy" could not resolve tribal rivalries. In Museveni's view, the continent's democracies are no more stable than dictatorships; wars between so-called democratic countries are just as frequent, and democracies have greater difficulty maintaining a stable economy, controlling the money supply, and maintaining low inflation. This view, although quite common, ignores the setbacks many African countries have had due to autocratic and self-centered regimes.

Tanzania

Tanzania gained independence in 1961, and Julius Nyerere, the country's first leader was the nation's "Founding Father." Under his leadership, Tanzania had one-party rule, which formally came to an end in 1995 with the first democratic elections.

In the past decade, per capita income grew at an annual rate of 3.5 percent, and in 2008 its per capita GDP adjusted for PPP reached $400, though its poverty rate at the international poverty line of $1.25 a day still increased from 77 percent in the early 1990s to 88 percent a decade later.

Today, the president is elected at the same time as the members of the National Assembly. The president has complete control over the legislative and executive branches; he is both chief of state and the head of the government, and he appoints the prime minister and selects cabinet members from the National Assembly. The president also appoints the judges for the Court of Appeals and the High Court. Opposition leaders have no power over political life and no influence on the government, as the president has controlled 93 percent of the seats in the Assembly since the elections of 2005. One party has dominated the multiparty electoral competition in Tanzania with no threat to the ruling party. President Jakaya Mrisho Kikwete, who took office in 2005, had enough partisanship in favor of his party that, regardless of the approval ratings of his job performance, he will certainly win reelection in the elections scheduled for October 2010. The economy is doing quite well, however, and during the 2000s it grew at an average rate of 4 to 5 percent. The country remains dependent on agriculture, including aquaculture.

Mozambique

Mozambique had a long period of civil war after it gained independence from Portugal in 1975. The conflicts ended in 1992 with a United Nations–backed peace accord between the two main opposing parties, and a new constitution that established a multiparty system. Since 1994 Mozambique has had three peaceful general elections and a presidential transition, and it remained politically stable. Under the country's presidential system, the president appoints the cabinet and chairs cabinet meetings. In 2004, the leading party successfully made a sensitive but peaceful transition of power, when the leader stepped down after 18 years in office and transferred the leadership to a successor from the same ruling party. The country's new president, H.E. Armando Guebuza, was elected in 2004 with 64 percent of the votes, more than twice as many as the opposition candidate, and in the parliamentary elections, the president's party won 62 percent of the votes.

Since the devastating civil war, Mozambique has been a strong economic and social performer and enjoyed a remarkable recovery, achieving an average annual economic growth rate of 8 percent between 1996 and 2008, and reducing the incidence of poverty by 15 percent between 1997 and 2003. Mozambique remains a poor country, however, and more than two-thirds of the population is below the poverty line, most working in subsistence agriculture.

Botswana

Botswana has become known as one of the world's great development success stories and Africa's greatest success in establishing democracy. Since independence in 1966, Botswana's leadership has adopted successful strategies to establish a multiracial and democratic society. Since then, Botswana had four decades of uninterrupted civilian leadership, becoming Africa's most developed country and one of the fastest-growing economies in the world, with its average annual growth rate of about 9 percent. Government investments in mineral excavation, principally diamond mining, made its diamond industry the country's main engine of growth. Politically the country is very stable and has regularly held free and fair elections. The electorate adopted a constitution that secures fundamental rights and freedoms. The Botswana Democratic Party (BDP) has been in power since the first elections, held on the eve of independence in 1965. Botswana has impressive track record of good governance and economic growth, supported by prudent macroeconomic and fiscal management as well as large investments in infrastructure, and developing health and education systems that include the provision of nearly universal and free education,. Nevertheless, unemployment remains persistently high, at nearly 20 percent, the poverty rate is over 30 percent, and most of the poor live in rural areas that have benefited much less from the country's rapid development. As a result, income inequality is extreme, and there is a large income gap between rural and urban populations.

Africans' mistrust in democracy

In the precolonial era, rivalry between tribes was sporadic and not deeply rooted because their very limited interactions created few frictions between them. Abundance of land and water resources gave no reason for competition between tribes, and the lack of roads left many tribes quite isolated from each other. Their isolation led also to the development of myriad tribal languages and distinct customs and social rules. Minerals and oil were of little use, and only when foreign powers began to covet these natural resources did they become valuable enough to instigate conflicts between tribes. Several decades after the African countries became independent, the spread of globalization and the growing world trade in these resources made them a major cause of violent rivalries between and within countries.

But tensions between tribes started to grow already under colonial rule. The new roads and railroads built by colonial powers to transport the continent's resources to the seaports increased the interaction, and also the competition, between tribes. The divide-and-rule strategy of colonial powers saw the fomenting of rivalries between tribes as an effective way to strengthen colonial control and prevent tribes unifying against foreign rule. Moreover, the colonial regime tended to favor the relatively larger and more powerful tribe in order to secure its support.

The animosity between tribes deepened after the African countries gained independence, when many old disputes created by the colonial regime came to the open, and their rivalries and mistrust often prevented new states from reaching agreements necessary to form a widely supported central government. Over time conflicts intensified due to disputes over increasingly scarce land and water resources that many felt were divided very unfairly by the autocratic leaders.

Already under colonial rule, and even more so under the autocratic leaders, the natural resources and the crops that were grown in the continent's fertile lands enriched some tribes much more than others, thus increasing inequality in their living conditions, economic power, and political influence. The more powerful tribes often seized leadership and became the ruling political and economic elite, while smaller tribes remained much poorer. Even today, in nearly all African countries the ruling party and more prosperous individuals are members of the dominant tribe. The scars from the conflicts and their entrenched animosities remain deep in the collective memory and continue to frustrate efforts to achieve national unity.

Africa's three "lost decades" of stagnation and growing poverty aggravated these tensions, deepening the inequalities and the divisions between peoples. In the past decade, as the economies of many countries resumed growth, income inequalities increased even further due to unequal distribution of gains from this growth; in the resource-rich countries the huge revenues accumulated from the exports of resources barely trickled down to the lower income groups and the rural areas. The World Bank estimates around three-quarters of revenues were accumulated by the top 1 percent of the population.

In rural areas, the population is too poor, too powerless, and too consumed by the struggle for daily survival to fight the highly corrupt elite protected by well-equipped security forces. In a few countries, like Sudan, Niger, Côte d'Ivoire, Rwanda, and to some extent Nigeria, conflicts escalated into armed struggle along ethnic and sectarian lines; in most other countries the poor rural populations were too powerless to stage any serious resistance.

In urban centers, in contrast, the rapidly rising number and power of young people who are increasingly more frustrated about their hopeless conditions, increase the pressure, sometimes violently on the government. These young people are better informed and much more in sync with their neighbors in the shantytowns, and in the larger cities they take the lead in the struggle against incompetent, corrupt, and autocratic leaders. Ever more aggressively, they demanded their share in the country's resources, better opportunities to find employment, and more government investments to improve conditions in shantytowns.

People are increasingly more frustrated that, despite the spread of democracy in Africa, power in most countries remains in the hands of the same autocratic leaders, the same ruling party and dominant tribe. In order to remain in power after democratic elections, vote-rigging became pervasive, increasing frustration, anger, and disillusionment with democracy among the minority groups left out.

In Accra, angry unemployed youths used force, threats, and intimidation against employees of the National Youth Employment Program and National Health Insurance Authority, demanding their firing. In Lagos, gangs often vandalize local stores, forcing many to close down. In Johannesburg, the more expensive stores are in large malls protected by security guards. In many large cities angry demonstrators blame their leaders for doing nothing to protect them from the high food prices or the threat of unemployment, and denounce the rigging of elections, the organisation of thugs to cause mayhem violence, and the refusal, to step down when their terms in office ends.

Angry demonstrations were conducted against Mwai Kibaki of Kenya and Robert Mugabe of Zimbabwe, who employed violence and intimidation against opposition parties after losing elections. As long as these leaders still hang on to power, it is not clear what will be the impact of such anger: Will these angry young men find leaders that will bring them together and change the political practices of the past, or will that anger explode and bring more violence and chaos? In many African countries elections have been an open struggle over access to the resources controlled by the state, and politicians resort to a variety of means to attain public office, including making many pledges (Mohammed and Nordlund 2007), or engaging in personal attacks. Voters had, therefore, to make their choice among candidates less on the basis of their policy positions and more on the basis of the candidates' assumed trustworthiness and reliability. Favoritism and explicit acts of vote buying (Schaffer 2007) and electoral violence remain common.

The elections in Nigeria in 2007 became a notorious example of deeply flawed democracy (Human Rights Watch, 2007). A bitter feud between outgoing President Obasanjo and Vice President Atiku Abubakar, an aspirant successor, dominated the election season. Dueling lawsuits, boycott threats, and shifting alliances between opportunistic political parties and factions created a chaotic atmosphere of uncertainty. On polling days, voting for president and National Assembly did not take place in quite a few polling stations in a half dozen states, since the electoral materials were not delivered. In numerous other locations across the country, ballot papers were misprinted or arrived late. In the southern Niger Delta zone, armed militias brazenly stole ballot boxes or substituted prestuffed boxes of their own. Opposition candidates were harassed or arrested, voters were turned away from polling places by gangs of young thugs, ballot secrecy was violated by party workers and police, and some 300 persons were killed in election related violence.

In the past decade, the transition to democracy has proved more frustrating and less beneficial than people had expected. A combination of several factors contributed to that frustration: The failure of government to improve the economy or even to protect the people against high food prices; the resistance of leaders to relinquishing part of their power and authority while making most elections merely a sham; and the slow pace at which changes in governance are taking place. On the positive side, the transition to democracy, even in a one-party system, does have the effect, however slowly, of obliging governments to be more accountable, more attentive to the demands of the people, and more aware of individual rights—mainly the result of greater freedom of the press, which exposes the government to harsh criticism. As more people come to realize that flawed elections are abusing them (even if they get some "share in the pie") and preventing any real change, they will be less tolerant of vote-rigging and bribery.

Do elections intensify tribal conflicts?

Inequality and tribal fragmentation proved to be major problems for leaders of opposition parties that sought to challenge leaders and tried to mobilize popular support. Elections along tribal lines left minority tribes highly fragmented and deeply divided and thus put in power, nearly unchallenged, the political leader who represents the dominant tribe and mobilizes additional support with favoritism. As democratic elections became more widely accepted, however, the minority tribes discovered the power they could master by forming an alliance of several tribes that could be a stronger and more effective opposition to the country's leader. With strong opposition, these minority tribes could no longer be excluded or ignored, and could even gain the majority of votes and the right to form a government.

In both Kenya and Zimbabwe, the opposition party won the majority of the votes but the elections were effectively stolen from them by the leaders of the ruling party. After the second round of voting which was clearly flawed and in which Presidents Mwai Kibaki and Robert Mugabe were declared the winners, they were forced by angry demonstrations to enter into long negotiations and to agree to a shared government. It was indeed unusual in Africa to have elections with two equally strong leaders competing against each other, and even the notion that power can be peacefully transferred to a rival party, thus also to a rival tribe, was unprecedented and difficult to stomach. The widespread evidence of rigging raised doubts among many Kenyans about the merits of democracy that left in power the autocratic leader (in a nominally less powerful role), but turned their country, formerly quite stable and for years Africa's main financial center, into a fragile state.

Another factor that stokes tensions is the high and rising income inequality that became extreme in urban areas, particularly in the resource-rich countries. In the rural areas, the inequalities between tribes are largely the result of preferential treatment by the countries' leaders in the allocation of land and water resources. Discrimination against minority tribes and the widespread use and abuse of favoritism aggravated rivalries that sometimes escalated into armed conflicts, particularly when rebel forces received support in arms and shelter from a neighboring country. These rivalries also prevent collaboration between tribes and hinder rural communities in forming a united front to present demands to the central regimes, to jointly use their resources, or to jointly build projects particularly essential to securing more effective use of dwindling water resources.

In urban centers, living together has reduced the tribal divides, although the scars of tribal animosities have not entirely healed. Paradoxically, but not unexpectedly, riots and demonstrations against the government became more common and aggressive when countries made the transition to democracy, particularly during the elections. Great hostility remained against ethnic groups that benefited from government largess and were employed by the government while most others were unemployed.

The downside of the democratic process in Africa that left in power autocratic leaders who employed vote-rigging and favoritism raised doubts in many African scholars about the merits of democracy for Africa. Obviously, the election process by itself, even when carefully observed, does not make the country truly democratic, and may even deepen the division between ethnic and sectarian groups. The Afrobarometer 2008 survey in 18 countries[10] indicates that while six in ten Africans still believe democracy is preferable to any other form of government, satisfaction with democracy dipped to 45 percent from 58 percent in 2001. Peter Lewis, among the researchers who conducted the survey in 2006, observed that while some countries gradually developed a more active and less hostile political life, others went through the routine of elections, but were disillusioned when governance did not seem to improve. According to the Afrobarometer survey, African voters are losing patience with flawed elections that often exclude popular candidates and are marred by serious irregularities and violations of the law.

Conflicts between formal state laws and informal traditions

In many African countries, the establishment of institutions of government, including an independent judiciary system to ensure the rule of law, faced difficulties whenever there was conflict between rules of the state and traditional tribal rules and customs. Tribal institutions were based on traditions that determined socially accepted norms for person-to-person relations, for the family life, and for the life of the community. Tribal institutions and norms also established rules that determined the rights and obligations of individuals to the tribe and the rights and obligations of the tribe to the individual. These traditional norms usually included the obligation to mutual help within the extended family in the village and between villages of the same tribe, and the obligation of the tribe to defend its villages against enemies from other tribes. The informal institutions determined also the group of elders that functioned as the court and were in charge of interpreting and enforcing the tribes' rules. These elders are, in today's terms, the tribal legislative and judiciary branches that have the authority to administer social norms and make decisions on tribal rules.

One reason for the considerable traditional authority given tribe's elders in interpreting the laws and making decisions on legal matters is that the traditional laws have not been documented, since in most, though not all, African countries, no writing system for tribal languages has been developed. Instead, the traditional legal system has been passed on from generation to generation by the elders who, in addition to their function as the court, had the authority to interpret traditional laws and adapt them to the needs of their times.

In the past, the traditional rules of the tribe were the only valid legal system. The colonial regimes did not infringe on the traditional laws or on the elders' authority. But in the modern state, frictions between traditional rules and the system of laws of the state are practically unavoidable, in part because the rules of the state must be much more comprehensive. In Africa, this friction was first and foremost the result of the different rules and social norms of the different tribes in that state, and the need to establish a unified system of rules on the relations between people from different tribes that would apply equally to all. In most cases this has been done not only by taking into account the power of each tribe and its proportion of the population, but also the preferential treatment given the dominant tribe, which usually was also the leader's tribe. A second reason was the need to determine laws about relations between individuals and the state that establish the authority of the state but recognize the rights of the individual. The third reason was the need to establish rules for the state institutions that determine their authority and responsibilities. The forth reason was the need to determine rules for the relations between enterprises and financial institutions. This system of laws was usually based on the legal system inherited from colonial authorities and has been changed only gradually and often much too slowly.

In addition to this system of laws, many rules were determined or changed by the autocratic leaders according to their needs, and these rules superseded or supplanted the rules of the state. These rules of autocratic leaders often exacerbated the conflicts between the tribal rules and the state laws, particularly in the rural areas, where tribal authority is most pervasive.

The traditional system remains strong and dominating in the social life of the community in rural areas, and the elders still have a pivotal role in settling disputes, approving decisions related to the family or the community, and so forth. In urban areas people from different tribes live together, and the state's laws dominate. The traditional rules and practices are still dominating in family life, the rules of marriage and divorce, the commitments and obligations within the family and between individuals of the same tribe, and even many rules that formally belong to the domain of criminal law are still based on traditional rules and norms.

Since tribal rules and norms are much less comprehensive, the traditional or religious courts sometimes operate side by side with the formal state courts. This division exists in many other countries in other continents. Legally, there is a clear division of authority, but the tribe's members tend to feel a much greater obligation to obey the informal rules of the tribe. South Africa has made a conscious effort to give a role and authority to tribal elders, particularly to set rules and make decisions on many personal and family issues. The tribe's elders then consult with representatives of the state's legal authorities, but in most cases they issue the final verdict.

Formal legal institutions have therefore always been foreign imports to African societies, particularly since they were successively replaced by other rules, and sometimes by the rules of other religions that were imported and enforced by the powers that conquered and ruled the African countries at different time periods. Ever since they gained independence, the African countries have determined and implemented their laws through their own institutions, although these were largely based on the systems inherited from colonial powers. This created frequent problems at first, because most African countries had only fragments of the legal institutions that make up the judicial branch; further, most countries established only very late a constitution and formal guidelines on how laws can be changed, and because autocratic leaders often changed the rules with a stroke of a pen—or a strike of a machete.

Structural reforms and the tribal divide

International development organizations that advised African countries on policy and economic reforms and helped them construct their institutions of government often failed to take into account the implications of the ethnic division of these societies, which were grouped into rather artificial nation states by the borders drawn by the colonial powers. They also did not take fully into account the unpredictable and arbitrary decisions that a central government run by an autocratic leader can make. In addition, the government institutions in these countries were plagued by corruption and there was no institution in the judiciary or the legislative branches to which they were accountable. Nevertheless, the international development organizations had no choice but to implement the reforms they designed or advocated with and by the country's existing institutions. These institutions were not only corrupt but also exceedingly incompetent, since the main criteria for filling the various positions were tribal affiliations rather than skills and experience; similarly, the main criteria for the division of power within and between institutions and among individuals was also influenced by tribal loyalties.

The institutions of the newly independent African states were thus effectively controlled by the ruling elite and by the members of their tribe, often at the expense of the smaller tribes. As a result, the authorities in institutions like the central bank or government ministries even implemented the reforms of the IMF and the World Bank with a clear ethnic bias, thereby distorting the intentions of the reforms and reducing their effectiveness. The failure to take into account this bias by designing reforms according to textbook principles that assume a priori that policies will be implemented equally and rules will be equally enforced and obeyed by all, was arguably one of the main reasons for the disappointing achievements of structural adjustment programs, even though the principles of the reforms seemed most suitable for the mode of operation of the economies of the African states.

Thus, for example, the plans of pro-poor growth policies were influenced by the bias in the allocation of resources for development projects and by the bias in targeting regional development programs. Even during the past decade, as the growth of most countries accelerated to record levels, the decline in poverty was very small, and rural areas were mainly affected by ripples of the growing economy, while prosperity concentrated in the urban centers and the main effect of this growth was to increase income inequalities.

Foreign investors encounter similar problems in dealing with the state institutions in many African countries or with the local economic elites, since the officials were often concerned mostly with their own interests and those of their tribes. The privatization programs that were part of the structural adjustments and the World Bank's sine qua non for economic reforms had the effect of transferring control from the government to private enterprises that were controlled by the economic elites, thus strengthening their dominance over the economy and increasing the monopoly power of these enterprises.

The absence of a well-established constitution that obligates the government and its institutions, determines clear limits on their power, and secures equal rights to all, made the state institutions and the system of governance a major handicap for these countries' development. Rules were changed arbitrarily and frequently by the leaders and implemented by institutions or bureaucracies in an onerous and corrupt manner.

Only in the past decade, when democratic regimes started to become the norm and gained force in more African countries, were basic laws formalized as part of a constitution and other laws became an integral part of the legal system. In a democratic system rules must approved by the legislative branch, and although this does not have much meaning in a one-party system, there are clear provisions that determined how and by whom the constitution and the rules of law can be changed. Quite a few of these rules, most notably rules that establish term limits, still have been changed. In some countries the electorate strongly opposed, though not always successfully, attempts of the leader to change laws on term limits. It is gradually being realized, both by many governments and the public, that a more stable legal system provides the necessary basis for a more stable system of governance and less arbitrary policy decisions.

Reducing civil conflicts: external "nation building" interventions vs. internal public pressure

> National and local ownership is critical to the successful implementation of a peace process. In planning and executing a United Nations peacekeeping operation's core activities, every effort should be made to promote national and local and ownership and to foster trust and cooperation between national actors. Effective approaches to national and local ownership not only reinforce the perceived legitimacy of the operation and support mandate implementation, they also help to ensure the sustainability of any national capacity once the peacekeeping operation has been withdrawn.
>
> United Nations 2008

The United Nations defines peacekeeping as "a way to help countries torn by conflict create conditions for sustainable peace" (www.un.org/Depts/dpko/dpko/). Peacekeeping would police a peace agreement, build trust among belligerents, and provide technical and logistical support for key transition activities like disarmament, demobilization and integration of combatants, and elections. Peace agreements between warring parties are normally not self-enforcing. Peacekeeping would provide a monitoring and enforcement mechanism.

After the end of the cold war, the UN shifted and expanded its field operations from "traditional" missions involving strictly military tasks, to complex "multidimensional" enterprises designed to ensure the implementation of comprehensive peace agreements and assist in laying foundations for sustainable peace. Today, peacekeepers undertake a wide variety of complex tasks, from helping build sustainable institutions of governance, to human rights monitoring, to security sector reform, to the disarmament, demobilization and reintegration of former combatants. In the past decade UN peacekeeping has increasingly been used to intervene in intrastate conflicts and civil wars, mainly to stop the massacre of citizens by the rival forces that the weak central regimes in these countries were not able to stop. In 2005, nearly 77 percent of all UN peacekeeping forces (or 50,000 out of a total of 65,000) were located in Africa, where the missions accounted for close to 75 percent of the UN's peacekeeping budget.

According to the United Nations peacekeeping operations, "fragile states" are conflict-prone countries and are seen as a potential threat to their own citizens, to neighboring countries, and perhaps even to world peace. In order to ensure their security these countries can be placed under trusteeship, with the intervention of a multinational force that must be authorized by the Security Council. This force would seek not only to maintain peace or ensure peace sustainability ("peace-building"), but also to rebuild the institutional capacity of these countries and establish an effective system of governance that is essential to preserving this peace for the long run ("state-building"). The current turmoil in fragile states, and the threat they create to their own citizens and citizens in other countries, provide a justification for international intervention and a framework to guide international assistance to these states. The need to extend the role of the peacekeeping force in fragile states beyond peace-building and peacekeeping operations has been recognized when it became clear these countries would need to establish an effective system of governance to preserve the peace; the two are therefore complementary operations. It remains to be determined, however, how far the state-building operation can go, and what should be the specific goals.

Paul Collier took these guidelines several steps further in *The Bottom Billion* and much more so in his later book, *Wars, Guns and Votes* (2009),m where he argues that in some countries—the countries of the bottom billion where the majority of the world's poor population lives—there is need for a wider external intervention that aims not only at stopping wars between countries and civil conflicts within countries through extensive external intervention, but also building systems of governance in countries that had been engaged in wars and civil conflicts, in order to sustain the peace. He estimates that intervention to build up a failed state and prevent another eruption of violent conflict may last up to ten years. The rather successful Operation Palliser that restored peace in Sierra Leone in 2000 is the model Collier has in mind, and he advocates that this example should be followed in other failed states, which include the majority of SSA countries. Collier dismisses the argument that such operations would amount to an infringement on national sovereignty, since in practice, he claims, this is the sovereignty of their autocratic leaders and not of their people.

Drawing on the successful experience with the intervention of British troops in Sierra Leone, Collier also advocates the use of similar international military intervention in other failed states, and according to his calculation that intervention is highly cost-effective. Civil conflicts have high direct costs by ruining a country's infrastructure, destroying entire neighborhoods in large cities, and disrupting agricultural production. Their negative effects often spill over to neighboring countries when rebel forces receive support and shelter from members of their tribe who reside there. In these cases the costs of the conflict escalate very rapidly, and peacekeeping operations are much more complex, last much longer, and require much longer presence of external military forces in the post-conflict societies.

Nevertheless, external interventions on a wider scale will meet strong resistance from regimes in these countries, unless the regimes reach a desperate state in which they lose control over large parts of the country and ask for that intervention, as did the governments of Sierra Leone and Congo D.R. Many other African countries, including Chad, have UN troops, but they are much smaller operations confined to local conflicts. It will take much more to make a wider intervention in Sudan, in Ethiopia, and even in Zimbabwe. The leaders in these countries will see this uninvited intervention as not only infringements of national sovereignty, or whatever is left of it, but also as a direct threat to them and their regimes.

In nearly all African countries, including most failed states, the leader remains firmly in control of the army, unless and until he is toppled in a military coup by another army commander. Moreover, in many countries the government was elected in democratic elections that in many cases were supervised by an international team of observers, although many elections were still flawed and vote-rigging was uncontrolled. In most of these countries the same leaders and/or ruling parties were elected, partly because elections were still along tribal lines, primarily in the rural areas, and partly because these leaders did all they could (and all that their money could buy) to secure their election. For these leaders and for most African people, what Collier effectively suggests is to impose Washington Consensus–type reforms under the threat of a gun.

Building up the state and restructuring the entire system of governance by an external intervention force is a great threat to these leaders, since it would erode their power and control over the country and may even risk their lives. They will therefore resist this wider intervention as forcefully as they can. Even in the case of a despotic, Mugabe-type leader who is clearly protecting his sovereignty rather than his people, the act of removing a democratically elected leader—regardless of how faulty his election was—is certainly contrary to the UN resolution quoted above, and no African or world leader would support it, even when it may be essential for the reform of the state's governance.

The limitations of external intervention to build up the state governance

There are indeed many humanitarian reasons to justify external intervention: since independence large population groups in many African countries have suffered extreme abuse of their basic human rights, and their leaders not only failed to protect them but often used the power of the state and its security forces to aggravate this abuse. Even in a country like Sudan, where President al-Bashir has been engaged for many years in two civil conflicts that became genocide and openly committed war crimes, an external, wide intervention to build the state would be opposed by all African and Arab nations. Leaders of other developing countries, as well as the leaders of China and Russia, would also vehemently oppose this intervention.

Nigeria is also included in the category of failed states, according to the criteria set by international organizations, but Nigeria does not meet the criteria set by Collier: with a population of more than 150 million, Nigeria is too large to make such an intervention feasible. In other words, size matters; the fate of the people matters less. What makes it worse in Nigeria is that the intervention force would be embroiled in a power struggle between Muslims in the North and Christians in the South, and the developed countries have had enough of that.

Chad is one of the examples Collier brings to make his case. There is, however, scant chance that international intervention will take place in Chad despite the appalling conditions of its people, and there is an equally small chance that an international force, if it ever arrives, will manage to establish even peace and security in Chad, let alone government accountability.

The mission Collier designs will not get off the ground because the conflict in Chad is a racial/tribal conflict that has been going on since the country became independent half-a-century ago, but which has deeper roots of animosity and rivalry. Chad became nominally democratic in 1996 and in 2005, after two flawed elections, President Idriss Deby (who had come to power in a military coup several years earlier) held a referendum that removed constitutional term limits, and in 2006 he won another controversial election.

The long and tyrannical regime of President Deby is not, however, the reason for the persistent civil conflicts in Chad. These conflicts are between Muslim Arabs and black African Christians and animists, and they have a long history of discrimination and exclusion that predates colonial rule, going back to the Arab slave trade and deep racial divides. Despite oil resources and large revenues from its export in the past decade, Chad is one of the ten poorest countries in the world. The majority of the population, including most Arab Muslims, is desperately poor, and around two thirds of the population live below the poverty line of $1 per day.

While the country's needs are compelling, it is hard to imagine any intervening force entering the country, fighting against the well-equipped army of President Deby, thanks to strong support from Libya, and in the process removing this democratically elected president from power, most likely by assassinating him. Even the Sudanese dictator al-Bashir, who is engaged in an extremely costly war with Chad, is not likely to support that intervention out of fear for his own life. This plan would encounter the strong opposition of all the African and Arab states, and the possibility of being caught in a conflict between Muslims and Christians would deter all developed countries that might be asked to send troops.

In fact, it is not even certain this intervention would do any good to the people of Chad, since it will further aggravate sectarian conflict, and it would certainly be opposed by the Arab Muslims, who would see this as an attack against them. They fully supported President Deby in the past elections because he gave them security, and they will always oppose any leader who is not an Arab Muslim, regardless of his qualifications. For the same reason, the Christian Chadians in the South would always oppose any leader who is Muslim, since no Muslim leader will give them security. Collier's claim that, "Military intervention, properly constrained, has an essential role, providing both the security and the accountability of government to citizens that are essential for development," is therefore utterly wrong. Accountability cannot be attained under the regime of President Deby, and neither he nor any other Muslim president can provide security to the black African Chadians.

Although income inequality in Chad is extreme and most of the country's high revenues are accumulated by its tiny elite and a meager share reaches the poor, it is wrong to see the civil conflict in Chad as a personal rivalry between an autocratic leader and the rest of the country, as Collier argues. It is a tribal–sectarian conflict, and therefore it is not even certain an external intervention force would be able to restore lasting peace in a country where racial/tribal animosities have been deeply rooted for centuries and armed conflicts last for decades; nor is it possible to imagine that against this background there is much potential to build an accountable system of governance, since that would require establishing some sort of a power-sharing agreement between the two camps. To maintain any peace, the intervention force may have to remain in the country for much more than a decade and effectively separate the two communities.

In both Sudan and Chad, the black African and mostly Christian tribes have practically nothing in common with, but much against, the Arab Muslims, and their enmity will prevent them from establishing any communal life and elementary collaboration necessary to form a state or reach an agreement on the structure of the government in that state.

The solution reached in Sudan to divide the country between North and South by 2011—although it remains to be seen whether President al-Bashir will abide by any agreement—is probably the correct solution also for neighboring Chad and also Niger. There is nothing wrong with a "two-state" solution for countries created by arbitrary colonial borders that locked within them extremely antagonistic racially divided peoples who have a long history of enmity, exploitation, exclusion, and incessant fighting. There is also nothing advantageous in insisting on keeping these irreconcilable enemies together, possibly separated by an international force that will have to remain there much longer than a decade. In all three countries, newly discovered natural resources are likely to create more difficulties and aggravate the conflicts, but with less ill-will and more imagination it should be possible to find some financial arrangement that would keep all parties content if they are separated into two states.

In Sudan, Chad, Niger and several other sub-Sahelian countries the racial/ethnic/religious divides are extremely deep and the scars are still bleeding. In these countries the process of state-building is practically impossible in the foreseeable future and even any kind of modus vivendi between the two communities is bound to be fragile. Also, the seemingly successful experience in Sierra Leone has left the country deeply divided.

These examples highlight a basic flaw in one of the basic assumption made by Collier that "in the small and fragmented societies of the bottom billion, power is personalized, and elites often have a distinct identity." In Chad, Sudan, Niger and most other African countries the power struggle is *not* personalized, even though big egos of big chiefs are involved. In none of these countries is the power struggle between the leader or the narrow elite and the rest of society; instead it is a power struggle between tribes, ethnic, or sectarian groups within these countries, and the leading tribe or sect in each of these countries is fully identified with, represented by, and supports the country leader.

The role of external intervention or even a UN peacekeeping force may be even more controversial in Guinea-Bissau, Togo, and Mauritania. These three countries had democratically elected governments that were toppled in military coups in the past few years. To restore democracy and then, perhaps, build the state, any external intervention would have to be engaged first in military operations against the security forces of the new regimes and remove the military leaders. In an article in the *International Herald Tribune*, Collier lamented the lack of action against the military coups that toppled democratically elected governments in these African countries, asking: "Why...did the United Nations not intervene militarily when the democratic government of Mauritania, another country in the bottom billion, was overthrown by a coup last month?" (*IHT* Sept. 22, 2008).

Restoring democracy has not been formally recognized as one of the missions of a UN peacekeeping force, and when elections are deeply flawed, as they were in these three countries, it is not even clear whether the elected government has the legitimacy to ask for external intervention. In

Mauritania, support was muted for the first democratically elected leader who was toppled in the coup, and few mourned the political demise of the prime minister who failed to deal with the food crisis. Nevertheless, there was broad public resistance to the coup d'état, after so many coups and coup attempts the country has experienced, and many people, particularly among the intellectual elite, expressed anger and frustration about the coup. Under strong public pressure, the new military regime was essentially forced to schedule new elections within less than a year. In other words, there was no need for UN military intervention. The people of Mauritania themselves proved to be the most effective (and cost-effective) way of achieving the result of restoring democracy.

Support and resistance to despotic leaders

Many leaders abuse their power to enrich themselves, and despite widespread favoritism only a small share of their country's riches trickles down even to poor people of the leader's own tribe. Nevertheless, these leaders are supported by their tribe because for them these leaders are better than the alternative of having the leader of the rival tribe as the country's leader. Even the most notorious and abusive African leader, Robert Mugabe, had the unwavering support of his tribe during the two rounds of recent elections because he gave them the public asset they were afraid to lose had the opposition leader (and the leader of the rival tribe) Morgan Tsvangirai been elected: security.

The experience of most African countries is very similar: in a multiethnic society more security for one tribe or ethnic group means, almost by default, less security for the others and greater risk that they will be discriminated against and excluded. With this background there are reasons to doubt whether the "bargain" Collier suggests can possibly work. According to the scheme Collier lays out, the international community would provide a security guarantee to a government in a poor country that operated by specified rules of governance, while reducing aid to that country in proportion to its increases in its military budget. Then, if there were a coup attempt against a government that made and adhered to its promises, Western countries would go in to overthrow the coup-plotters and restore the previous government.

The *conditionalities* in this scheme would require the international community to provide security guarantees to countries like Sudan, Chad, Guinea, Niger, and Guinea-Bissau provided their leaders operate by specific rules of governance designed in Washington or Oxford and if the leader in any of these countries spend any money to increase its military budget, the aid to his country would be reduce proportionally. All these countries are resource-rich and have enough resources for their military budget. The reduction in the aid money will therefore hurt only the countries' poor.

Collier does not make clear whether the bargain he suggests would include the UN peacekeeping operations in crisis areas like Darfur; the UN and then British peacekeeping operation in Sierra Leone had no strings attached, no bargain, and no conditionalities; its only goal was to stop the mass killing after a decade of civil conflict. In fact, in Sierra Leone there was not even any effective central regime to make a bargain with.

Moreover, the bargain Collier lays out violates the UN mandate for peacekeeping operations, and for that reason alone is not likely to get international support. For the Western countries providing security guarantees to the governments of failed states that would require sending troops "to overthrow the coup-plotters and restore the previous government" would mean more casualties among their troops, and among the countries' civilians who would be killed in this well-intentioned mission. On top of that, the bargain would not even have the support of the leading tribe in the country itself, since its members would worry that by gaining greater accountability (whose virtues *to them* are unknown) they may lose the security they now have while their leader is also the leader of the country. Western intervention is, therefore, likely to encounter strong resistance of the locals and possibly lend support to rebel troops that would make the whole adventure "good investment," as Collier calculates but unacceptable for all these other reasons.

There is also no doubt the elite of any of these countries, who now work in the government and in public institutions, will resist intervention. They have secured jobs that they received as part of the leader's favoritism, but may lose those jobs if new standards of accountability are introduced. They will also lose the benefits they now reap as their share in the country's rampant corruption. New standards of accountability that reduces corruption also will reduce their incomes.

The international experts that come with the external intervention force will not, therefore, receive much assistance from the country's present establishment, although they will have to rely on this administration and the public institutions to establish accountability, first because they know too little about the country, and second because they cannot replace the entire staff in all these institutions. One lesson from the unsuccessful experience of reforms designed by the Washington Consensus was that the implementation of the reforms must have the collaboration of management and staff in public institutions, since they are the ones who actually implement the reforms.

The plan to implement reforms by an external intervention force according to a set of guidelines designed by experts in Washington or Oxford is likely to encounter the same resistance as did the Washington Consensus reforms. The barely disguised hostile position Collier takes by suggesting that, "The evidence is against...internal solutions;...breaking the conflict trap and the coup trap are not tasks that these societies can readily accomplish by themselves" is in my view not only inherently wrong but, even worse, doomed to fail.

The concluding chapter suggests a different approach and takes a very different position: In my view, the *only* solution that can work is a solution that comes predominantly from within the country itself, and that solution cannot be imposed but must have the consent and conviction of these peoples that the coup trap, the conflict trap, and the trap of lack of accountability must come to an end because they are highly damaging for them. The peoples of Mauritania, Mozambique, Botswana, and Senegal had this conviction, and their countries ended or avoided these traps. The challenge of both the African Union and the donor countries is to create the conditions to provide the incentives that convince the peoples in the African countries that the cycle of conflicts and coups and abuse of power by officials they themselves elect is ruinous to their interests.

In his research, Collier discovered that "democracy" in bottom billion countries had a strong association with political violence—in part because it was "democracy" in name only (e.g., holding and manipulating elections to consolidate illegitimate power). Collier calls this "fake democracy protected by the sanctity of sovereignty." The same discovery and the same conclusions apply to the democratic process in Western European countries in the nineteenth century. To call the experience of African countries "fake democracy" because violence and manipulation were widespread in their very first rounds of election, is to ignore the lesson of history that transition to democracy is a lengthy process. Even equal voting rights to all were given in some European countries only after a process and a struggle that lasted nearly two centuries. Statistical calculations based on two to three "observations" over 15–20 years are entirely missing this lesson.

Collier correctly emphasizes that "We need to dismiss the illusion that elections are the milestone and face the long haul of building the economy." But he takes the argument too far when he asserts that "Electoral competition creates a Darwinian struggle for political survival in which the winner is the one who adopts the most cost-effective means of attracting votes.... Providing good governance is the least plausible way of winning an African election. Most African countries that profess democracy end up with an unviable halfway house without the capacity of autocracies to act decisively or the accountability of a genuine democracy." Again, this is the kind of statistical analysis that is based solely on past observations and makes no attempt to deviate from the linear trend line charted by past observations and instead use the experience of other countries and other time periods in order to make predictions about the future. The approval of "the capacity of autocracies to act decisively" ignores even the lessons of the African experience.

From the donors' point of view, decision for or against external intervention are even clearer. The "Iraq–Afghanistan syndrome" that haunts all leaders in developed countries will not make them enthusiastic supporters of any plan to send troops to failed states, or even to post-conflict countries, with the objective of providing more security in order to achieve greater accountability of the countries' leaders. Although the whole scheme certainly reflects the best of intentions, the plan to adopt the basic principles of centrally designed reforms that characterized the Washington Consensus, but which multiplies the difficulties several times over by requiring large-scale intervention with military forces, is not likely to fly.

It took the EU four years to make the decision to intervene in the crisis in the Balkans and stop the massacre in Bosnia, which was in their backyard. The massacre in Darfur continues uninterrupted as both the AU and limited UN forces prove totally ineffective. In Congo D.R. there are about peacekeeping 20,000 troops, but they are far too few to establish law and order in this large country, which is about a quarter the size of the United States; large areas are still under the control of warlords and of Rwandan and Ugandan troops who loot the country's resources. On top of all that, quite a few UN troopers are not benevolent angels: Many are involved in arms dealing, take bribes for supporting one rebel force or the other, and are heavily involved in drug-dealing and prostitution.

Collier recognized changes must come predominantly from within and cannot be imposed, but he argues that security in post-conflict societies may still require an external military presence. The Sierra Leone experience described in the next section shows, however, that despite the nearly decade-long intervention of UN peacekeeping and British troops, the security situation remains fragile and it will take much longer than a decade to achieve accountability.

Sierra Leone: mission accomplished—with external intervention

The success of foreign intervention by restoring peace in Sierra Leone is the most noted example of establishing peace in this type of operation. In practice, however, after more than ten years of state building with the help of UN and British troops, the achievements remain very tenuous. Although Sierra Leone has extremely rich natural resources, it is one of the poorest countries in the world (Box 4.5). Infant and maternal mortality rates are the highest in the world, and the country still ranks as the poorest on the United Nations Human Development Index. Its resources have been embezzled systematically by widespread corruption, nepotism, and fiscal mismanagement that eventually led to a decade-long civil war. A Truth and Reconciliation Commission set up when the war ended noted that corruption and the marginalization of ethnic groups were key factors that triggered the war in 1991. The commission warned that a return to the old ways might well send the state into

Box 4.5 Sierra Leone

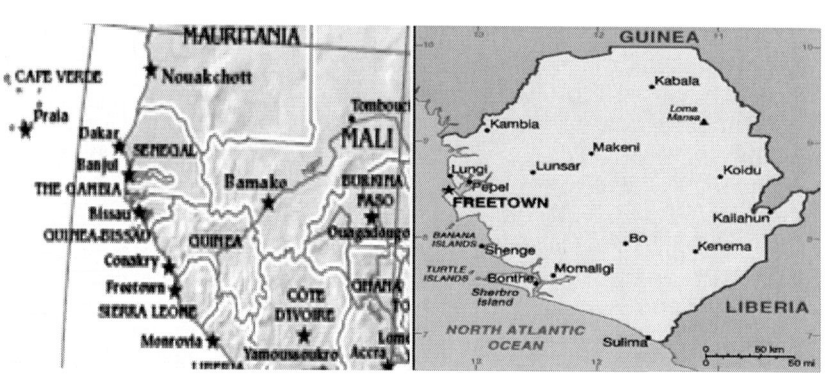

Map 4.8 Sierra Leone
Source: CIA, *The World Factbook* (2009).

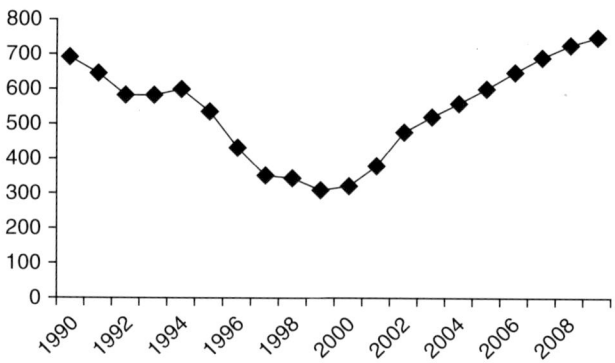

Figure 4.5 Average GDP per capita in Sierra Leone in US$ (in 2000 prices and exchange rates)
Source: IMF, World Economic Outlook (2009).

- Population: 6,5 million.
- Pop. annual growth rate: 2.28%
- Coastal length: 402km.
- GDP per capita UD$800 (2008 est.); Poverty rate: 70.2% (2004).
- Share of urban population: 38%.
- The main ethnic groups: Temne (30%) and the Mende (20%); no significant ethnic divide.
- Religions: 60% Muslim; 30% indigenous beliefs; 10% Christians.

- Natural resources: Rich mineral resources, particularly diamonds. Recently oil was discovered.
- Child mortality: 155 deaths per 1000 live births (2nd in the world).
- Youth unemployment: 80%.
- Civil war broke in 1991, followed by a series of military coups. Main reasons: High corruption and the influence of the civil war in Liberia. In 1998, the UN started to send peacekeeping troops that were later joined by British troops.
- Poverty rate (2008): 70%.

another round of anarchy and bloodshed. A brief review of the developments in Sierra Leone since the elections of 2007 shows this is a distinct possibility.

The civil war in Sierra Leone started in 1991, when the Revolutionary United Front (RUF) entered the country from Liberia, launching a rebellion to overthrow the one-party rule of the All Peoples Congress (APC), in power since 1967. The rebellion quickly developed into a campaign of violence aimed at controlling the country's diamond and mineral resources. The war lasted from 1991 until a temporary peace agreement was reached in 1999, after several African governments, together with the governments of the United Kingdom and the United States, and the UN secretary general's special representative intervened in the negotiations between the rival forces.

During the civil war, the RUF committed horrendous abuses; over 50,000 people were killed and over two million, a third of the country's population, were displaced. UN forces were sent to help the Sierra Leonean government, since the abuses still continued after 1999, and British troops were soon sent to assist the UN forces to end the war, and another peace agreement was signed in 2002. UN forces stayed in the country until 2005, and British forces still remained to help the government conduct, in 2007, its first postwar democratic election. The governing party accepted defeat and peacefully handed over power to the leader of the opposition. Even today, however, most of the population still lives in abject poverty, and youth unemployment is around 80 percent. Corruption is widespread, income inequality extremely high, and the country's political system remains fractured along tribal/regional lines.

Sierra Leone's neighbors, Angola, Liberia, Guinea, and Guinea-Bissau all have extremely rich oil and other resources, and they are all plagued with civil wars, a succession of military coups, and extreme poverty. In Angola, the civil war lasted 27 years and ended in 2002 with a fragile peace agreement. Angola is Africa's second largest oil producer and exporter after Nigeria, and after the civil war it grew at astronomical rates of over 15 percent per year, thanks to the commodity boom and a construction boom to resettle displaced persons. Angola is still one of world's most corrupt countries; its government lacks basic institutions, and is highly incompetent. The current peace attracts many foreign investors who seek to exploit the oil resources. Income inequality is extreme, and only a tiny percentage of the population benefits from the huge revenues.

The civil war in Angola started in 1975, after it became independent from Portugal. The war was between forces of the two main parties, whose leaders failed to reach an agreement on power sharing. Some 1.5 million lives may have been lost in this war, and 4 million were displaced during the quarter century of fighting. Only after Jonas Savimbi, the leader of one party, was killed in 2002 did the other party take control over the country. In September 2008 Angola held its first elections in 16 years, and the two parties both participated. The leading party was helped by the country's high rate of growth and won in a landslide. The elections were peaceful, supervised by an international team that praised the process, but shortly afterward the government went back to the old routine of high corruption and shared very little of the revenues from its oil exports with the more than 80 percent of the population that remains dismally poor.

Both Sierra Leone and Angola are still recovering from the damage of the prolonged civil wars, and their regimes remain fragile. In neighboring Guinea and Guinea-Bissau military coups continue unhindered. The institutions of government in all these countries barely function, and most transactions are still conducted by high government officials who secure their share.

The election control commission, National Elections Watch (NEW), which was established in Sierra Leone during the May 2002 elections illustrates the limitations of NGOs aimed at strengthening democracy. While the intervention of NEW helped ensure good conduct of the elections, the commission was quickly dissolved due to lack of funding and was therefore unable to oversee local elections held at the end the same year. President Ernest Bai Koroma from Sierra Leone, who ran in the election campaign in 2007 on a platform of fighting corruption, is widely accused of nepotism by rewarding his family members and cronies with lucrative contracts. The president apparently has long forgotten the promise in his inaugural address that "There will be no sacred cow in my regime. My ministers, my family and no one will be given preferential treatment. Everyone must face the law." In fact, companies owned by relatives and associates are exempted from export duties or customs charges. The president's sister quit her secretarial job to become a government contractor, using her influence without competing on public bids. Despite the country's resources, more than 50 percent of Sierra Leone's economy comes from donor assistance, and with the war long over and donor fatigue setting in, the poor are the ones bound to suffer from the looting and waste of the country's resources and from a decline in aid.

Conclusion

Only the pressure of the people in these countries can convince the public officials that stopping waste (and increasing the effectiveness) in public institutions is the only way to keep their positions; the only form of government that can give people the power to put this pressure on the officials and the leaders and make these demands is democracy.

So far, most elections in the African countries have been a struggle over access to the resources controlled by the state and over positions in public institutions that give a share in "the pie." Politicians, therefore, resort to everything they can muster in order to attain public office. In many countries that have made the transition to democracy, public officials continue to use a variety of unscrupulous measures to secure their election.

This must be seen, however, as an ongoing process still at its initial stage in most countries, and it would be wrong to consider the disappointing achievements thus far as the best the democratic process in Africa can do. The democratization process has not been easier, smoother, or shorter in Europe, and certainly not in Latin America. The process we now witness in Africa, disillusioning as it is, must be seen as a stage in that transition. As the people of Mauritania proved, if they are not timid or afraid to express their anger against yet another coup the almighty military leaders have staged, they can apply enough pressure to force new elections. It does not take much to predict that the next round of elections in Nigeria will not be as flawed as that of 2007.

If the people in government and public institutions come to realize their jobs are at risk and their election is not secured because the public is less tolerant of their corrupt and abusive use of power, then they will have to be at least more careful in their methods. Otherwise, they are bound to create a public outrage against them. This will not yet make them accountable in the Scandinavian sense of the term, but it is a small step in that direction.

With greater freedom of the press and more open public protests, public officials will be under tighter scrutiny and have less freedom to abuse their power; that would require them to comply with certain standards that at least have the pretense of greater accountability. This may not come out of their own new conviction of the need for accountability or higher standards of ethics, but it will nonetheless be the product of a more careful cost–benefit analysis that would convince them that election-rigging and fraudulence are likely to generate negative net benefits. Only the public in these countries can determine these costs and benefits that, over time, will take the system of governance in the right direction.

Despite many disappointments with the democratization process thus far, there have been several successful experiences in African countries that offer hope that a more accountable regime will come to power and break the cycle of conflicts, coups, and arbitrary abuse of power. If the leaders come to realize that their only way to stay in power is with public support, they are more likely to listen, respond to public demands, and make greater efforts to reduce corruption and waste. The example of Botswana shows that the conflict trap and the coup trap are not a preordained fate of these societies, and it is a task they can accomplish by themselves. In the historical process the developed countries themselves went through, primarily in the nineteenth century, democracy proved to be a strong force that gave people the power to demand competence, effectiveness, and accountability in government. In the African countries, that experience has been far too short to draw hasty conclusions that democracy has failed or is doomed to fail.

Notes

1. Gérard Prunier, *Africa's World War: Congo, the Rwandan Genocide, and the Making of a Continental Catastrophe*. Oxford University Press, 2008.
2. Sources: Eldis Reports on Conflicts and Security, War and militarization of mining in Eastern Congo, 2009.
3. At the time, the agreement was with the Organization of the African Union (OAU).
4. Paul Collier: *The Bottom Billion: Why the Poorest Countries are Failing and What Can Be Done About it*. Oxford University Press, 2007.
5. World Bank, *Breaking the Conflict Trap: Civil War and Development Policy*. June 2003, p. 168.
6. Nevertheless, the United States cut back on its peacekeeping operations in West Africa due to growing domestic pressures as an effect of the war in Iraq and put pressure on its foreign assistance funds.
7. Quoted by President Obama in his Nobel Peace Prize acceptance speech.
8. William Russell Easterly, *The White Man's Burden: Why the West's Efforts to Aid the Rest Have Done So Much Ill and So Little Good*. 2008
9. See also his article "Development in Dangerous Places," prepared for a forum on global poverty and intervention. See *BostonReview* July/August 2009.
10. The survey was based on interviews with 1,200 to 2,400 people per country.

Part V
The Fourth Wave of Democratization: Will Democracy Cement the African Multiethnic Nation State?

> And he shall see old planets change and alien stars arise,
> And give the gale his sea-worn sail in shadow of new skies,
> Strong lust of gear shall drive him forth and hunger arm his hand,
> To win his food from the desert rude, his pittance from the sand.
>
> From *The Voortrekker*
> Rudyard Kipling

5.1
The Transition of the African Countries to Democracy

As the world is now concluding the first decade of its voyage into the twenty-first century, there is optimism and conviction that on the wings of stunning technological innovations the journey to a whole new wonder world will not slow down. Despite gusty winds that shattered the global economy at the end of the decade in a series of economic crises, and explosive wars marked by the trauma of 9/11, hopes remained high. Against the daily background of new technology records in speed and height, however, the images of extreme hunger and poverty that continue to come from Africa cast a dark shadow on this journey and leave us all wondering how hunger can prevail in a world that has never been so rich, and the standards of living of most people have never been higher.

The answer to these questions is not only in the domain of economics, and it can only be understood when the failure of the continent's economies is combined with the social and political transformations African countries are undergoing. Despite the rapid growth of more than half the African countries during the first decade of this century, that growth barely had any effect on the standard of living of the vast majority of their populations, and the number of their poor continued to rise.

In the aftermath of the series of economic crises that paralyzed the global economy since the last years of the decade, and the spread of hunger as an effect of the food crisis, the G-8 countries convened again and pledged new resources to help the African countries renew their growth. They emphasized in particular the needs of the people in the rural areas who were caught between the entrenched high food and oil prices and the ominous global warming that threatens to have the most damaging effects on Africa. But in the countries themselves business was as usual: during the decade of rapid growth and mammoth revenues from the export of oil and other natural resources, the resource-rich African countries, with very few exceptions, did not investment in their rural areas, neither to increase yields nor to improve infrastructure. As a result, most of the increase in the number of poor and undernourished people during the food crisis was in the rural areas. Even if the additional aid pledged by the rich countries and the international development organizations is indeed given and reaches its destination, it will not have much effect on the poor, and will not make more than a dent on living conditions of hundreds of millions of people in rural areas.

The threatening recession in the coming years will not have the same form, however, as the stagnation in Africa during the three "lost decades" in the 1970s through the 1990s. The reason is the demographic and social changes that are taking place as an effect of the rapid growth of the urban population and the political changes in a growing number of countries as an effect of the weakening of autocratic regimes and the transition to democracy that in most countries is still in its early stage but, it makes people more aware of their power. The sociodemographic process on the one hand and the political process on the other hand reinforce each other and they are likely to be the forces that will shape and change African society in the coming decades.

The significance and depth of the transformation many African countries are now undergoing as an effect of these processes can be appreciated if viewed against the backdrop of the other fundamental changes African society experienced in the earlier years: Until the African countries gained independence, their tribal societies were entirely fragmented, consisting of many different tribes, each with its own social order and leadership, and remained unchanged for many centuries; most tribes had very little contact with each other, since they were separated by high mountains, deep rivers, heavy rainforests, or impenetrable deserts. Even when tens of thousands were caught and sold into slavery, most others knew next to nothing about it, and their isolation in small communities prevented them from joining forces and fighting the slave traders.

The colonial powers brought them gradually to the modern world by opening new roads that connected them and engaged them in trade, but only after they became independent were the African people forced to make the adjustments to the twentieth century, with independent states, more modern and complex economies, and closer interactions with each other and other continents, through trade and foreign investment. They had to make this transition and adjust their economies within few decades, whereas it took Europe nearly a millennium to make the very tumultuous transition from the "natural order" that was based on a rural society, feudal and serf systems, and small monarchies, to the world of the eighteenth and nineteenth centuries with more advanced economies, large kingdoms, and an industrial revolution that triggered a flow of migrants from rural areas to urban centers. In Africa people, tribes and states are still struggling with this transition, and so far only a small minority has benefited from it. Hunger and extreme poverty could, however, have been avoided in a continent that was then blessed with rich natural resources, fertile lands and plenty of water, but hunger and poverty were and still are widespread due to poor governance, self-centered leaders, and violent struggles between tribes and sectarian groups over power and control. As a result, most of these riches were accumulated by the leaders, their small circle of supporters, and their army commanders, while the majority of the population remained poor and lived in the rural areas.

The statistical analyses conducted in many studies on past economic trends of the African countries shed light on the dimension of the changes in the continent's economy, on the large and continuous increase in income inequality between and within countries, and on the deepening poverty. More recent studies endeavored to explain the reasons for these failures to spread the developments of African economies more widely and to reduce poverty. These studies concentrated on the function of the regime under autocratic leaders, their poor governance, and their failed economic policies. Other studies should examine also the reasons for their disastrous system of governance, which may be related to their fragmentation into ethnic and sectarian groups that did not develop a more cohesive society and determine the identity of African states. The main reason for their fragmentation was the process in which the states were established in territories determined by the arbitrary colonial border, but this territorial partition became also socially and politically divisive and confrontational only after the countries became independent states.

The lack of social, ethnic, or religious cohesion in these states' multiethnic and fragmented societies effectively triggered conflicts and competition between ethnic groups over control of territory and resources. There were also other reasons for the built-in conflicts in African societies, some of them are related to the specific conditions in different countries, including the personality of their leaders (primarily their "golden leaders" who led also their war of independence), their resources, and the regime established by the colonial power that had controlled their countries. Only a more complete analysis can identify the social forces that brought autocratic leaders to power in all the African countries and maintained the authoritarian system in most of them; their very fragile regimes; and the reasons for the intense social conflicts, the large number of military coups and the incessant wars that drained Africa of resources and impoverished its people.

This concluding part of this book provides a general survey of the main developments on the African continent—a survey aimed at providing an integrated framework for reviewing the economic, social, and political forces that have shaped these developments in the past and will have a long-lasting impact on the continent and its people. This survey draws the basic outline of the very fundamental adjustments the African people experienced and were essentially forced to go through in the past, and highlights their driving forces. This overview is therefore drawn with a wide brush and offers only a sketch of these processes, one that underlines the very fundamental transformation of the society, economy, and system of governance as they make the transition from their own isolated world and become part of the world of the twenty-first century.

The structure of the tribal society

The difficulties African peoples encountered in the transition from a tribal society to a nation-state were due not only to the multitude of different languages, ethnic groups, and religions brought together when the states were formed and their territories determined. By bringing together different ethnic groups into multiethnic states, they had complicated communication problems between people from different tribes, creating instinctive suspicion and often opening hostility between them. The most difficult problem, however, was the very different social order between the tribal society and the state. In the traditional tribal society members have close family relations and a long history of collaboration that cemented their cohesion and created instinctive trust. Equally important was their strong attachment to their territory and a strong sense of ownership of the land in which they had lived and cultivated for generations, and of the water and other resources in their territories. The lack of rural infrastructure and the natural boundaries between territories had isolated and limited interactions between tribes and, therefore, limited also their conflicts over natural resources, although they did not eliminate them altogether.

Due to that isolation and limited interactions, the African continent was inhabited by hundreds of tribes, each with its own customs, language, organization, and beliefs. Underneath their differences, however, they share several similar characteristics that make it possible to identify the general principles of their social, political, and economic institutions: First, in all tribal societies, the social identity had and still has well-defined territorial dimensions, and the administrative unit and social rules that define also the rights and obligations of the people in this community are territorially delimited; second the tribal system across the continent is based on quite similar principles and social norms. The tribal societies evolved, however, two very different directions by developing two different structures of social and political organization that were determined largely by the borders of their territories (Forester and Evans-Pritchard 1987):

The small tribes included a relatively small number of communities or extended families that concentrated in a small territory. Within this territory, social order was strictly maintained and the community and lineage principles determined, and these cemented their allegiance to the tribe and its leaders. The relations between communities that were part of the tribe were coordinated with, and dominated by, the relations with lineage groupings.

The tribe's elders were, and still are, both the governing administration and the judicial authority, and they rule according to a system of laws and code of ethics deeply embedded in the tribe's heritage and commonly accepted by all members. That system and the leadership to which all the tribe's members are strongly committed kept the tribe together, protected its members, and preserved the widely accepted social rules and standards. These norms and social rules determined, in turn, the rights and obligations of the members, the relations within the family, between families, with other members of the community, and between the communities that were part of that tribe. The tribe has clear and widely accepted ways of settling disputes under the authority and guidance of the elders, but the basic rules are sacred laws that are part of the tribe's heritage and religion.

Natural borders secluded the tribes within their territories, separated them from other tribes, and limited the interactions between tribes. This isolation led to the creation of a large number of different cultures, languages, social norms, and heritage. Disputes between tribes over land or water resources, particularly in the semiarid areas, were not uncommon, however, and they were the main reasons for tribal conflicts and ferocious wars. There were no arrangements, no rules, and no agreed-upon authority for settling these disputes, and the stronger tribe dominated, often absorbing the members of the smaller one. The Kikuyu, for example, migrated to their current location in Kenya about four centuries ago, and after conquering some of the most fertile lands now make up Kenya's largest ethnic group.

The large tribes were spread across much wider areas; they were large even in today's terms and included hundreds of thousands and even millions of people who lived in many small but closely interrelated communities and had a more complex political organization under a common leadership. The Zulu in South Africa became a population of nearly ten million whose shared identity had evolved over centuries; the Zulus absorbed many small neighboring tribes that had very similar languages and cultures, creating a large and powerful sovereignty under the rule of a single chief who united and governed them. The process by which the large dominion was formed by integrating many small dominions was very similar to the process in which the European monarchies were combined into a large kingdom.

These large African tribes, under the rule of the chief, had a structure and organization which was in many ways similar to that of a state. The chief was the executive head, the legislator, the supreme judge, the army commander, the spiritual leader, and even the principal capitalist of the whole community. The chief was vested with the economic and legal control over the entire land within the boundaries of the territory he governed, and all people within this territory were subjects of the chief and had the right to live in that territory by accepting his rule. Within this administrative area, social order was strictly maintained, and in the large dominions the chief even had a police force under his command to maintain order and with the authority to apply strict and severe penal sanctions, although such decisions had to be made by the chief, himself. Some scholars even referred to these territories as "sovereign states," although these states did not have any formal legal system or institutions other than their traditions and the unifying authority of the chief.

Even in the large dominions, there were no formal rules that determined relations between communities and tribes, since even in the larger tribes interactions between the smaller communities were sporadic due to the natural boundaries that determined their territories and separated them from each other. Their climatic and geographical conditions determined also their livelihood as nomads or farmers, and thus also their social organization. The limited progress of African societies and their primitive economies were largely due to the limited interaction between tribes that prevented them from engaging in trade outside their boundaries and thus gave them no incentive to develop more advanced and competitive production methods or any road infrastructure. They therefore lived on subsistence agriculture and produced their food using rudimentary production methods and very primitive implements.

The Yoruba in Nigeria and Benin also had a large population of more than ten million people, who shared the same language, although there were frequent disputes between different factions within this territory that had to be settled by the chief. In the seventeenth and eighteenth centuries, there was a single administrative government that controlled Yorubaland. Most of that territory is now in Nigeria, although the colonial borders divided that kingdom and therefore also the Yoruba people, among Nigeria, Benin, and several other neighboring states. The Igbo in Nigeria also had well-organized and orderly societies composed of hundreds of local communities and more developed trade networks but they did not have a unifying leader and did not develop the structure of a state.

The peaceful cohabitation of the members of the individual tribes and the limited interaction between tribes contributed to their security within their territory and to their allegiance and strong commitment to their tribe. In his book, *The Cement of Society* (1989), Jon Elster suggested the concept of the *coefficient of cohesion* that was based on the number of transactions between households and communities that live in a certain area. In Africa, the small territory in which most tribes lived enhanced the cohesion between the members of the same tribe because their work, social, and family relations were closely interrelated and involved all forms of collaboration. The cohesion between different smaller tribes remained, however, quite small even when they were members of a large tribe, partly as an effect of the natural borders that separated them and restricted their interactions; partly because family relations between members of the different smaller tribes were still uncommon, since these relations were determined and settled by the elders of each of the tribe; partly because their languages may still have had slight differences; and partly because there were no rules for the relations and interactions between individuals from different tribes and the chief settled only the relations and disputes between the tribes.

The development of the African dominion, particularly against the background of the development of the state in Europe of the eighteenth and nineteenth centuries, suggests the African dominion was in the process of becoming a state. That process was much slower in Africa, however, because the cohesion between tribes even within the same dominion or same large tribe remained quite small, and they had few incentives to develop a more formal structure that governed the entire dominion and determined the rules for interactions between individuals from different small tribes. In Europe, in contrast, the natural boundaries did not isolate the communities and the monarchies had extensive and frequent interactions that over time evolved into formal transactions that brought them to realize the mutual benefits of settling disputes in agreements that eventually led to the formation of agreed-upon rules and institutions that also minimized the damage of wars.

In the precolonial period, the tribes within the dominions of the Zulu, the Ngwato in southern Africa, and the Yoruba and Igbo in western Africa were in the early stages of forming a closer unity that could lead them to determine formal rules for their interactions that would resemble the rules of a state. These embryonic states preserved, however, the territorial integrity of the individual tribes; the chief was the unifying authority who governed all the institutions, including the legislative and judiciary authority; there was therefore no separation of powers and no independence to any of these authorities. Instead, the various duties, the special rights, prerogatives, and privileges, gave the chief the authority of a single unifying administrative government. The cohesion between tribes within the dominion was, therefore, highly dependent on the unifying power and authority of the chief, and conflicts between rival contenders to inherit the position of chief, usually members of the "royal" family, often divided the tribes within the dominion and led to fierce conflicts.

The process of forming a more unified structure and institutions in the dominion that could bring the individual tribes closer was still in its early stage when Africa was colonized in the nineteenth century. An evaluation of this process from a historical perspective must recognize that at each stage in this process the social structure was designed to meet as best it could the needs of the population and maintain the social order within the tribe and later between tribes within the dominion. The social norms within the individual tribes, and the rules for dispute settlement between tribes under the authority of the chief, made life in tribal communities quite stable and safe, and the evolving structures of tribal societies always had a high *coefficient of cohesion* and stable relations between tribes under the unifying power of the chief.

The lack of a writing system prevented the tribe's elders and the chief from documenting the legal system; nevertheless, the system of rules and social norms was well-preserved over time by the tribe's elders and by the strong adherence of the tribe's member to the basic principles and commandments. The tribes also had institutions and organized methods to cater for the welfare of all their members, protect them, and secure their safety. Although the history of African tribes, particularly the history of large dominions, had also many chapters of wars and conflicts over territories and resources, these wars were not nearly as devastating as wars in Europe.

The allegiance and strong commitment of the tribe's members to their tribal heritage and to their leaders reflected their unconscious but deep conviction that the social order and mutual guarantees of the tribe's members to the livelihood and safety of all offered the most secure and stable system for organizing their lives as individuals and as a community and for cementing social relations and mutual trust. During the colonial period the interaction between tribes became more frequent and intensive, in part due to the construction of new roads that gave access to many hitherto secluded rural areas, but trade between tribes remained very limited and most interactions were with the invading colonial powers and their trading companies. The majority of the African people therefore retained their tribal allegiance under colonial rule and later also in the independent states. The "divide-and-rule" tactics of the colonial administration, however, instigated rivalry between tribes and generated frequent and bloody disputes. The unity within the tribe was therefore the main protection of its individual members.

Many African leaders sought to bring progress to their countries by integrating them with the world economy and society and abandoning tribal heritage. For Kenyan president Daniel arap Moi the tribal system was the cancer of African society. In contrast, for Africa's "golden leaders," the first generation of the leaders of the independent states, from Kwame N'Krumah, Ghana's first president, and Patrice Emery Lumumba, the first elected prime minister of Congo, to Jomo Kenyatta, the first president of Kenya, the search for their common roots and their unifying socioethnic identity motivated them to strengthen their tribal heritage. These leaders were great supporters of pan-Africanism, and in their view the tribal social system gives Africa its historical identity and gives the African people their allegiance to Africa. They fully recognized that the African nation-states cannot be defined by colonial borders, and these borders dividing tribes between different states cannot create national solidarity.

From the tribal society to the state

As colonial rule came to an end and the African countries became independent, the vast majority of the population still lived in rural areas and maintained their organization and social structure as tribes, according to their traditions, social rules and norms, and under the authority of the tribe's elders. These rules were no longer suitable, however, for the much more complex structure of the state, for the many and much more complex interactions between peoples and communities from different tribes that became citizens of the same state, and for the relations between the tribe and the central authority of the state. The transition from the tribal to the state system of governance was therefore abrupt and traumatic.

Under the tribal system, individual tribes carefully and devotedly protected their territories, their living space for generations, and all households in each of these territories were of the same tribe. The colonial borders had paid no attention to the territorial integrity of individual tribes; consequently, these borders often cut their lands and divided their communities between different states. During colonial times, the borders did not have any significant political role and served primarily to mark the division of the continent's natural resources between colonial powers. When the African states became independent, these borders became the political borders that marked the territories of the new states and thus determined the boundaries of their sovereignty and control. Each leader was therefore keen to preserve the territory of his state and protect its borders, even though this territory was an arbitrary agglomeration of slices of territories of different tribes and therefore ruined the territorial integrity of most tribes. As a result, the population of most states consisted of fractions of many different tribes for which the new state became a macabre concentration of people from different tribes with different languages, cultures, heritage, and social structure.

The chaotic fragmentation of tribal territories that forced splinters of different tribes to live together in the same state only increased their alienation to the state and reduced their motivation to establish any collaboration or form any unity with members of other tribes who became their fellow citizens, but with whom they had no shared history or a unifying governing authority. Even the struggle for independence against the colonial power was conducted primarily by the larger tribe, while the smaller tribes were excluded both from the fighting forces that led the struggle and from the governing authority of the state that was formed when they became independent. As a result, frequent land disputes and civil conflicts have erupted and enmity between tribes was exacerbated.

The African autocratic leaders inherited the all-powerful and authoritarian system of governance from the African chiefs. There were, however, key differences between the two systems: The chief was the supreme leader of loosely integrated territories that unified many smaller tribes but preserved their territorial integrity and respected their leadership and social rules; the chief was widely recognized and obeyed by the tribes, and all their members who lived in the territory under his authority. The authoritarian leader of the newly independent states was, in contrast, the leader of fragments of many different tribes or ethnic groups that occupied territories that were different from the territories of their tribe. There were therefore many territorial disputes between the individual members and the communities of different tribes, but there were no rules and no unifying authority that could settle these disputes. To enforce his authority, preserve the territorial integrity of the state, and protect the state's border, the new leader used brute force. To settle land disputes between fragments of different tribes, the leader sided with the larger tribe, which in most cases was his own tribe, at the expense of the smaller tribes. The leader used military force to evacuate people from their homes and expel them from their territory in order to resettle people from his own tribe, thus creating deep enmities and sowing the seeds of many land disputes and conflicts in later years.

In comparison, the evolution of the feudalistic system in Europe during the Middle Ages was much more gradual and on the scale of equality between people, or Elster's *coefficient of cohesion* of the members of the community, Europe was at that time at a much lower level. Traditionally, feudalism was thought to be composed of reciprocal obligations in which the lord provided land to his vassals in exchange for military service; for Karl Marx this system manifested the power of the ruling class on account of their control of arable land that enabled them to exploit the peasants who farmed their lands (typically as serfs), and in his view this was therefore the embryo of industrial capitalism. There is still a debate among historians what exactly was the social and economic structure of the feudal system; there is no disagreement that in this system the vast majority of people were essentially slaves. It took Europe several more centuries to gradually liberate the serfs and many more years to gradually improve the living conditions of the peasants, but only with the onset of the Industrial Revolution could also the people in rural areas improve their own standards of living and gain their freedom.

In Africa, neither the formation of the independent states nor the establishment of central governments evolved gradually. All these developments were practically imposed upon the African people when the main colonial powers left the continent in the aftermath of World War II. and with the establishment of the independent African states under the pressure of African liberation movements. For most African people these developments were very dramatic, since the newly independent states effectively ruined territorial cohesion, separated them from their family members and forced many to move to new lands that were not theirs and live with people that were their rivals. The establishment of the African independent states in territories that were not integral parts of the territories of their citizens—behind borders arbitrarily carved out, and thus forcing millions of them to flee from their ancestral lands and, thereby, entirely transforming their entire way of life—was a shattering experience from the majority. As members of different tribes became citizens of the same newly independent states and subjects of the same central authorities because they happened to live in the same territory, according to the arbitrary borders determined by the colonial powers, these people clearly lost their homes. At the same time, the borders left little option to the leaders of independence movements but to divide the territory of many tribes among different countries and thus separate many of them from their communities.

In his classical book, *Freedom versus Organization* (1962), Bertrand Russell wrote: "Nations like people have a right to be free.... To force people to live under a government not that of their own nation was felt like forcing a woman to marry a man whom she hates. Love of home and love of family both have an instinctive basis, and together they form the foundation of love of country." The African tribes had this foundation and this love of their home that was built up over centuries. The new African states did not have this foundation, and most of their people were forced, often by evicting them from their homes, to live under an autocratic regime that was foreign and hostile to them.

To emphasize that a nation has a definition that is not merely economic, but is first and foremost a community of people who live in the geographical area that is and has been their forefathers' land and have strong sentiments of solidarity, Russell quoted the Italian philosopher Giuseppe Mazzini who wrote: "A nation is not a mere aggregate of individuals, but a mystic entity with a soul of its own. God divided humanity into distinct groups or nuclei upon the face of the earth, thus creating the germ of Nationalities. Evil governments have disfigured the divine sign. Nevertheless you may still trace it, distinctly marked out by the course of great rivers, by the direction of the high mountains, and by other geographical conditions" (p. 352). The African tribes clearly had this soul, but most of them were too small to create the germ of a nation; the divine signs that marked their territories were disfigured by colonial boundaries and became the borders of the African states, and these states did not have the soul that could bring their people together and establish a bond between them.

The principles of the nation-state recognize that a group of people who live in an integrated geographical area over which they have a legitimate claim as an integral part of their history and their common identity and who wish to form a government that will represent their identity and help them in building their homeland, has the right to be an independent state. In practice there are limitations to this principle, the main one being conflicting claims over this land, the size of that area, and the size of its population, which determine, in turn, their capacity to protect themselves and defend their homeland. A small group of people cannot form an independent state even if they meet all other criteria since it cannot protect its people. Most tribes could not therefore form independent states when they were opened to the outside world and no longer could be secluded and protected by their natural borders. With the construction of new roads, the development of advanced means of transportation, and the use of more destructive weapons, many small tribes had to, willingly or unwillingly, become part of the larger and more powerful tribe, while many others were expelled from their lands and enslaved or killed by their neighbors or by foreign powers that penetrated into their territories.

To build a nation that can protect itself but has high cohesion, the first generation of leaders of the African independent states made great efforts to establish national unity. Quite a few were captivated by socialist ideals and tried to establish the Communist economic system, which was entirely foreign and even threatening to the tribal system. Nevertheless, their charismatic personalities and the people's exhilaration when they became independent were strong unifying forces. In Zambia, for example, the first president, Kenneth Kaunda, made a point of implementing policies and using the tools of the state to promote national unity; with the motto "One-Zambia, One Nation" he took measures to forge the new nation by carefully maintaining an ethnic balance in his appointments to the cabinet and other key government positions.

For better or worse, tribalism remains, however, the fabric of African society and people's socioethnic identity is much stronger than their identity as citizens of the states. The tribal identity plays a key role in political conflicts and has been a crucial source of both solidarity and great enmity. This is the reason why voting in Africa and in many other parts of the world is so strongly along tribal or sectarian lines, and why people from the tribe of the ruling chief are loyal to him without any criticism (even in the extreme case of Robert Mugabe in Zimbabwe) and would not accept the transfer of power to the rival party that represents another tribe and thereby surrender their power to their adversaries. Even today a Kikuyu is more a Kikuyu than a Kenyan, a Zulu is more of a Zulu than a South African, a Sudanese has a fundamentally different allegiance depending upon whether he is a black African Sudanese from the south or an Arab Muslim Sudanese from the north, and even in Zambia, despite all the efforts of the legendary Kenneth Kaunda and the liberal governments that followed, a Shona is more Shona than a Zambian.

Tribalism is by no means unique to Africa. This is the power that dismembered Yugoslavia into several states, continues the radical nationalism of the remaining members of the separatist ETA group in the Basque country in Spain, maintains the near division of Belgium between the country's Walloon and Flemish that may well break up the country, and continued for many years the long and bloody war in Northern Ireland. It took Germany the traumatic experience of World War I to form "Ein Reich." The unique characteristic of the tribal division in Africa is the extremely large number of tribes that, until the last century, were separated from each other, but maintained their strong territorial integrity, their own language, their own culture, and their own heritage that formed their "mystic entity with a soul of its own." The large number of tribes and their small size made it necessary for them to collaborate with other tribes to protect themselves, but exposed many more to the brute force of external enemies, African and others, that showed no mercy in expelling them from their lands and killing many.

The challenge for African societies was, and still is, to change the colonial borders of their states in ways that can reduce rivalry between tribes and sectarian groups, increase the allegiance of their citizens to their state, and restore as much as possible the territorial integrity of the tribes. Sudan has been negotiating, since 2005, an agreement that will divide the country between the North and the South, but even that separation is by no means certain. The discovery of rich oil resource in the territory of South-Sudan further complicates this process.

In very few other African states is a significant change in the borders possible, however. The discovery of many new natural resources will certainly complicate this process; the massive migration from rural areas to urban centers create megacities in which people from different tribes are mixed together in ways that make it practically impossible to divide them between different states, even though tribal rivalries are still strong. The main reason is the small likelihood of reaching any agreement between the autocratic leaders on a significant exchange of territories and, even in countries that have made more substantive transition to democracy, it is bound to be very complex to reach an agreement on new borders that may force some people to move to another state after six decades during which they built homes and cultivated their lands.

Africa's greatest curse: its autocratic leaders

In the early days of the newly independent states, the cult of personality of the "golden leaders" was an effort to bring their peoples together. These leaders were more than political leaders and were very different from the leaders who came after them, both in their personal integrity and in their convictions and commitments. Since their struggle for independence against colonial rule, their main mission was to build the new African nation and new African identity. They did not see much difference between the different nations as determined by colonial borders but rather a pan-African identity: those who live in the entire African sub-continent. This group of leaders who fought together and became the leaders of the newly independent African states in the 1950s had a lot in common, both in their commitment to building the new African nation, and in their social beliefs regarding the relations between the nation and its people. In practice, their struggle for independence was for the people with whom they shared the same place of birth, the same tribal affiliation and territory they called home, but in theory or in their dreams they were fighting for all African people and for the entire territory they called "Black Africa." That was their real home, and they all shared the same dreams and the same home.

They were all in agreement that colonial borders and the countries that they define have no legitimacy. While they all fought with their tribe in the territory where their tribe lived, they did see their country as the territory the colonial power determined by their borders. In his book, *The Fate of Africa*, Martin Meredith quoted the British prime minister at the end of the nineteenth century, Lord Salisbury, who remarked, "We have been giving away mountains and rivers and lakes to each other, only hindered by the small impediment that we never knew exactly where they were."[1] The first decree issued by the first leader of independent Ghana, Kwame Nkrumah, was to replace the British name of his country, Gold Coast, by its ancestral name.

When the founding fathers, idealists and ideologues like Nkrumah or Kenneth Kaunda were replaced, many of them in military coups, by a new generation of leaders like Idi Amin of Uganda, or Jean-Bedel Bokassa of the Central African Republic, whom Meredith describes as "flamboyant, autocratic figure[s], accustomed to living in style, demanding total obedience." They had none of their predecessors' commitments and convictions and did not make any effort to promote national unity or build the pillars and establish the institutions of a state. In fact, for them national gain was a castle that had to be conquered since it contains many elements that are the enemy of the state. These are the minority tribes that from the start were antagonistic to the state since it had broken their territorial integrity. The legitimacy of their regimes or the support of their peoples did not concern them, both because they had the support of their tribe, and because they had the power of their army. Indeed, even those leaders who held national elections made sure that they would never be voted out of office.

The conflicts embedded in the boundaries of the African states and the distribution of the population in their territories were, from the outset, major impediments to their development, not only due to the arbitrary division of tribes among different states but more often due to the leaders who came to power by the support of the dominant tribe and controlled these states. These leaders, and those who came after them, enforced their own laws by brute force to strengthen their control, often using their own version of "divide-and-rule" to weaken opposition to their leadership. Instead of trying to find fair and acceptable settlement to the many land disputes between tribes, or form an arbitration process to settle these disputes, they frequently used these disputes to empower and give preferential treatment to their supporters and weaken the opposition to their regime.

The refusal of these leaders to make any territorial compromise or find any settlement to border disputes caused great damage to most African countries by triggering many confrontations and, sometimes, also wars. The resentment of members of the tribes that were discriminated against by these leaders made it impossible to build up and nurture their allegiance to their state. Their forceful intervention to impose settlements that favored their supporters, instead of building institutions and legal arrangements to settle disputes, increased the grievances of the minority groups and their opposition to the regime. Even the border dispute between Nigeria and Cameroon over control of the Bakassi Peninsula had to be settled by the World Court in 2002 because the two states and the AU were not able to settle it by themselves.

These leaders functioned also as the supreme legislative authority and determined the rules of the state, either to serve their own interests or to advance the interest of their supporters, mainly the members of their own tribe. These rules openly discriminated against the minority tribes and were imposed on them even when they were in contradiction to these tribes' own social customs and traditions, thus exacerbating their sense of discrimination, increasing their resistance to the authority of the state, and aggravating the rivalries between tribes.

Nearly all these autocratic leaders came to power in military coups, and during the first four decades after they became independent, the African countries saw more than a hundred military coups attempts, and more than half were successful. Patrick McGowan calculated the frequency distribution of the African military coups d'état from 1956 to 2001 and ranked the countries from the worst (Sudan) to the best (Botswana).[2] In each of the countries: Sudan, Ghana, Uganda, Burundi, Sierra-Leone, Benin ,and Nigeria there were more than 40 plots for military coups d'état from 1956 through 2001.[3] The struggle to hang on to power was thus an integral part of the regime in the African states that shed the blood of millions of people and wasted a huge part of their resources and turned nearly half the African countries into failed states. These leaders used their power to enrich themselves by looting their country's resources and their state's coffer. The blatant favoritism that they used to increase the support in their regime and weaken their opponents led to incessant civil conflicts and bloody and costly wars that took an extremely high toll in human lives and wasted their resources. These wars and civil conflicts, combined with profligate public policies, were the main reasons for economic stagnation and high and rising levels of poverty in the African countries.

These leaders did not initiate any economic reforms, did not make any investments to improve the rural infrastructure or provide social safety nets to the poor and malnourished people in their countries, and did not use their resources to support economic reforms that were initiated by the international development organizations and donor countries. Even when they accepted the conditions of the World Bank and the IMF in order to receive their aid when their countries were plagued with heavy debts, their administrations were not helpful in implementing these conditions, and most of the aid money was siphoned off in the administrative channels.

The multitude of conflicts and wars within and between countries that led to the death of millions of people, mostly civilians, and to the expulsion of millions others from their homes, their lands, and ancestral territories, many of them to refugee camps, was primarily because these leaders refused to reach any compromise or make any concessions that would reduce their power or weaken their control. Many armed conflicts were instigated by these leaders in order to gain control over natural resources in their own, or neighboring, countries or to strengthen their control over their countries' resources against domestic warlords and gangs and against armies supported by other countries. The huge natural resources in the Democratic Republic of Congo attracted many warlords who embezzled these resources to finance their military expenses and enrich themselves.

During the past decade, the huge revenues the resource-rich countries accumulated from the record rise in the prices of oil and minerals, from the ample new resources discovered in the past two decades, and from the flow of foreign investments made in the search for more resources, did not benefit the majority of the population and did not reduce the number of poor. Only few African countries took measures to protect their poor and secure their food supply during the food crisis, often under the pressure of violent demonstrations. Among the many countries that remained failed or fragile states, nearly half are resource-rich countries, including quite a few oil exporting countries, from Sudan and Chad to Equatorial Guinea. The continued civil conflicts in these countries swallowed a large portion of the revenues from their resources and did not allow them to establish law and order. Despite the spread of democracy, most elections were deeply flawed, and in the majority of the African countries the same autocratic leaders remained in power. As the first decade of the twenty-first century comes to an end it is hard to avoid the conclusion that for most African countries, and for the majority of the African people, this was another lost decade in which far greater opportunities than at any time in the past were wasted.

The main reason for this disappointing conclusion of the decade, after a very promising beginning and jubilant reports of the World Bank and the IMF, is the extreme inequality in the distribution of the wealth that was accumulated during the decade. The major share of that wealth was wasted on the continued civil conflicts and on the escalating crime in most urban areas; the other share was seized by the countries' leaders, their close circle of supporters, and by the political and economic elite. Only a very small share trickled down to the poor and to the rural producers, and only meager investments were made to improve the countries' infrastructure in urban and rural areas. According to World Bank estimates, more than 80 percent of the revenues of the oil exporting countries were amassed by the top 5 percent of their population. Even the estimates of these countries' income inequality are most likely highly slanted, because these estimates are based on the income and expenditures surveys and the countries' economic and political elite is either not included in these surveys or is not reporting their true income. The enormous wealth Nigeria's former president, Olusegun Obasanjọ, amassed in foreign banks in excess of more (most likely much more) than six billion dollars, is only part the country's oil revenues that found their way to foreign banks.

Ending the addiction to aid

Despite the commitment African leaders made at a meeting in Accra, Ghana, in September 2008 to "take action to accelerate progress," when the full effects of the food crisis became evident, it has also become clear that most resource-rich countries did not take any action or assumed any responsibility to care for their poor, despite the wealth they have accumulated. As a result, most countries remained dependent on aid to provide food to their impoverished and malnourished populations.

The African leaders made even more specific pledges at that meeting: "We will need to address three major challenges to accelerate progress on aid effectiveness:

- Country's ownership is key.
- Building more effective and inclusive partnerships.
- Achieving development results—and openly accounting for them—must be at the heart of all we do."

In fact, the leaders of the aid recipient countries had already made similar commitments at the Monterrey Conference in March 2002 and at the Paris Conference in March 2005, in which these pledges were formalized in three action principles—*ownership, alignment, harmonization*—but in all too many countries, including the oil exporting countries, these principles were not accompanied by action and their poor continued to depend on aid.

The possibility that much will change in the next food crisis are very slim. Most of the aid money given to the government in these countries is siphoned off in the administration maze, and only a small portion does indeed reach the target population. Aid donors have realized this misuse and are giving more of their aid directly to the target population. They may also try to channel more aid through the tribes' leaders, but the countries' leaders are likely to object to arrangements that bypass the normal channels of government institutions and are likely to see these arrangements as an infringement of their sovereign rights and interference in their internal affairs. Given the rich countries' aid fatigue and their own huge needs due to the global economic crisis and their huge debts, the African countries themselves, perhaps through the institutions of the AU, must take responsibility for ensuring just distribution of the available aid money.

5.2
Can Democracy Help the African States to Cement Their Multiethnic Societies?

In his famous and award-winning book entitled *The Third wave: Democratization in the Late Twentieth Century* (1991), Samuel Huntington analyzed and evaluated the wave of democratization that took place between 1974 and 1990, which he saw as the most important global political development of the late twentieth century. Africa was the only continent that went against this wave. Nearly all the new countries that became independent between 1956 and 1970 became authoritarian shortly after independence, most after military coups. Botswana was the only African country that consistently maintained a democratic regime.

In Huntington's words, "The decolonization of Africa led to the largest multiplication of authoritarian governments in history" (21). In the third wave of democratization, approximately 30 countries in Europe, Asia, and Latin America replaced authoritarian regimes by democratic ones. The movement toward democracy that seemed to become an almost irresistible global force moving from one triumph to the next was not able to move the African continent. While democracy won in nearly half the world states, in Africa 33 newly independent countries moved toward an authoritarian regime.

New embryonic democracy started to emerge in Africa in the 1990s, and by mid-2000s more than 40 African countries instituted democratic elections and made a transition to democracy. The elections were deeply flawed, rigging was common, and freedom was strictly curtailed; many countries had one-party elections that elected the same leaders but now gave them the legitimacy tag of "democratically elected."

The rapid growth of most African countries in the past decade gave a boost to the forces in their society that demanded a transition to democracy but also the resistance of others afraid to lose their advantages and preferential treatment in the transition. The growing pressure of donor countries and multinational NGOs was the main driving force that gave incentives and put pressure on African leaders to hold democratic elections. Most leaders resisted that change, but acquiesced to international pressure although they conducted the elections in ways that made sure they were reelected. This, however, was only the first round in the transition to democracy, and the second and third rounds already held in many countries clearly show this is a slow process that is nonetheless moving forward and already has had an impact on quite a few countries that have reached a stage in which a reversal of the process is bound to be much harder than in the past.

Alternative scenarios of future political developments

The transition to democracy in Africa in the coming decade is likely to progress more rapidly in some countries but may come to a halt in many others, depending on several internal and external factors. Internally, that process depends on the pressure the social and political forces that call for this transition can exert relative to the resistance of the more adamant autocratic leaders and of other local interests. The pro-democratic forces are driven by the growing impact of the middle-class and by the influence of the minority tribal and sectarian groups that see that transition as essential to continue the country's economic development and to reduce discrimination. The anti-democratic forces are first and foremost the dominant tribal and sectarian groups that want to maintain their power, and the leading economic elite that see a democratic regime as a threat to their monopolistic control of the country's resources. They are likely to receive the support of the multinational corporations that are using, and gaining the most from, these countries' resources.

The main struggle between the pro- and anti-democratic forces will be conducted in the urban areas, not only as a result of the growing share of the urban population in the African countries' general populations but also because the urban populations will be the most powerful political force. In the urban areas, however, the support of democracy depends also on the extent to which the democratic regime will be able to maintain law and order. If the inevitable conflicts between opposing factions in a democracy will lead to an increase in crime and a deterioration of personal security than more people in the urban areas are likely to support a "strong leader" who will put an end to the chaos in the streets.

On the external front, the main support in the transition to democracy will come from the donor countries that are democratic themselves and support the pro-democracy movements world-wide. The international development organizations are also likely to support the democratic regime and may deny support to countries that are controlled by an extremely dictatorial regime as the one in North Korea. On the other hand, both donor countries and international organizations may continue to support countries that have an autocratic regime if that regime is more open, especially in the media, and is perceived to be the best guarantee to peace and stability in the country and in the region. Perhaps the most obvious example is the regime of Hosni Mubarak in Egypt.

Two other factors on the external front that will influence the transition to democracy are the emerging countries and the African Union:

- The emerging economies, primarily China and Russia, support many autocratic leaders on all continents, in part because these leaders give them access to their countries' natural resources, and in part because these leaders offer attractive economic deals in exchange for support of their regimes. Equally important is the fact that China itself is not democratic and it therefore either hesitates or openly refuses to implement sanctions against countries that have autocratic regimes, like the regime in Iran. Another emerging economy that will have an impact on that process is, obviously, South Africa, which has a direct effect on the other African economies, and its leaders are directly related to, familiar with, and affected by the political struggles in other African countries.
- Equally important is the position of the African Union. Although the AU as an institution made many pledges to support the process of democratization in Africa, the leaders who must make a unanimous decision whether or not to implement sanctions against leaders who are overtly anti-democratic and use force to suppress the pro-democratic movement in their countries, have refused to make that decision. Even in the extreme case of Robert Mugabe, who openly rigged the elections in Zimbabwe, the leaders of the AU countries refused to implement sanctions, in part because many of these leaders have autocratic regimes in their own countries and were against that precedence.

Several other factors are likely to make the transition to democracy in Africa haphazard and tenuous:

- On the economic front, the anticlimactic conclusion of the past decade, the threat of a deepening global recession, and the huge domestic debts of the rich countries that committed large financial resources to the IMF are likely to slow down the growth in the African countries and will certainly reduce the flow of aid from the donor countries. This may be less damaging to the resource-rich African countries, including the countries in which new resources have been discovered, but it is likely to be highly damaging to the resource-poor African countries and even more so to the poor populations in all African countries, primarily in the rural areas, who will suffer the most from the decline in aid. These trends are likely to weaken the pro-democratic forces that received their greatest boost from the resumption of growth in their countries during the past decade, since their struggle against the autocratic regimes in their countries is likely

to weaken when their economies are in decline and growth is highly unstable due to the instability in commodity prices in world markets.
- The demographic and social changes marked by the rapid increase in the urban population will increase the power and influence of the urban populations, but it may not increase by much the share and the influence of the middle class. The reason is the slow growth and even stagnation in most economic sectors other than those related to their countries' primary resources. In particular the industrial sector will remain undeveloped and unable to become more competitive in the world markets despite the rise in wages and other costs in China. The main reason is the small investments even in labor-intensive industries in most African countries, in part as an effect of their decaying infrastructure and in part as an effect of the rising transport costs that will send more industries to the Eastern European countries. Although the improvements in education in many African countries, particularly in the urban areas, are a strong incentive for local industries, the gap in the standards of education between Asian countries, including China and India, and the African countries will continue to grow. Moreover, many of the better-educated youngsters in Africa are likely to increase their efforts to migrate to other countries in other continents due to the dismal opportunities in their own countries. The more educated are usually also the greatest supporters of democracy, but as they leave their countries the pro-democratic movement is likely to weaken.
- In the urban centers the waves of migrants from rural areas are turning more cities into a megalopolis in which the country's security forces have no control and violent gangs establish their own law and disorder. The tribal divides between people in cities who share the same neighborhoods in the same slums are gradually declining, even though such divides surfaced in the 2007 elections in Kenya. They remained dominant also in the elections in most countries, primarily because the majority of the population still lives in the rural areas and their voting is persistently along tribal lines. As the tribal divide in the cities is gradually declining, however, the income divide between rich and poor is sharply rising, while the middle class remains scanty. The antagonism of the poor to the government and the economic elite has become explosive in several countries during the past decade, due to highly corrupt control by the rich over the distribution of the country's revenues from the export of its resources and the huge wealth the economic elite amassed during the commodity boom.

The anger of the poor has become more threatening to the central regime with rises in food prices during the food crisis; violent protests have forced the leaders in several countries to resign, and have led to military coups in several others. Although most people in the urban centers have little hope to find adequate work that will enable them to improve their living conditions, and they are not willing to accept the extreme income and wealth inequalities or passively accede to the rampant corruption that is nothing but blatant robbery of their country's resources by the small elite and the country's leaders, they have not managed to join forces and build the necessary power to force a change in regime. Instead, they have been divided into small armed gangs or even joined the small armies of local warlords in order to rob the rich or gain control over the natural resources of their own country or neighboring countries. Their violent protests, armed gangs, pirates, and warlords can only deter foreign investors and may make more African countries failed states that cannot establish law and order.

Only a few African countries can therefore expect any authentic change in the political regime, a transition to a functioning democracy, and free and fair elections that will come together with improvement in the economic conditions and a decline in poverty. While more minority groups in a growing number of countries would no longer be willing to accept their deprivation and discrimination, only few would be able to form an alliance with other minority groups in order to increase their impact on the regime.

- Migration from rural areas—where food security is deteriorating due to worsening climatic conditions—either to the urban centers or to neighboring countries, is also likely to grow in the coming decade. That migration may also increase instability in the rural migrants' home country and may lead to civil conflicts and confrontations in the neighboring and better-off countries where the new migrants may threaten the jobs of the local urban population and the agricultural resources of the local rural population. Migrants from other countries are almost always treated as second-class citizens; some countries also impose fees for residency permits that must be renewed annually. Employers who want to employ foreign workers for posts in certain professions, particularly skilled workers, must give priority to local workers; otherwise they have to provide acceptable reasons for employing foreign workers. Migrants to rural areas are not allowed to acquire land, and they must therefore cultivate marginal lands. The fight for the right to use the increasingly limited agricultural resources is likely to intensify as these resources become scarcer. The problems faced by migrants are also due to lurking fears about security. In some countries locals may spread rumors about an Islamic plot (as they did in Côte d'Ivoire) or instigate xenophobic attacks against foreign corporations that exploit their country's resources.
- In countries where the division between population groups is quite clearly along racial or sectarian lines, an agreement like the one in Sudan to divide the country between Arab Muslims and mostly Christian black Africans is likely to be of great concern to the authorities in several neighboring countries. The agreement in Sudan is an unprecedented break of

the territorial boundaries set by the colonial powers, and in several other countries where the population is also divided along tribal, sectarian, or racial lines (including Niger, Mauritania, Nigeria, and Côte d'Ivoire), the group (or groups) that currently feel exploited and excluded may raise a similar demand. The demand for a "two states solution" may further intensify their fighting in order to reach a similar agreement and destabilize the country.

The shape of the democratic reforms in Africa

The transition to democracy in the African countries were preceded by developments very similar to those in many other developing countries that went through a similar process. The East Asian countries, for example, became highly authoritarian in the 1960s and 1970s, some of them after a brief experience with democracy. Over time they moved from autocracy to a semi-democratic government but maintained the one-party system. Some moved to multiparty elections, but only in the 1990s; few others still maintain the one-party system but have given more civil rights to their citizens and greater freedom of speech and freedom of the press; and several others, most notably North Korea, remained strictly autocratic. The democratic reforms in the countries of the first group were in line, however, with their citizens' demands for civil, religious, and (gradually) more political rights. Most Latin American countries made frequent transitions from authoritarianism to relative democracy, mostly as an effect of their volatile economic conditions, but over time even most of their autocratic leaders came to accept that their citizens have certain basic, inalienable rights that no regime can deny. In quite a few other countries, including Singapore, Cuba, Russia, China, and Vietnam the government concentrated its efforts and resources on promoting economic growth, while still limiting the political liberties of their citizens, since they consider these restrictions a legitimate, and to some extent necessary, price for giving their citizens economic security.

The democracy African countries established was very different from a European-style democracy, even though the latter was the model donor countries promoted and demanded. In most African countries the elections turned into a struggle for power and for the amenities public office provides. In fact these countries had a similar struggle under the autocratic regime, but then it was usually settled in a military coup rather than in elections. For the politicians, this was a struggle over the access to the resources controlled by the state, and they resorted to a wide variety of means to attain public office. Most elections were flawed: rigging, favoritism, vote buying, and electoral violence are still common, and in quite a few countries elections are for a single party. Only in less than a handful of countries was there a peaceful transfer of power to the leader of the opposition.

It would be, however, a mistake to dismiss the importance of this transition of African countries to democracy and the changes it has already brought and can still bring. After all, also in Europe that transition was not smooth and flawless. In France the voting system was based on property qualification for half a century until the "universal" right to vote for *men* was introduced in 1848; until the end of the nineteenth century, electoral mobilizations were largely based on tangible benefits, favors, and primary loyalties. In the African countries the democratic regime is too young to make any judgment about developments in the future; people do not yet have enough experience with the new system, are still too suspicious about the regime, and have little trust in election results. The longer-term impact of democracy cannot therefore be judged on the basis of the flaws in the early rounds. Donor countries and scholars who want to see tangible results fast, and statistically significant proofs that progress has already been made, must acknowledge that democracy is a slow "learning" process of both the governor and the governed.

In most African countries democratic elections did not secure the stability and sustainability of the regime—as they do in countries that have longer experience with democracy. In the latter, democracy increases the stability of the regime by conferring legitimacy to the government and thus ensuring voters' support. The "democratic" elections in Kenya, Nigeria, and Zimbabwe did not bring more stability or more effective governance, but an increase in the awareness of the elected leaders of the will of the people. In these elections the autocratic leaders or ruling powers remained in power (albeit after major rigging and gross violations of election rules), but in Kenya and Zimbabwe mass protests forced the ruling leaders to form a coalition government with the leaders of the opposition, and in Nigeria the newly elected leader took active measures to combat corruption.

In the African countries the first impacts of the democratic elections were greater freedom of the press, greater involvement of the population in the political process, more active participation in voting, and often also open protests against flawed elections. These developments may actually *destabilize* the autocratic regime and its sustainability by shattering its legitimacy. Although public protests and critical press reports have limited power at the early stages of the transition to democracy, they do have an impact on the political process: There is no doubt that without their influence, Robert Mugabe would not have agreed to a shared government with opposition leader Morgan Tsvangirai in Zimbabwe, and President Mwai Kibaki of Kenya would not have agreed to a shared government with opposition leader Raila Odinga.

In rural areas the impact of the democratization process is much smaller. In the past two decades and, even more so in the next decade, more young people are migrating to the urban centers, the population that remains in rural communities is aging, their food security is declining, and their poverty is increasing. They barely have access to the press or to the other media, and they are therefore much less and much later informed. Their hard work, their struggle with shrinking resources, and their isolation reduce their interest in the political process. At the same time, though, the growing competition over agricultural resources involves them in more intense competition and conflicts with neighboring tribes over the shrinking land and water resources and, in extreme cases, forces them to migrate to other regions. This is a highly damaging process, not only to their livelihoods, but also to their perception of discrimination and isolation. Their allegiance to their tribe remains strong, but their tribe may have been divided in the past by the colonial border between different countries and is therefore much weaker.

The leader's favoritism to the dominating tribe in the allocation of water or arable land may become much more important due to the dwindling agricultural resources, and confrontations between tribes may become more frequent and violent. These confrontations will further impoverish the rural populations and are likely to spill over, not only to neighboring countries, but also to the urban centers where allegiance to the tribe remains strong and agriculture serves as a household level buffer by providing inexpensive shelter, food, and employment for unemployed laborers from urban areas in times of crisis, thus acting as their safety net.

The dubious significance of democratic elections

In his book on democratization in the late twentieth century (1991), Samuel Huntington maintained that "open, free and loyal elections constitute the essence of democracy and are a *sine qua non*." In the Western liberal democracies the virtues of the election process (namely the extent to which they are open, free and loyal), not only determine the legitimacy of the elected government, but also guarantee this government will operate and fulfill its duties according to liberal principles and maintain the rule of law, the separation of power, and the protection of the basic liberties of its citizens. Huntington is using a more formal definition of the term "democratically elected government" and maintains that:

> Governments produced by elections may be ineffectual, corrupt, shortsighted, irresponsible, dominated by special interests, and incapable of adopting policies demanded by the public good. These qualities make such governments undesirable, but they do not make them undemocratic.

This raises, however, questions and even doubts about the desirability of democracy and the gains to society from a democratically elected government that is ineffectual and corrupt. Can a government that has been democratically elected but is ineffectual, corrupt, shortsighted, and thus undesirable still claim to have legitimacy because it has been democratically elected? For the voters themselves, the act of voting is to some degree a gamble and a hope that the government they elect will *not* be ineffectual, corrupt, shortsighted, and thus undesirable. If their gamble proves correct they will remain loyal to the government, continue to support it, and the government will remain their legitimate representative. If their gamble proves incorrect they no longer may continue to support that government since it will no longer be their legitimate representative.

Is this government still democratic even though it is no longer the voters' legitimate representative? Formally it is. Since elections are not, and cannot, be held daily but only once every four or five years, that government remains "democratically elected" throughout its term in office, even though shortly after the elections it proved to be undesirable. Moreover, constitutional democracy puts restrictions on the power of the government to implement policies that are undesirable to its citizens, ineffectual, and corrupt.

In parliamentary elections in which the voters do not elect the government directly, the government that turns out to be undesirable may lose its majority in the parliament in a no-confidence motion, and may be forced to resign. In the British system, Parliament is then dissolved, new elections held, and voters have an opportunity to elect another government (through the Parliament) they will have greater confidence in to be their legitimate representative and conduct desirable policies.[4] In fact the constitutional rule that introduces the "vote of no confidence" reflects the recognition that voters may have erred in their gamble in the elections, and gives them the opportunity to correct their error. The "undesirable" government may then lose its legitimacy with the vote of no-confidence and thus also lose its claim to be a democratic representative of the people. This rule, and the threat of a vote of no-confidence, prevent the government from conducting undesirable policies and thus forces the democratically elected government to be liberal and implement desirable and uncorrupt policies during its term in office. In this system "Liberalism and Democracy Can't Have One Without the Other" (Marc Plattner, *Foreign Affairs,* March/April 1998).

The formal interpretation of the term "democratically elected," according to Huntington is thus devoid of any ethical content, and the constitutional motion of a vote of no-confidence reaffirms the demand that the government must be, and must remain, an authentic representative of the will of the people and have their support not only on the day of the elections but during its entire administration. This supervision of the parliament over the government guarantees that in Western societies the terms "liberal democracy" cannot be separated and the essence of democracy is not only the administration of "open, free, and loyal elections" but also a "government that maintains the rule of law, the separation of powers, and the protection of basic liberties of its citizens."

In other societies, however, this definition may no longer hold either because they are not democratic or because they are not liberal. In countries that have elections for a single party, the government will always receive the majority of the votes and a parliamentary no-confidence motion is not even possible. These countries cannot be considered democratic, however, regardless of their policies. Several African countries held single-party elections, and President Museveni of Uganda even argued that multiparty elections are not suitable for Africa (although in Uganda the president is elected in a popular vote among several candidates). Several countries nominally have several candidates but only one candidate receives the vast majority of the votes: In Egypt, the constitution was changed in 2005 so that they have direct elections of the president in a multicandidate popular vote, and Hosni Mubarak was reelected as president by 89 percent of the vote. In Angola, the first democratic elections in 16 years were held in 2008 and regarded by international observers as reasonably fair; the ruling party, the MPLA won more than 80 percent of the vote, but after the elections civil and political liberties were limited. Can the MPLA still be regarded as a legitimate representative of the people? The question in a country like Angola is how to keep open an effective vote of no-confidence that will prevent the government from limiting civil liberties. In a one-party system, this of course is impossible; in a country where the government wins 80 percent of the vote this is equally impossible.

In a country where the voting is along ethnic lines, the leader or party that represents the larger ethnic group always has the majority of the votes. In this country, the government always has a majority of the votes, both in the parliament and among the voters. This government can conduct corrupt, shortsighted, and irresponsible policies, be dominated by special interests, and/or violate human rights (primarily of the members of the minority groups), and is still assured of receiving the support of the majority of the votes—from the members of the larger ethnic group—not only in the elections but also at any time after the elections. This government is essentially the government of, by, and for the larger ethnic group. According to Huntington's definition, it is still democratic but in most cases it is not liberal. In this country there is therefore an inherent contradiction between these two terms. More diverse societies are less likely to have this contradiction, the threat of a vote of no-confidence is effective, and the government is obliged to be liberal throughout its term in office. More monolithic societies are likely to lose the power of this threat and therefore change the character of their regime.

In many African countries, particularly in the fragile states, great efforts have been made by the donor countries to secure elections that are open and free by bringing in teams of international observers to supervise the elections and monitor the counting of the votes. Since the elections were adamantly and consistently along tribal or sectarian lines, the same autocratic leaders were usually elected and their policies remained ineffectual, corrupt, dominated by special interests, and therefore illiberal, even though they had at all times the support of the majority of the voters. The same has happened in several Middle Eastern countries, and however ineffectual the policies of the government of Iran can be, it must also be recognized that this government was democratically elected. The same has also happened in voting for parliament in Palestine, where Hamas received the majority of the votes, but for various technical reasons has not been recognized as the government of the people.

Obviously, neither in Africa nor in the Middle East was this the intention of the donor countries when they demanded democratic elections but, since the larger ethnic or sectarian group of voters remained loyal to their leader, he was democratically elected. The members of the tribe of Robert Mugabe continued to vote for him even though they were fully aware of the great damage his onerous policies cause Zimbabwe and formally he can therefore claim he was democratically elected. In voting along tribal lines voters express not only their support for their leader but also their fear that if the leader of the other tribe is elected he would be even more harmful to them.

Loyal voting along tribal lines is the main obstacle to change a corrupt and clearly "undesirable" regime in many African countries and to assure this government will remain liberal. In the Muslim countries in Africa, the Middle East, and Asia democracy faces similar problems when voting is between representatives of the Shiite and the Sunni sects. Sunni voters will elect Sunni representatives who will in turn elect a corrupt and ineffectual government (or worse), because they would not vote for the Shiite party that they perceive as more damaging to their interests. In most African countries deep animosity between tribes frustrates efforts to engage them in a productive dialogue, form collaboration between them, and strengthen their common interests, since collaboration would require them to reach a compromise with the other tribe(s) that their leader is likely to reject.

Can African democracy be "illiberal"?

In his article on "illiberal democracies" Fareed Zakaria (1997) argues that "a political system (is) marked not only by free and fair elections but also by the rule of law, a separation of powers, and the protection of basic liberties, religion and property." In practice, however:

> Democratically elected regimes, often ones that have been reaffirmed through referenda, are routinely ignoring constitutional limits on their power and depriving their citizens of basic rights and freedoms. From Peru to the Palestinian Authority, from Sierra Leone[5] to Slovakia, from Pakistan to the Philippines, we see the rise of a disturbing phenomenon in international relations—illiberal democracy[;] for almost a century in

the West, democracy has meant *liberal* democracy—a political system marked not only by free and fair elections, but also by the rule of law, a separation of power, and the protection of basic liberties of speech, assembly, religion and property." (Zakaria, 22).

The concept of illiberal democracy combines several ethical criteria in the evaluation of a democratically elected government along the lines of the Western democracies where, as quoted earlier: liberalism and democracy cannot have one without the other; the two are essentially synonyms. In the African countries (and in some, but not all the countries mentioned by Zakaria) where the government is democratically elected by the voters of the larger ethnic group, it will continue to win the majority of the votes even if it ignores the constitutional limits on its power and deprives some of its citizens of their basic rights and freedoms. Hence, the rise of illiberal democracy is *not* "a disturbing phenomenon in international relations," but an *inevitable* outcome of the spread of democracy to countries in which the government will be democratically elected and gain a vote of confidence at all times. In these countries the main criterion of voters is not whether their candidate maintains the rule of law, the separation of powers, and the protection of basic liberties, religion, and property, but whether the candidate represents their ethnic or sectarian group and, therefore, their specific interests. The other criterion is whether a government of the *other* party will better serve their interests or will things be worse for them.

This raises questions of whether the insistence of the donor countries on holding elections in countries that have one-party elections or in countries that have a dominant ethnic or sectarian group—and in which the majority of the voters will therefore continue to vote for the leader of their ethnic or sectarian group irrespective of its policies—does indeed serve the best interests of the country, and whether under these conditions elections are at all desirable even when they are free and fair. The instinctive answer is, no. But then how else should the leader of that country be elected? Who else can determine for these voters how to elect a leader who will maintain the rule of law or protect their basic liberties?

In fact, in these countries the elections in themselves and possibly even democracy in itself, may sometimes be *undesirable*—at least in the view of the donor countries—first, because a government that ignores its constitutional limits and deprives its citizens of their basic rights and freedoms is undesirable, and second because by holding the elections the government receives not only the legitimacy of its own voters but also the recognition of the international community of its legitimacy. That legitimacy will entitle the country to various benefits from donor countries and from international organizations, thus making it easier for that government to continue its practices of ignoring constitutional limits on its power and depriving its citizens of their basic rights and freedoms.

An ethnonationalist government that has been elected democratically in these countries is often dominated by powerful socioethnic groups that openly discriminate against minority groups, depriving them of basic rights and freedoms (favoring members of their own group by establishing theirs as the language of the state and their social rules for the relations among people, on the way people dress and the relations in the family as the rules of the state). Among minority groups, these measures are bound to increase the sense of discrimination and alienation from the state and may consequently destabilize the country.

The central tenet of socioethnic identity is that people who are members of one socioethnic group should be allowed to maintain their identity and should not be dominated by another socioethnic group. One, and sometimes the only, way to protect and secure their independence and to prevent the possibility they will be dominated is to separate them physically from the state in which they are dominated (because they are a minority) and to give them their own state. People who have the same socioethnic identity and the well established perception that they are discriminated against or dominated by the ruling socioethnic group *because* of their different identity, are likely also to demand their own territory as the home of their socioethnic group. This, they feel, is the only way to reduce the discrimination against them, allow them be free to keep their heritage, language, and sometimes also their religion.

This solution can have considerable limitations, however: This "ethnic federalism" may subject the entire territory to discrimination and thus make it even less beneficial. In Ethiopia, the Ethiopian Peoples' Revolutionary Democratic Front (EPRDF), led by its chairman and prime minister, Meles Zenawi, has radically reformed Ethiopia's political system. The regime transformed the hitherto centralized state into the Federal Democratic Republic and also redefined citizenship, politics, and identity along ethnic lines. Yet, there is growing discontent with the ethnically defined states, the rigid grip of the EPRDF on power and fears of continued interethnic conflicts that will effectively increase their discrimination. The transition to a federal state was led by the leading Tigray People's Liberation Front (TPLF) by creating nine ethnic-based regional states and two federally administered city-states that resulted in a highly asymmetrical and unequal federation that combines populous regional states in the central highlands with sparsely populated and underdeveloped ones.

The election of a government that is likely to be illiberal but can nonetheless be reelected even if it indeed proves to be illiberal is less common in countries with a multiethnic and multisectarian society where voting is *not* persistently along tribal, ethnic, racial, class, or religious lines. This, however, was the case in Yugoslavia when the country was ruled by an autocratic leader who essentially imposed his control over the different ethnic-sectarian groups, but when the autocratic regime collapsed, the country was fragmented into several different countries. In multiethnic countries democratic elections may also generate conflicts between members of different groups, either because the members of the minority group will always protest against the imminent election of the leader of the majority group who will always discriminate against them and exclude them from any position in the government, or because members of the two largest ethnic groups are likely to be in constant conflict with each other.

Donald Horowitz (1994) and Zakaria (who quoted him) even raise the obvious question: "What is the point of holding elections if all they do is to substitute a Bemba-dominated regime for a Nyanja regime in Zambia[,] neither incorporating the other half of the state" One answer can be that holding elections in Zambia is still better than making an arbitrary choice of the regime, provided the two groups are committed to respecting the outcome of the elections. Another answer can be that holding elections is, in fact, worse because neither group will accept a regime dominated by the other group.

One can also ask: What is the point of holding elections in Burundi if all they do is elect the same Hutu leader? It is still better, however, than holding elections in a country such as Rwanda in which the Hutu and the Tutsi live together, with growing ethnic tensions that caused ongoing hostilities for decades, culminating in the genocide of Tutsis and moderate Hutus. In Burundi, the first democratically elected Hutu president was assassinated in October 1993, also triggering widespread ethnic violence between Hutu and Tutsi. An internationally brokered power-sharing agreement in 2003 between the Tutsi-dominated government of Burundi and the Hutu rebels paved the way for a transition process that led to an integrated defense force, established a new constitution in 2005, and elected a majority Hutu government.

In most countries democracy will not necessarily increase the cooperation between groups and may even intensify the rivalry between them. Hence, Horowitz concluded, democracy "is simply not viable in an environment of intense ethnic preferences." According to this criterion, democracy is not viable in Africa, the Middle East (contrary to the Bush plan for Iraq), Central Asia, and quite a few countries in Latin America (and Belgium?). And yet, the elected parliament in many African countries is forcing the government to be more attentive to the demands of minority groups, since the potential of minority groups to form an alliance with other tribes (Nyanja and the Tonga in Zambia) that will give the alliance a majority in parliament has led to competition between tribes and their leaders who seek the support of minority tribes.[6]

While the experience in Rwanda and Burundi as well as in several other countries proves the transition to democracy is by no means a panacea, and despite the disappointing performance of one or two rounds of elections (and in some countries even three), held so far in the over 40 African countries that have made the transition to democracy, these are almost inevitable difficulties in the transition to democracy—difficulties most countries have experienced, but over time will for the most part be overcome. It would therefore be, in my view, a grave error to ignore or dismiss the potential advantages of democracy over the longer run. The possibility to form an alliance between different tribes in a "National Rainbow Coalition" was realized in Kenya only in the elections of 2002, but collapsed in the elections of 2007. Nevertheless, democracy has been advantageous to many countries by reducing the power of an autocratic leader. The greater freedom of the media in a democracy has made it both the unofficial auditor as well as the ombudsman of and for the people in curtailing the reckless or corrupt waste of government resources.

The political developments in Africa in combination with demographic and social changes marked by a growing urban population that is politically more active, more aggressive, and better informed, are the forces that may, over time, bring the advantages of democracy to the continent. The greater freedom of speech and of the media have given power to the people in many African countries, from Mauritania to Zimbabwe, to demand more democracy and less corruption. More open and fair elections and greater protection of human rights will also, over time, have the effect of reducing the hostility of the minority groups and their sense of marginalization and exclusion.

Democracy in all these countries is still at a very early stage and, in spite of everything, is therefore very fragile. Democratic elections are an obvious and necessary first step, but in themselves they may not sufficient. Both the donor countries and the African Union must play an active role to protect this process and ensure that the elected government will indeed preserve, maintain, and protect the basic rules of the constitution and the human rights and the liberty of its people.

Notes

1. Martin Meredith, *The Fate of Africa: From Hopes of Freedom to the Heart of Despair; A history of fifty years of independence,* 2006.
2. McGowan, P. J. "African military coups d'état, 1956–2001: frequency, trends and distribution," *Journal of Modern African Studies,* 41, 3 (2003), pp. 339–70.
3. On the other hand, in the past five years the presidents of three African countries, Togo, Guinea, and Gabon, died in office, after a cumulative 104 years in power; two of these leaders, Omar Bongo of Gabon (42 years) and Gnassingbé Eyadéma of Togo (38 years), were succeeded by their sons. Similar scenarios seem to unfold in several other countries where the presidents are grooming their sons.
4. In Germany and Spain a vote of no confidence requires the opposition, on the same ballot, to propose a candidate of their own, whom they want to be appointed as successor by the respective head of state, thus requiring the motion of no confidence to be at the same time a motion of confidence for a new candidate.

5. In Sierra Leone the president has been elected since 2007 by popular vote, and in the elections held that year President Koroma was elected in the second round by 55 percent of the votes while the leader of the opposition received 45 percent of the votes.
6. This criterion by itself suggests that this has the potential of establishing a more democratic government in Afghanistan than in Iraq.

References

African Development Report 2008/09. *Conflict Resolution, Peace and Reconstruction in Africa.* Addis Ababa, 2009.
Afrobarometer. "The Quality of Democracy and Governance in Africa: AFROBAROMETER Round 4," *Working Paper No. 108* (2008).
Anand, S., and A. Sen. "Human Development and Economic Sustainability," *World Development*, Vol. 28, pp. 2029–49 (2000).
Barro, R. "Democracy and Growth," *Journal of Economic Growth*, Vol. 1, No. 1, pp. 1–27 (1996).
Bigman, D. (ed.). *The Impact of Globalization on Strategies of Rural Development and Poverty Alleviation in Developing Countries.* CAB International, 2002.
Bigman, D. *Globalization and the Least Developed Countries: Potentials and Pitfalls*, CAB International, 2007.
Bigman, D. "The Food Crisis in Retrospect: What have we learned? Can it Happen Again?" *CAB Reviews: Perspectives in Agriculture, Veterinary Science, Nutrition and Natural Resources* (2009).
Blattman, C., and E. Miguel. "Civil War," The Center for Global Development (March 2009).
Bratton, M. "Vote buying and violence in Nigerian election campaigns," Working Paper No. 99 AFROBAROMETER Working Papers (June 2008).
Bratton, M., and R. Bhavnani. "Voting in Africa: Ethnic, Economic, or Strategic," Working Paper, Michigan State University (2009).
Burnside, C., D. Dollar. "Aid Policies and Growth," Policy Research Working Paper, No. 1777. Washington: World Bank (1997).
Burnside, C., D. Dollar. "Aid, the Incentive Regime and Poverty Reduction," Policy Research Working Paper, No. 1937. Washington: World Bank (1998).
Burnside and Dollar: W. Easterly, R. Levine, D. Roodman. "New Data, New doubts: A Comment on Burnside and Dollar's 'Aid, Policies, and Growth,'" NBER Working Papers, No. 9846 (2000).
Centre for International Cooperation and Security, Department of Peace Studies. "The impact of armed violence on poverty and development," (March 2005).
Chua, A. "World on Fire," New York: Doubleday, 2003.
Clark, G. *A Farewell to Alms*. Princeton University Press, 2007.
Collier, P. Development in Dangerous Places, *An article of Development in Dangerous Places, a forum on global poverty and intervention.*
Collier, P. "Natural Resources, Development and Conflict: Channels of causation and Policy Interventions," World Bank (2003).
Collier, P. "Economic Causes of Civil Conflict and their Implications for Policy." In *Leashing the Dogs of War: Conflict Management in a Divided World*, USIP Press Books (2007).
Collier. P. *The Bottom Billion: Why the Poorest Countries Are Failing and What Can Be Done About It*. Oxford University Press, 2007
Collier, P. *Development in Dangerous Places* prepared for *a forum on global poverty and intervention*. BostonReview July/August 2009.
Collier, P. *WARS, GUNS, AND VOTES: Democracy in Dangerous Places*. HarperCollins, 2009.

Collier, P., D. Dollar. "Can the World Poverty cut in Half? How Policy Reforms and Effective Aid can meet International Development Goals," Policy Research Working Papers Series No. 2403 (2001).

Collier, P., and J. W. Gunning. "Explaining African Economic Performance," *Journal of Economic Literature*, Vol. 37, No. 1, pp. 64–111 (1999).

Collier, P., and A. Hoeffler. Draft chapter for the *Handbook of Defense Economics* Department of Economics, University of Oxford (March 2006).

Collier, P., A. Hoeffler and D. Rohner. "Beyond Greed and Grievance: Feasibility and Civil War," Faculty of Economics, University of Cambridge (2006).

Collier, P., and B. Lomborg. Does Military Intervention Work? http://www.project-syndicate.org/contributor/759 (accessed in 2008).

Collier, P., and N. Sambanis (eds.). Understanding Civil War (Volume 1: Africa): Evidence and Analysis. The World Bank (2005).

Daniel Kaufmann, D., A. Kraay and M. Mastruzzi. "Governance Matters VII: Governance Indicators for 1996–2007," *World Bank Policy Research* (June 2008).

Daniel Kaufmann, D. Aart Kraay and Massimo Mastruzzi. "Governance Matters VIII: Governance Indicators for 1996–2008," *World Bank Policy Research* (June 2009).

Davidson, B. *The Black Man's Burden: Africa and the Curse of the Nation-State*. New York: Random House, 1992.

de Zeeuw, J. "Projects Do Not Create Institutions: the Record of Democracy Assistance in Post-Conflict Societies," *Democratization*, vol. 12, no. 4 (August 2005).

DFID. "Why We Need to Work More Effectively in Fragile States," London (2005).

Drezé and A. Sen. *Hunger and Public Action*.

Dye, K. "Corruption and Fraud Detection by Supreme Audit Institutions," Policy Research Papers, World Bank (2007).

Easterly, W. R. *The White Man's Burden: Why the West's Efforts to Aid the Rest Have Done So Much Ill and So Little Good*. Penguin Books, 2008.

Easterly, W., and R. Levine. "Africa's Growth Tragedy: Policies and Ethnic Divisions," *Quarterly Journal of Economics*, Vol. 112, No. 4, pp. 1202–50 (1997).

Easterly, W., and R. Levine. "It's Not Factor Accumulation: Stylized Facts and Growth Models," *The World Bank Economic Review*, 15(2): 177–219 (2001).

Elster, J. *The Cement of Society: A Study of Social Order*. Cambridge: Cambridge University Press, 1989.

Food and Agriculture Organization of the United Nations (FAO). *World agriculture: Towards 2030/2050*. Rome: FAO, 2006.

Food and Agriculture Organization of the United Nations (FAO). *The State of Food Insecurity in the World Economic Crises—Impacts and Lessons Learned*. Rome 2009.

Foreign Policy, Failed States Index, Various years.

Forester, M., and E. E. Evans-Pritchard (eds.). *African Political System*. International African Institute, 1987.

Fukuyama, F., *State-Building. Governance and World Order in the 21st Century*, Ithaca, Cornell University Press, 2004

Garcia, M., and J. Fares. *Youth in Africa's Labor Market*. World Bank, 2008.

Ghazvinian, J. *Untapped: The Scramble for Africa's Oil*. Harcout Books, 2007.

Hall, Robert H. E., and C. Jones. "Why Do Some Countries Produce So Much More Output per Worker Than Others?" *The Quarterly Journal of Economics* 114(1): 83–116 (1999).

Harris, J. R., and M. P. Todaro (1970). "Migration, Unemployment and Development: A Two-Sector Analysis," *American Economic Review*, 60: 126–142.

Hass, P. *Crude World: The Violent Twighlight of Oil*. Knoff, 2009.

Horowitz, Donald. "Democracy in divided societies," in Larry Diamond and Mark F. Plattner. *Nationalism, Ethnic Conflict and Democracy*, Baltimore: The Johns Hopkins University Press, pp. 35–55, 1994.

Huntington, S. P. *The Third Wave: Democratization in the Late Twentieth Century: Democratization in the Twentieth Century*. University of Oklahoma Press, 1991.

IFPRI. *Assuring Food and Nutrition Security in Africa by 2020* (August 2005).

IFPRI. *Taking Action for the World's Poor and Hungry People* (December 2007).

Intergovernmental Panel on Climate Change (IPCC, UNEP September 2007).

Jeffrey S., J. Stiglitz, and M. Humphreys. *Escaping the Resource Curse*. New York: Columbia University Press, 2007.

Kaldor, M. "New and Old Wars: Organized Violence in a Global Era," Standford: Standford University Press, 1999.

Kaufmann, D. "Myths and Realities of Governance and Corruption," World Bank, working paper, 2005.

Kaufmann, D. "Corruption, Governance and Security: Challenges for the Rich Countries and the World," World Bank, 2004.

Kaufmann, D., A. Kraay. "Government Indicators: Where are we? Where should we be going?" *World Bank Research Observer*, Vol. 23(1) (Spring 2008).

Kaufmann, D., A. Kraay, and M. Mastruzzi. "Governance Matters III: Governance Indicators for 1996–2002," World Bank policy research working paper, No. 3106 (2003).

Kaufmann, D., and P. C. Vicente. "Legal Corruption," World Bank working paper (2005).

Lavallée E., M. Razafindrakoto, and F. Roubaud. "Corruption and Trusts in Political Institutions in Sab-Saharan Africa," *AFROBAROMETER WORKING PAPERS* (2008).

Lustig, N. "Coping with RISING Food Prices: Policy Dilemmas in the Developing World," working paper 164, cgdev.org (2009).

Maass, P. *Crude World: The Violent Twilight of Oil*. Knopf, 2008.

Mansfield, E., J. Snyder. "Democratization and War," *Foreign Affairs*, no. 74 (1995).

NEPAD. *The New Partnership for Africa's Development*. (October 2001).

ODI: Opinion. *The First Millennium Development Goal, Agriculture and Climate Change*, October 2007.

Paarlberg, R. *Starved for Science: How Biotechnology is Being Kept Out of Africa*. Harvard University Press, 2008.

Pardey, P. G., J. M. Alston, and R. R. Piggott (eds.). *Agricultural R&D in the Developing World: Too little, Too Late?* Washington, D.C.: International Food Policy Research Institute, 2006.

Pardey, P. G., N. Beintema, S. Dehmer, S. Wood. "Agricultural Research: A Growing Global Divide?" Washington,D.C.: International Food Policy Research Institute. (August 2006).

Plattner, M. "Liberalism and Democracy: Can't Have One Without the Other," *Foreign Affairs* (March/April 1998).

Pratt, A., X. Diao and Y. Bahta. "How Important Is a Regional Free Trade Area for Southern Africa? Potential Impacts and Structural Constraints," Discussion paper, IFPRI (2009).

Purohit, M. "Corruption in Tax Administration," Policy Research Papers, World Bank (2007).

Ravallion, M., S. Chen, and P. Sangraula. "New Evidence on the Urbanization of Global Poverty," World Bank Research Brief (March 21, 2007).

Rodrik, D. *Thinking About Governance* (March 24, 2008).

Rodrik, D., A. Subramanian and F. Trebbi.. "Institutions Rule: The Primacy of Instituions over Geography and Integration in Economic Development," NBER Working Papers, w9305 (2002).
Rosegrant, M. W., S. A. Cline, W. Li, T. B. Sulser, R. A. Valmonte-Santos. *Looking Ahead: Long-term Prospects for Africa's Agricultural Development and Food Security.* 2020 Discussion Paper 41. Washington, D.C.: International Food Policy Research Institute, 2005.
Rotberg, R.. "Nigeria: Elections and Continuing Challenges," *Council on Foreign Relations Special Report No. 27* (April 2007).
Sachs, Jeffrey D. *The End of Poverty: Economic Possibilities for Our Time.* New York: Penguin, 2005.
Salih, M.A., S. M. Mohammed and P. Nordlund. *Political Parties in Africa: Challenges for Sustained Multiparty Democracy.* Stockholm: International IDEA, 2007.
Schaffer, F. (ed.). *Elections for Sale: The Causes and Consequences of Vote Buying.* Boulder, Colorado: Lynne Rienner Publishers, 2007.
UN World Water Development Report. "Water in a Changing World," 2009.
UN. *The UN Millennium Development Goals Reports.* New York.
UNCTAD, database www.unctad.org/fdistatistics (accessed 2008)
UNFPA. *The State of World Population 2007: Unleashing the Potential of Urban Growth,* 2007.
United Nations, 2008. *United Nations Peacekeeping Operations: Principles and Guidelines.* New York: United Nations, Department of Peacekeeping Operations, Department of Policy, Evaluation and Training.
USAID. "Fragile States Strategy," 2005.
World Bank. "Assessing Aid," Washington, 1998.
World Bank. "Can Africa Claim the 21st Century?" Washington, D.C., 2000.
World Bank. *Breaking the Conflict Trap: Civil War and Development Policy,* June 2003.
World Bank. *Global Economic Prospects 2007: Managing the Next Wave of Globalization.* Washington, D.C., 2007.
World Bank. *Global Economic Prospects 2008: Technology Diffusion in the Developing World.* January 2008.
World Disasters Report 2007, http://www.ifrc.org/publicat/wdr2007/index.asp (accessed).
Zakaria, F. "The Rise of Illiberal Democracy," *Foreign Affairs*, pp. 22–43 (1997).

Index

Abubakar, Atiku, 254
accountability, 15, 224, 242, 267
administrative costs, 126, 128
Africa
   see also specific countries; Sub-Saharan Africa (SSA)
   agenda for, 51–4
   doing business in, 128–9, 160–4
   economic growth in, 3–4, 5
   heritage of colonial rule in, 32–4
   impact of climate change on, 46–7
   map of, 1
   poverty in, 91–2
African dominion, 283
African Economic Community (AEC), 136
African farmers, 75–80
   see also agricultural sector
   increased production for, 83–9
   small-scale, 79–80
   trade and, 80–3
African society, changes in, 5–7, 14–17, 23, 27–8, 297
African Union (AU), 72, 127, 172, 195–6, 201–2, 210, 214, 231, 296
Africa-to-Africa trade, obstacles to, 122–7, 135–7
AFRITACS, 162
Afrobarometer survey (2008), 256
agricultural exports, 80–3
agricultural products, 61, 166, 169
agricultural sector, 40, 131
   impact of climate change on, 17–19, 46–7, 57, 96–7
   increased production in, 69–70
   productivity in, 61, 75–80, 138–9
   reforms, 72–5, 83–91
   reliance on, 94
   small-scale farms, 79–80
   ways to increase yields in, 83–9
aid, *see* foreign aid
al-Bashir, Omar, 9, 11, 184, 187, 263, 264
Alliance for a Green Revolution in Africa (AGRA), 89–91

al-Qaeda, 215
alternative energy, 40, 114
Amin, Idi, 290
Angola, 131, 146, 212–13
   civil war in, 272
   conflicts in, 16
   economic growth, 35
   elections in, 303
Annan, Kofi, 73, 89
arms trade, 131
Asian countries, 159–60, 241–2
AU, *see* African Union (AU)
authoritarian regimes, economic reforms by, 11
autocratic leaders, 7–15, 21, 33, 42, 75, 175–6, 220, 233, 245, 253, 254, 256, 284–5, 289–93, 296

Bangladesh, 160
banks, 162, 229
Bédié, Konan, 182
Belgian Congo, 189
Belgium, 13
biofuel, 40, 71–2, 85, 101–2, 109, 114
birth rate, 44
The Black Man's Burden (Davidson), 31
blogs, 8
Bokassa, Jean-Bedel, 290
borders
   arbitrary, 122, 175, 265, 289
   disputes, 19, 199–202, 290–1
   flow of migrants across, 126
   legacy of colonial, 196–202
   natural, 281
   trade and, 123–5
Border War, 196
Bosnia, 269
Botswana, 13, 143
   democracy in, 15, 172, 252
   economic growth in, 10, 93–4
   natural resources, 35
The Bottom Billion (Collier), 10, 119, 147, 202, 228, 261
brain drain, 94, 297
bribery, 135, 147, 161, 239, 241

316 *Index*

Brown, Lester, 59, 60
Burundi, 140, 189
business climate, 129, 160–5
business start-up costs, 163

CAADP, *see* Comprehensive Africa Agriculture Development Program (CAADP)
Cameroon, 200
canals, 110
capital flows, 37–40
Central African Republic, 131
cereal prices, 108
cereal production, 69, 102
Chad, 13, 186–7, 203–4
   conflicts in, 262–5
   oil resources, 35
   revenues of, 14
children, malnourished, 42–4, 68, 78
Chile, 11
China, 15, 17, 27, 60, 101, 112, 115, 128, 137–8, 160, 296, 297
cholera, 78
Christians, 23, 264, 298–9
cities, 22
   see also urban areas
citizenship, 230
civil conflicts and wars, 3, 5, 14–16, 49–50, 94–5, 146–7, 164, 171–3, 176–7
   autocratic leaders and, 292
   caused by deprivation and exclusion, 180–8
   in Chad, 262–5
   climate change and, 19
   colonial borders and, 196–202
   costs of, 20
   in Côte d'Ivoire, 182–3
   democracy and, 244–74
   effects of, on economic growth, 49–51
   elections and, 255–60
   external intervention in, 260–72
   failed states and, 214–18
   food production and, 74
   food shortages and, 111
   in Great Lakes region, 188–9
   human capital costs of, 208–10
   impact of, 206–43
   inequalities and, 210–14
   in Namibia, 196
   in Niger, 210–14
   during post-independence period, 33
   poverty as cause of, 202–5
   reducing, 260–9
   roots of, 20–1
   in Rwanda, 188–94
   in Sierra Leone, 269–72
   in Sudan, 183–8
   tribal roots of, 177–80
   two-state solutions to, 29–30, 265
Clark, Gregory, 75–6
class wars, 29
climate change, 5, 15
   doubts over, 115
   impact of, 17–19, 46–7, 95–7
   threats from, 57–64
climatic conditions, 119
Club of Rome, 60
coalition governments, 26–7
coastal access, 123, 124, 127, 130
coastal countries, 123, 128, 132
coefficient of cohesion, 282–3, 286
coffee, 80–1
collaboration, need for multinational, 97–9
Collier, Paul, 10–14, 51, 119, 120, 124, 127, 128, 142, 143, 145, 146–7, 169n2, 202, 203, 218, 228, 242–3, 261–2, 265–9
colonial rule, 6, 12, 13, 21, 31, 244, 253, 278, 284
   borders created during, 122, 175, 196–202, 265, 289
   heritage of, 32–4
   landlocked countries and, 129
   Rwandan genocide and, 189
commodity crisis, 4–5, 40–2, 101, 115–16
commodity futures, 103–6
commodity prices, 4–5, 17, 27, 41, 80, 93, 103–6, 144
Common Market for Eastern and Southern Africa (COMESA), 134, 136
communication, 139
comparative advantage, 143
competitiveness, obstacles to, 160–3
Comprehensive Africa Agriculture Development Program (CAADP), 89–91, 111

conflicts, *see* civil conflicts and wars
Congo Democratic Republic, 13, 23, 145, 190–6, 215, 269
Congo Kinshasa, 31
Consultative Group on International Agricultural Research (CGIAR), 96
contraceptives, 63
contracts, 164, 166, 168, 229
copper, 10–11
corn, 102
corruption, 5–7, 11–13, 94–5, 139, 145–7, 149–50, 152, 160, 161, 164, 225, 227, 238–43, 259
Côte d'Ivoire, 222, 249
    conflicts in, 16, 182–3
    map of, 183
    per capita income, 49
Country Policy and Institutional Assessment (CPIA), 223
credit, 229
crime, 15, 22–3, 215
cropland, 140
crop varieties, 91
cross-border migration, 54, 120, 126, 131
cross-country roads, 19
cross-country trade, obstacles to, 122–6

dams, 110
Darfur, 131, 177, 185–8, 205, 208, 243, 267, 269
Davidson, Basil, 31
debt crisis, of 1980s, 3–4, 15, 33–4, 42
debt relief programs, 37–40
Deby, Idriss, 263–4
democracy
    in Botswana, 252
    civil conflicts and, 244–74
    debate over Western-style, 245–8
    economic reforms and, 11–12
    fake, 268
    good governance and, 145
    illiberal, 304–8
    merits of, 11–12
    mistrust of, by Africans, 252–5
    in Mozambique, 251–2
    multiethnic societies and, 294–308
    in Senegal, 249–50
    spread of, 5, 7–9, 15, 23–7, 171–2, 294–5

    in Tanzania, 251
    transition to, 24–6, 147–8, 151–2, 171–3, 207–8, 236, 244, 245, 248–52, 273–4, 277–93, 295–9, 307–8
    in Uganda, 250–1
democratic elections, 299–308
democratic reforms, 299–301
Democratic Republic of Congo (DRC), 13, 18, 23, 145, 190–6, 215, 269
demographic changes, 5–6, 8, 27–8, 31, 157, 297
deprivation, conflicts caused by, 180–8
desertification, 97
de Soto, Hernando, 163
despotic leaders, 266–9
development plans, 19–20
diamonds, 10, 11, 17, 143
diarrhea, 78
discrimination, 256
disease, 44, 78, 120, 141–2
Doha Round, 41, 81, 85, 108, 113, 126
donors, 73, 141, 217, 220, 240, 243
    credibility with, 151
    election demands from, 9
    partnership with, 166
drinking water, 46, 139
drought-resistant crops, 58, 110
droughts, 15, 18, 46, 110, 120, 218
Dutch Disease, 142

East African Community (EAC), 134
East Asia, 11, 22, 128, 159, 241–2
Easterly, William, 39, 206, 241
Economic and Financial Crimes Commission (EFCC), 152
economic development, 19–20, 31
economic growth, 3–5, 16–17, 27, 28, 31, 34–7
    geographical obstacles to, 121–38
    government institutions and, 226–30
    impact of global financial crisis on, 40–2
    living standards and, 92, 93
    obstacles to, 119–20, 160–4
    overcoming obstacles to, 97–9
    spillover, 127
    strategies for sustained, 91, 95–7
economic institutions, 162
economic policies, 3–4, 15, 41–2
economic reforms, 3–4, 11, 16–17, 160–1

economic refugees, 156
ecosystems, 58
education, 78, 137, 141, 164–5
Egypt, 120
Ehrlich, Paul, 60, 63
elections, 7–9, 15, 172, 268–9, 292, 297
  democratic, 23–6, 299–308
  fraudulent elections, 9, 16, 24, 25, 244, 254–5, 273
  in Nigeria, 150–1
  tribal conflicts and, 255–60
electricity, 139, 141
elites, 6, 14, 29, 206, 259–60
Elster, Jon, 282, 286
emergency aid, 218–19
endemic corruption, 238–43
End of Poverty (Sachs), 120
energy resources, 114–15
environmental challenges, 6, 150
Eritrea, 13, 16, 131, 140, 200
ethanol, 85, 101–2
Ethiopia, 140, 306
  border disputes, 201
  floods, 58
  governance in, 225–6
  oil resources, 35
ethnic fragmentation, 207
European Union (EU), 102, 109, 269
exclusion, conflicts caused by, 180–8
expenditures per-capita, 96
export processing zones (EPZs), 166
export revenues, 5, 15, 35–6, 81
exports, 42, 49, 80–3, 84
external intervention, in civil conflicts, 260–72

failed states, 13, 15, 23, 36, 127, 162, 203–4, 214–18, 222, 263
famine, 19, 22, 33, 60, 61, 69, 71, 209, 218
farmers, *see* African farmers
farm subsidies, 73, 81, 102
fertilizer prices, 40, 114
feudalism, 286
financial markets, impact of food crisis on, 102–6
financial sector, 162
First Congo War, 192
fiscal policies, 41, 143
floods, 15, 18, 57, 58, 120, 141

food crisis, 71, 74, 77, 85, 98–118, 249–50, 277, 292, 293
  coping with, 109–13
  impact on financial markets, 102–6
  impact on political stability and trade policies, 107–8
  lessons learned from, 100–2
  repeatability of, 113–16
  world trade and, 111–13
food distribution, 69
food exports, 80–3, 84
food imports, 77, 78
food insecurity, 55
food prices, 4, 13–14, 40, 42, 60, 65, 68, 71, 77, 88, 93, 100–2, 108
food production, 64, 65, 69, 71–80
  changes in distribution of, 109
  climate change and, 96–7
  low productivity in, 138–9
  small-scale farming and, 79–80
  ways to increase, 83–9
food security, 46, 88–9, 94, 298
  decline in, 120
  impact of climate change on, 57–64
food shortages, coping with, 109–13
food supply, 17–19, 60–3, 65, 98
foreign aid, 14, 37–40, 111, 142, 218–22, 228, 240–3, 277–8, 293
foreign banks, 33
foreign direct investments, 17, 37–40, 165
foreign investments, 5, 37–40, 49–50, 51
fossil fuels, 114–15
fragile states, 130–1, 204, 214–18
  conditions for aid to, 218–22
  criteria for, 217
  definition of, 215
  elections in, 303–4
  governance of, 223–6
  list of, 216
  peacekeeping operations in, 260–1
fraudulent elections, 9, 16, 24, 25, 244, 254–5, 273
freedom of expression, 8
free markets, 72–3, 128, 229
free trade, 81–2, 112–13, 127–8
Frontier Economies, 38, 39, 49, 94, 103, 211
Fukuyama, Francis, 230

Gabon, 146, 223
Gandhi, Mahatma, 62–3
gangs, 22, 23
General Agreement on Tariffs and Trade (GATT), 113, 125
genetically modified crops, 46, 63, 71
genocide, 187–94, 208
geographical obstacles, to growth, 121–38
Ghana, 92, 103, 160–1, 222
  democracy in, 15
  governance in, 225
  macroeconomic stability, 94
  natural resources in, 17
  poverty in, 93
Ghazvinian, John, 146
Global Competitiveness Index, 161, 240–1
Global Competitiveness Reports, 161–2
global economy, 15
Global Environment Outlook (UN), 59
global financial crisis, 4, 15, 27, 40–2, 67–8, 172
globalization, 111–12, 113, 125
Global Monitoring Report (2008), 67
global trade, 41
global warming, *see* climate change
Goferis, Benedikt, 169n2
gold, 11, 17
"golden leaders," 175–6, 233, 279, 284, 289–90
good governance, 145, 223, 225, 228–9
governance
  bad, 12–13
  criteria of, 223–6
  definition of, 235
  good, 145, 223, 225, 228–9
  industry and, 128
  limitations of external to build up, 263–6
  quality of, 227
  weak, 34
government
  accountability, 242
  corruption in, 161, 164, 238–43
  effectiveness, 224, 227
  role of, in food production, 72–5
government institutions, 162, 163, 165
  building, 230–2
  conflict between informal traditions and, 256–8

corruption in, 259
deterioration of, 232–6
elites and, 259
failures of, 76
public trust in, 236–8
quality of, 227
role of, 226–30
weakness of, 162, 163, 165
Great Lakes region, tribal wars in, 188–9
greed, 143–4, 145, 147
Green Revolution, 17, 43, 63, 65, 68, 73, 76, 83, 154
gross domestic investment, 42
gross domestic saving, 42
growth potential, 161
Growth Tragedy, 206–7
Guebuza, H.E. Armando, 251
Gueï, Robert, 183
Guinea, 13, 16, 221, 272
Guinea-Bissau, 13, 172, 221, 243, 265, 272

Haass, Peter, 150
health care, 141
Heavily Indebted Poor Countries (HIPC), 34, 74
Heckscher-Ohlin model, 143, 167
Herbst, Jeffrey, 194–5
HIV/AIDS, 143
Horn of Africa, 130, 200, 222
Horowitz, Donald, 307
housing prices, 103
human capital, 208–10
hunger, 17–18, 42–4, 67–9, 91–9
Huntington, Samuel, 11, 294, 301, 302
Hutus, 188–90, 192, 204, 307

Igbo, 283
illiberal democracy, 304–8
imperialism, 31
imports, 42
income disparities, 4, 5, 14, 18, 23, 29, 45, 47–51, 75, 92–3, 210–14, 256, 279, 292–3
income per capita, 48–9, 50, 96, 131, 212
income taxes, 62
independence movements, 175–6
independent states, formation of, 284–9
India, 101, 137, 160, 297

industrial-based economies, 75–6, 78, 94
industrialization, 154, 159–69
industrial parks, 165
Industrial Revolution, 22, 75, 159
industrial sector, 44
industrial zones, 128
industries, local, 166–7
inequality, 4, 5, 14, 18, 23, 29, 45, 47–51, 75, 92–3, 210–14, 256, 279, 292–3
infant mortality, 150
inflation, 40
informal traditions, conflicts between state laws and, 256–8
infrastructure, 51, 72, 76, 82, 83, 110, 111, 124, 135–6, 138–42, 160
institutions, *see* government institutions
Intergovernmental Panel on Climate Change (IPCC), 18, 46, 57, 95
Internally Displaced Persons (IDPs), 18, 208
International Development Assistance (IDA), 218
International Food Policy Research Institute (IFPRI), 78
International Monetary Fund (IMF), 4, 33, 36, 42, 75, 76, 235, 243
International Organization for Migration, 18
Internet, 139
investment opportunities, 37–40, 103
Iran, 115
Iraq, 115
Iraq-Afghanistan syndrome, 268–9
irrigation, 110
Islam, 23, 29
Islamic fundamentalism, 114

Johnson, Gale, 61, 64
judiciary system, 229, 232–3, 239

Kabila, Joseph, 193, 194
Kabila, Laurent, 192, 193
Kagame, Paul, 39–40
Kahl, Colin H., 202
Kaunda, Kenneth, 288
Kenya, 13, 103, 140, 222
  conflicts in, 16, 178–80
  corruption in, 161
  demand for reforms in, 15–16
  elections in, 9, 255–6, 297, 308
  food prices in, 14
  governance in, 225–6
  internally displaced persons in, 18
  map of, 179
  per capita income, 48–9
  poverty in, 93
  protests in, 7
Kenyatta, Jomo, 32, 175, 180, 284
Kibaki, Mwai, 27, 178, 254, 255, 300
kidnapping, 22
Kikuyu, 178–9, 281, 288
Kipling, Rudyard, 31, 275
Krugman, Paul, 125

labor, 143
labor force, 164–5
landlocked countries, 13, 14, 51, 119–20, 122–5
  poverty trap and, 127–32
  regional trade agreements and, 132–8
laws, 229, 239
leaders
  autocratic, 7–15, 21, 33, 42, 75, 175–6, 220, 233, 245, 253, 254, 256, 284–5, 289–93, 296
  despotic, 266–9
  military, 176
  post-independence, 175–6, 233, 279, 284, 289–90
Leopold (king), 13
Levine, Ross Eric, 206
Libya, 264
Limits to Growth, 58–9, 65, 69–72, 96
living conditions, 131–2
  economic growth and, 92, 93
  urban, 6, 7, 28
local industries, 22, 166–7
location, 122
Lumumba, Patrice Emery, 284

macroeconomic policies, 15, 167
Madagascar
  demand for reforms in, 15–16
  macroeconomic stability, 94
maize production, 72–3
malaria, 44, 78, 120, 141–2
malaria vaccine, 243
Malawi, 72–3, 210
Malaysia, 128
Mali, 15
malnutrition, 19, 42–4, 65, 68, 70, 77–8

Malthus, Thomas, 17–18, 61–3, 65, 75, 80
Marx, Karl, 286
Mauritania, 13, 172, 265–6, 273
  demand for reforms in, 15–16
  economic growth, 35
Mauritius, 172
Mbeki, Thabo, 161
McGowan, Patrick, 291
media, freedom of, 8
medicines, 141, 142
Meredith, Martin, 290
middle class, 29
Middle East, 115
migration, 5
  climate change and, 18–19
  cross-border, 54, 120, 126, 131
  rural-urban, 5–7, 21–3, 31, 44–5, 51–4, 119, 120, 131–2, 154–7, 297, 298
  spatial distribution and, 122
military coups, 9, 11, 24, 29, 32–4, 131, 145, 172–3, 176, 220, 244, 290, 291
military intervention, in civil conflicts, 260–9
military leaders, 176
militias, 22–3
Millennium Development Goals, 27, 65–9, 74, 85
Miller, 144
Mills, Greg, 195
minerals, 10
minority tribes, 26–7, 256
Moi, Daniel arap, 180, 284
Mombasa, 124
monetary policies, 41
moral restraint, 62–3
Morel, Edward, 31
Moreno, Ocampo, Luis, 187
mosquito nets, 141–2
Moyo, Dambisa, 39
Mozambique, 127
  democracy in, 15, 251–2
  food prices in, 13–14
  per capita income, 48
Mubarak, Hosni, 296, 303
Mugabe, Robert, 9, 11, 16, 27, 201, 242, 254, 255, 288, 300, 304
multicountry collaboration, 19
multiethnic societies, 294–308
Multi-Fiber Arrangement (MFA), 137
Multilateral Debt Relief Initiative (MDRI), 34

multinational collaboration, 97–9, 135–6
Museveni, Yoweri, 250–1
Muslims, 23, 29, 182, 186, 264, 298–9
Mwanawasa, Levy, 10–11

Nairobi, 124
Namibia
  border war, 196
  democracy in, 15
Nasser, Gamal Abdel, 32
National Elections Watch (New), 272
nation-states, formation of, 284–9
natural disasters, 18
natural gas, 17, 35, 114, 129
natural resources, 5, 32, 123
  competition over, 15
  conflicts over, 19
  as "curse", 142–53
  demand for, 17
  discovery of new, 17, 35
  exploitation of, 143–4, 253
  use and abuse of, 10–12
  using, for industrialization, 166–7
Neo-Malthusians, 63–4
nepotism, 240
New Partnership for Africa's Development (NEPAD), 85, 166, 167
Ngwato, 283
Niger, 13, 131, 221
  conflicts in, 49–50, 181–2
  crime and violence in, 23
  natural resources, 35
Nigeria, 13
  border disputes, 200
  business obstacles in, 163–4
  corruption in, 94, 146, 149–50, 152
  crime and violence in, 23
  demand for reforms in, 15–16
  democracy in, 15
  elections in, 9, 150–1
  as failed state, 263
  foreign investment in, 49–50
  government of, 229, 247
  growth potential, 161–2
  kidnapping in, 22
  map of, 148
  oil resources, 10, 17
  poverty in, 50, 93
  protests in, 7, 16
  resource curse in, 148–53

322 Index

Nile Basin Initiative, 136
Nile project, 19
Nkrumah, Kwame, 32
nonfragile states, 130–1
Nyerere, Julius, 32, 74, 251

Obasanjo, Olusegun, 94, 148–51, 240, 254
O'Connell, Stephen A., 169n2
Odinga, Raila, 27, 178
official development assistance (ODA), 37
oil exporting countries, 4, 35, 47, 50, 94–5, 115, 146, 161, 292–3
oil prices, 40, 42, 114, 115, 144, 152–3
oil resources, 10, 17, 35, 114–15, 129
Operation Palliser, 261
Orange Democratic Movement, 180
Organization of African Unity (OA), 245
Organization of the Islamic Conference (OIC), 249
organized crime, 147, 215
outsourcing, 167–9
overpopulation
    food supply and, 63–4
    water scarcity and, 59–61
Overseas Development Assistance (ODA), 38, 39
ozone layer, 97

Pakistan, 160
palm oil, 114
pan-Africanism, 284
paradox of plenty, *see* resource curse
Paris Club, 150
peacekeeping operations, 260–72
per capita income, 48–50, 131, 212
pirates, 130
policy reforms, 219
political instability, 224
political stability, food crisis and, 107–8
political transformation, 23–7
poor
    anger of, 297–8
    food shortages and, 18
    increase in, 5
    protests by, 29
    urban, 20
The Population Bomb (Ehrlich), 60, 63
population growth, 21
    food supply and, 61–3

limits to, 60, 63–4, 69–75
rate of, 70
in urban areas, 154–7
post-independence period, 32–4, 175–6, 233, 279, 284–9
poverty, 3–4, 15–18, 39, 278–9
    conflicts and, 14, 202–5
    distribution of, 79
    incidence, 96
    measures of, 92–3
    rise in, 42–6, 91–2, 176
    rural, 158–9, 203–5
    urban, 21–3, 28, 158–9, 297–8
poverty alleviation, 20, 65–9
    in rural areas, 52
    in urban areas, 53–4
poverty traps, 10, 119–20, 127–32
Preferential Trade Agreements (PTAs), 133–4, 136
pregnancy-related deaths, 78
press, freedom of, 8
prices
    commodity, 4–5, 17, 27, 41, 80, 93, 104–6, 144
    food, 4, 13–14, 40, 42, 60, 68, 77, 93, 100–1, 102, 108
    oil, 40, 42, 114, 115, 144
privatization programs, 239
production, 61–3
    agricultural, 69–70
    costs, 160
    outsourcing of, 167
productivity, 61, 75–80, 137–8
Program for African's Seeds Systems (PASS), 90–1
progressive taxes, 62
property rights, 11, 163, 168, 229
protests, 7, 16, 29, 254–5
public health spending, 141
public institutions, *see* government institutions
public sector ethics, 225–6

rainfall, 57, 96
rain-fed agriculture, 80
rainforest, 10
real GDP, 35, 50
reforms, demand for, 6, 7, 15–16
refugees, 156, 208
regional technical assistance centers, 162

regional trade agreements, 127, 132–8, 230
regulations, 126, 135, 160, 164
regulatory burden, 225, 227, 228
religious animosities, 23
remittances, 5
remote regions, 13–14
rent-seeking, 143–4
residential property prices, 103
resource curse, 119–20, 142–53, 188
resource-poor countries, 123, 129, 211, 296
resource-rich countries, 4–5, 11–15, 17, 20, 34, 36, 38, 41, 47–9, 51, 123, 129, 211, 292
resources, *see* natural resources
road infrastructure, 51, 72, 82, 124, 135, 139, 141
Ruanda-Urundi, 189
rule of law, 225, 229, 232–3, 239
rural communities, 5–6
  impact of climate change on, 17–19, 58–9
  lack of development in, 20, 154
  poverty alleviation in, 52
rural population, 155, 157
rural poverty, 78, 158–9, 203–5, 300–1
rural roads, 13, 14
rural-urban migration, 5–7, 21–3, 31, 44–5, 51–4, 119, 120, 131–2, 154–7, 297, 298
Russell, Bertrand, 287
Russia, 296
Rwanda, 58, 72, 171, 177, 269
  facts about, 192
  genocide in, 188–94
  macroeconomic stability, 94
  map of, 191

Sachs, Jeffrey, 39, 51, 67, 120, 124, 126, 138, 228, 241, 243
Salisbury, Lord, 290
schools, 78
scientists, 73
Second Congo War, 192
Seeds of Change (Brown), 59
Seko, Mobutu, 192
Senegal, 92, 103, 222
  democracy in, 15, 172, 223, 249–50
  poverty in, 93

shantytowns, 23, 28, 53
Sharia law, 23
Sierra Leone, 131, 212–13, 238, 262, 267
  conflicts in, 16, 271–2
  corruption in, 272
  elections in, 272
  external intervention in, 269–72
  facts about, 270–1
  map of, 270
skilled labor, 94
slave trade, 6
small and medium-sized enterprises, 165
small-scale farms, 79–80
socialism, 32–4, 175
social safety nets, 111
social welfare, 62, 63
socioethnic identity, 306
Somalia, 13, 131, 207
  as failed state, 214–15
  food crisis in, 71
  internally displaced persons in, 18
  pirates in, 130
South Africa, 14, 296
  border war with Namibia, 196–7
  corruption in, 161
  democracy in, 15
  governance in, 225
  macroeconomic stability, 94
  migration to, 131
  protests in, 7
  rural-urban migration in, 22
South Asia, 44
Southern African Development Community (SADC), 192, 196
Southern African Development Coordinating Conference (SADCC), 196
Southern African Power Pool, 136
South Korea, 11, 116, 128
south-to-south trade, 137–8
spatial factors, 121–2, 124–5
speculation, 103–6
stagnation, 3–4, 16, 28, 31–7, 77–8, 84, 100, 149–50, 176, 206–7, 228, 253, 278
staple foods, 84
state institutions, *see* government institutions
states, formation of, 284–9
stock market index, 39

structural adjustment programs, 33–4, 74, 82–3, 172, 239
structural reforms, 258–60
Sub-Saharan Africa (SSA)
see also Africa; specific countries
economic growth in, 3–4, 91–2, 93
living standards in, 93
poverty in, 91–2
Sudan, 13, 131
conflicts in, 15, 16, 29–30, 177, 183–8, 265, 298–9
corruption in, 11, 94–5
division of, 29–30
economic growth, 35
elections in, 9
facts about, 185
food shortages in, 58
internally displaced persons in, 18
map of, 184
oil resources, 35
Suez Canal, 119, 130
Supreme Audit Institutions, 234–6

Tanzania, 13, 15, 74, 160–2, 251
tariffs, 135
tax administration, 234
taxes, progressive, 62
tax rates, 161
technical assistance, 162
technological progress, 164–6
terrorist organizations, 215
textile manufacturing, 22, 94, 137–8
Togo, 13, 172, 265
Toure, Sekou, 171
trade, 49, 116
agricultural sector and, 80–3
costs of cross-border, 133
cross-country, obstacles to, 122–7
food crisis and world, 111–13
free trade, 81–2, 112–13, 127–8
global, 41
impact of food crisis on, 107–8
intraregional, 135–7
local, 82
outsourcing network and, 167
regional trade agreements, 132–8
south-to-south, 137–8
trade agreements, 112–13, 132–8, 165–6, 230
trade barriers, 135
training programs, 164–5

transnational corporations (TNCs), 167
transportation infrastructure, 51
transport costs, 14, 124–8
tribal conflicts, 21, 23, 33, 145, 177–94, 244–5, 255–60, 281
tribal loyalties, 24, 288–9
tribal rivalries, 32, 248–9, 253
tribal rule, 244, 252–3, 257–8, 278–9, 283–4
tribal societies, 6, 12, 280–4
Tsvangirai, Morgan, 16, 27
Tutsis, 188–91, 192, 204, 307
2020 Vision for Food, Agriculture, and the Environment (IFPRI), 87–8
two-state solutions, 29–30, 265

Uganda, 13, 162, 222
crime and violence in, 23
democracy in, 250–1
floods, 57, 58
internally displaced persons in, 18
macroeconomic stability, 94
natural resources, 17
poverty in, 92–3
unemployment, 4, 7, 15, 22, 28, 53, 156, 158
United Nations, 260, 261
United States, 102, 103, 109, 137
United States Agency for International Development (USAID), 142
uranium, 10, 17, 35, 143
urban areas
crime and violence in, 22–3
growth of, 5–6, 21–3, 154–7
living conditions in, 6, 7, 28
migration to, 5–7, 21–3, 31, 44–5, 51–4, 119–20, 131–2, 154–7, 297–8
poverty alleviation in, 20, 53–4
poverty in, 15, 21–3, 28, 158–9, 297–8
protests in, 254–5
tribal conflicts in, 256
unemployment in, 4, 156, 158
violence in, 254
urban industrialization, 159–69
urbanization, 6–8, 21–3, 53, 120, 154–7
urban poor, 20
US aid programs, 73
US dollar, 104

violence, 6, 7, 16, 22–3, 29, 178, 224
voice, 224

vote-rigging, 8, 16, 24, 25, 148, 256
voting process, 9
voting rights, 24

Wade, Abdullah, 245, 246–7, 249
Washington Consensus, 4, 219, 243, 267, 269
water, 46
water-borne disease, 78, 141
water scarcity, 59–61, 85, 97
Watson, Peter, 136
West African Pipeline, 136
Western-style democracy, 245–8
World Bank, 4, 13, 33, 36, 72, 74, 75, 76, 91–2, 95, 111, 243
World Development Report (2008), 76, 83
World Development Report (2009), 121, 124
World Economic Indicators, 92–3
World Economic Outlook (WEO), 131
World Food Program (WFP), 57–8

World Trade Organization (WTO), 113, 125

Yar'adua, Umaru Musa, 16, 94, 151–2
Yoruba, 282, 283
Yugoslavia, 207

Zakaria, Fareed, 304–5, 307
Zambia, 13, 72, 222, 288
    revenues of, 14
    use of natural resources in, 10–11
Zenawi, Meles, 306
Zimbabwe, 13, 242
    corruption in, 11
    demand for reforms in, 15–16
    elections in, 9, 16, 255–6
    internally displaced persons in, 18
    protests in, 7, 16
    revenues of, 14
Zulu, 281, 283, 288